Re...

GOD

Render unto
GOD

Economic Vulnerability, Family Violence, and Pastoral Theology

James Newton Poling

with contributions by
Brenda Consuelo Ruiz
and
Linda Crockett

WIPF & STOCK · Eugene, Oregon

Wipf and Stock Publishers
199 W 8th Ave, Suite 3
Eugene, OR 97401

Render Unto God
Economic Vulnerability, Family Violence, and Pastoral Theology
By Poling, James Newton
Copyright©2002 by Poling, James Newton
ISBN 13: 978-1-62032-030-3
Publication date 3/1/2012
Previously published by Chalice Press, 2002

To Nancy Werking Poling

Contents

Acknowledgments

Special thanks to all those persons and institutions who supported my research and writing for this project:

Colleagues and institutions in Nicaragua since 1991: AEDAF, *Asociacion Evangelica de Asesoramiento Familiar,* The Protestant Association for Family Counseling; CEPAD, *Consejo de Iglesias Evangelicas Pro-Alianza Denominacional* (The Ecumenical Council of Protestant Churches); Rector Debora Garcia, the faculty, staff, and students at El Seminario Bautista Teológico (The Baptist Theological Seminary).

Garrett-Evangelical Theological Seminary, for a sabbatical leave during spring quarter, 2000, and for funding several of my research trips to Nicaragua, and the United Methodist Church for sponsoring a student trip to Nicaragua in 1999.

Colgate-Rochester Divinity School, Lowell Fewster, and the American Baptist Churches of America for sponsoring my first trip to Nicaragua in 1991 and funding several subsequent trips.

Brenda Ruiz for her friendship and counsel over ten years of collaboration.

Linda Crockett for her friendship and sharing her life, her writing, and herself with me and others.

Scholars who read, responded, and edited my manuscript in various stages: Nancy Poling, Ulrike Guthrie, Pamela Couture, Brenda Ruiz, Linda Crockett, Sarah Rieth.

Students in my classes who have responded to my developing ideas.

Introduction

In Mark 12:13–17, Jesus' enemies try to trick him by asking whether one should pay taxes to Caesar. If he says yes, he alienates his followers who hate the tax system. If he says no, he jeopardizes himself with the authorities. Jesus takes a coin and asks his accusers: "Whose head is on this coin?" They say, "Caesar's." Jesus says: "Render unto Caesar that which is Caesar's and unto God that which is God's."[1]

Ever since this story was recorded, religious leaders have debated how believers should relate to economic and political systems. Some argue that Jesus' message was primarily concerned with personal spirituality and that he intended his followers to cooperate with those in authority. Others argue that Jesus was a brilliant debater who knew how to avoid the rhetorical trap set for him. These followers understand his statement as a moral commitment to justice and solidarity with the poor and the vulnerable.

I begin with this story to illustrate the ambiguous history of religion as a resource in the lives of those who are vulnerable in society. On the one hand, religion often serves the interests of the dominant classes at the expense of working-class and poor people by sanctioning established authority and power–Render unto Caesar that which is Caesar's. On the other hand, religion often serves as a source of empowerment and resistance for those who suffer violence and oppression–Render unto God that which is God's. This tension within religion is a topic and the title of my project.

I have taken as my moral commitment and my research sample those persons who suffer economic vulnerability and family violence, particularly women and children in working-class and poor communities of various cultures. We can learn much about the gospel from studying those who live in the extreme vulnerability of interpersonal violence aggravated by economic oppression. For such persons, what is the difference between religion that aggravates the suffering of persons and religion that empowers persons in these circumstances?

In my previous research I discovered that male dominance and white supremacy create vulnerable populations who have few resources for preventing and vindicating their experiences of violence, and suggested alternative religious ideas and practices that arise from the resistance of these populations to oppression.[2] In this book I extend my

1

research to discover how economic vulnerability among working-class and poor women and children in European American, African American, and Latina/o cultures exacerbates experiences of family violence, and what role religion plays in empowering them and their families.

I follow three methods of research: (1) *Case studies in collaboration with victims and survivors of family violence and their advocates.* I develop case studies with survivors of family violence who live in situations of economic vulnerability in various cultures. These are based on my fifteen years of clinical experience in the field of family violence education and advocacy. (2) *Review of research and literature on economic vulnerability, family violence, and religion.* I engage in interdisciplinary conversations between religious studies, theology, and the social sciences. (3) *Creative and practical theory building as a basis for future studies.* The result will be a theoretical framework that can be further tested empirically.

Social Location and Accountability

I am a middle-class, European American male, a graduate school professor, an ordained minister in the Presbyterian Church (USA), and fifty-nine years old. I am doing research across ages, genders, cultures, and economic classes; therefore, I must be accountable to the groups most affected by this research. I am accountable to the family violence movement of survivors and their advocates by submitting my work for their critical feedback. Some of this is accomplished in this book through coauthoring with survivors, giving the survivors final say over the content and context of their stories. Some of this is accomplished through submitting my work to advocates and scholars with long experience in the family violence movement. I have developed a covenant of responsibility with particular scholars from the groups I am writing about, namely, European American, African American, and Latina women: they have given me critical feedback on my work, and I have changed what they decided must be changed.

This project challenges many of the assumptions of my personal life. As a white male in the first world, I live at the pinnacle of the global political economy, and my religious imagination is shaped by decades of education and indoctrination into male dominance, white supremacy, and class privilege. The partial transformation of my consciousness is due to the confrontative love of many friends over many years. They sensed the internal contradictions in my life and values and loved me enough to challenge me to new awareness of God's action in my life. I am most clearly indebted to Brenda Consuelo Ruiz and Linda Crockett for their collaboration in this work, and to a whole host of other faithful persons who have influenced my life. I pledge myself to continue to be accountable to those who have experienced oppression and have survived to give guidance to those who have ears to hear and eyes to see.

Preview of the Book

The *first chapter* of this book will focus on definitions. What do we mean by economic vulnerability? How is such vulnerability created and maintained? How is economic vulnerability related to family violence, that is, how does economic vulnerability create conditions of violence, and how does economic vulnerability aggravate the problems that are present when persons live in fear of violence? How can pastoral care and counseling be a resource that empowers persons in situations of economic vulnerability and family violence? What obstacles must the ministries of care overcome to follow the mandate to care for all God's children?

Stories of Pastoral Care

During fifteen years as pastor, therapist, advocate, and activist in the family violence movement, I have formed long-term relationships of mutuality and trust with many survivors of family violence from European American, African American, and Latina/o communities. I draw on this experience to develop in-depth case studies as an empirical base for my book. Collaboration and mutual accountability are paramount in the writing of these case studies. I have used this method in previous studies of gender and race and feel confident in its efficacy for understanding these issues. *Part 1* includes three chapters about specific pastoral care contexts. In *chapter 2* Brenda Consuelo Ruiz, pastoral counselor in Managua, Nicaragua, describes three cases and the context for her ministry of care, especially for women in situations of extreme poverty. In *chapter 3* Linda Crockett describes her experience of survival within a European American family where violence was practiced and justified as normal. Her awakening through the courage of peasant resisters in El Salvador strengthens the North-South dynamic in this book and illustrates a model of accompaniment across cultures, races, and classes. In *chapter 4* I describe my own recent pastoral counseling practice with working-class white men who had been convicted of sexual offenses with children. Pastoral theology, the biblical and theological foundation for care and counseling in the church, provides the context for affirming and challenging present practices of care.

These examples of pastoral care in situations of economic vulnerability and family violence give a rich base for the main questions guiding this book: What do people experience when they are economically vulnerable? How does economic vulnerability contribute to experiences of violence in families and communities? How are economic decisions made that determine the vulnerability of the world's population? How can religion be a resource of support for those who seek a better life in situations of economic vulnerability and family violence?

Economic Analysis

Pastors and pastoral counselors underestimate economic vulnerability and family violence because of the difficulty in understanding the macrosystems that create the economic conditions for people's lives. The large movements of natural resources, capital, and labor around the world are difficult to fully understand even for economists. In *part 2* we examine the academic discipline of economics in order to get some perspective on how economic vulnerability for so many people is created and maintained. In *chapter 5* we look at the reality of economic inequality itself. How are the resources of the world distributed? How many people live at the median income of the United States, currently $29,605? How many people live on less than $2 per day? What are the quality-of-life issues resulting from these differences? How can we compare the economic life in developed versus poor countries when the reality of life is so different? What does it mean to be poor in the United States? How are economic factors related to family and other types of violence?

Chapter 6 examines the discipline of economics as an explanation of how economic systems work. Our primary focus is market capitalism, the dominant system that affects the lives of people in the world today. We look briefly at the history of this field as it developed in Western society, whose issues determine the important debates about economic development today. *Chapter 7* examines a Christian critique of market capitalism, paying particular attention to the work of John Cobb and Herman Daly, including their alternative model for evaluating economic development. After this foray into the macrotheories of economics, we look at several places in the world to see how these economic theories actually affect the lives of people. The country of Nicaragua provides an important case study for understanding situations of extreme poverty and how decisions made in the North create such massive suffering in the South. In spite of the relative wealth of persons in the United States, even here large groups of people live in economic vulnerability. We close this chapter by looking at how this is possible.

Resistance to Capitalism

To hear the macroeconomists speak, we might be tempted to think of those who are economically vulnerable as passive. In many economic theories, the masses of people are commodified as laborers, consumers, or collateral concerns. For example, when measuring economic output for the Nicaraguan economy, farm laborers who work for $1 per day are counted as contributing to economic productivity, while peasants growing beans for their families and receiving no wages are not counted. Among people who live in vulnerable situations, there is much creative activity that I call resistance to capitalism. I am especially interested in the actions of persons who experience both economic vulnerability and family violence. First, there is the resistance of survival and revolt: many people manage to survive in spite of the dehumanizing conditions of their lives; some people revolt to overthrow the systems that create misery for so many. Second, people organize alternative institutions with different values from the greed and competition of capitalism. Cooperative endeavors exist in every community, where people work together for the general welfare and where profit is not the core value. Third, people develop alternative visions of human life that are based on economic justice and nonviolence. In *part 3* we look at such forms of resistance to capitalism in Nicaragua and in the United States, focusing especially on projects developed by women and those in African American communities.

Theological Reflection

In *part 4* we move to the explicitly religious dimension of our project: How has the Christian tradition been a resource for persons who experience economic vulnerability and family violence? In this section, we proceed on the assumption that Christian churches and theologians have always lived with an acute tension. The church began as a persecuted group whose leader had been tortured and killed, and most churches eventually adopted the cross as the central icon of worship, piety, and practice. But what does the cross mean? The Christian church has always found a way of surviving within the social, political, and economic systems of its time, often by becoming an integral part of the power structures of society itself. Yet Christians in every generation have sought to return to the roots of the faith in the prophetic and persecuted Jesus and the disciple community. The tension between accommodation to the social order and critique and revolt against that order is central to the history of the Christian church. The same thing is true in relation to market capitalism and its successes and failures.

Some Christians place themselves squarely within the capitalist system and advocate its expansion, believing that all human beings will prosper as capitalism prospers. Other Christians see market capitalism in the twenty-first century as an evil force that must be opposed and challenged at every opportunity. Most Christians are somewhere in between.

I am skeptical of capitalism as an economic system and of its value for humankind, primarily because of the massive human suffering in the world during the twentieth century. I place myself among those who try to resist capitalism's dominance in the world. If the people of the world can establish a humanistic and ecological value system with widespread support, then capitalist markets will have their place, as I argue in *chapter 7*. Capitalism must be dethroned from its stature as a religious idol to a penultimate system of economic development, and we need to find the religious resources of our traditions that might contribute to such changes. *Chapters 11 and 12* examine such resources from the Christian biblical tradition, with a focus on the gospel of Mark and the life and work of Jesus. *Chapter 13* continues this discussion by turning toward the church as the body of Christ, the ongoing witness to the values of economic justice and nonviolence.

Transforming Pastoral Care

In *part 5* we return to the principles and practices of care at a micro-level of personal and interpersonal interaction. How can the people who tell their stories in *part 1*, the ones who have resisted economic vulnerability and family violence, be empowered by pastoral care and counseling? Just as the church itself has been too often captivated by the dominant economic and ideological order, so pastoral care and counseling has functioned with middle-class, individualistic values that too often put the responsibility for change on persons who seek care. We must begin by listening and validating the experiences of oppression of many persons who seek our help, and revise our theories and practices so that their resistance to economic vulnerability and family violence is strengthened.

Rather than support the dominant order, pastoral care should have as its goal the transformation of persons and communities toward economic justice and nonviolence, as Jesus taught in his life and by his death on the cross. Pastoral counselors must ask themselves: What do we render to God? Should we serve Caesar and reap the economic privileges of such collusion with injustice, or should we serve God and risk our economic and physical lives for the sake of the gospel? While our calling does not always come to us in such clear choices, we must remember that our commitment to love God is always primary, and this commitment means that we often must resist the evil systems of this world for the sake of the gospel.

An Invitation

I expect that many readers will be concerned about the central questions of this book, issues of the vulnerability of so many people in the world because of economic injustice and family violence. Many readers will want to think more carefully about how Christian churches can improve their understanding and practices of care for those who are vulnerable. Many of us have been vulnerable at times in the past because we are children, women, African American, Hispanic, or poor. We remember the gospel messages about God's compassion for the poor and the divine justice that is part of God's character.

However, many readers may feel challenged by the complexity of the analysis in this book. How can we possibly expect ourselves to understand the abstractions of modern economic theory, the flow of capital and resources around the world, the deep roots of interpersonal violence in families, and the complications of a cross-cultural interpretation of the scriptures? It sometimes seems to be too much, and we feel overwhelmed by the enormity of the task.

My witness is that there is a sense of freedom in facing the complexities and ambiguities of this topic and coming to a new set of priorities about economic life from a Christian perspective. Every day we are bombarded by messages from global capitalism about values that we know are false. We know in our hearts that capitalism is a force that frequently challenges the core values of Jesus Christ. Even though it is difficult, it is important to attempt to understand the systems of power of our day, and to find the simple biblical values of faith, hope, and love. It is important that we not give in to the temptation to throw up our hands and yield to the demonic pressures of modern society. So I invite you on an adventure into the stories of those who are vulnerable, into dialogue with those critics who have analyzed economic theories, and into encounter with those biblical interpreters who re-present Jesus for our generation. The task is daunting, but the goal is important. As we stretch our imaginations, we will come to new understandings of what God's love means for the whole world, and find a new place where all people can be gathered into one community of love and justice.

Part I: Principles of Pastoral Care

1

Economics, Violence, and Care

Introduction

Several years ago I counseled with a man with significant pathology. Ken was abusive to his wife and children, unable to hold down a job, and deceitful with most everyone in his life. He was diagnosed with Borderline Personality Disorder and illustrated his individual problems in almost every session over three years. He skipped sessions, came late, refused to engage with me, and denied the seriousness of his difficulties. Surprisingly, however, we formed a strong bond that gave me access to his inner world.

Ken was a perpetrator of violence against his wife and children. He alternately threatened them, withheld resources, manipulated their vulnerabilities, and sexually abused his young daughter. While he felt significant guilt and shame about his behaviors, especially after he was arrested, spent time in jail, and faced a long period of probation, he had great difficulty looking at the history and context of his abuse and making the necessary changes. He taught me much about how violence is intertwined in the lives of some men and their families, and how difficult it is to change.

Beyond individual and family pathology, I learned from Ken about the social pathologies of class oppression: how some welfare workers infantalize clients until their mistreatment of persons becomes a self-fulfilling prophecy; that there is a system of corporations that counts on an endless supply of skilled, lower-class men who are forced to work at low wages and can be discarded depending on the cycles of business; and much more.

Maintaining empathy with Ken through the ups and downs of his life was a challenge for me as a professional pastoral counselor. I had been

9

trained in diagnosing pathology and maintaining an ethical perspective on destructive behaviors toward others. But I had not been trained in analyzing the class issues in his social context. For example, if he became enraged and quit a job because he was expected to work long hours in a cold and unsafe garage for low pay and to absorb abuse from his supervisors, should I understand his behavior as adaptive or defensive? It was both, of course, but my training had not provided the tools of social analysis to carefully sort out the interlocking developmental and class issues.

Ken confronted me with class issues that also challenged my pastoral and theological diagnosis. I understood that he was engaged in sin when he abused his wife and children and when he refused to accept adult responsibility for himself and fulfill his covenantal responsibilities. I could see that his dysfunction was a result of intergenerational evil in the past because of his background in an abusive family of origin. Ken's healing depended on an empathic relationship with a surrogate parental figure, his courage to tolerate the pain of personal conversion and change, and the presence of a community of support for the future. I gained understanding about how God was calling Ken out of his evil circumstances into a more loving life in relationship with others and with God. But I was frustrated by my inability to bring into the therapeutic relationship an analysis of the institutions that oppressed Ken and others like him and kept them in a vulnerable state. How was God confronting these institutions and calling the larger society to become more empathic and nonviolent?

The field of pastoral care and counseling has been slow to understand, diagnose, and provide competent treatment for survivors and perpetrators of family violence. Likewise, our theories and practices do not adequately take into account the economic vulnerabilities of working-class and poor clients. I have too often focused in my pastoral counseling practice on individual and family healing and salvation, while many of my clients were bombarded with social forces that set them back daily. One of the problems of being a professional pastoral counselor is that I am mostly protected from such forces through adequate salary, health insurance, good housing, education, safe communities, and stimulating work. Unless economic vulnerability is built into our theories, I do not have the existential experience for identification with many of our clients.

How does our pastoral theology help us to understand economic vulnerability and family violence? As Ched Myers says in his book *Binding the Strong Man,* Jesus was from the peasant class and represented its economic and political interests in his ministry. His resistance to the elite and managerial classes enabled his community of origin to challenge the social realities of his day and opened up the forces of a populist movement whose ideas have transformed the world. Jesus' effectiveness in bringing these social interests into the public arena through a nonviolent movement for change led to opposition from the elite leaders and eventually caused his death.[1]

In the spirit of Jesus, pastoral counselors need to serve all the people of God, including the majority, who are working class and poor. I challenge readers to reexamine all assumptions that create gaps between economic classes and ostracize many people who seek justice and healing from the church.

Definitions

The purpose of this section is to define and clarify the key terms in the title of this book and discuss their interrelationships: economic vulnerability, family violence, pastoral theology, and intercultural care.

Economics and Vulnerability

An *economy* is a complex system of material activities and exchanges that determines how wealth and resources will be created and distributed within the population. It is a system that organizes human desire, deciding what values and behaviors will shape the personal experiences of groups.[2]

Whenever people gather into communities of mutual material support, they develop patterns of activity and exchange, such as raising chickens and exchanging eggs with someone who raises cows and barters with milk, or exchanging care between the younger and the older generations. As these interpersonal systems extend into larger areas, they develop into complex exchanges between tribes, nations, and, since the sixteenth century, privately owned transnational corporations.

For example, in a village economy, one peasant makes candles and exchanges them for eggs and milk from another peasant. In an international economy, English mills make woolen cloth and exchange it for Portuguese wine. In a just world, all groups would benefit, because each would produce products for a reasonable price and would improve the quality of their lives through exchanges with other groups. Local communities could specialize in certain skills and yet have access to the material goods produced by others.

After the problem of total stagnation of economic life, or loss of all productivity,[3] one of the most difficult problems in any economy is unequal distribution. What happens if one peasant can unilaterally control the rate of exchange, such that half as many candles will buy the same amount of eggs and milk? What happens if Portugal fears for its safety on the seas unless it gives in to the demands of English mills on the exchange rate? Superior military force and consolidated political power distort the exchange rates and create disadvantages for those who are vulnerable. Within the information economies of the twenty-first century, inequality is a major problem. The poor workers of the world have very little influence over the value of their labor, the fair value of natural resources in the local community, or the cost of products they must consume in order to survive. The study of the complex interrelationship of capital, labor, and land (natural resources and environment) is the essence of economics, and the inequality that some groups experience in these interrelationships constitutes economic vulnerability.

Economics is the academic and professional study of economies, that is, the development of theories that explain how various economies work, including the smallest village exchanges in many informal economies and extending to the global financial and information networks.

The word *economy* can probably be traced back to the Greek word *oikonomos,* "one who manages a household," derived from *oikos,* "house," and *nemein,* "to manage." From *oikonomos* was derived *oikonomia,* which had not only the sense "management of a household or family" but also senses such as "thrift," "direction," "administration," "arrangement," and "public revenue of a state." The first recorded sense of our word *economy,* found in a work possibly composed in 1440, is "the management of economic affairs," in this case, of a monastery. *Economical* also includes the meanings of "thrift" and "administration." What is probably our most frequent current use, "the economic system of a country or an area," seems not to have developed until the nineteenth and twentieth centuries.[4]

In chapter 6 I review the history of economics as a theory and a social science discipline, which, as the above history of the word shows, is mostly a nineteenth- and twentieth-century development. The task of economics as a scientific discipline is to understand how wealth and resources are created and distributed in a population, and to develop policies that will provide the most benefit for the most people. Economists often disagree about the best ways to create and distribute wealth.

Poverty is a condition created by the failure of the economic system. The consequences of poverty are sometimes hidden, because poverty can last for generations, and people adapt in creative ways in order to survive. For those who are poor, the economic system does not provide adequate food, water, housing, clothing, and health care, with resultant trauma and declining quality of life. In such situations, violence is often a daily experience, not only the violence of being without resources but the reactive violence that comes when people reach the limits of their ability to adjust psychologically. Some poor communities develop resilient attitudes and behaviors that enable them to survive in economically difficult times. For others, the breakdown of personality, family, and local community actually contributes to interpersonal violence.

In developed countries, economic vulnerability has additional meanings, namely, the lack of control over one's daily life. In Western nations, high wages for certain jobs and minimum wages for others have changed the formula for poverty. In contrast to the absolute poverty in many underdeveloped countries, it is possible to be poor in a developed country if the cost of goods and services exceeds the income in a family. I examine the relative poverty in rich countries more closely in part 3. Even when families have high incomes from wages when evaluated on a global scale, their economic lives can be problematic. For example, during the last two hundred years millions of people have been forced from traditional agricultural communities into industrial factories against their will. While their wages are higher than before, the quality of their lives has been reduced. Urban slums can be dreadful places to live, even when wages are higher. Many writers illustrate these tragedies in their novels.[5] More recently, capitalism has embarked on a concerted effort toward temporary and part-time employment, which provides decent wages on an unpredictable basis only, and the resulting insecurity makes family life very difficult. Pastors and counselors particularly need to be sensitive to various kinds of economic vulnerability facing people.

> *Economic vulnerability* is defined as the limits of the resources and adaptability of the community or an individual when faced with potential threats, which in other words means a community's ability to absorb the changes that a disaster causes in its particular milieu.[6]

When a community is faced with hunger, illness, unemployment, need for education, violence, natural disaster, or other crises, what are the limits of resources that it can draw on, and what are the consequences of these limits for the well-being of the people?

> A community's risk of being affected by [an event] is defined by calculating the potential action of a given *threat* in the light of the region's particular conditions of *vulnerability*. The risk will be determined by the extent of the threat to [the community] and by its vulnerability to that threat. It is the reduction of vulnerability that explains why different [communities] have different risks when faced by the same threat...Disasters occur when extreme...events create situations that exceed a given [community's] capacity to absorb and survive the ensuing upheaval.[7]

Jose Luis Rocha and Ian Criostoplos wrote the above incisive paragraph to explain the tremendous number of deaths, injuries, and damaged property in poor countries from natural disasters such as floods, earthquakes, and volcanic eruptions, especially in contrast to rich countries, where such consequences are vastly reduced. They define the concept of vulnerability that we need to understand better. Vulnerability does not mean weakness, since some vulnerable people have survived threats that would destroy other people. Vulnerability does not mean moral choice, since moral choices depend on the history and culture of a community. Following what is defined as moral in the history and religion of a particular community does not necessarily lead to decreased vulnerability. For example, the Nicaraguan Roman Catholic Church teaches that artificial birth control is immoral and allows couples only the option of abstinence during fertile periods in order to limit family size. Yet the rapid growth of the population causes much suffering in a country with inadequate food, shelter, and health care. Being moral according to the church increases vulnerability rather than reducing it.

Vulnerability refers to the limits and adaptability of the resources that a community has accumulated over time. In this sense vulnerability is a condition of being human in a world where danger exists. Vulnerability is what theologians call finitude, the fact that human beings are limited in what they can achieve and in what they can endure. Human bodies and spirits are limited in the face of threats such as illness, violence, and death.

Not all vulnerabilities are equal. A family living in a brick house on a hill probably will not suffer the same consequences from a flood as a family living in a cardboard shack in a riverbed. The family on the hill has reduced its vulnerability to floods, while the family in the riverbed has not. There may be many reasons for the difference in vulnerability between these two families, but economic and political decisions are critical to the safety of populations. One must have access to capital, ownership of land, and education to build or rent a brick house on a hill, and without such resources, a family might be forced to live in the riverbed because that is the only space left.

Many families lived at the base of the Casita Volcano in Posoltega, Nicaragua. Because of the excessive rain from Hurricane Mitch on October 26–30, 1998, the whole mountainside gave way and buried eight communities and two thousand people.[8] Even a family in a brick house on the hill would not have been safe, because the mountainside itself could not hold up after forty inches of rain fell. For many years before this tragedy, the people who lived on this mountainside were vulnerable, but the massive tragedy of more than two thousand deaths had not happened there before, so they were not completely aware of their vulnerability. In a more developed country, zoning laws might have prevented housing from being constructed on such a site, and the tragedy might have been minimized.

In other parts of Nicaragua and Honduras much of the damage occasioned by the hurricane was brought about by the heavy deforestation caused by transnational companies' having clear-cut the mountains and shipped the wood products to the North. More recently, poor people have cut trees down for firewood or used fires as a cheap way to clear the land. The same economic vulnerability contributed to the lack of community resources to rescue disaster victims, to recover dead bodies, and, later on, to help the victims reconstruct their houses, find new jobs, and so on. To this day, thousands of hurricane victims in Nicaragua are still living in houses made out of cardboard and plastic and are making a living from charity or delinquency.

I define economic vulnerability as any situation in which the dominant economic system causes an insecurity and a lack of resources that make daily life desperate for people, or whenever the economic system imposes control and restrictions that deprive people of life, liberty, and the pursuit of happiness—in a word, whenever it threatens people with the loss of their humanity.

Family Violence

All those without power and privilege are the most vulnerable and the most likely to be victimized by sexual and domestic violence.[9]

Family violence is a pattern of assaultive and coercive behaviors, including physical, sexual, and psychological attacks, as well as economic coercion, that persons use against members of their family or household.[10]

Family violence is one form within a larger class of violence. Violence can be defined in terms of the damage it creates, the context in which it occurs, or the intentions of those who perpetrate it on others. The English word *violate* comes from the Indo-European root *weie*–"vital force." From this we get such words as "vim, violate, violent, from Latin *vis*, force, with irregular derivatives *violare*, to treat with force, and *violentus*, vehement."[11] The first dictionary definition of violence is "physical force exerted for the purpose of violating, damaging, or abusing." Other meanings include: damage resulting from a storm; "abusive or unjust exercise of power"; and "abuse or injury to content or meaning."[12] In these senses, the word allows us to define violence as physical, sexual, and psychological attacks—if they contain vital force, if there is damage or likely damage, and if there is an intention of harming and controlling another through such acts.

Violence and the threat of violence are the main strategies of war and military force: unless one complies with certain demands, the consequence will be damage to one's body or person. Violent crime is the use of force to obtain something, whether money, sexual access, or revenge, or is random aggression against someone. Often the threat of violence suffices to obtain control and compliance, especially if such threats fit within a believable pattern of violent behaviors.

Throughout this book, I will use the word *violence* to refer to any use of vital force to damage and/or control persons or groups of persons. In this sense, an economic system that is supported by political and military institutions can be violent. The massive poverty in the world is not just the result of unfortunate weather in certain places and inadequate skills of certain populations. Massive, long-term poverty that threatens life and health is the result of systematic control of people by economic institutions supported by military force. The damage is not difficult to observe–high infant mortality, illnesses caused by unclean water and inadequate food, and the breakdown of families and communities with resulting family violence. The agents of economic violence are sometimes more difficult to identify, especially since the dominant institutions control the public media and sources of information and knowledge.

In addition to war and political and economic oppression, there is interpersonal violence when one or more individuals control and exploit other individuals. One of the most frequent places of occurrence of interpersonal violence is within the family. The lifetime rates of family violence range from 25 to 50 percent in most sample populations.[13] That is, 25 to 50 percent of the persons in a population will experience some form of family violence during their lifetime.[14] These statistics increase or decrease depending on several factors. Any person can be vulnerable to family violence in any family of any social class. We also know that family violence increases during times of community stress, including economic depression and war; but such violence decreases in situations where women and children are empowered by culture, laws, and social support. In communities of every social and economic class, a significant percentage of persons will experience family violence. This is a major challenge for those in the caring professions and for the church that is engaged in caring for its members and persons in the community. One purpose of this book is to improve the church's knowledge of economic vulnerability and family violence so that the church can provide resources for those who need it.

Women and children are often more vulnerable to family violence than men. This means that an analysis of economic vulnerability and family violence must include a gender focus.

> Why is a gender focus so important? Many people, particularly men, insist that it is just a fad, but that is not the case. Particularly during a disaster, women are more vulnerable than men. Worse still, the men in their own families are the ones who make them more vulnerable. Women social workers belonging to a Masayan NGO (non-governmental organization) observed that the women in the emergency shelters "were busy with domestic chores while their husbands were getting drunk." Similar attitudes were observed during Mitch. Because "boys don't cry,"

when men are driven to it by their powerlessness in the face of a disaster, they tend to "balance up" their emotional imbalance, which they do not know how to handle, by abusing their power. Studies demonstrate that both violence against women and children and sexual violence rise sharply during emergencies caused by natural disasters.[15]

The relationship between economic vulnerability and family violence is complex, and class prejudice often causes middle-class readers to assume that the lower classes are more violent than others. This false perception is the result of faulty analysis, including the confusion of the damage from economic violence itself. People who live in desperate poverty suffer many difficulties in their lives, mostly the result of the oppression of poverty itself. I will explore this reality in chapter 5 on the unequal distribution of wealth and vulnerability. The United Nations Human Development Report has systematized the damages people experience from poverty.

Family violence occurs in every social class and every culture that we know about.[16] The desires of some people to threaten and coerce others do not correlate with any social category. In fact, the most violent persons in history have been rulers of governments and military forces who have caused the deaths of millions of people. And we know from various biographies that such rulers were often violent with their partners and families as well. Names such as Hitler, Stalin, Idi Amin, and other well-known tyrants make the point. Leaders in democratic countries have also lived with contradictions in their lives. Many of the "founding fathers" owned slaves and depended on violence and the militia to defend their property rights. The violent system of slavery created the context in which these men could force their will on others. It is not accurate to simply equate family violence with economic vulnerability.

However, violence intersects with economic vulnerability in several important ways. First, as I show in part 1, women and children in working-class and poor communities have few defenses against male violence in the home. While the incidence of violence may not be greater among the poor, women and children who are poor have fewer choices when confronted with violence. In chapter 2, Brenda Consuelo Ruiz presents three cases of women who decided to stay in violent relationships because they could see no other way to feed their children, and because the legal system in Nicaragua provided no protection. These cases are important because they show how economic vulnerability can aggravate the problems of violence. However, many poor women do leave violent relationships, and many non-poor women stay in violent relationships.[17] Poor women often develop inner psychological and spiritual resources that help them resist violence and survive in ways that are not understood by scholars who study these subjects.[18]

A second way that economic vulnerability and family violence are related is that the violence of poverty has a disintegrating effect on some persons and families. Many communities have resisted the economic violence of capitalism in creative ways, and they have engaged in alternative institutions and visions that provide hope for the future. However, for other people, poverty is so damaging that it leads to disintegration of personality, one symptom of which is violent behaviors perpetrated on others. The danger is not just the existence of poverty at some point in a person's life but also the cumulative effects of poverty over generations. A young child who loses a parent to a nutrition-related illness and is not cared for by another adult will suffer long-term trauma that will have various consequences, including an increased risk for violence. A soldier who returns from war to a situation of poverty is more likely than other men to engage in family violence, continuing the behaviors of rape and threats that were taught and expected during military actions. Poverty is violent, and its long-term consequence is an increase in violence for particular individuals.

Another way to understand the interaction of economic vulnerability and family violence is to look at the experience of children.

> Children's poverty is conditioned by two overlapping categories of poverty—material poverty and the poverty of tenuous connections. Children's flourishing is envisioned in two normative frameworks: children's social ecology and children's rights...Children's poverty must be overcome by building relationships with vulnerable children. This work of care is a means of finding God...Through this work of care—by practicing the means of grace and the work of mercy and piety—the church can genuinely transform itself and influence society and culture.[19]

Pamela Couture's work closely parallels what I am saying in this book: economic vulnerability and family violence have devastating consequences for children and adults and must be a priority of concern for the church. In global terms, the vulnerability of children does not correspond exactly with material poverty. Some nations have higher quality of life for children with moderate resources, and some nations have lower quality with more resources. The difference depends on the distribution of resources and the conscious care that the society focuses on the needs of children. However, most of the extremely poor countries have low quality of life for their children because poverty itself is devastating in its consequences for children and adults alike. In the United States, the injustice of resource distribution and the insensitivity of some areas of the country to children mean that the quality of life for some children is low. Infant mortality rates in some areas of the United States are as high as 15 per 1,000 births, and the number of children living in poverty is as high as 40 percent in some states.[20]

Many children are vulnerable because they live in poor families headed by women.

> Three gender-related conditions contribute to the poverty of women and children: [U.S.] women's wages are stretched because women are more responsible for dependent children than men; women's wages have remained consistently lower than men's wages, roughly two-thirds that of men; women are likely to be persistently poor when they live in poor communities where community institutions have declined.[21]

Many children are vulnerable because of tenuous connections with family and community.

> The poorest children in [U.S.] society are those with only tenuous connections to their families and communities. Homeless children often live with their families but are unable to access community services in a reliable way. Street children may have tenuous links to family and community. Children in foster and group home care receive community services but may have little or no contact with their families.[22]

Couture suggests that pastoral care must be adapted to respond to children who are economically vulnerable and subject to family violence. In order to do this, pastoral care should challenge the way churches raise money and the way health care is delivered, and must avoid becoming subject to the values and rhetoric of capitalism. As capitalism takes over the delivery of health care services, with profit as the primary motive, care for the whole population is no longer the top priority. "The more pastoral care and counseling is drawn into the formal economy, however, the narrower its clientele and the less likely it is to be able to fulfill its ethical mandate to provide care as an extension of the congregation to all persons, regardless of their ability to pay."[23] Couture concludes:

> My hope is that in the new era, pastoral care and counseling will be as acutely engaged in informing itself about the structural situations that create suffering as the ecumenical, relief, and humanitarian agencies have been—and that we will share responsibility for the rearrangements of the economy that are presently occurring, rearrangements that have ramifications for children abroad and in the United States.[24]

Pastoral Theology

Pastoral theology is a set of beliefs, attitudes, and behaviors motivated by the Christian gospel and practiced by Christian communities to provide care for all people–resources for survival and healing, trustworthy community, and empowerment for justice-work on behalf of others.[25]

Pastoral theology is a Christian term that has a long history within the life of the church. From the Indo-European prefix *pa-* meaning, "to protect, feed,"[26] pastor originally comes from the Latin, *pastor,* or shepherd.[27] Pastor became the term that designated the leader of a local congregation and, after the Protestant Reformation, included the functions of protection, feeding, and caring activities of the whole people of God, the priesthood of all believers. Seward Hiltner defined pastoral theology as the theory and practice of care, with a special emphasis on starting from theological foundations and returning from practice with theological insights.[28] The field of pastoral care has expanded its concerns beyond professional and ordained pastors to include the congregational care practiced by the whole community.

The content of care involves providing resources for survival and healing, trustworthy community, and empowerment for justice-work on behalf of others. Providing resources for survival and healing is the most traditional definition of pastoral care. This includes the general care of a congregation through visitation, prayer, worship, and other rituals. It also includes the practices of pastoral counseling and psychotherapy, wherein people meet on a regular basis with trained professionals for support, consultation, and advice on dealing with their personal problems.

Trustworthy community is a necessary requirement for quality human life. The needs of children, who require tender and solicitous concern,[29] teach us the most about the need for community. But we also learn about adult needs for community during times of crises such as trauma, illness, grief, and other difficult times. Even beyond times of obvious need, adults and children benefit from communities who are truthful and safe and do not favor important people over those with less power. Survivors of family violence need trustworthy community because their own families have turned against them, and they must have other places to find support and understanding. Persons who live in the midst of economic vulnerability need trustworthy community because they need places where they can be relieved from the pressure of survival and can gather their resources for fighting another day.

Empowerment for justice-work on behalf of others is also a goal of pastoral care. Having received care at crucial points in one's life, acting out that care on behalf of others is the final stage of healing. Sometimes this is as simple as visiting and praying with others who suffer. Sometimes it means engaging in nonviolent action to challenge social injustice. We understand family violence today because survivors themselves organized shelters and began advocating for justice for women and children who were caught in family violence. We understand the violence of poverty today because the poor themselves have organized revolts and alternative institutions for their own liberation. The church, in its caring ministry, is called to engage in justice-work on behalf of those who are economically vulnerable and caught in situations of family violence. Apart from a concerted effort to change society, the caring ministries toward individuals will be empty.

Intercultural Care

As its economic system of capitalism has become a global empire, the United States has become a multicultural society, and various groups have become assertive against the hegemony of the European American culture. The cultural parochialism of much of the U.S. church's theology and practice has been clearly identified. In this book I attempt to respond to this challenge by using an intercultural method. Most obviously, I will give sustained attention to three cultures that are not dominant in the U.S., namely, the African American culture, Latino/a culture, and the emerging women's culture. However, I need to define more clearly what I mean by culture and how this reality affects the method of our work. Emmanuel Lartey, pastoral theologian from Ghana who has taught in England and the United States, is a leader in developing an intercultural approach to pastoral care and counseling. This long quotation gives several important principles that guide our work:

> By culture I shall be referring to the way in which social groups develop distinct patterns of life and give "expressive form" to their social and material life experience…The culture of a group of persons is the particular and distinctive "way of life" of the group. This includes the ideas, values, and meanings embodied in institutions and practices, in forms of social relationship, in systems of belief, in mores and customs, in the way objects are used and physical life organized. It has to do with the way in which patterns of life are experienced, understood, and interpreted. These structures and their meanings influence the ongoing collective experience of groups. They also, on the other hand, limit, modify and constrain how groups live and interpret their life experiences. Moreover, there is a constant historical interaction taking place between people and their changing social environment and circumstances. Culture is therefore never static. Instead there is a continual interplay resulting in dynamism, adaptability, re-interpretation, re-formulation and change. There is certainly continuity, but this is itself continually challenged by changing circumstances, so that new forms of expression, new perceptions and creative interpretations are emerging all the time.[30]

Lartey articulates the following three principles that are important for our work:[31]

1. *Contextuality*, which means that every description of the life of persons must be understood within the cultural context where it takes place. In this volume, this will be done as much as possible by relying on descriptions from persons within particular cultures. It is difficult for persons outside the culture to understand the complex symbols, languages, and histories that create certain events.

2. *Multiple perspectives*, which means that there can be no dominant, universal perspective from which everything can be clearly seen. In this book, four perspectives are represented: African American, Latino/a, women-culture, and white, male, professional U.S. culture

3. *Authentic participation*, which means that the narrator cannot write about a culture based on books and library research alone. The written language communicates only a small percentage of cultural reality. I understood this much better after visiting Nicaragua, Korea, and Ghana. I felt the impulses of culture more strongly than I had ever felt them before, and I knew instinctively that I would have to visit many times to begin to get even a glimpse of the richness of the history and communal life of each culture.

Based on his definition of intercultural pastoral care and counseling, Lartey redefines pastoral care:

Pastoral care consists of helping activities, participated in by people who recognize a transcendent dimension to human life, which by the use of verbal or non-verbal, direct or indirect, literal or symbolic modes of communication, aim at preventing, relieving, or facilitating persons coping with anxieties. Pastoral care seeks to foster people's growth as full human beings together with the development of ecologically holistic communities in which all persons may live humane lives.[32]

Notice the changes from the definitions I use in the previous section. As Lartey attempts to define pastoral care for an African and intercultural world, he significantly changes the focus of care itself. Instead of "motivated by the Christian gospel," he suggests "people who recognize a transcendent dimension to human life." This opens up dialogue with African Muslims and religious leaders of African traditional religions who also have theories and practices of care, but are not motivated primarily by the Christian gospel. The interreligious dimension is critically important in our world today, especially if we want to find ways of addressing economic vulnerability and family violence.

Lartey also changes "theories and practices of care" to a more holistic focus on a range of activities that are often ignored in pastoral theology, namely, "activities [that are] verbal or non-verbal, direct or indirect, literal or symbolic modes of communication." This part of the definition challenges the Eurocentric understanding of pastoral care, and forces the caring person to attend much more systematically to multiple types of communication, which are more easily accessible in African than in European cultures.

Lartey's goal is "to foster people's growth as full human beings together with the development of ecologically holistic communities in which all persons may live humane lives." He has again moved away from an exclusively Christian focus for the sake of interreligious dialogue and has included a focus on the natural environment, so important for people who live in poor nations where the environment has been devastated by capitalism.

Intercultural care is the systematic attempt to give voice to multiple cultures in order to undercut the dominance of Western culture and economics, and to empower indigenous cultures that have important resources for the future of the world.

Ambiguities of Relating Economics, Violence, and Care

Having defined the key terms, I need to acknowledge certain ambiguities in bringing together these topics, namely, economic vulnerability, family violence, and pastoral theology.

All pastoral care occurs within an economic context, and much pastoral care occurs across economic and class lines. We need to explore how issues of pastoral care are affected by the economic and class contexts of human life, and what pastoral care might look like if economics and class were built into the theories and practices of pastors.

What are the differences between the disciplines of economics and pastoral theology? The first and most obvious difference is between the interpersonal relationships of pastoral theology (micro-systems) and the global systems of economics (macro-systems). Pastoral care is usually understood as the theory and practice of immediate care provided by a Christian community for its own members and those in the surrounding community. Caring often influences participation in social justice ministries by providing resources, leadership, advocacy, and personal involvement. But such activities, while motivated by care, are not usually called pastoral care.

While every household has an economy, that is, a system of material exchanges for creation and distribution of wealth based on normative images of human desires and behaviors, economics is almost always defined as a global system that can only be understood by elite professionals with higher education. Figuring out how to relate such micro- and macro-systems is difficult. While I show that economic resources have dramatic effects on small interpersonal units such as households and local communities, it is difficult to understand how economic systems work and how small units of persons can influence the economic systems that influence their way of living.

A second difference is the histories of the academic disciplines that have defined pastoral care and economics. Pastoral care developed in the twentieth century in dialogue with the social sciences, especially psychology, and it almost always focuses on the individual within a small interpersonal network of relationships. Economics, on the other hand, developed in dialogue with political philosophy and mathematics, and it almost always focuses on the relationships between large institutions and nations. Economics tends toward the "hard sciences," with quantitative measures, in contrast to psychology with its "soft science" of interviews and the self-reports of individuals. Economics and psychology are nervous allies on a few topics, but basically ignore each other. Economics assumes a general concern for care, but infrequently asks how such care takes place within small social units such as families and interpersonal groups. Psychology often submits to the dominant economic system by providing research that endorses its rightful influence in individual life, for example, by interviewing consumers on which products they prefer. Until the rise of Liberation movements of the late twentieth century, the psychological literature rarely raised critical issues about the dominant system of economics.

A third difference between pastoral care and economics is at the level of assumptions. Pastoral care has assumed a love-ethic based primarily on the analogy of parent and young child. Because twentieth-century psychology developed out of a fascination with how children grow and the long-term consequences of childhood experiences, care usually has been understood as the care of a mature person for one who is less mature, therefore an asymmetrical relationship. Such relationships require what one author called "solicitous and tender concern"[33] for the other. Caregivers must "take care"[34], "be careful," and "do no harm."[35] Thus, caring has been seen as a stereotypical feminine value, as a mother caring for an infant. By analogy, even adults need "tender, loving care" to survive in a cold, hard world. By contrast, economics has always been about power–the power to create, the power to decide what happens, the power to make difficult decisions even when the results might hurt someone. Thus, economics is understood as a masculine, public activity that cannot be too concerned about care. The creation and distribution of wealth is not about making sure everyone feels okay, but about doing the hard thing without too much regard for interpersonal values.

Yet the dichotomy between pastoral care and economics has never been total. Persons who care for others have always been concerned for the others' economic situations. Social workers who start out in counseling relationships often become involved in advocating for economic change on behalf of the people they have become attached to.

Genuine care includes the whole person, and households with low income and/or large debts need care for their economic situations as well as their interpersonal relationships. Likewise, economics always includes concern for the everyday lives of people. Every economist includes in her or his argument an assumption that her or his theories are the best way to provide care and resources for the most people. There is no legitimate economic theory that tries to justify itself on the amount of suffering it creates for people. In this sense, care for people is one of the arguments for every economic system. Economics is important to care, and care is important to economics.

The question for this part of our work is this: How are pastoral care and economics related to each other at the level of interpersonal relationships and face-to-face communities, and how are they related at the level of macro-systems that function at national and global levels? Answering this question is important for both care and economics.

At this stage, I face a challenge in the way I have been proceeding. There are no universal definitions of pastoral care and economics, but only definitions that have been constructed in particular historical and social contexts. I am talking about pastoral caregiving that has developed in the United States during the twentieth century, and I am talking about capitalism as the dominant economic system and its theory as developed in the United States and Europe in the last three centuries. One can discuss the relationship of U.S. pastoral care and U.S. capitalism in several ways.

In one sense, U.S. pastoral care and U.S. capitalism are *complementary developments*. They developed during the same period within a similar cultural context. U.S. capitalism is a public ideology/theology that sets the terms for how the material world is understood and managed. U.S. pastoral care is an ideology/theology that tends to the more private wounds of people whose lives are circumscribed by U.S. capitalism. These two systems of belief and practice have coexisted and supported each other for centuries. Pastoral care has listened to the suffering of people and has offered interpretations that give individuals the responsibility for accommodating rapid social change. By focusing on childhood experiences, emotions, and feelings of guilt and inadequacy, pastoral care has provided religious sanction for the individualism that fuels capitalism. No great protest to U.S. capitalism has come from the pastoral care community. In fact, pastoral care specialists have benefited economically by providing services that capitalism is willing to pay for through government and private health insurance policies.

In another sense, U.S. pastoral care is a *form of resistance* to U.S. capitalism, its deficiencies, and its evil effects. As capitalism drastically changed the everyday lives of people in the United States, moving them from farms to cities, from cottage industries to factories, from local to anonymous communities, from interpersonal to technology-oriented networks, pastoral care tended to the suffering of persons and thematized their complaints against the economic system. In the early years of the twentieth century, pastoral care specialists attended to persons in hospitals and prisons, bringing their unhappy plight to the attention of the public and spearheading a move to provide more resources for these vulnerable populations. In the middle years of the century, pastoral caregivers were active in the civil rights and peace movements, interpreting the needs of people for social justice within a caring perspective. Since 1970, feminist pastoral caregivers have brought to the public's attention the complaints of women about unequal work, domestic violence, sexual abuse, harassment, and discrimination, and have advocated changes in laws, customs, and personal habits in all people. Pastoral caregivers have been active in intercultural counseling with ethnic minorities in the United States. Economic dislocation of immigrants and refugees brings a high need for caregiving and also makes possible political movements for economic empowerment.

Pastoral care itself is an ambiguous phenomenon in U.S. society, especially in relation to U.S. capitalism. In some ways pastoral care has been a movement that helps people adjust to the economic system without regard for its justice or injustice. In other ways, pastoral care has been a movement of solidarity with the people, encouraging their resistance to injustice, and providing resources for survival, healing, and empowerment.

In the rest of this book, I explore this complex relationship between pastoral care and economics in the United States, in Nicaragua, and globally, and I ask how we can develop theories and practices of care that take the economic realities of everyday life more seriously as the context for care.

Conclusion

In this chapter I have defined some of the key terms that are important throughout this book: economic vulnerability, family violence, pastoral theology, and intercultural care. I have discussed some of the problems in each of these definitions and some of the tensions in their relationships with one another. In chapter 2, I examine case material of persons who have experienced the first three of these realities. The persons who have shared their lives with us have experienced economic vulnerability in Nicaragua and the United States; their lives have been profoundly shaped by family violence; and they have sought pastoral care for healing and survival. I invite you to listen intently to these voices within their cultural and religious context before I turn to the debates among scholars about the best way to provide care for vulnerable persons in various economic and family situations.

2

Pastoral Counseling of Domestic Violence Victims in Nicaragua
Brenda Consuelo Ruiz

Three Cases

Margarita[1]

Margarita was a petite, slender woman of thirty-six when she first came for counseling in 1995. She had been married to Carlos for fourteen years and had separated from him four years before. She worked as a store clerk and earned little money. She and her husband had three sons, who were fifteen, thirteen, and twelve at the time.

Margarita came from a Christian family. She was the fourth of eight children, and because her parents were poor she was given away when she was three years old to a childless aunt who had more economic resources. Her aunt took good care of her material needs, but did not attend to her emotional needs. She would not let her see her family and would not let her cry when she was lonely. Margarita felt isolated from her parents, brothers, and sisters and felt even more so after she was sexually abused by two uncles and a stepbrother, abuse she first disclosed in counseling. She felt guilty for not having been able to defend herself and also for becoming distant from her siblings.

Carlos, the husband, was the third of seven children. He had been abused as a child and had to start working at a young age to support himself. He had used a lot of drugs during adolescence and had been under psychiatric treatment for depression for some time. Carlos was abusive of Margarita. Their oldest son remembers seeing Carlos chase Margarita around the house with a knife, and he was still afraid of his father. Margarita said Carlos would often parade around right in front of her with other women and that he badly abused the children.

Carlos left for Honduras, looking for a job and for psychiatric treatment, and there he found another woman who was willing to mother him more than Margarita and started to live with her and her young daughter. Whenever he came to Nicaragua he wanted to sleep with Margarita and acted as if they were still a happy couple. Margarita had difficulties asking him to leave, because he was helping her support the family and because she felt her sons needed a masculine role model. She came in for counseling because she was feeling depressed and because the children were aggressive toward one another. She realized the marriage was not viable anymore, but it took her nine months of therapy to initiate the divorce.

When Carlos realized that she was preparing to divorce him, he blamed her for their problems and threatened to withhold the money she needed to support the children. Margarita feared that she would be forced to let the children live with him and this other woman in Honduras. Margarita could not stand the thought of losing her children because she could not support them. She considered stopping the divorce procedures because of his threats, but decided to go on because of the abuse. Carlos then tried to manipulate her by acting sick and begging her to take care of him. Margarita became confused and was only able to stand her ground through much coaching from her counselor. Her counselor encouraged her to make use of all her spiritual resources as well as legal advice. After many months she managed to secure alimony payments and to limit Carlos's visiting rights.

Carlos in the meantime tried his best to turn the children against her. Margarita neglected herself in order to meet her children's demands and became sick. She had to stop the divorce procedures temporarily in order to buy medicine. Her husband weaseled out of his financial obligations with the family and with other agreements on many occasions, but with the continuous support of her counselor and much prayer Margarita persisted with her demands. At the end, she was able to achieve a good relationship with her children and to develop a life for herself.

Margarita was in therapy on and off for three years. It was no easy task for her. Even though the counseling center she attended charged low fees, many times she had a hard time deciding what was more important: buying food or shoes for her children or coming in for a counseling session. But she was thankful for her twenty-eight sessions, because they had helped her regain her dignity and self-esteem, to gain a better perspective on her life, and to feel God's love surrounding and sustaining her at all times. Even though the most significant support she had received from her church was only that neither the pastor nor the congregation had condemned her for divorcing her husband, her deep personal spirituality had helped her survive this ordeal.

Soledad

Soledad remembers living in a rural area when she was young, but she cannot remember how old she was when her mother gave her away as a maid the first time. She only remembers that she had served and had been abused by several different families by the time she had turned eight and her mother decided to give her to her sister (Soledad's aunt), who in turn gave her to another family she knew. Her new employer gave her such a bad beating once that Soledad was in a public hospital for six months with a lung injury. Luckily, poor people at that time did not have to pay anything at public hospitals, and as she began to get better, she earned her stay by helping the nurses do small chores.

After that she worked for a family who treated her well but refused to put her in school. Her mother came to get her once, and Soledad tried to commit suicide so that she would not have to go live with her mother. She remembered that her stepfather had threatened to rape her and her mother had not believed her when she related it. She knew she could not count on her mother's love or protection, for in every place where she had worked her mother had not come to visit her, only to get the salary Soledad had earned. In the end, the mother was successful in forcing Soledad to come to live with her.

She continued working as a maid through her adolescent years and she fell in love with a boy from the neighborhood. But in exchange for some money, her mother had arranged for an older man to come visit them and spend the night with Soledad. The man raped her, and the mother gave Soledad to this man as a live-in companion. This man turned out to be a good provider, and he and Soledad had five children. Her oldest daughter was born when Soledad was fifteen. But Soledad never learned to love this man. After several years he became a womanizer and left her for another woman. He never contributed to the family again in any way.

Soledad was forty years old when she came in for counseling in 1998. Even though the center charged low fees, her salary as a maid would have made it hard for her to pay for the counseling. Her employer paid for her. Her presenting complaints were sudden crying spells, irritability, and numerous conflicts with her adult children, who all lived under the same roof with her.

When she and her sons and daughters came for family therapy the conflicts and personal suffering became evident. The youngest daughter (eighteen) had tried to commit suicide because the mother continuously rejected her boyfriend and fought with her all the time. The youngest son (twenty-one) was aggressive after a head injury caused by a car accident. He had also used drugs when younger. The oldest daughter (twenty-five) fought with the second one (twenty-two) over disciplining her children, especially her twelve-year-old son, who in turn complained that his mother did not love him. The oldest son (twenty-three) was depressed frequently, had a drinking problem, had made several suicide attempts, and became aggressive when drunk. Both of the sons were unemployed and continuously fought with their sisters over food, space, use of electricity, and so forth. All the children agreed that the mother was emotionally inexpressive, and several said that they did not think their mother loved them.

With tears in her eyes Soledad said that she loved her children very much but that she did not know how to express it. Her mother never taught her how to be a loving mother. She had done the best she could to raise her children as a single mother, working long hours as a maid in order to feed her children. She confessed that one thing that angered her was that her children had not done well in school. All her life she had yearned to go to school and learn how to read and write, but never had the opportunity. Now her children had the chance to get an education, but they were not taking advantage of it. She, in turn, felt that they did not love her.

During the next several sessions, the therapist explained that Soledad could very well have been killed by all the abuse she suffered as a young girl but that God preserved her life and must have an important purpose for her. Even though Soledad was a non-practicing Catholic, she firmly believed in God. The therapist also explained that abuse in early life can have serious consequences later on, but she congratulated Soledad for trying to be a better mother than her own mother had been. She also explained how poverty, crowded living conditions, and unemployment erode people's self-esteem and how important it is for family members to try to help one another out in order to survive. Together the family explored ways in which each family member could contribute to support one another, to express their love for one another, and to build a better family life.

During the next few months some changes started to take place: the youngest daughter started to do better in school and to help around the house a little more, and Soledad started accepting her daughter's boyfriend a bit more. The youngest son helped take care of the children in the household and took on some of the house chores; the sisters paid him, so he had some spending money. The oldest daughter was still bitter but continued her job as a schoolteacher and decided to go to night school, so she had less time to fight with the others. The second daughter got herself a job as a maid and had a boyfriend; she had some money of her own and could afford to pay her brother to do the housework. The oldest son decided to go to Costa Rica to try to find a job.

This family had a long way to go when they stopped therapy, but they had begun to experiment with alternative ways to survive and to relate to one another.

Juana

Juana was a thirty-six-year-old woman from a rural area who sought counseling for the first time in September 1997. She was depressed and had made suicidal gestures on three occasions. Her self-esteem was very low. Julio, her live-in companion, had abused her emotionally for sixteen years with several incidents of threats and physical abuse.

Juana was brought up in a conservative Protestant home with no father present. Her family was extremely poor, and she was able to graduate only from junior high school. She decided to marry her first boyfriend even though she was not in love with him so that she could escape her repressive environment. That marriage lasted only two years, until she met Julio and fell madly in love with him. She abandoned her husband and came to live with Julio.

She knew Julio was a womanizer. In fact he had many short-lived affairs while they were together, but he was a good father to their five children, and she loved him. He had recently developed a degenerative bone disease, and Juana expressed that she was willing to give up her life in exchange for his. Her main presenting concern was that he seemed to be in love with a university classmate, a relationship that had lasted for at least three years.

She only paid the equivalent of US $1 for every therapy session. That was all she could afford, because she had to pay the bus fare from her hometown into Managua out of her meager resources. After the first few sessions, she realized that she needed to value herself more. The therapist encouraged her to see the abilities and strengths she had within herself even though she was playing the role of a doormat in her relationship with Julio. She helped Juana understand that it was not healthy to direct her anger against herself, but that it was better to direct it where it belonged, at her partner.

Juana and her therapist talked about how she could start a little business to gain economic independence from Julio and how she could survive emotionally without him. They also talked about how God loved her and had provided her with people who would help her. But her friends were not from the Pentecostal church she attended. According to her church she was "living in sin," and she did not dare to mention her abusive situation to the pastor or other church members, because she knew she would be condemned right away and that her situation would be viewed as a punishment from God for her "sinful behavior."

Slowly she began to defend her rights and detach herself from this hurtful relationship. It was a difficult struggle, because she had depended totally on this man, both emotionally and economically. Deep down she still loved him desperately, but rationally she knew this was not a healthy relationship for her and that changes needed to be made. She began confronting him about his behavior with less guilt and more confidence. She told the therapist she had decided she would not allow him back into her life unless he respected her and loved her as she deserved and unless he decided to quit the other relationship. With this she discharged herself from therapy.

Two weeks later she came back to the counseling center. She was extremely emaciated and pale. She said she had done something terrible: she had taken a whole bottle of sleeping pills after a big fight with Julio, during which he had threatened to kick her out of the house and take the children away. Her adolescent sons had been acting up lately, and her little business was not doing well; she was desperate about all her problems. Luckily Julio was around when she took the pills and was able to take her to the hospital to have her stomach pumped. She was unconscious for three days, but soon after she had regained consciousness she was discharged from the hospital because the doctors had declared themselves on strike, demanding better salaries and working conditions. Back at home she became worse and had to be taken to the emergency room again. She was hospitalized again for a few days and then was discharged to her mother's home, where she was lovingly cared for by her family and friends.

With the help of her therapist she was able to see that God loved her and had preserved her life and had given her a second opportunity, and that what had happened had given her the chance to experience how much her family and friends really cared for her and were willing to support her. She also was able to see for herself that Julio was not a person she should have been willing to give her life for.

Her recuperation, both physical and emotional, was slow; she was vulnerable for a long time. But with much prayer and the help of her family, friends, and therapist, she started to take some firm steps toward establishing independence from Julio. She gave away the bed she had shared with Julio for all their life together, got herself a new one, and rearranged the furniture. She explored different alternatives to generate income. She investigated the process to demand alimony and slowly allowed herself to express her anger toward Julio. One of her turning points came when she was so angry with him that she ripped and burned a bunch of papers Julio still had in her house. Last time she came for therapy she was wearing a simple but elegant dress. She commented that Julio was still trying to get her out of the house but that she was sure she would not allow it. That was the last time Juana was seen in the counseling center.

Recurring Themes

There are several recurring themes in these three cases:

- All the clients wanted to break the cycle of violence. None of them wanted her children to experience what she had gone through.

- In all three cases, the women had few economic resources available to them to escape from or confront the violence at home. The state did not provide a safety net either.

- The counselor at times felt overwhelmed by the heaviness of her client's abuse and the few alternatives of economic survival. There were not many other places these women could go to for help. The injustice and the unnecessary suffering were particularly burdensome.

- In all the cases the church as an institution played an innocuous role at best. The women had not shared much, if any, of their stories with their pastors, church leaders, or ecclesial communities.

- Long-term therapy was not a possibility for any of the women. That was a luxury none of them could afford, either money-wise or time-wise. In situations of poverty such as these, the best a therapist can strive for is short-term intervention.

- Each of the clients had a tremendous personal and spiritual inner strength that became evident when the woman needed to tap into it. Part of this strength came from a profound faith tested over the many years of suffering and from the strong ties with their extended families and friends.

The Cases at the Counseling Center

The author of this chapter works part time in an ecumenically based counseling center whose main purpose is to attend to the counseling demands of low-income families. The cost of a therapy session is nominally the equivalent of US$9, although the majority of the clientele pay less than that. Many, such as Juana, pay the equivalent of US$1, and some are seen for free if the situation requires it.

Of the 162 cases seen by the author from 1993 till the end of 1999, 100 had directly to do with domestic violence (61.7 percent of the cases). Of these, 53 involved violence against children and adolescents taking place at the time or during the childhood of the clients, and 47 were cases of partner violence.

The cases involving domestic violence had the following characteristics:

1. Most of the families were poor and had many children (such as Margarita's family of origin, her husband's, and their nuclear family).

2. The biological father was either physically or emotionally absent (such as Soledad's), many of them were unemployed, and quite a few of them were alcoholic.

3. The mothers had usually achieved a low academic level (Soledad and Juana), and many started having children when very young (Soledad).

4. In many of the cases members of the extended family raised the children, most frequently the grandmother or an aunt (as in Margarita's case). Many family conflicts arose from excessive control of adolescent children by an older grandmother or aunt, especially in the case of conservative Protestant families.

5. In the cases where the mother was raising the children alone, the oldest child was usually parentified; there was a lot of neglect of the children's needs as the mother usually had to work long hours to support the family (as in Soledad's family). These homes usually had great economic limitations, and oftentimes the older children had to work from an early age to support themselves (as Carlos did).

6. In most of the cases it was at first difficult to identify the situation as one of domestic violence. Most victims tended to justify the behavior of the aggressor either by blaming it on external factors (ignorance, stress, alcoholism, the devil) or blaming themselves.

7. In a good number of cases the mother had several successive husbands or lovers with the hope that the man would help her raise her usually large family. This often lent itself to sexual abuse of the stepdaughters, as it did in Soledad's case.

8. Many of the parents had been directly abused as children or had witnessed their mothers being abused. In many of the cases the abuse went back to the grandparents' generation, as it did for Margarita's husband.

9. A significant number of fathers and older sons were veterans of the Contra War whose aggressive or withdrawn behaviors were the result of war trauma.

10. The symptoms most often experienced by the abused women were: depression, addictions, suicide attempts, sexual dysfunctions, psychosomatic complaints, and other psychiatric symptoms.

11. The children often experienced the following symptoms: aggressiveness, behavioral problems, low achievement in school, substance abuse, promiscuity, and vagrancy.

12. Other than the counseling center, these women had few other options where they could go to get adequate help.

For the reader to understand the full implications of the above-mentioned characteristics and their consequences on the prevalence of domestic violence, we need to describe the socioeconomic situation that the majority of the Nicaraguan population faces.

The Socioeconomic Situation of the Nicaraguan People: Massive Poverty

Nicaragua is a small country (about the size of New York State) of five million people situated in the middle of Central America. According to the Basic Indicators Report of the Situation of Health published by the World Health Organization in 2000, Nicaragua has a per capita income of US$452, making it the third poorest country in Latin America[2]. But even this low per capita income does not quite reflect the reality of the majority of the population if one takes into account that the 1998 annual report of the Pan American Health Organization shows that the wealthy Nicaraguans (20 percent of the population) have 60.5 percent of the total per capita income, whereas the poorest of the poor (20 percent of the population) receive only 2.8 percent of the total income[3]. The 1999 United Nations World Population report says that 78 percent of the urban population lives in actual poverty, and of these, 43 percent live in chronic poverty.

At least 50.1 percent of the economically active population is unemployed and sub-employed.[4] A significant percentage of the poor (about 60 percent) are women, especially single mothers.[5] One of the reasons for this is that many more women than men are involved in the informal market, which pays salaries that are 30 percent lower than those of the formal market. The second reason is that Nicaragua has one of the highest population growth rates in Latin America and in the world (2.9 percent) and the highest percentage of adolescent mothers in Central America as sex education is inadequate and access to contraceptives is still limited. The fertility rate for 1998 was 3.9 children per woman.[6] The sheer survival of the family, then, depends often on having two adult incomes. That is one reason why so many women in Nicaragua are willing to put up with a lot of abuse from their partners.

Women ordinarily work under very harsh conditions. Maids, for example, generally make about fifty dollars a month, work more than fourteen hours a day, often seven days a week, and their legal rights are hardly protected. They are often subjects of sexual harassment or abuse by the men in the houses in which they work, and very rarely have access to social security or other benefits.

Of the population under the age of fifteen in the rural areas, 80 percent are poor, which means the survival of the family depends also on children being incorporated very early into the labor force, even though in recent years it has been illegal to hire children younger than fourteen years of age. In 1996 the Ministry of Labor did a census that showed that 20 percent of children between the ages of ten and eighteen held full-time jobs, but figures from the National Coordinator of NGOs that Work with Children and Adolescents show that more than 40 percent of the children are involved in the labor force. Children may work in the family's small business (tortilla making, carpentry shop, small farm, etc.); pick coffee, cotton, or tobacco in large farms; or they may be involved in child prostitution or working as maids for higher income families.[7]

As happens in other countries where child labor is common, abuse of these children starts very early, be it by their bosses or family members. Many of the children are sexually abused. The many cases that are cited in the Nicaraguan newspapers of pregnant adolescent girls whose fathers or other relatives force them to have sex with them are not thinking of buying Levi jeans or Nike shoes with whatever money they can get from the abusers, but are thankful for the food that they, their mother, and their siblings eat that is provided by the abusers. The abused children's very own survival and that of their siblings stand in the way of denouncing the aggressors.

The World Bank and the International Monetary Fund reported in 1998 that Nicaragua had an illiteracy rate of 34 percent and that illiteracy was predominantly higher in the rural areas (46 percent). Education is not mandatory, and the majority of schools have been privatized with tuition and fees out of the reach of most of the low-income population. In 1999 only 52.2 percent of school age children were actually enrolled in school. Only one out of every hundred children who enters the school system manages to graduate from the university sixteen years later.[8] Many more girls than boys drop out of school.[9] Something that makes these figures especially serious is the fact that the Nicaraguan population is predominantly young, with 53 percent of the population younger than eighteen.

The country does not have a welfare system, and the social security program is painfully inadequate, so there is not a safety net that can help ameliorate the consequences of such dire poverty. One of the direct consequences of the high level of unemployment has been the migration of young people from rural areas both to urban areas and to other countries in search of jobs and a better future. Out of Nicaragua's population of five million, approximately one million work in another country (mostly in Costa Rica and the United States). These workers were able to send back to their families approximately US$600 million dollars in remittances during 1999 (compare with US$500 million the country received for its exports that same year).[10] Although this heavy migration contributes to the economic survival of the families, it also contributes to the destruction of families' networks that in the past have contributed to the emotional and cultural survival of these families.

Health care is not readily available for the great majority of people. About 66 percent of all births take place under very risky conditions; the infant mortality rate is five times higher than that of developed countries; and maternal deaths are ten times higher than in countries in the North.[11] There are only five medical doctors and three and a half nurses for every ten thousand inhabitants. The caloric intake of the population is lower than the average for Latin America, and the protein intake is very similar to that of poor African nations.[12] One out of every four children younger than five suffers from some degree of malnutrition, and one out of three children of that same age suffers from chronic malnutrition.[13]

About 34.7 percent of the population have no access to potable drinking water, and even fewer have access to electricity; 55 percent of homes have dirt floors.[14] Before Hurricane Mitch killed thousands of people and made tens of thousands homeless in 1998, only 20 percent of the population lived in adequate housing. Disasters such as flooding and earthquakes have aggravated already terrible living conditions.

Living on less than a dollar a day is no easy feat, even in Nicaragua. Having to do so not only accounts for hunger, malnutrition, diseases, and lack of education and health care for children and adults but also for a desperate need for survival—almost at any cost. A woman who has two or more small children, does not have a place to live, has never worked outside her home and has no marketable skills, reads and writes with great difficulty or not at all, and does not have extended family nearby and no welfare system to rely on will be greatly tempted to endure significant amounts of violence from her partner.

The high incidence of natural disasters (earthquakes, tidal waves, volcano eruptions, hurricanes, floods, droughts, etc.) by no coincidence affects the poor the most and has contributed greatly to this growing poverty and emotional instability and, therefore, to the resulting prevalence of domestic violence. Another important factor has been the war of insurrection that took place between 1977 and 1979 to oust the Somoza dictatorship, during which at least one out of every five Nicaraguan families lost a family member. In the 1980s the Contra War (financed largely by the U.S. government) left 17,100 people dead and many more thousands wounded, displaced, and disabled.

This harsh economic reality and its consequences are not only due to a national situation but also to an unjust international economic order. Nicaragua has one of the highest per capita foreign debts in the world. During 1998 it allocated more than 50 percent of the value of its imports or 75 percent of collected taxes to service the foreign debt. In other words, for every dollar the country invested on health or education, five dollars were allocated for paying the services, not even the principal of the debt itself.[15]

A Highly Patriarchal Society with a Religious Justification of Domestic Violence

Patriarchy was well established when Nicaragua and all Central America gained independence from Spain in 1821.

> By all accounts, the men who went to La Española during the first ten years were the most selected collection of rabble that was ever put together: ex-soldiers, ruined noblemen, fortune seekers, criminals and convicts.[16]

> Together with the gold, the females constituted the main part of the war booty or the easy prey of the "caballeros" appetite or their lack of ethical pruritus to abuse of their physical superiority.[17]

The Spaniards despised the natives, especially the women. The frequent practices of rape against the indigenous women created the so-called Mestizo race (90 percent of the actual Nicaraguan population), and racism accompanied this oppression, resulting in the denigration of the Mestizo populace. The annihilating abuse that the Indians experienced at the hands of the Spanish had devastating consequences for families in which abused men frequently abuse women and children. The cycle of abuse from the violence of the male conquerors to male dominance within indigenous families has contributed greatly to the development of "machismo" in Latin America.

> The Spanish conquerors were men coming from a society ferociously hierarchical, not only by customs but by the prevailing laws. This hierarchical organization was considered fundamental for maintaining the social, political, economic, and moral order in society; and it was difficult even to imagine an alternative then.[18]

Machismo had its theological basis in a type of religiosity the indigenous population was forced to accept (they were given this choice: either baptism into the Catholic faith or a horrendous death). The Catholic church taught that women were inferior to men and that children, particularly indigenous and Mestizo children, were created by God to be good household or field laborers to earn their way into heaven.

"Macho" men traditionally feel the most macho by establishing sexual relations with as many different women as possible, by begetting as many children as possible, by being aggressive, and by drinking the most alcohol. There is no surprise, then, in the high rates of single mothers, fatherless children, alcoholism, and domestic violence in Nicaraguan society today. Being sensitive, loving, tender, vulnerable, and affectionate are "feminine" characteristics, not likely to be found in a real "macho" man.

As the Protestant denominations made their appearance in our country (late 1800s and early 1900s), they brought with them not only the "good news" but also fundamentalist teachings about the men being the family head, the submission of women, and the necessity for suffering to purify the soul. Many Protestant churches adhere to these teachings to this day, making it actually sinful for a woman to consider leaving her abusive husband, as she would be violating God's will concerning the permanence of marriage. In many of these churches a woman is taught to believe that a non-Christian husband can be saved by her sacrifice and that her highest calling as a Christian is to forgive her husband continuously for any wrongdoing, even if her life or the life of her children is at stake. The same applies if the abuse comes from the pastor or another male authority figure in the church.

In trying to change this situation, churches in Nicaragua need to look critically at the many ways in which they have contributed both wittingly and unwittingly to situations of violence against women and children, not only by their theological teachings but also in the ways they have silenced and blamed the victims, sided with the perpetrators, and denied the existence of domestic violence in their midst. The churches have to repent of those sins. They also need to reread and reinterpret the Bible through women's eyes, learning about the many cases of violence against women and children described in the Bible and how famous male figures in the Bible were perpetrators or at least accomplices in situations of violence. They need to examine and imitate the example of Jesus as a defender of women and children.

Churches also need to offer restitution to the victims by offering free or affordable counseling services for the victims, by establishing support groups in the churches, by constructing shelters or becoming temporary shelters themselves, by finding ways to confront the perpetrators, and by revising their by-laws to deal appropriately with cases of domestic violence. They also need to educate their membership about issues related to domestic violence, such as healthy family living, self-esteem, interpersonal communication, creative resolution of conflict, and so forth, to prevent future situations of abuse. And last but not least, the churches need to maintain a prophetic ministry to denounce social and political structures that contribute to the violation of the rights of women and children.

There are a few para-ecclesial organizations in Nicaragua that are doing a lot of work in the area of domestic violence and a few others that support this work at least indirectly. The Protestant Association for Family Counseling (AEDAF) has done systematic workshops with women, pastors, and church leaders on domestic violence and related issues. Organizations such as these are usually underfunded (AEDAF had to close its offices in 2000 because of funding difficulties) and understaffed but nevertheless committed to ministry to the victims and survivors. And yet they seem like a very small ray of hope in the midst of such great darkness of structural and domestic violence.

Inadequate Ways to Deal with Domestic Violence

It was not until the 1980s and 1990s that domestic violence was talked about as such in Nicaragua, and not till 1996 (and then it was thanks to the efforts of the National Network of Women Against Violence) that reforms to the laws were passed in which domestic violence was regarded as a punishable act and regulations were established to prevent it. But passing laws and actually enforcing them are two different things. Many of the steps in the legal process from the complaint of a victim until the aggressor is actually convicted are easily compromised and turned to the abuser's advantage.

Women have difficulty initiating legal procedures to defend themselves against violent spouses because they have difficulty identifying their experiences as domestic violence. Many women have internalized the patriarchal belief that a man has a right to abuse his wife if she does something he does not like. Many children have been taught that whatever punishment their parents administer is for their own good and that this is how parents show they care for their children.

A research study done with children and adult victims of domestic violence in Nicaragua in 1995 showed that women and children were most likely to acknowledge that they were being victimized by their spouses and parents in cases of high-intensity physical aggression. The cases of emotional violence and low-level physical violence were more difficult to identify, especially in families where hierarchical relationships were well established and the victim depended economically and emotionally on the aggressor.[19]

The legal process still has many problems. It is not user-friendly for women who live in or are from rural areas and who depend on their husband entirely or for those who have a low academic level. Some city women who happen to have a job outside the home can sometimes not afford to take time off work to invest in the legal process, especially if they have husbands who are continuously threatening to kill them or take their children away from them if they denounce them publicly.

A 1995 study in Nicaragua showed that only five out of a hundred abused women go to the police to file a complaint. Only 12 percent of the filed complaints are processed by the legal system, and of these, only a small segment of abusers are convicted, the majority with a short sentence.[20] Since the legal system does not actually provide adequate protection from violence, the majority of women ignore the law that supposedly defends their right to a life of nonviolence.

The new laws do not make it mandatory for community leaders to support women and to denounce what is happening. So many horrid stories of abuse remain hidden in the offices of teachers, pastors, priests, or counselors as they encourage the victim to denounce the abuser on her own, or as more often happens, suggest that the victim remain silent either because they are not believed or to protect the perpetrator.

The law needs to be revised, and the reporting of domestic violence, especially against children, needs to be made mandatory for teachers, counselors, pastors, social workers, nurses, doctors, police, and so on.

Nicaragua has only one shelter in the entire country, and it has space for only twelve women. Nicaragua needs a system of shelters where women and children can go when their lives and health are in danger. The victims look to their families for help, but many times they are told the abuse is their fault or that women's role in the world is to suffer. This is especially the case if there has been abuse in the family of origin.

Domestic violence was declared a public health problem in Nicaragua in 1996, but the health system is still not prepared to respond adequately to the victims. Programs and procedures still need to be elaborated and put into practice, and the health personnel as a whole needs to be sensitized. There have been some efforts from nursing schools in the country to help prepare nurses to deal with domestic violence cases, but these very same nurses often find themselves frustrated when the system does not respond to the needs of the victims. Many of them have seen the victims, both women and children, come bruised and wounded time after time, until they finally come as corpses. Some have collaborated to denounce the cases and have watched how they fall through the cracks of bureaucracy and corruption.

In a country where the basic needs of the majority of the population are still unmet, it is difficult to make domestic violence as a priority. In a context where the structural violence is so blatant, it is easy to classify domestic violence as a minor problem. It takes our commitment to change this situation.

In this chapter we have tried to illustrate with specific cases how economic vulnerability makes it very difficult for women and children who are being abused to leave their abusive environments. We have also shown how this economic vulnerability is not brought about by individuals' shortcomings, but by misguided national policies, by an unjust international order, and by a wrongly interpreted religiosity. As Christians we need to address all these scenarios if we really want to make a difference in the lives of thousands of abused women and children and to prevent future abuse cases.

3

A Story of Healing and Liberation

Linda Crockett[1]

"At the heart of war is rape."

I was in a war zone in El Salvador with a church delegation when I first heard these words in 1989. A friend shared them with me to assure me I was not going crazy.

I was frustrated and frightened. The nightmares, headaches, insomnia, difficulty in concentrating, and intrusive memory fragments of rape and childhood sexual abuse that I began to experience after my first trip to El Salvador two years before were becoming progressively worse. Thoughts about my mother's suicide a long time ago were on my mind with increasing frequency.

At the same time, I was working hard to help build an interfaith solidarity network in Pennsylvania to accompany Salvadoran refugees struggling to rebuild their homes in conflictive zones. I was also holding down a full-time job and trying to raise two teenage sons. I was angry with myself for not having better control over what was happening inside of me. I wanted to direct my energy to the Salvadoran struggle—not focus on my own pain.

Although I did not yet comprehend it, my entry into accompaniment of the Salvadoran poor in the context of the war had triggered an activation of the interior conflictive zones that are the inheritance of every untreated survivor of childhood sexual abuse. A child who is sexually abused learns to survive in a war zone. Unprotected, he or she is subject to psychological, physical, and spiritual destruction—particularly when the abuse occurs within the context of the family itself.

In 1989, I experienced the conscious memory of being raped by an acquaintance when I was twelve and of being molested during the course of an entire summer when I was five by an older teenage cousin and two of his friends. I had never talked about these experiences, minimizing

42

their significance and impact. I was unaware that other, more profoundly painful memories of sexual abuse at the hands of my mother lay deeply buried behind the walls I built as a child in order to survive.

I did know that something deep inside of me was badly broken. It seemed as though if I just concentrated on the work in El Salvador, somehow I could keep from facing the pain that kept surfacing in so many ways. I spent time writing in my journal each night, reflecting about what it means to see God through the eyes of the poor, sometimes working through my own political analysis as I followed the trail of blood and tears from El Salvador to Washington, D.C.

Suddenly, as though my mind had disconnected from my hand, I would be writing about being badly hurt as a child, with no one to help or comfort me, wishing I could be invisible, wrapping myself in an imaginary world to escape from the reality in which our family lived. I wrote about how it felt when my father stopped holding or touching me after discovering that the son of his sister had molested me, withdrawing from me as though I had become unclean. I would be disturbed and ashamed when I found myself writing about these things in my journal. I believed that they had no place there.

I had not yet understood that the God who accompanies the poor is also the God of raped children. I was beginning to make that connection in El Salvador.

● ● ●

I grew up in a war zone in a rural community in Pennsylvania. The neat brick walls of the house my father built with his own hands belied the violence committed within, unseen by the casual passerby.

Surrounded by tranquil meadows and bordered by woods, the only other nearby houses were those occupied by my father's siblings. My grandfather deeded parcels of land to his children. Raised to be deeply suspicious of "strangers," most of the siblings chose mates from the same county and built homes within the matrix extending out from their birthplace. The community was aptly named "Greenville." In the 1950s, a narrow dirt road was the only means of passage through the lush green foliage and lily-covered creek that bordered at least one property line of each of the siblings' houses.

My uncles worked in factories. My father was a carpenter. During the day, my aunts spent their time at my grandmother's house baking, cleaning, gardening, and gossiping. On the rare occasion when a stranger happened to walk down the dusty road, the women quickly locked the doors, drew the shades, and hid under beds. Anyone outside the family was not to be trusted.

It was into this enclave that my father brought my mother as a young, pregnant bride. Stationed at a Virginia naval base, he met her in a waterfront bar owned by her mother. By day, she sold bait, tackle, and cold beer to the locals, whose pickup trucks usually surrounded the ramshackle structure. At night, the bar was a favorite party spot for sailors such as my father, who considered the owner's pretty teenage daughter to be an added attraction. By various accounts, my mother was the life of many a party on the small piece of land jutting out into the bay on which the bar perched, somewhat precariously, on long stilted legs.

The abrupt transition to the conservative, Pennsylvania Dutch community composed of her new husband's family resulted in complete culture shock. Although the aunts refrained from hiding under the bed in her presence, it was clear they looked askance at her makeup, skimpy clothes, cigarettes, and barroom vernacular. The Old Testament was frequently quoted in Greenville; passages about the wickedness of Sodom and Gomorrah were among my father's favorites. A normally quiet man, when he talked about the "Good Book," he often worked himself into a frenzy. Pounding the table with his fists, he would shout at the top of his lungs about the terrible judgment awaiting anyone who violated even one of its tenets. My father's god ruled by fear, inflicting harsh punishment for any violation of his law.

My mother despised her new home. She was isolated and completely out of her social environment, with no support other than my father. She lacked education, job skills, and money. One of nine siblings, her childhood had been characterized by poverty and abuse. Her father, who was exceedingly kind to his dogs, was brutal with his children, especially when he was drinking. And there were not many days he was sober. When she reached puberty, she escaped her father's violence by fleeing to stay with an older sister in another state. Her mother, after years of enduring her husband's drunken rages, managed to scrape together enough money to buy a run-down bar at the water's edge when the marriage finally dissolved. When my mother reached eighteen, she joined my grandmother, spending the evenings with sailors eager for her company.

The child who grew in her womb was the reason she married my father, who promised that after I was born he would take her back to Virginia to live. He did not keep his promise, and it was the source of countless fights as the years wore on and my mother's hatred of Greenville grew. She threatened to leave and take my younger sister, brother, and me with her. He reminded her she had no money and would be destitute. Other than money, where we lived was the only thing my father controlled. Everything else became my mother's domain. Especially the children. And her control of us was absolute.

It was not until twenty-two years had gone by that my father kept his promise to take her back to Virginia, returning her body to the shores of the Atlantic to be buried. A superstitious man, perhaps he took seriously her vow that if he buried her in Greenville, she would haunt him for the rest of his life.

• • •

I was thirty-two years old when I first entered the war zones of Central America. At the time, I was chairperson of the evangelism committee in the Lutheran church I attended. The pastor habitually stuffed my mailbox with all the appeals for help that he deemed not relevant to our rural congregation. Time after time, I would bring proposals to the leadership that would have involved our church in social justice ministries. I was largely ignored. The pastor counseled that the congregation, which was founded before I was born, was not mature enough to make a commitment to this kind of work.

One day, my mailbox contained a letter that changed my life. It was a plea from Salvadoran Lutheran Bishop Medardo Gomez for accompaniment of his people in the midst of a war in which more than 60,000 civilians had already been killed. He wrote that his people were walking the way of the cross and that they did not wish to walk alone. As brothers and sisters in Christ, they asked that we walk with them. I could not have found El Salvador on a map. But that letter found its way into my heart. Although I did not recognize her then, the child within me who had never been protected understood the urgency of the cry of the Salvadoran poor. I felt compelled to respond without fully comprehending why. Understanding would come only after I plumbed the depths of my own pain, remembering abuse I had forgotten in order to survive.

I immersed myself in learning about the situation in El Salvador. For generations, a wealthy Salvadoran minority had exploited the economy for their own benefit. The vast majority lived in abject poverty. In the 1970s, Christian communities formed in which people began to view their reality through the lens of the gospel. They were encouraged by nuns and priests fervent in their embrace of the preferential option for the poor boldly proclaimed in Vatican II. The traditional church teaching to accept suffering on Earth and focus on reward in heaven was critically examined by illiterate peasants. Lack of schools, medical care, and land led to increasing discontent. A growing conviction that it was not the will of God that their children die from poor nutrition in a country so rich in resources led the poor to organize themselves to demand economic justice.

Vigils, demonstrations, and speeches were met with military violence. Community leaders were "disappeared" by shadowy groups for which the government disclaimed responsibility, despite the fact that they operated with impunity in areas controlled by the army. The leaders' mutilated bodies were often returned to the streets of their communities in an attempt to terrorize people into silence and submission. Some of the poor, convinced that peaceful protest would never result in social change, took up armed resistance. Civil war began.

In the early 1980s, the United States aligned itself with the Salvadoran government. In the context of the cold war, the struggles of the poor in Central America were viewed as communist inspired. Funds flowed to the military.

My pastor was alarmed when he realized I would not be dissuaded from involvement. I was trying to live what he preached from the pulpit. I felt abandoned and confused by his response. Fortunately, one woman from my church and a few others scattered across a one hundred–mile region felt called to respond. We found one another and spent months in prayer, discussion, and reflection. We invited people from other states who were doing the work of accompaniment to talk with us. Ultimately, five of us decided to form a delegation and go to El Salvador. A Catholic sister whose love for the Salvadoran poor seemed boundless would be our guide.

When it was clear that we were going with or without the support of our home congregation, the church leadership finally allowed us to take a second offering one Sunday to help defray our expenses. Several men were vocal in their opposition to women going to a war zone. Some said we were being duped by communist propaganda. Their wives did not put money in the plate when it was passed. But a few stuffed bills into our pockets furtively on the way out, along with handwritten greetings to give to Salvadoran women.

A service of blessing was held the week before we left. But the official message was clear. This was not the ministry of the church. It was a personal calling.

● ● ●

I walked through the doors of Resurrection Lutheran Church in San Salvador for the first time in October 1987. A portion of the church had been damaged by a bomb just days before. The government viewed churches that advocated justice for the poor as a threat to the country's stability, which depended on a labor pool competing for work at wages so low that their children died from malnutrition. Members of the church were being targeted by death squads. As U.S. citizens, we were witnesses that could not be as easily silenced by the military government.

That night, our delegation accompanied members of the church as they gathered for a prayer vigil. Stone-faced soldiers with machine guns surrounded the church. We sat in a circle to symbolize our equality as we prayed, talked, and sang. People told stories of family members who had been tortured and murdered because of their work for justice in poor communities. They understood the oppression and poverty in which they lived to be similar to the conditions under which Jesus ministered during the Roman occupation. Jesus was persecuted because he fed the poor; he denounced the rich for their abuse of the vulnerable; he healed despite prohibitions in the law; he taught the outcasts they had value in the eyes of God. The authorities believed his actions inflamed the public, so they assassinated him, just as they were doing now to those who took up his work. The parallels brought chills to my body, even in the 100-degree heat.

The gospel was alive in the hope, struggle, and resistance of the poor who gathered in the church that night. There was no separation between what was preached from the pulpit and the commitment required of those who did the work of God. The church's pastor had been captured and tortured by death squads two years earlier. For the first time, I was with people who were continuing to write the Bible as they lived it. They became my teachers. Eventually, they opened me to my own pain so I could heal.

• • •

The God who walked with the poor and inspired their work for justice was not the God of law and judgment my father shouted about. The term *battered-child syndrome* was developed in 1961 when I was six. A social awareness of the need for protection of children from physical abuse was germinating. My father was very upset by this. He muttered that the government had no right to interfere with family "discipline" of children. His terse admonition of "what goes on in this house *stays* in this house" was repeated so often to my brother, sister, and me that it became a mantra we lived by. Along with his conviction that state intervention in families was communist inspired was his unshakable belief that he was a good man because he read the Bible, worked hard, and attended church.

Each Sunday morning, our family dressed up in clothes we could not afford and went to worship services at a church where seating was predicated on social class. The town's elite sat in the front rows by unspoken, common assent. Ushers quietly and efficiently shepherded everyone else to other pews. No velvet cords were needed to reserve the rows closest to the pulpit. It was understood by the parishioners: no one other than the town's "first families" sat in the front pews.

In the car on the way home, my parents would inevitably begin to fight. Sunday morning screaming and cursing seemed more ferocious to me than verbal battles the rest of the week. It was as though all the tensions that ran just below the surface of our family as respectable and Christian were magnified by this weekly ritual. The explosion usually came as soon as we cleared the parking lot. Within a few minutes, my mother's increasing agitation was met by my father's sullen silence, which only enraged her further.

As an adult, I continued to attend worship services out of habit. I instinctively honed in on the ugly realities behind the masks many parishioners wore in the churches I attended. Racism, greed, love of money, and scorn for those unlike themselves were evident by peering behind only the first layer of pretense in parishioners. My childhood had trained me well for this. And it also led to the cynical conviction that no one actually tried to follow the Jesus who loved children and the poor, who lived without material possessions, who made it clear that blood ties were not the definition of family. Despite what was preached from the pulpit or droned in liturgies, this Jesus was not taken seriously.

Among the Salvadoran poor, however, there was little pretense. Masks were few. The Jesus who befriended those at the margins of society was loved and emulated. In El Salvador, Jesus was alive in a way I had never encountered him in churches in the United States.

• • •

One day I visited a Salvadoran community of people who had been displaced by the war. The majority were women, children, and the elderly. They were struggling to survive on a scrap of land at the edge of a conflict zone. Many of them were living under shelters of plastic and tin. The army came to the community one day and rounded up all the people. They began to interrogate them, accusing them of supporting the FMLN armed resistance. After a few days of occupation and harassment, the soldiers finally left, taking with them all the food and the few tools the community had. They also took some prisoners. One of the captured was an old woman.

She was imprisoned for several months. During her captivity, she was badly tortured. She was eventually released and returned to the community as a living reminder of the military's power. The trauma of the torture had seriously damaged her mind. She could no longer function. She was filled with guilt and pain because under torture, she had made false confessions, agreeing that she and everyone else in the community her torturers named were connected to the FMLN.

She could not sleep at night. Instead, she stumbled from shelter to shelter, begging endlessly for forgiveness from each family she might have betrayed.

I asked the people, "What did you do? What happened to this woman?" I will never forget the answer given to me by one of the community leaders. A lay catechist, in a worn and faded shirt, a man full of faith, said to me: "We healed her. It cost us a lot, but we healed her."

My mother had periods of psychotic behavior. She had just been released from the care of a psychiatrist and was taking medication when she killed herself when I was twenty. By that time, I had a three-year old child. My mother left behind a broken family, including my twelve-year-old brother and sixteen-year-old sister. She left me with the scars and wounds of years of physical and sexual abuse, most of which I could not begin to remember until the interior walls began to crumble in El

Salvador more than a decade later. No one could heal her, not doctors, not hospitals, not medication.

And here I was, listening to this campesino tell me that his community had healed a woman who was deranged by torture. When I was able to speak, I asked him how they healed her.

He said they were not sure what to do at first. But they instinctively understood that she needed to be listened to and she needed to be held. They organized themselves so that someone was with her twenty-four hours a day. She was never left alone. They talked to her, encouraging her to spill out the pain, the rage, the grief. They held her like a child and let her cry. Eventually she recovered from her trauma and was healed.

The catechist explained how her healing was costly for the community. Their survival depended on the labor of each person in the fields where meager crops grew. Every day that someone sat with the woman was a day of lost labor, which meant less food. And they had no assurance that the time they were investing in her healing would yield fruit and eventually restore her to them. It was a risk with no guarantee of success. How is it that a community of peasants with no medical training knows how to heal a woman severely traumatized by torture? Why were they willing to risk this?

It cost that community a great deal to heal their wounded member. But they did it...with love, patience, and faith in a God who walks with those who have no one else to depend on, and who cries out for justice.

● ● ●

Our initial delegation of five blossomed into an organization committed to accompaniment and to ending U.S. military aid. I returned to El Salvador repeatedly during the next six years to be with the poor as they buried their dead and searched for family members who had been "disappeared." To offer what small protection I could with my physical presence. To let them know they were not alone.

There is nothing worse than suffering alone, believing yourself to be abandoned by the world. The child in me who I thought was dead knew this. She had suffered alone for years. And she began her journey of resurrection in El Salvador.

The poor prepared the way for my own healing journey to begin. As I accompanied them, I learned about hope, community, and resistance to unjust power. Values imposed by my parents and reinforced by culture and the church–such as unquestioning obedience to authority, the privacy and privilege of the nuclear family, and submission to suffering– were slowly transformed. I began to understand that God was not in an irrevocable alliance with the powerful.

It was in El Salvador that I encountered the God who weeps at the exploitation of the vulnerable, the God who is outraged at the violence inflicted by those who abuse their power and authority.

In many ways, El Salvador felt like home. I was on familiar turf: lies, deception, violence. But most of all, the mask the government wore to hide its atrocities from the rest of the world felt intimately familiar to me long before I comprehended why it did. Abusive parents carefully construct masks to hide the truth and preserve social standing. My parents struggled up from poverty to reach the lower middle class. We lived in a tiny three–room bungalow without indoor plumbing. When I was nine, we moved into a large house my father built, converting the bungalow into a garage. On the outside, the handsome brick house looked good. Inside, we had a few pieces of broken furniture and one paycheck that never quite stretched a whole week. My mother begged my father to let her buy a rug, a sofa. He refused, pouring all our money into what could be seen from the outside. To my father, appearances were important. The handsome brick house was not a home, but a mask. It covered the atrocities that were committed inside with a cloak of respectability.

And most people prefer to accept the mask that camouflages evil than to attempt to look beneath it. I saw it in El Salvador. I lived it as a child.

Although my relatives whispered that my mother was "not well" as she became increasingly hostile and reclusive, none of them questioned why blankets covered the windows of our house on certain afternoons when I came home from school. Although they muttered their suspicions after an emergency trip to the doctor to stitch up my badly cut genitals when I was not yet two years old, no one demanded to be allowed to see me when my mother declared I could have no visitors for a few weeks. None of the doctors who became aware of my abuse later when I was hospitalized at age twelve were able to remove me from my parents' control. My father's threat of a lawsuit because they dared to suggest I was abused by my mother intimidated and silenced them. Too often how parents treat their children in the privacy of their home is, in my father's oft-repeated words, "nobody's business."

Like many survivors of abuse, I coped by a variety of methods as I grew to adulthood. During adolescence, I was attracted to abusive environments filled with drugs, violence, and men who seemed to instinctively know I was vulnerable. No one had ever taught me that my body was mine. I let anyone have it. I did not feel it was really connected to me.

I married at seventeen, pregnant with my first child. I broke a years-long drug addiction on my own because I did not want to hurt the tiny creature growing inside me. We moved into a tiny trailer on a rented lot. Our only living room furniture included a small, hard sofa; an old stereo; and a huge cardboard box of records. Our neighbor regularly urinated just outside our bedroom window and frequently exposed himself to children. I didn't know anything about pregnancy or how to care for the baby who would soon be born. I had never been protected as a child. But I understood one thing: I had to protect the new and fragile life within me.

I did everything within my power to create a safe place for this son and the one who followed four years later, including taking various low-wage jobs to put food on the table. Eventually, I took a secretarial position in a corporation and worked my way up to department manager, eventually being named a corporate officer. I taught myself whatever I needed to know, devouring books and absorbing information until I acquired an expertise in a part of the company no one else had. I gave up any dream of higher education. Emotional and economic survival took everything I had.

Yet I moved through early adulthood in a dissociative haze. I have little memory of major family events. Emotionally, I was numb. I was compelled to secretly hurt and punish myself. Sexual pleasure and pain were intricately linked. My mother had taught me well. I was unable to make love with my husband unless I imagined I was being beaten and humiliated. Greatly troubled, I finally sought the counsel of our pastor. His advice was to act out some of the fantasies with my husband to reinvigorate our sex life, as long as nobody got seriously hurt. Although my husband was at first reluctant to hit me, the pastor's advocacy of it legitimized it. I discovered I responded sexually to pain in fantasy, but in reality I was devastated. I was inexplicably addicted to pain. Many times I wanted to die.

Part of me, though, was extremely high-functioning no matter how awful I felt. That part was not present in my intimate relationships. It came out only for work and allowed me to excel in the corporate environment that demanded detached emotions and accommodation to a structure steeped in patriarchy and class privilege.

Although I had always remembered the molestations and rape by those outside my immediate family, it was not until El Salvador brought me from numbness into pain that I began to remember the sexual abuse by my mother. As I listened to the stories of torture survivors, memories long quiescent began to stir. I fell into what seemed to be a waking nightmare. Most of my childhood up until the age of twelve was like a blank page. I didn't remember, because I could not bear to know what happened to me and continue to live. Repression and denial have their place.

It was not until I absorbed enough of the courage and hope taught to me by the Salvadoran people I accompanied that it was safe to begin to remember my own abuse at the hands of my mother. We think of men as the primary abusers. But women can, *and do,* sexually and physically abuse not only their sons but also their daughters.

In 1992, I made a conscious decision to heal, and entered therapy. I knew I needed someone with an understanding of Central America and its importance to my own process. A friend told me about Jim,[2] a pastoral counselor who had been to Nicaragua.

I wrote him a letter, explaining about the pain and memories that had begun to surface in El Salvador, and my need to heal in an environment with a therapist skilled in working with abuse issues who would also honor the importance of my connection to the Salvadoran people.

One week later, Jim called me. He said he was deeply moved by my letter, and he hoped he could help. He had a warm voice and an easy laugh. I felt strangely at ease talking with him. We agreed to meet in a few days.

When I met with Jim for the first time, we talked for two hours. It felt as though his gentle questions went inside me to a place no one else had ever been before, yet I did not feel violated. When the session was finished, I was exhausted. I asked if he would feel comfortable working with me. He was silent for a moment. I steeled myself for rejection. Then he said, "No. Not exactly comfortable. Listening to your pain makes me feel like you do when you listen to the suffering of Salvadorans."

In a daze I asked if I could come for sessions every three weeks. My budget was strained from the trips to El Salvador, which involved personal expense. Jim said there was a fund established at the counseling center I could use to defray the cost. He didn't think it was a good idea to wait three weeks before coming again. I made an appointment for the next week and quickly left. I had no way of knowing it then, but the relationship in which I would eventually come to feel safe enough to allow the raped child to surface and heal had just been born. I did not know it would take years of struggle. I did not know that I would become as attached to and dependent on Jim as a child to her mother, allowing him to re-parent me as I grew slowly to health and autonomy. I only knew I wanted to be "fixed" in no more than a few months. I needed to get back to El Salvador. I had wasted enough time on my own pain.

• • •

As I was buffeted in the storms of healing, the traumatic memories that I had split off in order to survive burst through my defenses. My body retched memories. Remembering anal rape, I bled from my rectum. Remembering how my mother tied my hands with a piece of rope, my wrists either pounded with pain or hung limp and numb. I do not know how this is possible; I just know that it happened. The details of a bedspread, the pattern of the wallpaper, the clarity of a beer bottle on the floor on which I focused during the abuse were thrust into my consciousness with terrifying vividness.

The ways in which I was hurt by my mother do not fit readily into the sad categories of what we have reluctantly come to recognize as common acts of sexual abuse. Some of the abuse was highly ritualized. I was tied down and ordered not to make a sound while my mother stimulated my body and then punished me for responding. When I came home from school and saw the windows darkened with blankets, I knew I was going to be hurt. But I had nowhere else to go. By the time I reached third grade, I thought being tortured was normal. I believed that all mothers who loved their daughters did to them what my mother did to me. My mother assured me they did.

As I struggled to survive the remembering, I discovered that like the Salvadoran woman who had been tortured, I also needed to be held and touched in nurturing ways. A gay man I met when he was working in El Salvador with victims of war became my adopted big brother and best friend. He spent hours at a stretch, in the United States and in El Salvador, listening to my emerging pain and rocking me like a child. Telling me fiercely I was beautiful, loved, and would heal, Gary encouraged me to claim my own tears and anger. His accompaniment helped me tremendously in validating the connections between my own pain and the suffering of the Salvadoran people. By holding me and listening to me, he enabled me to trust physical and emotional intimacy with a human being in a way I never could before.

When he returned to his church in Chicago after spending several years as a volunteer mission worker in El Salvador, he revealed his sexual orientation to the congregation. He hoped to create a space where he did not have to hide his true identity to be welcomed and affirmed. The result was that he was banned from holding any leadership position in the church. He was not even permitted to be a lay reader during worship. Eventually he left the church.

In the wilderness that is called healing, I encountered many others who, rejected and scorned by society, sought sanctuary within the church and found none. The culture has grown increasingly hostile to survivors who speak out about their abuse. Well-funded organizations of primarily affluent people claiming to be falsely accused by their adult children of sexual abuse sprang up in the late 1980s after many survivors came forward to speak publicly about their experiences. They coined the term "false memory syndrome" and fed it to the media, where it was largely picked up uncritically as though it were a medically accepted diagnosis rather than a political phrase.

On TV and in national magazines, photos appeared of well-dressed, gray-haired professionals who claimed their children's memories of abuse were "implanted" by conniving therapists. One backlash organizer was fond of asking, "Do we look like child abusers?" The appeal to class worked well, creating a public climate of suspicion toward adults who spoke of being abused as children.

Finding little safe space in society and being estranged from their families, some survivors hoped the church would provide a safe space where they could tell their stories and be affirmed in their quest for healing. Many left with new wounds after they discovered, as did gays and lesbians, that the church was not a place of nurture for them.

I count myself among those who find no place within the institutional church. The friends who walked with me in Salvadoran war zones were active in their churches and committed to social justice. Yet they could not accompany me as the war zones I lived in as a child opened up, and the storms of healing buffeted me and anyone close to me in their relentless fury. They could listen to the stories of Salvadorans tortured by the military. But they recoiled from my stories of torture by my mother. Gary was the only friend who did not abandon me and stood fast even when the agony of healing made me withdraw from him.

One of the painful things for me when I was attending worship services was the frequent use of parent images of God. I felt fear when a liturgy directed me to pray to a father-god, or an inclusive language text named god as mother. Those who have been abused by mothers and fathers cannot easily take comfort in god-as-parent imagery. The reality of sexual and physical abuse of children by their families is seldom talked about in churches. I have never heard a sermon about incest. I feel betrayed when I hear the commandment "Honor thy father and mother." Where is the command to honor the children?

I no longer expect to find God in most U.S. churches. The god I learned to know and love in El Salvador walks with those whom society deems to have little value. The poor. The abused. Gays and lesbians. The vulnerable elderly. And, especially, the children. I walk with them and dream of a church where everyone puts their chairs in a circle and is equal.

4

Pastoral Care and Vulnerability

All those without power and privilege are the most vulnerable to and the most likely to be victimized by sexual and domestic violence.[1]

Who Are the Vulnerable?

Family violence destroys persons in many different social locations. Whether poor or rich, female or male, and regardless of culture, religion, ability, and so forth, people need to be protected from violence and given resources for healing when it strikes. Economic vulnerability often deprives people of the resources they need for full human development and maturity and thus results in additional risks of violation of persons and groups. Economic systems determine opportunities for basic nutrition, safety, employment, health care, education; lack of these resources does violence to persons of all ages. The church needs to engage in a more profound understanding of how economic systems create vulnerability for persons and communities and to offer its care for healing and empowerment.

Survivors of economic vulnerability and family violence often demonstrate amazing resilience in coping with the violations. Survivors survive–they learn how to counter some of the negative consequences of violence by drawing on inner resources and resisting the intentions of their abusers. They protect others–siblings, children, the vulnerable– through cooperating and organizing for safety. They seek justice by bringing their complaints to the community, where they hope to be vindicated and have the injuries healed. They thrive through healing relationships, education, and productive work in the community. The resilience of survivors is an important resource of understanding the nature of economic vulnerability and family violence.

Margarita, Soledad, and Juana were abused as vulnerable children and deprived of necessary resources for their development. Later they were threatened and abused as vulnerable women in relation to men who were willing to use their physical and legal power to control the women's lives. While the types of sexual and physical abuse these three endured happen to women in many social locations, economic vulnerability contributes another layer of oppression. The practice of making children work for wages is considered necessary in many poor communities, a practice that makes the children vulnerable to sexual and physical abuse because of the situations in which they are forced to work. Margarita, Soledad, and Juana all tried to escape the violence they experienced in childhood and as adults, but they had limited choices. If they escaped from one situation, they often put themselves in danger from another direction. And the fact that they had responsibility for children made their vulnerability especially high.

Margarita, Soledad, and Juana were all resilient in the midst of oppression. They fought back against their abusers and sought new opportunities for their futures. They protected their children from similar kinds of abuse, even while they sometimes acted out their own frustration and anger with their children. They divorced abusers; they filed police reports; they sought pastoral counseling; they changed themselves so they could have the inner strength to cope. They were determined to make life better for themselves and their children, even while the structures of the economic system were stacked against them.

Linda was held "captive"[2] in a home by several layers of vulnerability–her age, her physical size, her level of maturity, the mental illness of her mother, the insensitivity of her father, and the economic and cultural isolation of the extended family. Linda did not live in dire poverty as Margarita, Soledad, and Juana did in Nicaragua; her needs for food, shelter, and clothing were met. However, economic vulnerability was a strong factor in creating the culture in which her family lived, and the most basic need of safety from violence was not met. Since Linda's family was working class, they lived defensively against the class humiliation that they felt, within a "poverty of tenuous connections."[3] The class isolation especially affected Linda's mother and prevented her from receiving the diagnosis, treatment, and accountability she needed to become a healthy person. Linda became the child victim of the tangle of family pathology that kept her captive. It is impossible to understand Linda's experience without an analysis of her vulnerability caused by economic situations and family violence.

Linda was also resilient. She developed a rich inner life of benevolent figures to protect her from her mother's violence. She married young and stopped her risky behaviors with sex and drugs in order to protect her children from abuse. She succeeded in her corporate job so she could have a reliable economic base. She engaged in justice work in solidarity with the peasants of El Salvador, who had much to teach her about survival and justice. Finally, she sought the resources of a healing community of four pastors and counselors (a pastoral counselor, an activist for justice in Latin America, a massage therapist, and me), even when she knew that her healing journey would cause her additional pain and struggle.

Economic vulnerability and family violence have not been adequately integrated into the theory and practice of pastoral care and counseling. I will illustrate the truth of this statement in the rest of this chapter in several ways: First, I will briefly describe my own experience of pastoral counseling with men who grew up in economically vulnerable and abusive families. Second, I will examine two authors in pastoral care who have helped us to thematize economic vulnerability and will attempt to see how their analysis can help us understand the pastoral issues we are addressing.

My Pastoral Counseling Experience

When we examine issues of family violence, victims and survivors take precedence because they need the advocacy of church and society to redress the abuse of power that has devastated their lives. But we also must ask about the needs of abusers, both men and women, who are products of the family and social systems that perpetuate interpersonal violence. Linda's mother is an example of an abuser who most likely was victimized by her family of origin and the male subculture she grew up in and who internalized her abuse so totally that she herself became a perpetrator. We know that family violence has long-term effects on personal development and that an important minority of victims become abusers.

> It is estimated that about one third of children who are abused or exposed to violence as children become violent themselves in later life. Later involvement in violence is only one of many potential outcomes of growing up in a violent home. Clearly, not all men who are abused or exposed to violence as children later perpetuate violence against their intimates, just as only a minority of women exposed to violence between parental figures later become involved in relationships with violent men. Similarly, not all men who physically or sexually assault their wives come from homes in which they had experiences with interpersonal victimization. Nonetheless, being assaulted by or witnessing assaults among family members in childhood or adolescence appears across empirical studies as a primary risk factor for later involvement in abusive relationships for both women and men.[4]

In addition, we know that economic vulnerability leads to traumatic experiences that have long-term effects in the lives of persons. Margarita, Soledad, and Juana not only faced family violence but were forced to work as children in unhealthy and dangerous situations, and they faced insurmountable economic obstacles as adults trying to raise their families. The men they coupled with also lived in economically vulnerable situations and had survived difficult and abusive childhood experiences.

Vignettes

Men who sexually abuse children come from every economic class, race, and culture. However, the court system has a class bias, which means that men with money can afford good lawyers and find ways around the laws. As a result, poor and working-class men are overrepresented in prisons and court-ordered treatment programs for family violence offenses. Most of my work with child abusers and batterers has been with poor and working-class men. Most of the men I counseled had spent time in jail, from a few weeks to several years.

Ronald: "If we get laid off, we can always work as greeters at Wal-Mart." This was the standing joke for Ronald and other white men who worked in the delivery warehouse of a large supply company. As the company was bought and sold on the international market, layoffs were frequent and indiscriminate. All the men and women who worked there were insecure, and since their jobs involved no special skills, there was little hope of finding another with the same pay and benefits.

Ken: "I got so mad that I had to quit so I wouldn't hurt someone." Ken repeated the same cycle every few months. He was a semi-skilled white mechanic who could only get work at national franchises that installed cheap tires and mufflers. The companies depended on a quick turnover of workers in order to pay deflated wages and no benefits. Given the terrible ways workers were treated, and the cold and dirty working conditions in the garage, it was no wonder that Ken became enraged and quit on a regular basis. The family survived because his wife had worked as a secretary for several years in an office where she was not treated with respect. He projected his rage onto his family, abused his daughter, and was on probation for child abuse.

Randall: "One of the worst times of my life was when I saw the police pick up my father out of the gutter and take him to jail. He was the town drunk." Randall, a white pastor who was sixty, remembered vividly this event that occurred when he was eight. Old enough to be humiliated, he remembered the experience because his family also lost its home and moved in with relatives, where for the next three years an older cousin sexually abused him. Until Randall attended college and graduate school and became a professional, he never had any economic or emotional security.

Philip: "Mostly I remember my grandmother and her sister physically fighting until they were exhausted." Philip, a young African American who grew up in rural Alabama, escaped to college and seminary, but he never recovered from his violent and impoverished childhood. His father abandoned the family during Philip's infancy, and his mother died when he was nine. As an adult his depression sabotaged all other achievements he accomplished. He sexually abused two children and ended up in prison with a long sentence of four to twelve years. As an African American adult who has served a long time in prison, he will likely be economically vulnerable the rest of his life.

These four men experienced economic vulnerability during their childhood, and three were economically insecure as adults. Their economic vulnerability was compounded by abuse from adults in their extended families and in the community. In adulthood, during times of crisis, three of the men sexually abused children, thereby passing on the trauma they had experienced. Fortunately, their behaviors were reported to authorities, and they were forced to be accountable for hurting other persons.

Class and Violence in Pastoral Care and Counseling

In her article "Hard Work, Hard Lovin', Hard Times, Hardly Worth It: Care of Working-Class Men,"[5] Judith Orr gives attention to working-class men and the challenges they face because of their economic vulnerability. While the U.S. Census defines class mainly in terms of occupation, income, and education, more recent scholarship also includes privilege and the exercise of power. That is, working-class people do not have access to the same privileges, and they are not likely to be able to control their work environment on a daily basis.

Those in the working class take orders frequently and give orders rarely. They expect to give deference rather than receive it. Yet under patriarchy men expect to give orders and receive deference. Thus, working-class men live in the intersection of conflictual relations of economic production, reproduction, and consumption, which constitutes a nexus of power relations. Class is not merely a matter of having or not having power. It is an antagonistic field of struggle.[6]

Given a definition of class that focuses on the intersection of work, education, income, status, and control of one's time and energy, Orr estimates that 59 percent of the U.S. workforce is working class.[7] The myth of the middle class is an oppressive system for men and women who have little control over their economic and personal lives. Orr develops a grid to help us understand how gender, power, and personality theory intersect with issues of class and economic vulnerability.

First, in the U.S. economy, women in general are more economically vulnerable than men, who are more likely to have jobs and adequate income to survive. However, many working-class men have vulnerabilities similar to women; thus, they face economic dangers and threats to their gender identity as men. They experience labor differently, depending on various factors: whether work is paid or unpaid or is public or private; whether or not it requires training; whether workers receive equal wages, training, promotion, and benefits; and whether work leads to influence over the family budget and sharing of housework.[8] During times of affluence, such as the year 2000 in the United States, such vulnerabilities are often hidden, but they reappear with a vengeance during times of capitalistic recession. When markets are shrinking, many men and most women discover that they are expendable.

Most of the male abusers I counseled did not have the resources to escape the criminal justice system because they were economically vulnerable. Many of them were forced to change jobs during therapy, often at great risk to themselves and their families. They were marginalized workers whose economic survival depended on the state of the general economy. In good times, they could manage; in bad times, they were likely to be laid off, and they had few resources to draw on. This state of vulnerability contributed to their general insecurity as persons, as men, as providers for their families. The violence they imposed on their families was not that different from the abuse they experienced at work and the insecurity they lived with every day.

Second, Orr states, men and women are differently affected by the hierarchies of power and authority at work and in the family.

> Social power is composed of force and of the ability to define a situation, to set the terms of understanding and discussion, to formulate ideas, and to assert morality. Within the family it includes control over decisions about the children's school or apprenticeship as well as personal independence from put-downs and violence. In the workplace it includes freedom from arbitrary authority, such as rough treatment by bosses as well as being heard by unions.[9]

Men who are mistreated at work are likely to reproduce the hierarchies at home that make them feel important and in control. Thus, at home they often treat their female partners as powerless employees in a way that mirrors the class differences between people in the workplace. The U.S. economy creates hierarchies among men that result in layers of power and vulnerabilities, and divides them into groups that Orr defines as white, heterosexual, professional men; respectable working-class men; and poor and near-poor white men, racial minorities, and gay men.[10]

Many of the men I worked with could be termed "near-poor" because of the jobs they held. One of my clients, who abused a young child, was a truck driver when I first saw him and made an adequate salary to own a small home. However, he was treated disrespectfully at work because he did not own his truck and because he did not have enough seniority to have choices about his working conditions. He was given the most difficult assignments, night hours, and runs that were not financially profitable. Soon after he began therapy, he lost his job because of a downturn in the business. Next he worked with a local contractor, a poor manager of his business, who did not pay employees for weeks at a time. At one point, I had to inform his boss that he was in physical danger because my client was building up so much resentment that he threatened to assault him. The traumas of losing his job and then working for an incompetent boss overwhelmed his ability to handle his rage at work and at home. Rage about his childhood and class situations fueled his abusive behaviors toward children and toward other men.

Third, Orr says that men and women are differently affected by the structures of desire, which includes

> desirability of another, the structure of homosexual/heterosexual relations, the antagonism of gender, trust/distrust and solidarity/ jealousy in relationships, and the emotional relationship of child rearing...The structure of desire within the family includes access to adequate contraception, the right to abortion, control of one's sexuality, and the right to initiate and leave relationships. The structure of desire within the workplace is evident in freedom from sexual harassment and differential benefits to employees in differing family relationships.[11]

The structure of sexuality at work differs greatly for men and for women. Men who are in positions of authority in relation to women are more likely to sexualize their relationships and cause a hostile environment for women who are trying to work. The laws against sexual harassment and abuse at work from Title VII of the 1964 Civil Rights Act were designed to make the workplace safe for women. Men who are economically vulnerable have a reputation for being crude in their sexualized behavior toward women. This class bias serves the interests of elite and professional social classes who can pass themselves off as "not too bad." By comparison, however, it is true that some economically vulnerable men do engage in sexual harassment as a way to compensate for their own insecurities at work, and in imitation of the structures of domination and control that are created in the economic system itself.

Stan Gray tells the story of what happened at Westinghouse when a group of union women won the right to come to the shop floor and work alongside men with the same working conditions, wages, and grievance procedures. At first the men were threatened and used all forms of sexual and gender harassment to push the women out. "Part of the fight to identify the women as co-workers was therefore the battle against calling them 'cunts' or 'bitches'...[After limits were set against such harassment] the focus shifted to other areas. Many men came back with traditional arguments against women in the workforce. They belong at home with the kids, they're robbing male breadwinners of family income."[12]

Through a most ambiguous intervention, the union organizer shamed the men into behaving:

> I decided to take this one step further and use some intimidation to enforce the basics of public behavior. In a tactic I later realized was a double-edged sword, I puffed myself up, assumed a cocky posture, and went for the jugular. I loudly challenged the masculinity of any worker who was opposed to the women. What kind of man is afraid of women? I asked. Only sissies and wimps are threatened by equality. A *real man* has nothing to be afraid of; he wants strong women.[13]

By appealing to the homophobia and fragile masculinity of the workers, the organizer was able to win temporary "protection" of the women from harassment and mistreatment. In effect, the organizer had sexually harassed the men in order to stop them from sexually harassing the women. While painful to hear, this example illustrates the power of sexual and gender dynamics at the workplace, and how economic vulnerability interacts with the micro-relationships between men and women.

In summary, Judith Orr has suggested that economic vulnerability works in complex ways for women and men. For women, economic vulnerability reinforces the vulnerability of gender and class issues and creates the possibility of trauma and long-term consequences. For men, economic vulnerability seems to contradict the male gender expectations of one who is supposed to have power and control over self and others. Working-class men often experience the threats of unemployment and inadequate economic resources; they often face mistreatment and domination from bosses and coworkers; they often engage in sexually harassing and abusive behaviors in order to identify with the male subculture with its rights to domination over women. This short discussion shows some of the complex interactions between class and gender in the workplace.

Pamela Couture has organized her writing in pastoral care around the economic vulnerability of women and children. In *Blessed Are the Poor?*[14] she argues that the church has underestimated the oppression facing women and children in economically vulnerable situations. By overemphasizing the ideal of "self-sufficiency,"[15] public policies in the United States have unfairly blamed women for their own vulnerability, using the rhetoric that welfare and other entitlement programs create dependency and thus expect too little from women who are poor. The welfare reforms of 1996 and the family-oriented tax code revisions have aggravated the vulnerability of women, who are responsible for the care of most children.

Couture asks: "What creates the widespread *vulnerability* of the female-headed household to poverty?"[16] She gives four answers to this question:

1. "Female-headed households are vulnerable to poverty due to the sexual and racial divisions of labor that continue to give women a secondary place in the socioeconomic structure of the United States."[17] As we will see in the following chapters, women are concentrated in low-paying service jobs in the United States and in the informal economy in poor countries. These gender cages limit the economic resources they can acquire and create economic vulnerability.

2. "In addition, due to child-custody and support practices, female-headed households usually carry heavier economic and emotional responsibilities for children than do male-headed households but have access to fewer economic resources."[18] Most children live with their mothers because of the concern of mothers for their children and because of social policies that expect mothers to care for their children even without a larger circle of supportive community. The economic system expects informal supports to provide what the system itself will not provide: adequate child care, education, and respite care. This issue is especially dramatic in Nicaragua, where mothers often have to organize their own schools to educate their children, even while they are selling goods in the informal market so they can survive day by day.

3. "Furthermore, women in female-headed households are less able to compete for higher places in the economic structure because their responsibilities for children conflict with their availability for economic competition."[19] Because the economic system makes no provision for larger support systems for mothers, women have little time and energy to become economic agents and improve their economic condition.

4. "Finally, the macroeconomic processes of advanced capitalism have depleted the communities where female-headed households are most concentrated, particularly in the inner city."[20] In the United States, poor women tend to live in areas

with low-cost housing, where public policies have resulted in a concentration of poor families. The economic and institutional supports for these communities are inadequate for families.

Couture summarizes these arguments under three themes: "the economic situation facing all women as women; the economic situation facing women who mother; the economic situation facing black women."[21] She concludes that the rhetoric of gender equality is empty unless there is attention to issues of economic vulnerability for women.

These lessons teach us that deceptive illusions of equality are produced when women declare themselves equal without restructuring workplace policies, or when one woman gains pay or position equal to her many male peers but women's labors and insights are generally devalued or romanticized, or when many women spend their lives caring and providing but die lonely or early.[22]

In contrast to self-sufficiency, Couture suggests the image of "shared responsibility"[23] between individuals, communities, and economies. This is a provocative image for the reform of pastoral care as well. How can pastoral counselors, whenever they are providing care for persons who are economically vulnerable, see themselves as part of a community of shared responsibility?

Conclusion

The first section of the book has presented case studies from three different social locations: Brenda Ruiz's practice with poor women in Nicaragua; Linda Crockett's personal experience in a white, working-class family; and my own practice of pastoral counseling with working-class men who have become abusers. I examined some of the ways that family violence intersects with economic vulnerability, a nexus that is often overlooked in pastoral counseling theory and practice. With the help of Judith Orr and Pamela Couture, I have identified some issues that need to be addressed so that the care of the church can be extended to families in vulnerable situations.

● ● ●

The next section of the book shifts the discussion from the micro-level of personal, family, and interpersonal relationships to the macro-level of economic systems and theories. In our pastoral work, we see the effects of economics and violence in personal and family life, but our theories and practices are sorely lacking in understanding how the larger systems affect persons and small groups. Even in the macro-level discussion, we continue to ask questions about how economics and violence affect individuals and families, since this is our primary focus.

Part II: Economic Analysis

5

The Connection between
the Unjust Distribution of Wealth
and Vulnerability

Introduction

Margarita, Soledad, and Juana suffered from economic vulnerability and domestic violence in Nicaragua. They were fortunate to find the skills of a pastoral counselor who helped them begin to sort out the multiple forms of oppression that affected their lives and endangered their children. Linda suffered from domestic violence within a white working-class family isolated by ideologies of the privacy and self-sufficiency of the home and gender oppression. Her story stands as a beacon of light to all children who grow up to be wounded adults seeking healing. Ronald, Ken, Randall, and Philip suffered from economic vulnerability in the United States. Fortunately, they found the skills of a professional pastoral counselor who provided some support along the way.

In this chapter, I explore the connection between unequal distribution of wealth and violence. Starting with Nicaragua as a representative case study from the two-thirds world of global poverty, I try to understand the facts about how wealth and violence are present in the world. Then I look at some statistics from the United States that point to the inequalities of wealth and violence between groups. As pastoral counselors come to a better understanding of economic vulnerability and family violence, they will be able to provide empathy, resources for healing, and empowerment. The United Nations Human Development Report of 2000 provides the statistics to illustrate the unequal distribution of poverty and violence. I argue that the inequalities between the United

States and Nicaragua and within groups in the United States are the result of decades of systematic oppression that we characterize by the term *economic dominance.*

There is a saying in Nicaragua: "When the United States catches a cold, Nicaragua catches pneumonia." It means that Nicaragua's economy is almost totally dependent on the U.S. economy. When the U.S. suffers a slight recession, Nicaragua falls into an economic depression. What is the effect of 50 or 150 years of unequal and unjust economic development? What happens to a population where 43 percent have lived on $1 per day for 20 years, while a majority of the U.S. population has the accumulated resources of $29,000 per person per year? The result is a discrepancy of resources that determines other choices. Accumulation of wealth shows up as land ownership—non-nationals own a large percentage of Nicaragua's land, while non-nationals own a small percentage of U.S. land. Such wealth shows up as military dominance. The U.S. has invaded Nicaragua five times to influence its political and economic situation, while Nicaragua has never invaded the U.S. Wealth shows up as freedom from indebtedness—the U.S. has a per capita debt of $12,000,[1] 40 percent of annual average per capita income, while Nicaragua has a per capita debt of $1,200, three times the annual average per capita income.

In addition, the U.S. aggressively influences the economy of Nicaragua through the International Monetary Fund and the World Bank. Through mandatory "restructuring plans," these powerful agencies have imposed such policies as increasing taxes, reducing social services, privatizing the major industries and utilities, and aggressively imposing free trade rules to allow U.S. capital free access to Nicaraguan labor and natural resources. The result is increasing dependence on the U.S. economy at all levels without regard for the human development needs of the Nicaraguan people. The UNHDP reports that the U.S. has a Human Development Index of 0.927 and Nicaragua's is 0.631.

Likewise, within the United States, the economic vulnerability of the indigenous peoples, African Americans, Hispanics, and other groups is the result of centuries of oppression—seizure of land, forced migrations, slavery, sharecropping, and systematic discrimination that outlawed and limited land ownership and capital accumulation. In later chapters we examine these military and legal strategies by looking at grassroots resistance movements. For now, it is enough to say that the economic dominance of certain elite classes has resulted in generations of economic vulnerability for much of the U.S. population.

United Nations Human Development Report 2000

The United Nations defines vulnerability according to the Human Development Index (HDI). The HDI is a set of quantitative measures that evaluates how well the people are doing in various countries in the world. The authors of the 2000 report stated their goals and defined the normative values of human life in the table of contents for their annual charts and graphs of human development indicators:

Monitoring Human Development: Enlarging people's choices

- to lead a long and healthy life

- to acquire knowledge

- to have access to the resources needed for a decent standard of living

- while preserving it for future generations

- ensuring human security

- and achieving equality for all women and men[2]

Of the various ways to measure the quality of human development, one measure is capital, or economic resources (a decent standard of living). But longevity, education, security, gender equality, and preserving the natural environment are also important. The advantage of the HDI is that it takes into account a wide range of human values, interests, and needs. Human beings cannot be reduced to only one measure of value, such as per capita income, and averages of economic factors do not give a full picture of the quality of individual human lives. Quality human development depends on multiple resources for responding to the various human vulnerabilities that come with finitude in a world that can be dangerous. (In chapter 7 I discuss the alternative model called "The Index of Sustainable Economic Welfare [ISEW]," developed by John Cobb and Herman Daly, which has similar goals of measuring the impact of economic development on human and natural environments.)

> The HDI is based on three indicators: longevity, as measured by life expectancy at birth; educational attainment, as measured by a combination of adult literacy (2/3 weight) and the combined gross primary, secondary, and tertiary enrollment rate (1/3 weight); and standard of living as measured by real GDP per capita PPP$. (GDP = gross domestic product; PPP$ = "purchasing power parity in dollars").[3]

With this scale, it is possible to make a rough estimate of the available resources and vulnerabilities of particular nations, and certain populations within each nation. By comparing an index that is based on life expectancy, educational achievement, school enrollment, and economic resources, the United Nations hopes that the world can improve the quality of life of all the world's people. Not included in the mathematical formula for HDI, but included in the UN discussion are attention to gender equality, environmental concerns, violence and safety concerns, and levels of poverty in the world.

Economic Vulnerability and Violence in Nicaragua

Nicaragua is a very poor country, the third poorest in the Western hemisphere. Based on 1998 figures, Nicaragua ranked 116th on the HDI out of 174 countries, with a score of 0.631 on a scale of 0.0 to 1.000.[4] This compares to the United States HDI score of 0.929.[5] This means that Nicaragua has a shortfall in human development of 36.9 percent, while the U.S. has a shortfall of 7.1 percent.[6] A shortfall in development shows the relative extent to which the basic needs of some groups of people in a country are not being met. The following figures from the UN Human Development Report 2000 are based on statistics taken before the impact of Hurricane Mitch in 1998, which killed several thousand people and left more than 100,000 Nicaraguans homeless. Agriculture was disrupted, and the annual productivity dropped significantly afterward.

What does an HDI score of 0.631 mean for the people of Nicaragua? First, we look at the figures that make up the HDI score and then examine some of the ways this reality affects the everyday lives of people. *Longevity* (1998): In Nicaragua, the life expectancy at birth was 68.1 years compared with 76.8 years in the U.S.[7] *Educational attainment* (1998): The literacy rate for adults was 67.9 percent, and the school enrollment rate for children was 63 percent.[8] *Standard of Living* (1998): The income per person based on the gross national product was $452.[9]

Longevity: This related to infant mortality and living conditions for the people. It is a way of measuring the health of the people in general. For example, in 1997, 40.8 percent of Nicaraguans did not have access to safe water, and 80.2 percent did not have access to adequate sanitation.[10] Such conditions contribute to the mortality rate. In 1997, 36 percent of children under five were malnourished because of food shortages, and their short- and long-term health were threatened.[11] A contributing factor to longevity is adequacy of diet, which is directly related to standard of living. The adequate diet is defined as 2,150 calories per day, which must include 54 grams of protein. The average Nicaraguan in 1995 was getting 73.3 percent of the calories and 82.8 percent of the protein needed for health. The result of inadequate diet is that 24.8 percent of the children show some retarded growth.[12]

Educational Attainment: Education is a resource that can reduce vulnerability and enable people to survive threats to their health and safety. According to the above statistics, in 1998 32.1 percent of adults were illiterate[13] and 37 percent of school-age children were not attending school.[14] The correlation of this figure with the extreme poverty rate is not coincidental, since illiteracy contributes to poverty by limiting access to knowledge and employment, and poverty contributes to illiteracy, since adults and children living in extreme poverty must work in informal markets for survival. Children who work to survive do not go to school. Children whose families break down under the stress of poverty sometimes become street children who survive any way they can. When we add the information revolution of computers and the Internet, the lack of education in such areas as information about agriculture and the environment that could better sustain the population leads to critical shortages of knowledge that increase vulnerability to various threats. However, education in an underdeveloped country such as Nicaragua does not solve the problems of unemployment and lack of land necessary for survival in an agricultural economy.

Standard of Living: Even though the per capita annual income of $452 is very low, it is deceiving, because this average is not distributed evenly among the population. Between 1987 and 1998, the richest 20 percent of Nicaraguans consumed 55.2 percent of the national income, while the poorest 20 percent consumed 4.2 percent of the income (or $87 per year per person).[15] In 1993, 43.8 percent of the Nicaraguan people lived on less than $1 per day, and 74.5 percent lived on less than $2 per day.[16] In addition to this high level of poverty, in 1998 the national debt was $5.968 billion, or 229 percent of the GNP of the country, and the ratio of the debt service was 25.5 percent of all exports of goods and services.[17] The debt equaled $1,243 per capita for a population of 4.8 million, or the equivalent of three years' income for every person in the country.[18] Food is expensive because Nicaragua produced less than 100 percent of four of eleven basic foods in 1995; even so, the large agricultural corporations export thousands of tons of needed food to other countries in order to raise money for private and public use, such as repaying the national debt;[19] 18 percent of imports in 1997–98 were food products.[20]

Another factor affecting the general economic situation in Nicaragua is the declining standard of living for the people. The *annual growth rate* of the Nicaraguan economy was minus 3.4 percent from 1975 to 1996, with an annual average range of inflation from 13.49 percent in 1990 to 7.2 percent in 1996.[21] From 1975 to 1998, the population increased from 2.5 million to 4.8 million, an average of 2.9 percent per year or 92 percent in twenty-three years. Local Nicaraguan sources estimate that as of 2001, the population of Nicaragua had grown to 5.5 million. Nicaraguans spend almost all their income on survival needs, mostly food, with little left over for housing, health care, and education. Trade, especially in light of the so-called Free Trade policies of the U.S., affects the standard of living. In 1997, Nicaragua imported 66 percent of its needed products, and exported 41 percent of what it produced. This compared with 13 percent imports and 12 percent exports for the United States in 1997.[22] Nicaragua's high level of trade means that needed food is exported at cheap prices and imported at high prices, making food more expensive than most families can afford.

Remittances (capital coming into Nicaragua from relatives living in foreign countries): The Economic Commission for Latin America and the Caribbean (CEPAL) did a study in December, 1999, that shows that 20 percent of the Nicaraguan population have come to the United States and Costa Rica (legally and illegally), and many send back money to their families in Nicaragua. At least U.S.$200 million comes from Costa Rica and between U.S.$400 to 600 million comes from the United States.[23] In 1999, 500,000 illegal emigrants went from Nicaragua to Costa Rica; 6,000 Central Americans were detained at the U.S.-Mexican border. The $500 million equals 60 percent of Nicaraguan exports and is more important than international aid. However, remittances come directly to the population and have immediate effects on the local standard of living.[24]

These figures point to high economic vulnerability for Nicaraguans. The double tragedy of these figures is that certain parts of the population suffer added vulnerability because of gender and age. In 1998 women, on average, made only 41 percent of the income that men made, which had a direct adverse effect on children.[25] Many women are single because of domestic violence and abandonment, thus increasingly vulnerable, with their children, to many threats.

The UN Human Development Report has a section on human security, which it defines as "safety from such chronic threats as hunger, disease, and repression; protection from sudden and hurtful disruptions in the patterns of daily life—whether in homes, in jobs, or in communities. Such threats exist at all levels of national income and development."[26] It is important for our purposes that this index includes domestic violence ("disruptions in homes"). While the UN report does not give statistics on all the indices, such as crime, car accidents, suicides, divorces (all of which would be helpful to know, but which are hard to study in a poor population), the figures we do have tell a sad story. Annually thousands of Nicaraguans have been killed or affected by disasters. Earthquakes, hurricanes, volcanic eruptions, floods, and droughts have a dramatic impact on vulnerable populations, who have little protection against such threats. "In 1972 an earthquake destroyed the capital, Managua, killing 15,000 people and leaving 170,000 homeless."[27] Because the aid money from the international community was stolen by the Somoza family, downtown Managua has not yet been redeveloped and is filled with empty lots and unsafe buildings.

In addition to natural disasters, Nicaragua has experienced thousands of deaths, disabilities, and displacements caused by war. The revolution, the murders by the Guardia Nacional of the late 1970s, and the U.S.-sponsored Contra War of the 1980s were devastating to the country. Two reports show the effects of this war:

[The War of the 1980s], according to the UN Economic Committee on Latin America (CEPAL) report, left: 40,000 dead

(1.5% of the population); 40,000 children orphaned; 200,000 families homeless; 750,000 persons dependent on food assistance; 70% of the main export, cotton, not planted; 33 percent of all industrial property destroyed; $1.5 billion worth of physical damage; and an external debt of $1.6 billion.[28]

April 30, 1986. Nicaragua presented a statement of 258 pages describing the acts of which it accused the U.S. and the legal arguments with which it maintained that the U.S. government had violated international law. If the U.S. were found guilty, Nicaragua would claim U.S.$320 million in compensation...By 14 votes to one, the Court decided that the USA is under obligation to the R. of Nicaragua for injury caused to Nicaragua.[29]

The U.S. has never paid Nicaragua for any of the damages assessed by the World Court. In addition to the 1972 earthquake and war from 1975–1990, Nicaragua experienced a devastating hurricane, Mitch, in 1998, which left thousands dead, injured, homeless, and traumatized. Mitch destroyed much of the fragile infrastructure of the countryside, and little has been repaired in spite of extensive international assistance.

Family Violence: The UN HDI includes domestic violence as a concern in its section on safety. Because the report contains no statistics on the rates of domestic violence in Nicaragua, we rely on studies that have been done by social scientists in Nicaragua. In chapter two, Brenda Ruiz presented statistics on sexual and domestic violence in Nicaragua. Some studies find that more than half the women are confronted with violence from a husband, partner, or boyfriend at some time in their lives. More than half the children experience and/or witness family violence.[30] These figures are not necessarily higher than the figures in populations with more economic resources, but they have drastic consequences. Women facing domestic violence from partners face very difficult choices about how to feed, clothe, and house their children and themselves if they lose the economic support of their male partners. In many cases, women stay in abusive relationships because they have no resources to support their choices. As I have pointed out, many women leave their partners anyway and try to develop networks of family and friends to get by. But when the entire population lives in extreme poverty, there are few resources to share. Lack of choices when living in a situation of survival increases the vulnerability to suffering. It is not the threat alone that causes the suffering, but the combination of the threat of violence with the vulnerability that comes with lack of economic resources.

In summary, these figures show that wealth and violence are unequally distributed in this world. Our theories and practices of pastoral counseling vastly overestimate the choices that people have in their lives by emphasizing autonomy and attributing suffering to lack of maturity.

At the same time we underestimate the vulnerability of oppressed populations by focusing too much attention on the intrapsychic dynamics of individuals within families. Our challenge is how to establish more accurate diagnosis and treatment plans that take into account the vulnerability and resources of people in situations of economic oppression.

Economic Vulnerability and Violence in the United States

At first blush, the economic figures from the United States indicate that there are fewer problems with resources and choices in people's lives. However, the averages cover up some significant problems regarding economic vulnerability. We will look first at the macroeconomic figures, and then do further analysis on the location of inequalities that are problematic.

The United States ranked third on the 2000 HDI with a score of 0.929, behind only Canada and Norway,[31] although the United States was first in GNP with U.S.$7.9 trillion, followed by Japan with U.S.$4.089 trillion and Germany at U.S.$2.179 trillion.[32] This compares with the combined GNP of U.S.$5.698 trillion for all of the medium and low developing countries in the world (129 countries), 20 percent of global GNP with 54 percent of the population.[33] The United States generates and spends 28 percent of the income of the entire world with only 5.5 percent of the world's population.[34] A further analysis of control of accumulated global resources through transnational corporations would show that the U.S. is the dominant economic power in the world with influence far beyond the statistics seen here.

Ranking third out of 174 countries on the HDI is not a problem for the United States since the differences between the most developed countries are small. *Longevity* (1998): The life expectancy at birth was 76.7 years, compared with 67.9 in Nicaragua.[35] *Educational attainment* (1998): The adult literacy rate was 99 percent (Nicaragua = 63.4 percent), and the school enrollment rate for children was 94 percent (Nicaragua = 63 percent).[36] *Standard of Living:* the per capita income was $29,683 (Nicaragua = $452).[37]

Where do we begin to find the economic figures that describe the vulnerability of some groups in the United States? There are several places where inequality shows up in the UN Human Development report.

Gender Inequality: The United States ranks thirteenth on the Gender Empowerment Index (GEI) with a score of 0.707 on a scale where gender equality would be 1.000.[38] (Nicaragua is not ranked because of lack of data.) There are gender differences in access to wealth: the female average real GDP is $22,565 compared with the male average real GDP of $36,849 for a rate of 61 percent female/male income.[39] Women do not have equality with men in such areas as politics (women make up 12.5 percent in legislatures) and management positions (women constitute 44.4 percent of administrators and managers, a figure that decreases at higher levels of income and status).

While the figures from the 1998 U.S. Census estimates do not correspond exactly to the HDI figures, the U.S. Census figures give a clearer picture of gender and racial inequality. In the U.S. 12.7 percent of the total population, or 34,476,000 persons, live below the poverty level. Poverty correlates with race in the following way: 10.5 percent of whites live in poverty, 26.1 percent of blacks, and 25.6 percent of Hispanics (any race). Poverty correlates with age in the following way: 18.9 percent of children, 6.9 percent of persons 45–54, and 10.5 percent of those over 65 live in poverty. Poverty correlates with gender in these ways: of married couples in households, 5.3 percent live in poverty, in contrast to 29.9 percent of all single female heads of house; 40.8 percent of black single female heads of house; and 43.7 percent of Hispanic single female heads of house.[40]

Poverty Level in the U.S.: The United States ranks eighteenth in the world in terms of the absence of human poverty in an industrialized country.[41] The Human Poverty Index for industrialized countries (HPI-2) is based on four factors: the percentage of people not expected to survive to age 60, the level of functional illiteracy, the long-term unemployment, and level of poverty. Income poverty in industrialized countries is defined as the "percentage of people living below the poverty line, set at 50% of the median disposable personal income."[42]

- 12.4 percent of the U.S. population is not expected to survive to age 60, twenty-third among highly developed countries.[43]

- 20.7 percent is functionally illiterate, eleventh among highly developed countries.[44]

- 0.4 percent has been unemployed for longer than 12 months.[45]

- The poorest 20 percent of the U.S. population averages $5,800 per year, while the richest 20 percent averages $51,705, a ratio of 19 to 1.[46]

- 12.7 percent lives below the poverty level (less than half of the median per capita income).[47]

Military spending: The United States spends $277 billion on its military and exports over $10 billion in military hardware,[48] compared with $6.8 billion in development assistance to other nations, of which only $1.36 billion goes to the least developed countries.[49] U.S. military spending is more than the total GNP of the least developed nations of the world ($136 billion, 34 nations), and 0.4 percent of that amount is in the form of development assistance.[50]

The United States has intervened militarily in Nicaragua five times since 1850, most recently by funding, training, and advising the Contras in their war against the Sandinista government, which had been duly elected in 1984. In the war of 1985–90, 36,000 people were killed; this has become one of the central traumas affecting the development of Nicaragua. The minus 3.4 percent growth in the GNP in Nicaragua since 1985 can be attributed to the Contra War and the exploitative economic policies of the United States in the 1990s. Nicaragua borrowed money to defend itself, and has borrowed money since to repay debts and try to feed its people.

Family Violence in the U.S.: In spite of its economic wealth, and the relative wealth of the majority of the U.S. population, the prevalence of sexual and domestic violence is not so different from the same kinds of violence in less developed countries. Between a third and half of all women report at least one incident of sexual or domestic violence during their lifetime; a third of girls have an experience of sexual violence before age 18.[51]

Using conservative definitions of rape and using conservative methods of collecting and interpreting data, Mary P. Ross reviews 20 empirical studies and estimates that at least 14 percent of all women have experienced a completed rape as adults. Results of the studies range from 8 percent to over 20 percent.[52] This is an astounding percent of the female population. Adding attempted rapes doubles the number of victims in most studies.

Estimates of physical abuse of children range from 200,000 to 4 million cases per year. The National Committee for the Prevention of Child Abuse estimates that more than 1 million children are seriously abused per year, including 2,000–5,000 murders of children.[53] Women are significantly involved in the physical abuse of young children where they are the primary caregivers. However, men often abuse young children and are responsible for the majority of cases of abuse of older children and adolescents. Estimates of child sexual abuse range from 12 to 28 percent of girls and 3 to 9 percent of boys. This means 210,000 cases per year, of which 44,700 per year come to the attention of some professional person such as a teacher, pastor, physician, or social worker.[54] Most experts believe that most physical and sexual abuse of children is never reported to authorities.

"We found that someone getting married runs greater than a one in four chance of being involved in marital violence at some time in the relationship."[55] In addition, live-in and dating relationships are also dangerous, because the rates of violence are almost as high.

The credible research on male violence indicates that at least 25 percent of women and children in the U.S. will be victims of physical or sexual violence by men, resulting in substantial physical and psychological injuries, either as children facing physical, sexual, or emotional abuse or as adults facing assault, battering, rape, or psychological control. These statistics do not diminish with social class, race, religion, or faithful church attendance, though they do correlate with gender (women are more frequently victims than men).

Summary

The statistics from the UN Human Development Report help us to see the great discrepancy between the United States and Nicaragua on the HDI, and they also suggest ongoing economic inequalities within the United States between various groups according to gender, race, age, and class. In a world where there are various threats to human safety and thriving, vulnerability helps conceptualize the consequences of various threats. When one has resources, the threats can be anticipated and choices made about what kind of life one wants to lead. When resources are limited by poverty and lack of resources, threats that become actual can be devastating, whether it is Hurricane Mitch, which killed 10,000 people and displaced hundreds of thousands in Central America, or domestic violence, which affects the health and future of one-third and more of all women and children in the world.

These figures illustrate the relative suffering of the people living in these two nations, but it does not tell the story of how these inequalities came to exist and how they are maintained for the present and future. In the next chapter, we explore some of the theories of economics that explain the unequal distribution of wealth and vulnerability in our world, and what some Christian theologians have said about these theories. In order to understand the meaning of pastoral care for those who are vulnerable, we need to understand the economic systems that make people vulnerable. And we need to understand how pastoral care can become a ministry of empowering people to reduce their vulnerabilities and increase their agency as children of God, even while they live in a world with many dangers, toils, and snares.

6

Theories of Capitalism and the Distribution of Wealth

Introduction

Christian and Jewish religious leaders have been troubled for generations by the unjust distribution of global wealth and the resultant vulnerability. They have drawn on the prophetic writings of Amos, Jeremiah, and other Hebrew Testament books to show God's displeasure over economic exploitation of the poor by the rich.

> Woe to him who builds his house by unrighteousness,
>   and his upper rooms by injustice;
> who makes his neighbors work for nothing,
>   and does not give them their wages...
> But your eyes and heart are only on your dishonest gain,
> for shedding innocent blood,
>   and for practicing oppression and violence.
>
> (Jer. 22:13, 17)

Many Christian theologians have argued that the unjust distribution of wealth and the vulnerability that results are against the spirit of Jesus, who came from the poor and advocated their just cause in his teachings and symbolic actions.

> "Blessed are you who are poor, for yours is the kingdom of God.
> Blessed are you who are hungry now, for you will be filled.
> Blessed are you who weep now, for you will laugh...
> But woe to you who are rich, for you have received your
>   consolation.
> Woe to you who are full now, for you will be hungry.
> Woe to you who are laughing now, for you will mourn and
>   weep."
>
> (Luke 6:20–21, 24–25)

76

While economic justice and God's love for those who are vulnerable are well-established themes in theology and ethics and in the actions of the churches over the generations, there is great difference of opinion among theologians about the best way of reaching these goals. For Christians at the beginning of the twenty-first century in the Western world, the debates are about capitalism, an economic system that has created the greatest accumulation of wealth and technology in history, but which also has coexisted with the greatest inequities and violence in history. The question for this chapter is how Christians should understand the contradictions of capitalism, and what practices Christians should recommend for the churches. In other words, what is our analysis of capitalism with its contradictions of wealth and injustice, and what is our plan for furthering the hope for justice that the prophets and Jesus called for and promised? How we answer these questions will have a direct impact on our theories and practices of pastoral care. As Christians, we are called to care for the whole world and for all people in every circumstance. What kind of pastoral care is needed in a world where so many people are economically vulnerable and living with the danger of violence? How do the economic systems affect the daily lives of people in different social classes, and how can we take these effects into account when people come to the church for pastoral care? To answer these questions, we must understand something about the macro-systems that create the context for the economic lives of individuals, families, and local communities.

"The principal goal of development policy is to create sustainable improvements in the quality of life for all people."[1] This requirement is met by the creation and distribution of goods and services that meet people's needs, and by economic systems that empower the nobler desires of humans, such as love and justice.

Pastoral theology is an interdisciplinary project that works to understand and improve care for people and communities. We must stretch ourselves to understand the complex debates that occur in other disciplines. As we do so, we discover that we have our own contributions to make to the debates and their outcome for people. In the sections that follow, I rely on secondary resources, that is, economists and theologians who interpret the primary texts and debates about economics.

We must try to be responsible with the materials of economics without shrinking from the moral obligation to represent justice from a Christian perspective. Daniel Finn warns against the tendency of non-economists who oversimplify the complexities because they don't know the history and theories of economics; some theologians too "readily [wade] into economic policy issues without apparent effort to become fluent in the continuing economic conversation."[2]

John Cobb says in response, "Those of us who are fundamentally opposed to the globalization of the economy will not be persuaded by

[Finn's] arguments, but we will have to formulate our objections to increasing international trade more carefully, and we will be helped by Finn to do so more accurately."[3]

We hope to take economists seriously on their own terms, and also to respond out of our understanding of the values of justice from the Christian gospel.

A Brief History of Market Capitalism and the Theories of Economists

Given the above theological vision of economic life, we need to enter into a dialogue with economists who have defined the basic terms that shape our understanding of economics today. For this section, I rely on the historical narrative by Robert Heilbroner, *The Worldly Philosophers*.[4] What does the discipline of economics say about the best ways to create and distribute wealth for the human community? Heilbroner begins his narrative about the nature of economics with the question: What is a market?

> [A market is an] arrangement in which society assured its own continuance by allowing each individual to do exactly as he saw fit–provided he followed a central guiding rule. The arrangement was called the "market system," and the rule was deceptively simple: each should do what was to his best monetary advantage. In the market system the lure of gain, not the pull of tradition or the whip of authority, steered the great majority to his [or her] task. And yet, although each was free to go wherever his acquisitive nose directed him, the interplay of one person against another resulted in the necessary tasks of society getting done.[5]

Although there have been bartering markets of exchange since the beginning of recorded history, there was no comprehensive theory of markets until recent centuries. That is, individuals and societies traded with one another and tried to gain advantages that would help them accumulate goods, but the abstract ideas of land, labor, and capital and the mechanisms for their interaction came into being only in the sixteenth century and afterward. As long as land was controlled by elite nobility and not available for competition; as long as labor was tied to serfdom to serve the will of the dominant classes; as long as money could not be loaned with interest because of church rules, then a market economy could not yet exist.[6]

Land, labor, and capital–these are the basic requirements for market capitalism according to economists. Land is defined as an inert body of natural resources that can be exploited for goods and for profit. Labor is a network of "job-seeking [persons] in which individuals sell their services to the highest bidder."[7] Capital is not just money or profit, but money that is available for "new and aggressive use" within a system that allows interest and profit.[8]

Within the medieval economic system, land, working people, and money were present, but, according to Heilbroner, they were regulated by a social system of kings, lords, and peasants according to traditions that governed their usage and interaction. The Enlightenment provided the intellectual climate in which market capitalism could develop.

The first architect of market capitalism, *Adam Smith* (1723–1790), postulated "the invisible hand" that allowed interaction between land, labor, and capital for the purpose of creating wealth. Smith believed that the prices of products were determined by the relative contributions of land, labor, and capital (or profit).

> The real value of all the different component parts of price, it must be observed, is measured by the quantity of labor which they can, each of them, purchase or command. Labor measures the value not only of that part of price which resolves itself into labour, but of that which resolves itself into rent, and of that which resolves itself into profit.[9]

An "invisible hand" that functioned by three principles controlled the balance between three economic factors: the self-interest of individuals, the competition between them for profit, and the equilibrium of supply and demand. As individuals sought profit through rent, exploitation of nature, selling labor, or investment and interest on capital, they competed with one another to drive prices up and down and generate a sufficient supply of goods and services. The result was the creation of wealth that was shared by a large population and an increased standard of living.[10]

The transition from a medieval economy to market capitalism required the freeing of land from domination by kings and lords, the freeing of labor from serfdom, and the freeing of capital from rules against investment and usury (interest). This required the overthrowing of a system that had been in place for centuries. Historians refer to this long period of transition by several names– Renaissance, Reformation, and Enlightenment. England was one of the first countries to benefit from this new theory of economics, and the wealth it generated in the eighteenth and nineteenth centuries made it the most powerful empire in the world. However, there were problems with Adam Smith's description of market capitalism that had to be faced by later economists. A brief review of these debates can be helpful, because the problems identified continue to haunt us.

Thomas Robert Malthus (1766–1834) was concerned about the problem of poverty for the majority of the population. He thought that when people moved from serfdom and sharecropping to factory jobs, the wages they obtained tended to drop toward subsistence, that is, the lowest wage that would prevent starvation. Because laborers were in great supply, and because the birth rate of the population was high, factory owners had no motive to provide additional wages beyond subsistence. Hence, he predicted that capitalism would never move the majority of the population beyond poverty. Unlimited labor would never be able to compete with the owners of capital.[11] While western Europe, the United States, and Japan have shown that capitalism can create wealth for the majority of its domestic population of workers, the rapid move of factories to the two-thirds world in the late twentieth century raises Malthus-type fears again. How can wages remain at a high level under capitalism when there is an endless supply of poor people in the world who must work for survival? The stagnation of workers' wages in the United States in the last twenty years may show that Malthus's fears about the causes of poverty are still relevant.[12]

David Ricardo (1772–1823) was concerned about the negative effects of competition among the actors within market capitalism– namely workers, capitalists, and landlords. Given that these three groups have competing interests, what prevents class warfare that destroys society and the economic system? This problem seemed to be happening before his eyes when he saw that landlords had a monopoly on land that kept rents, and therefore food costs, high, but did nothing to increase production.[13] What Ricardo did not realize is that the relative political power of these landlords, industrialists, and workers can change over time. The stranglehold that landlords had on rents in the nineteenth century was broken when they lost political power and their land became available for sale at market prices. The problem of land monopoly was transformed when capitalism created competition and shifts in power alliances. However, the issue of class conflict came up again in Marxist theories of economics, and the life and death struggles for survival between social classes are still present in the contemporary global scene.

Two other problems become apparent. First, Ricardo wondered what happens to capitalism when the basic needs of the people for food, shelter, and security are met. Doesn't this mean that capitalism will stagnate and the amount of wealth will decrease? Where are the markets for the surplus after the population is satisfied? A new idea from Jean-Baptiste Say suggested that "the desire for commodities is infinite."[14] The desire of people for goods and services does not end when food, housing, and security needs are met. As we know today, the consumer economy knows no limits as long as advertising can create new needs. But what happens to the people when false needs are created? This is a twenty-first–century question.

Second, Malthus was troubled by the boom and bust cycles of capitalism wherein times of prosperity are followed by collapse and widespread poverty. The extreme rhythms of capitalism created a pessimistic attitude in the population that could defeat the success of the markets to regulate wealth.[15] The depressions and recessions of the twentieth century, and the collapse of the Asian economic miracle in 1998 are examples that show the continuation of the problem.

The pessimism of Malthus and Ricardo led to the thought of the utopian socialists of the nineteenth century, including *John Stuart Mill* (1806–73), who suggested that economic wealth must be guided by the values of the community. Under capitalism, wealth can be used for selfishness and domination, but it can also be shared among the people if there is a community of sharing and altruism. In response to this analysis, many nineteenth-century utopian communities were developed in Europe and the United States where workers were given adequate housing by owners of factories, cooperatives including workers as owners were created, and there was an air of optimism that capitalism and Christian values could be combined.[16] If competition and supply and demand could be combined with the altruism of religious people, then the accumulated wealth could raise the quality of life for everyone. The idea that a community of values can make capitalism work in a humane way for people and the environment is an important part of the debate among contemporary Christian thinkers.

Karl Marx (1818–1883) rejected the utopian vision because he believed that the problems of capitalism were not so easily solved by the force of will or by altruism. In spite of the good intentions of Mill and others, Marx saw a destructive class conflict between workers and capitalists that would lead to revolutionary change. According to Marx, the value of a manufactured product is the amount of labor it requires. In order for profit to investors to exist, workers must be exploited and paid less than the value of the products they have created. This exploitation sets up a class conflict that leads to class warfare. Capitalism is inherently destructive of human life and leads to rebellion as people begin to realize the depth of their oppression. His solution was socialism (or communism), an economic system in which the workers and owners are the same group, and they can organize so that the profit of labor benefits everyone. Capitalists cannot be trusted to create and distribute wealth for the benefit of the people. Only socialism (a planned economy controlled by workers) can organize the system for the benefit of people. The bureaucratic nations created in the name of Marx have not succeeded in solving the economic problems of the world, as we are especially aware since the changes in the USSR in 1989. According to Heilbroner, Marx is important not only for his critique of capitalism but because he invented the critique of economics itself.[17]

The nineteenth century saw another development in the understanding of economics, namely, its change into a science with a special connection with mathematics. This has led to an increasing reliance on economics as a quantitative theory with a highly abstract quality. Mathematics has become the central tool of modern economics and is indispensable to understanding the complex interrelationships.[18] What would we do without mathematical concepts such as gross national product, per capita income, annual inflation rates, and consumer price index?

John A. Hobson (1858–1940) declared that imperialism was one of the primary problems of market capitalism in the late nineteenth century.

> Between 1870 and 1898 Britain added 4 million square miles and 88 million people to its empire; France gained nearly the same area of territory, with 40 million souls attached; Germany won a million [square] miles and 16 million colonials; Belgium took 900,000 miles and 30 million people; even Portugal joined the race, with 800,000 miles of new lands and 9 million inhabitants… John Stuart Mill called the colonies "a vast system of outdoor relief for the upper classes."[19]

Hobson argued that the creation of the colonies by European nations was not just a result of greed, but an extension of the logic of market capitalism. The unequal distribution of wealth within nations, and between nations and colonies, was not an accident, but a result of the profit motive as a dominant value. The problem is that consumption in the host country will never be sufficient to sustain high profits on investments. The rich will always look outside their own communities for investment opportunities where the margin of profit is much higher. This is the motive for imperialism–"the endeavor of the great controllers of industry to broaden the channel for the flow of their surplus wealth by seeking foreign markets and foreign investments to take off the goods and capital they cannot use at home."[20] The result is a race among the rich countries for dominance in the world, with its cutthroat competition and continual war. The original colonial period of capitalism lasted from the sixteenth century through the twentieth as Spain took over Latin America and the Caribbean; Britain, Holland, and Russia staked out claims in Asia in competition with Japan; and Africa was carved up among France, Belgium, and several other countries. One result of this competition between nations and growing colonial wealth was a long history of European wars. The gold from Latin America ended up in England as British industry provided the arms Spain needed to conduct its costly wars. Competition within the European nations culminated in the two World Wars of the twentieth century and the ensuing Cold War that dominated the last half of the century.[21]

This argument is very familiar today because it was taken up by Lenin and other Marxist economists and was made a cornerstone of the debate between capitalism and communism. On the basis of this argument, many newly independent colonies turned to the Soviet Union for help in the twentieth century because this analysis seemed to fit their situation. They sought freedom from the Western colonial system by making contracts with the Soviet Union. However, they often found themselves part of another empire with characteristics similar to the one they were revolting against. We see this argument reappearing as the poor countries again criticize neocolonialism and neoliberal economics in the late twentieth century after the collapse of communism in the Soviet Union and Eastern Europe.

The defense of contemporary neoliberal economists is that empires were fueled by greed long before capitalism and that exploitative imperialism is not a necessary ingredient of capitalism. Heilbroner suggests that the military expansionism of the United States in the last half of the twentieth century has been ideological, to defeat communism, rather than in service of economic gain. That is, the negative side of imperialism is due to human sin, not to any inherent weakness in the theory of market capitalism. "It is a direct political, rather than an indirect economic, form of foreign domination."[22] We shall return to this debate later when we consider the causes of the unjust distribution of wealth between rich and poor countries in the early twenty-first century.

Heilbroner then shifts the scene to the United States and the work of *Thorstein Veblen* (1857–1929), who wrote during the time of robber barons Rockefeller, Morgan, Carnegie, and others. Veblen saw these successful capitalists as predators who were more interested in power than in productivity. In fact, they often destroyed businesses for the sake of the profit that came from chaotic markets, rather than trying to maximize the production of goods and services. This was the time of the Christian "social gospel" movement that attempted to diminish the ills of capitalism such as child labor, dangerous working conditions, and low wages. Many laws were passed that challenged capitalistic exploitation of the poor with no accountability. Heilbroner suggests that Veblen's critique of exploitative capitalism supported the rise of a movement led by humanistic values. Veblen also foresaw the impact of science and technology as a source of productivity for economics.

One of Veblen's important observations was that profit did not accrue to industrialists through production of goods and services, but through their ability to profit from the disruptions to production that they could manipulate. Buying and selling corporations could be more profitable than buying and selling commodities. John D. Rockefeller did not profit by producing oil, but by manipulating the oil markets so that his companies profited from the changes. His monopolies gave him the power and the leverage to drive prices up and down in ways that he could profit from, even if such manipulation caused a reduction in the amount of oil products available to the consumer. Disrupting a stable market that guaranteed the oil supply was often more profitable for Rockefeller than producing and distributing the oil itself, because he could buy and sell stocks to benefit from the differences in the market prices. Only his dominance as a producer enabled him to be able to do this.[23]

According to Veblen, these predatory practices are encouraged by the logic of capitalism, which puts maximum value on profit in a competitive environment. We see a return to such practices in the day traders and the buying and selling of productive companies by transnational corporations. The stock market in the twenty-first century seems to have been motivated more by disruptions in monetary values than by the production of goods and services for the population. Veblen predicted that such predatory habits would undermine the ability of a capitalistic economy to support any population over the long term.

John Maynard Keynes (1883–1946) was a leading U.S. economist of the early twentieth century. He began writing during the period of prosperity of the 1920s and was one of the leading commentators during the Great Depression. "America [United States] in the late 1920s had found jobs for 45 million of its citizens to whom it paid some $77 billion in wages, rents, profits, and interest."[24]

The 1920s were a great time of optimism and expansion for the elite and the middle class. But capitalism was about to face one of its greatest challenges–the Great Depression. In October and November, 1929, "$40 billion of values simply disappeared. By the end of three years our [average] investor's paper fortune of $21,000 had diminished by 80 percent; his original $7,000 of savings was worth barely $4,000."[25] These changing statistics had dramatic impact on working people in their everyday lives.

> In Muncie, Indiana. . . every fourth factory worker lost his job by the end of 1930. In Chicago the majority of working women were earning less than twenty-five cents an hour, and a quarter of them made less than ten cents...In the nation as a whole, residential construction fell by 95 percent. Nine million savings accounts were lost. Eight-five thousand businesses failed. The national volume of salaries dwindled 40 percent; dividends 56 percent; wages 60 percent...the national income precipitously fell from $87 billion in 1929 [to $39 billion by 1933]... Over half of the prosperity of only four years back had vanished without a trace; the average standard of living was back where it had been twenty years before. On street corners...14 million unemployed sat, haunting the land.[26]

Keynes's challenge was to explain how the U.S. economy could move from prosperity to depression in such a short time. There was nothing in economic theory to explain what had happened. His explanation went something like this: Capitalism grows through savings, which are reinvested in new production. As long as the national income is high and savings are invested in growth, the economy will grow. But when income is low, saving is also low, and there is no capital for investment in the economy. The problem is that capitalism can only be self-sustaining when there is a continuous flow of capital between producers, consumers, savers, and investors. When this flow is interrupted, income drops and there is no fuel for economic growth. In the 1920s, savings in the U.S. population was high, and money was available for the stock market, which soared in paper value. However, after the crash of the stock market and the closing of the banks, the savings of most people disappeared and they spent all their income on necessities. This loss of consumer demand contributed to a stagnation of the economy, a fate that is deadly for capitalism, which depends on the constant flow of capital from land to labor to profit.[27]

Keynes saw that capitalism was a system of complex interrelationships in which high savings encouraged lower interest rates that led to borrowing for investments. If the whole economy slowed down to its subsistence level, there would be no investment and growth. Workers who have no jobs cannot spend for consumer goods, which lowers the demand for production and results in the loss of more jobs. Without demand for products and services, business has no market for its products. People without money to spend and save provide no impetus to the economy; in fact, they drop out of the economic equation, and the market collapses. And when demand stagnates on a worldwide basis, even the lure of imperialistic expansion disappears. Just as wealth is created during times of prosperity, wealth can disappear during times of stagnation.[28]

Keynes became an adviser to U.S. President Franklin Roosevelt and urged the government to increase its pattern of borrowing and investing money to "prime the pump" of capitalism. He argued that if workers have no income and cannot save, then the government should borrow in order to stimulate the economy. The debt can be paid back through increased taxes when the economy is strong. The New Deal was a program of work projects to put people to work, and Social Security forced people to save so money would be available for investment. The increase in government spending in preparation for World War II started the U.S. economy running again and led into the biggest gain of wealth in the history of the world.

> The world is more prosperous, with average per capita incomes having more than tripled as global GDP increased ninefold, from $3 trillion to $30 trillion, in the past 50 years. The share of people enjoying medium human development rose from 55% in 1975 to 66% in 1997, and the share in low human development fell from 20% to 10%.[29]

Keynes is a controversial figure today because of his support of government as an aggressive actor in the economy. Since 1980, some economists have advocated for smaller government and more trust in global capitalism. Whether the new laissez-faire theories will last and prove Keynes wrong is yet to be tested.[30] Keynes's legacy of government spending influenced U.S. government policy from 1930 until 1980, when it was successfully challenged under the administration of President Ronald Reagan, who was guided by an image of the free market ideas developed by economists such as Milton Friedman and the University of Chicago School of Economics.

Contemporary debate about economics continues between the "free market" economists, who trace their roots to Adam Smith, and "democratic socialists" (Joseph Schumpeter and others). Meanwhile, the role of technology in market capitalism has escalated with the global network of computers.

Summary

In this chapter I have looked at the history of the academic discipline of economics and its various explanations for how wealth is created and distributed. I showed that scholars anticipated in the past many of the current problems of capitalism and that capitalist assumptions about land, labor, and capital continue to influence the imagination of the people, especially with capitalism's emphasis on self-interest, competition, and supply and demand. Capitalism has been contested over many centuries for its values of greed and competition, its tendency to exploit those who are poor and vulnerable, its expansionistic needs, and its insensitivity to environmental degradation. Yet in spite of these critiques, capitalism has emerged as the primary economic system of the twenty-first century because of its ability to produce wealth and encourage individual creativity and freedom. For many, democracy and capitalism seem to go together, and they appeal to a wide range of the world's population.

In the next chapter, I examine the debates among contemporary theologians about the contributions and limitations of capitalism. These issues are important for those of us interested in pastoral care of persons with economic vulnerability and abuse issues, because they help us understand the context for the individuals and families we care about.

7

A Christian Critique of Market Capitalism

Market capitalism is a complex system of material activities and exchanges that determines how wealth and resources will be created and distributed within the population, and a system that organizes human desire, deciding what values and behaviors will shape the personal experiences of groups.[1]

What are the causes and consequences of the inequalities of wealth in the world today, and how do these inequalities shape the human urge for dominance and control? The brief history we have just reviewed suggests some hunches.

If Adam Smith is correct that capitalism depends on self-interest, competition, and supply and demand, then the human imagination will be greatly affected. Self-interest does not provide a basis for empathy for others, but leads one person to see another in utilitarian terms. Competition creates winners and losers who can easily see one another as adversaries rather than companions. Supply and demand turns economics into mathematics, with reduced space for the affective lives of people and the complex informal economics of everyday peasant life. The culture of capitalism dramatically affects how people understand themselves and one another.

If Malthus and Ricardo are correct, class conflict is inevitable as people find themselves trapped in situations with no way out. While industrialists seek an endless supply of workers at cheap wages to make a profit, laborers are often forced to live at subsistence levels. Class antagonism fueled by economic inequality, religious fervor, and race and gender prejudice contribute to frequent episodes of war and other types of violence for many people in the world.

Marx and Hobson believed that capitalism is destructive of human community and eventually self-destructive. Even though their prophecies about the demise of capitalism have been incorrect so far, their insight that capitalism has self-destructive tendencies must be taken seriously. The dominance of consumer economics transforms human beings into collectors of useless possessions and isolates them from the suffering of others. The fact that half the world's population lives at or below subsistence poverty is a sign that capitalism has not provided for the needs of the world's population. Regional war based on racial, ethnic, and religious differences is one of the major fears of elite capitalists in the U.S.

Veblen struggled to understand the problems of capitalism in the United States, especially the tendency of industrial leaders to gamble their assets and disrupt production of goods and services for the sake of personal wealth and power. Do the transnational corporations make their money by increasing economic production, or by disrupting trade through corporate mergers and takeovers in the global free market? Keynes discovered that government investment for the sake of production is one way to stimulate the growth of capitalism and decrease the risk of a major depression. Is the government's role to prevent monopolies and maintain competition or to extend corporate control over labor and natural resources to increase their profit without increasing production? These ideas are frightening today as we think of the free markets and information technology of the twenty-first century, and the human and environmental costs of expanding market capitalism.

Theologians and ethicists are currently debating whether the distribution or production of wealth, sometimes called "distributive justice" and "productive justice" should receive priority. The recent history of progressive theology puts strong emphasis on the fair distribution of wealth as a corrective for the unjust distribution of economic resources, an inequity that is characteristic of many different economic systems, including market capitalism. In line with much of Latin American and African American Liberation theology, the emphasis on "distributive justice" includes a preferential option for the poor as a measure of the justice of the economic system itself.

Finn emphasizes distributive justice and gives several principles that are important: the priority of God's reign over all institutional forms and individual decisions; the love of neighbor and a preferential option for the poor; the commitment to sustainability; stewardship of the environment; a concern for fellow citizens and foreigners: moral equality and difference; the role of science as a partner with ethics in making competent decisions.[2]

Ethicists such as David Krueger, Max Stackhouse, and others argue that more attention must be given to productive justice, and they challenge the exclusive emphasis on distributive justice. They are concerned that the church must encourage the creation of additional wealth in order to provide resources for an increasing global population. Krueger discusses five ethical principles that should guide Christians in a discussion of how wealth can be increased:

> This pursuit of wealth, in the form of goods and services, is properly guided and restrained by at least the following five moral considerations: (1) that it be efficient (and thus profitable and competitive); (2) that its products be beneficial and not harmful to users and society; (3) that in its relations with various constituent or stakeholder groups, it adhere to basic standards of productive justice; (4) that it support the creation and effective administration of appropriate countervailing institutions, e.g., democratic governments, regulatory agencies, and non-governmental organizations (NGOs), whose combined efforts aim to realize the well-functioning of civil society; and (5) that its activities aim toward environmental sustainability and sustainable development.[3]

In the discussion that follows, I confess that I am more interested in the distribution than production of economic goods. I am concerned about the exploitation of the poor that has accompanied the growth of market capitalism in the last two hundred years and continues to this day. It does not seem right that the U.S. gross national product has increased from $39 billion in 1933 to $7.9 trillion in 2000, yet half the world's population lives in extreme poverty. However, I acknowledge that Christians must be concerned with both the production and the distribution of wealth, and that ethical concerns must guide our thoughts and actions in both areas. I remind the reader of my primary purpose in writing this book: How do economics and violence affect the everyday lives of people who look to the church for care and counseling?

John Cobb and Herman Daly

John Cobb has emerged as one of the primary theological critics of market capitalism and free trade. With economist Herman Daly in an important book, *For the Common Good,* he criticizes the individualistic assumptions of contemporary economic theories and develops an alternative model for evaluating the human impact of economic activity.

> The world that economic theory normally pictures is one in which individuals all seek their own good and are indifferent to the success or failure of other individuals engaged in the same activity. There is no way to conceive of a collective good—only that there can be improvement for some without cost to others. Even this theory of social gain is possible only by neglecting relative status along with feelings of good will and ill will. It

would be difficult to imagine a more consistent abstraction from the social or communal character of actual human existence![4]

Cobb and Daly contrast individualism with the idea of "persons-in-community." Rather than being defined as laborers and consumers under capitalism, people should be defined as persons-in-community who are complex beings with many values, goals, and hopes. People should not be reduced to their roles as cogs in an economic machine, but should be seen as persons made in the image of God with vocations to love, work, and serve in a world defined as hopeful.

> *Homo economicus as self-contained individual* is the modern economists' model of the human being as consumer. Human beings as workers are those who sell their labor to the highest bidder. Since workers cannot be separated from their labor, they themselves function as commodities. The sale of labor is for the sake of gaining the income with which one can be a consumer. Hence there is a close connection between the two roles, both of which involve the element of seeking one's own maximum gain.[5]

> *Homo economicus as person-in-community* is equally relevant to people in their roles as consumers and as workers. Both are constituted by their relations to others. Although some may have to work at meaningless or socially destructive jobs, suffering discomfort and boredom, this is a sign of the failure of the economy, as is the poverty that precludes the ability to benefit from the market. The goal of an economics for community is as much to provide meaningful and personally satisfying work as to provide adequate goods and services.[6]

Economic theory quantifies the economic activity of individuals into a mathematical figure called the gross national product, that is, "the summation of the increase of goods and services acquired by the individual members...Per capita gross national product is the total production of the nation divided by the number of people in the country...[which] ignores the diversity of cultural and national societies."[7] This calculation lends itself very well to mathematical modeling, but human relationships do not figure in the calculations. Thus, *Homo economicus as self-contained individual* is not a full picture of human life and value.

In contrast to forms of capitalism that tend to encourage short-term profit for those who are aggressive in their marketing, and using the narrowest possible set of values, Cobb and Daly propose that an economy should meet the following criteria:

(1) It takes the long-run rather than the short-run view; (2) it considers costs and benefits to the whole community, not just to

the parties to the transaction; (3) it focuses on concrete use value and the limited accumulation thereof, rather than on abstract exchange value and its impetus toward unlimited accumulation.[8]

As an alternative to gross national product, Cobb and Daly have developed a mathematical model of economic development, called the Index of Sustainable Economic Welfare (ISEW). Its purpose is similar to the United Nations Human Development Index (HDI) reviewed in chapter 6. Both try to measure the qualitative and quantitative benefits of economic and political systems. I will not unpack their idea fully here, but I can give some of the primary criteria to show how relationships and other human qualities can be taken more seriously in economic theory.

In the Index of Sustainable Economic Welfare (ISEW), measures of personal consumption, for example, are decreased by measures of income inequality, because not all people benefit from a general increase in consumption. Some hidden benefits not counted in GNP, such as household labor, street and highway construction, and public expenditures for health and education, are important in the ISEW. On the other hand, some hidden costs that are often included as positive values in the GNP are counted as negative in the ISEW, for example, costs for advertising, commuting, auto accidents, water pollution, loss of land resources, depletion of nonrenewable resources, and long-term environmental damage. According to Cobb and Daly, while United States GNP rose 320% from 1950 to 1986, the ISEW rose only 136%. Comparing these two measures, one finds that the GNP overestimates the improvement in quality of life for human beings by 2.3 times. That is, GNP measures many factors that actually have negative impact on the quality of human life and the natural environment and thus encourages such negative development in spite of the human costs involved.[9]

We can see from this brief summary that the usual ways of measuring economic growth actually contribute to economic inequality and vulnerability. We need to understand this process better so we can provide better pastoral care for people who are victims of these distorted ways of measuring economic prosperity. How can the economy be doing well, yet many people be economically vulnerable and threatened with violence and death?

Two-Thirds World Poverty

So far in chapters 6 and 7 I have discussed economic theory from the perspective of the so-called first world, which has 23% of the world's population and controls 81% of the global economy.[10] Global GNP does not measure the everyday subsistence of people living in poverty because most peasants survive in informal economies where they do not own land, invest capital, or work at jobs for wages, and thus their economic activity is not counted as a part of GNP. In effect, the global economy would look much different if the discipline of Western economics measured all forms of economic life.

To understand the relationship of market capitalism to two-thirds world economics, we can look closely at the experience of people in countries such as Nicaragua. Then we can begin to understand the conditions under which Margarita, Soledad, and Juana live, and the obstacles they face when they try to seek pastoral care for the trauma of domestic violence. How do macroeconomic systems determine the choices they face in their lives? How can informed pastors use their knowledge of economics to empower Margarita, Soledad, and Juana?

Following World War II, after many decades of colonialism in which Europe, the United States, and Japan directly controlled and exploited many vulnerable countries in the world, the colonies began to move toward political independence. The rich countries, thereafter, changed their strategy from direct military and administrative control to indirect economic control. The imperialism that Hobson identified in the nineteenth century began to take on a much different shape.

Development of New Global Economic Institutions

The crucial organizing meeting for the postcolonial global economic system occurred at Bretton Woods, New Jersey, in 1945, where three international agencies were formed. The General Agreement on Tariffs and Trade (GATT) was organized to encourage international trade and resolve disputes between nations and multinational corporations. The International Monetary Fund (IMF) was organized to respond to currency problems in nations that might inhibit international trade. The IMF provides consultation services and short-term loans for resolving crisis situations so poorer countries can remain part of the global trading markets. The International Bank for Reconstruction and Development (World Bank) "makes long-term loans to developing countries to fund projects that will advance their economies."[11]

According to Cobb, Christians in the United States basically supported these agencies and their international policies on the assumption that their primary goals were (a) to resolve international disputes and therefore decrease the possibility of military conflicts, and (b) to provide financial consultation and resources that would help the poorer countries develop so they could raise the standard of living for their people. Alleviation of poverty in the world was a primary goal of many Christians, and these agencies seemed to be the best hope for such changes.

From 1945 to 1970 Christian leaders overlooked some of the problems. In addition to the authoritarian regimes in many poor countries and the violations of basic human rights, there were also questionable economic practices.

These policies required the shift of agriculture from subsistence farming to agribusiness, meaning that force often had to be used to remove peasants from their land. In order for the products to compete on the world market, industrial development entailed very low wages and hard working conditions. Labor, therefore, could not be allowed to organize to protest conditions and demand a larger share of the profits...Prior to the seventies few [U.S. Christians] noticed the rapid exploitation of nonrenewable resources and the deterioration of the natural environment that were involved in economic development. These were additional costs borne by the poor. Today we realize that they have global consequences.[12]

The consequences of the policies of GATT, IMF, and the World Bank were isolated successes in South Korea, Taiwan, Hong Kong, and Singapore, but continuing and increasing poverty in most other poor countries in Asia, Africa, and Latin America.

In the early 1970s, a shock hit the global economic system, that had drastic consequences for the poor countries of the world. The United States and Europe went through a period of high inflation and high interest rates, which raised the cost of loans for countries who depended on borrowing to keep their economy working. This was also the time of the oil shortage caused by the control of supplies by the Organization of Petroleum Exporting Countries (OPEC). The shortage drove up the cost of oil, which poor countries could not afford. However, by this time many countries were dependent on agribusiness with its demand for oil for machinery and fertilizer. These additional costs raised the cost of production and decreased trade opportunities, thus creating financial difficulties.[13]

Another consequence of the OPEC oil shortage was a windfall of money to the oil-producing countries. Billions of dollars in excess income came to countries and corporations without sufficient investment opportunities for their money. They placed much of their money in U.S. and European banks, which then looked for places to invest. This problem reminds us of Hobson's analysis of causes of nineteenth century imperialism. The excess profits could not be absorbed in the industrial countries, so they were invested overseas. This is one of the motives for imperialism, to put excess profits to work so they will generate more profit, the logic of capital as a commodity.

During the 1970s, U.S. and European banks began to invest in the poor countries of the world the extraordinary profits from oil sales. In the rush to find investments, the banks did not always take care to see if the loans were wise, especially if the loans could be secured by government guarantees. The social power of business leaders in poor countries meant that they could easily get government guarantees, and billions of dollars flowed into the poor countries.[14]

The result of this policy on the part of the commercial banks was a vast increase in Third World debt. Between 1973 and 1983 it rose sixfold, from 150 billion dollars to 900 billion dollars. Most of the increased indebtedness was to commercial banks. When certain governments, such as Mexico, began showing signs of inability to pay around 1980, commercial bank lending to Third World countries declined drastically and the rate of increase of debt slowed dramatically. Nevertheless, ten years later the total debt has increased another 400 billion dollars to 1.3 trillion dollars. Current third world indebtedness in Jan. 2000 is $2.0 trillion, equaling 42.8% of GNP.[15]

Where did this money go? Did it do anything to raise the quality of life in poor countries? Cobb lists seven places where the money went: (1) to fund legitimate projects; (2) to pay for needed imports such as oil; (3) to support government-run businesses that were rarely efficient; (4) to purchase luxury imports for the middle class; (5) to purchase military hardware; (6) to build popular monuments for political purposes; (7) to enable capital flight from the wealthy elite to northern banks for safe keeping.[16]

> Government officials and associated elites wasted or stole large amounts of the borrowed funds, which consequently generated no increase in wealth. Yet these loans must be paid back at interest–not by those few who benefited, but by the general public, who received none of the benefits. The benefits were privatized, and the costs socialized.[17]

During the 1980s, the debt crisis among the poor countries had become an important public issue, and eventually Christians began to see that the IMF and World Bank were not necessarily benevolent institutions organized to help the poor of the world. Rather, their goal was to provide for trade and financial stability that almost always favored the rich nations. After World War II there was much investment of capital in the poor countries of the Southern Hemisphere, but after 1980, the results of those investments resulted in a large flow of capital from South to North. Susan George summarizes the new situation in this way:

> According to the Organization for Economic Cooperation and Development, "between 1982 and 1990, total resource flow to developing countries amounted to $927 billion," much of it in loans that must be repaid with interest. During these years "developing countries remitted in debt service alone $1,345 billion (interest and principal) to the creditor countries." This involves a transfer of $418 billion in addition to uncalculated payments of "royalties, dividends, repatriated profits, underpaid raw materials, and the like."[18]

Between 1982 and 1990, $418 billion was transferred from the poor countries to the rich countries, not counting the trade imbalances that result in hidden money flowing to the Northern rich nations. This figure challenges the notion that the IMF and World Bank are primarily designed to help the poor countries begin to develop. This transfer comes at a time when large majorities of people in many countries live on less than $2 per day,[19] not enough to provide food and housing. The poor countries are subsidizing the rich countries at a time when the poor countries can least afford it.

> By the mid 1980s, interest payments on the debt they owed to foreigners more than offset inward flows to many countries, draining them of resources needed for development. Yet, in the absence of reforms in the international lending system, the debtor nations had to pay their debts in order to remain creditworthy and not become "economic pariahs."[20]

This is why John Cobb said that most of the poor countries would be better off if the United States and other rich countries just left the poor countries alone rather than trying to help them. Investment and charity from the North is very expensive. "This investment and aid have destroyed the self-sufficiency of nations and rendered masses of their formerly self-reliant people unable to care for themselves...We think in the long run it is better to de-link their economy from [the U.S. economy]."[21]

The response of the IMF to the debt crisis of the 1980s was "Structural Adjustment," meaning "adjusting" the local economy so that debt payments receive priority and can be paid on time. In order to repay the debts, the poor countries must raise the money (in dollars) through international trade, and they must reduce their domestic expenses so they can make their payments.[22] Developing countries are encouraged to make the following changes in order to increase trade and reduce expenses:

- Devalue the local currency so that exports will be cheaper on the international markets.

- Freeze wages so that inflation will not immediately raise the prices of exports and make them less competitive on the international markets.

- Increase exports that can be easily obtained, such as selling timber and other raw materials that do not require high capital investments. (Some countries rely on drug traffic to increase exports.)

- Privatize government corporations, which creates immediate income and makes such corporations more efficient.

- Reduce government expenditures, which are usually in education, health care, and social welfare.

- Legislate free trade, which minimizes labor and environmental regulations and is attractive to foreign investments; this also makes exports more attractive to foreign-owned businesses within the country.

Evaluating the programs of the IMF and World Bank

As financial plans, the IMF structural adjustments have been successful in terms of the amount of money that developing nations have been able to pay on their debt. As we saw above, the result of these policies since 1982 has meant the payment of "$1,345 billion (interest and principal) to the creditor companies."[23] The troubling issue is the increase in misery of the world's poor. In the previous chapter, the United Nations Human Development Report clearly shows the decreasing quality of life in many of the poorest countries in the world. There have been declines in health, nutrition, education, employment, and family income. All these statistics have human faces that Christians must see.

In defense of its policies, the IMF argues that the pain of debt repayment and structural adjustment is temporary in order to put the poor countries on a firm fiscal foundation according to market principles. However, such arguments do not remember the history of how and why such loans were issued in the first place, and what happened to the money. Only small amounts of money were spent for economic development. Much money was wasted on military hardware, worthless buildings, projects for political purposes, and capital flight that benefited only the elite.

Whatever the intentions of the policy makers in the IMF and the World Bank, as well as in the U.S. government, their responses to the debt crisis preserved a dominant-subordinate relationship among rich and poor nations. To many in the debtor countries, it revived memories of the injustices of colonialism and recreated a dependency that endangers the equal dignity and solidarity of peoples. Poor nations are already too dependent on the dominant lenders of the North not only for loans but for the terms of loan repayment.[24]

Another aspect of North-South economic relations is environmental degradation that too often occurs with capitalist expansion of free trade. The Presbyterian Report of 1996 identifies pollution, resource exhaustion, and threats to biodiversity as particular problems that need urgent attention. The loss of national environmental regulations in the new organization of the global economy is an important political issue.[25]

Within the World Bank, there is a vigorous debate about the future of macroeconomic development policies. The 2000 preliminary report, issued in January, 2000, raises serious questions about previous policies. Some statements create the impression that change at the macro level could be in the works.

> The principal goal of development policy is to create sustainable improvements in the quality of life for all people. While raising per capita incomes and consumption is part of that goal, other objectives–reducing poverty, expanding access to health services, and increasing educational levels–are also important. Meeting these goals requires a comprehensive approach to development...The idea that development has multiple goals and that the policies and processes for meeting them are complex and intertwined has provoked an intense debate on the wisdom of traditional development thinking. This introduction...emphasizes the need to reach beyond economics to address societal issues in a holistic fashion.[26]

Whether alleviating poverty and improving the quality of life for the world's poor is a goal of the IMF, World Bank, and other international agencies is not clear. What does seem clear is that the dominant economies of the North seem to do fine with the new rules of free trade and economic development. The recent formation of the World Trade Organization does not seem to be a good omen, especially since the poor countries, labor unions, and environmental groups are not represented.

Several movements are challenging the Northern dominance of the Southern countries. Jubilee 2000 is an international movement to forgive the debts of the poorest countries. Supported by many non-governmental organizations (NGOs) and many democratic socialist countries in Europe, this movement has made some headway as a political movement, and some forgiveness of debt has occurred. Certain economists suggest nationalist rather than neoliberal responses to the crisis of the poor countries.

> A "nationalistic" strategy favors (1) greater decentralization at all levels...(2) widespread popular participation in decisions from below...and (3) a high priority to making small agricultural production more productive...The smaller farm sector will aim, at first, at satisfying the basic needs of those working in it, and later, at creating an expanded base for economic well-being.[27]

In summary, market capitalism has increased the misery of the two-thirds world since World War II through investments that favored agribusiness instead of peasant farms; exploitation of natural resources rather than sustainable use; undemocratic, elite governments; and unmanageable debts. The result is a net flow of resources from the poor to the rich countries of the world, not only in debt repayments, but also in trade, labor, and natural resources. Banks with money to lend have gotten good returns on their investments in the South, even after many defaults on unfair debts. In the next chapter, we will examine more closely the effects of such macroeconomic policies on the people of Nicaragua.

Economic vulnerability has a history that needs to be understood by Christians who care about people in the world. There are systemic reasons why so many are poor and economically vulnerable. The myths about overpopulation, backward cultures, and pagan religions cannot be used to explain global poverty. Education and conversion to Christianity will not bring an end to global poverty. Rather, we have to look critically at global market capitalism, its history, theory, and values to understand the injustice in the world today.

Poverty in the United States

There is some tendency to think of the population of the United States as relatively well off. However, poverty in the U.S., and other industrialized countries does exist. It is important to understand the relationship between the extreme poverty of the poor countries and the relative poverty of the U.S.

> The economic relations of the ghetto to White America closely parallel those between third-world nations and the industrially advanced countries. The ghetto also has a relatively low per capita income and a high birth rate. Its residents are for the most part unskilled. Businesses lack capital and managerial know-how. Local markets are limited. The incidence of credit is high. Little savings takes place and what is saved is usually not invested locally. Goods and services tend to be "imported" for the most part, only the simplest and the most labor-intensive being produced locally. The ghetto is dependent on one basic export–its unskilled labor power.[28]

Using a scale that compares family income, education, and health care, the desperately poor of many countries in the world are more vulnerable than most of the U.S. population. However, we also have to look at economic vulnerability from a contextual perspective. What does it mean to have an income of $10,000 if housing costs $12,000 and if a family is in debt for $5,000? The imbalance between income, expenses, and debt means that many U.S. families are economically vulnerable. The United Nations Human Development office defines poverty in the developed countries as one-half of the median income of that nation, or $14.40 per day in the U.S. in 2000.[29] This means that people who try to survive on this amount of money will be excluded from participating in many of the opportunities of that society and will be deprived of food, housing, health care, education, and safety at a basic survival level.

Daniel Patrick Moynihan disagreed with the conservatives when he argued that the economic inequality of African Americans was not caused by heredity and lack of intelligence, but by the environmental effects of slavery and racism itself. He said that because the oppression of slavery and racism prevented African Americans from owning property and learning capitalistic skills, this population cannot compete as well in the capitalist U.S. While his emphasis on environmental factors that have a history in systemic oppression has a certain logic, he tended to put too much blame and responsibility on the African American family. He believed that when racism was eliminated by the civil rights acts, the African American family became the main cause of poverty. He was particularly troubled by single mothers, who, he said, destroyed the self-esteem and maturity of African American men so that they did not have the skills for jobs in the marketplace. His solutions were harsh and punitive, for example, decreasing welfare payments to single-parent families to encourage two-parent families, and providing incentives for young African American men to enter the military so they could learn discipline and gain marketable skills.[30] This liberal argument about race helped create the ideas for the 1996 welfare reform under the Clinton administration, the so-called "workfare" program.

Both conservative and liberal theories attempt to hide the systemic effects of white racism and the fact that capitalism depends on the existence of a large labor pool at low wages. If African Americans can be blamed for their exclusion from the benefits of capitalism, then capitalism as a system can remain legitimate in the eyes of the majority of the population. The same elitism that creates colonialism and defines the majority of the world's poor as nonpersons also ignores the economic vulnerability of African Americans within the United States. Racism justifies and excuses capitalism both at home and abroad for its oppression of people of color.

African Americans were slaves for three centuries in the United States. African people were bought and sold as property, and they had no rights to have property or accumulate wealth themselves. In fact, laws were established to limit the wealth and economic opportunities of free blacks before and after the 14th amendment. Manning Marable, in *How Capitalism Underdeveloped Black America,* gives one of the most astute descriptions of poverty among African Americans.

Once "freed," Black Americans were not compensated for their 246 years of free labor to this country's slave oligarchy. Their only means of survival and economic development was their ability to work, their labor power, which they sold in various forms to the agricultural capitalist. Sharecropping and convict leasing were followed by industrial labor at low wages. When Blacks performed the identical tasks that whites carried out, they were paid less than "white wages." Even when Blacks acquired technical skills and advanced education, they were still paid much less than whites who possessed inferior abilities. At every level of development, white capitalists accumulated higher profits from Blacks' labor than they gained from the labor of whites. Throughout the totality of economic relations, Black workers were exploited– in land tenure, in the ownership of factories, shops, and other enterprises, in the means of transportation, in energy, and so forth. *The constant expropriation of surplus value created by Black labor is the heart and soul of underdevelopment.*[31]

In their book, *Black Wealth/White Wealth: A New Perspective on Racial Inequality*, Melvin Oliver and Thomas Shapiro[32] also discuss the history of black underdevelopment by capitalism in the United States. They reject the traditional liberal and conservative arguments that racial inequality is inevitable because of racial or environmental reasons, arguments that continue to serve the interests of the ruling classes today. Rather, they argue that the racial inequality between whites and nonwhites in the United States has a history that can be understood and changed. According to Oliver and Shapiro, the following legal forms of discrimination have kept many African Americans in poverty:

1. The Homestead Act of the nineteenth century was a major source of wealth for the majority white population. Through free land grants to families who were willing to settle on the frontier, three-fourths of colonial families became landowners. Because of slavery and legal restrictions on free blacks, African Americans did not become landowners during this period.[33]

2. Reconstruction after the Civil War was a time of hope for many former slaves because of laws that were passed and the establishment of the Freedmen's Bureau, whose purpose was to provide economic support for African Americans. General Sherman's Order 15 "confiscated plantations and redistributed them to Black soldiers."[34] Later laws overturned Order 15 and many black soldiers had to give up their land.

> Real access to land for the freedman had to await the passage of the Southern Homestead Act in 1866, which provided a legal basis and mechanism to promote black land ownership…The amount of land was substantial, a total of forty-six million acres. Applicants in the first two years of the Homestead Act were limited to only eighty acres, but subsequently this amount increased to 160 acres. The Freedmen's Bureau administered the program, and there was every reason to believe that in reasonable time slaves would be transformed from farm laborers to yeomanry farmers.[35]

However, the end of Reconstruction in 1877 destroyed any hopes that the majority of former slaves would become landowners. Those who did manage to get some land were faced with violence and insurmountable obstacles from banks, politicians, and white-owned institutions. As Ida B. Wells later proved, one of the primary purposes of lynching was to destroy the economic leaders of the black community so that blacks would be helpless in the face of white domination.

3. "Jim Crow" laws instituted at the end of the nineteenth century also served to prohibit the successful economic growth of the black community. Segregation at every level meant that black businesses and farms were excluded from the growing market economy.

> Beginning in Tennessee in 1870, white Southerners enacted laws against intermarriage of the races in every Southern state. Five years later, Tennessee adopted the first "Jim Crow" law, and the rest of the South rapidly fell in line. Blacks and whites were separated on trains, in depots, and on wharves. After the Supreme Court outlawed the Civil Rights Acts of 1875, the Negro was banned from white hotels, barbershops, restaurants, and theatres. By 1885 most Southern states had laws requiring separate schools. With the adoption of new constitutions the states firmly established the color line by the most stringent segregation of the races; and in 1896 the Supreme Court upheld segregation in its "separate but equal" doctrine set forth in *Plessy v. Ferguson.*[36]

In the twentieth century, the federal government was a major actor in preventing black economic development. Oliver and Shapiro review several programs of the government that discriminated against African Americans during the twentieth century and significantly reduced their ability to develop an economic and political base.

4. The Social Security Act in 1935 was designed to help bring the U.S. economy out of the Great Depression and provide a way to save for retirement. However, the law was designed in discriminatory ways, excluding agricultural and domestic workers, tying benefits to lifetime wages, and giving additional benefits to men who had military service and were unionized.

> Thus blacks were disadvantaged in the New Deal's legislation because they were historically less well paid, less fully employed, disproportionately ineligible for military service, and less fully unionized than white men...they also paid more into the system and received less—because of the flat rate. Single Black women do not share in spouse's benefits.[37]

5. The Federal Housing Act of 1934 was passed to increase the possibility of home ownership for U.S. citizens, and its success brought millions of families into the middle class for the first time. Equity in their

homes has become the largest single source of wealth for most U.S. families. However, particular policies that favored the suburbs, single-family detached homes, highway construction, and tax deductions for suburban businesses, benefited white families more than black families. In addition, restrictive covenants, supported by bank and insurance redlining, legally excluded blacks and made suburban home ownership practically impossible for African Americans. Forced to live in the center of large cities, many African Americans saw their home values decline along with city services, and many lost their homes through foreclosure for these institutional reasons.[38]

6. "When it was first passed, [welfare] was intended for 'a white widow and her children' and Blacks were excluded until the mid 1960's."[39] Most welfare recipients are white women and children, and existing on welfare is a very difficult life. In the white public imagination, the typical recipient of the AFDC Welfare Program is a poor black woman who is probably committing fraud against the government and does not deserve the money she receives. In 1980 Ronald Reagan explicitly campaigned against the "welfare queen." The facts are much different. The use of residency requirements that limit mobility, requirements that no man be in the house, and an "assets test" to find if there are other resources give social workers extensive power over the everyday lives of people. Welfare has been a system designed to keep people in poverty rather than help them over hard times so they can find their way again.

"Between July 1972 and 1992, the combined [monthly] value of AFDC and food stamps for a three-person family with no countable income dropped 26% on average, from $874 in July 1972 (measured in 1992 dollars) to $649 in July, 1992."[40] This represents an annual 1992 income for three people of $7,788, or $2,596 per capita per year, or $8.00 per day per capita, or one-half the UN poverty rate of $14.40 per day for the U.S.

Since the welfare reform law of 1996, the situation of many poor people has deteriorated. "From 1995–1999, roughly 2 million families with average incomes of about $7,500, lost about 8 percent of their income. This happened because they lost more in benefits, both welfare and food stamps, than they gained in earnings from work."[41]

7. The Internal Revenue Code is another U.S. law that discriminates against African Americans. The lower tax rates on capital gains and the deduction for home mortgages and real estate taxes discriminate against African Americans and prevent their accumulation of wealth.[42] Over time, these differences result in the greater discrepancy of wealth between white and black families.

Our data show that among high-earning families ($50,000 a year or more) 17 percent of whites' assets are in stocks, bonds, and mortgages versus 5.4 percent for blacks. Thus while race-neutral in intent, the current tax policy on capital gains provides disproportionate benefits to high-income whites, while limiting a major tax benefit to practically all African Americans...This amounts to a $54 billion tax break, about $20 billion of which goes to the top 5% of taxpayers.[43]

Oliver and Shapiro summarize their findings: there are three reasons for the injustice of black and white wealth in the United States: (a) African Americans have historically been excluded from employment, land ownership, and investments through legal and illegal means since slavery was abolished; (b) African Americans suffered discrimination by housing, tax, and welfare regulations during the twentieth century; (c) African Americans have not been able to pass on wealth from generation to generation, thus blocking one of the main paths to wealth within the white community.[44] The life of poverty in the United States is brutal. Trying to live on $14.40 per day or $5,800 per year, which 12.7% of the U.S. population is trying to do, when the cost of living is more than two times as much, is too much for many people.

> Oppressed people learn strategies for survival; if they do not learn they perish...At the highest level of underdevelopment, the daily life of the Black poor becomes a continuous problematic, an unresolved set of dilemmas which confront each person at the most elementary core of their existence. The patterns of degradations are almost unrelenting, and thrust upon every individual and family a series of unavoidable choices which tend to dehumanize and destroy many of their efforts to create social stability or collective political integrity.[45]

Conclusion

In this chapter I first looked at the debate among theologians about capitalism and its strengths and limitations in relation to the Christian gospel. John Cobb and Herman Daly have developed an alternative to the Gross National Product: The Index of Sustainable Economic Welfare. With this tool, they recommend basic changes in the way capitalism is understood, and suggest ways that local communities can be empowered to manage markets for their benefit rather than their destruction.

Second, I looked at international development policies, especially as they affect small, poor countries such as Nicaragua. I showed that the policies of the International Monetary Fund and the World Bank–namely, free trade, privatization of utilities and industries, debt repayment, and smaller governments–have not reduced poverty, and that there are major disagreements among international scholars about how best to proceed. Some theologians and economists oppose global capitalism itself because of its history of exploitation of the poor, and proposals that return to national and regional autonomy are seriously entertained.

Third, I looked at poverty and the unequal distribution of wealth in the United States. I looked particularly at the African American community and the history of violence and discrimination that has made large parts of their community poor. This history shows the tendency of market capitalism to exploit those who are vulnerable in various ways, and the impact of white supremacy on the lives of people of color.

• • •

Part 3 of the book focuses on capitalism as a system that organizes human desire, deciding what values and behaviors will shape the personal experiences of groups. We can see capitalism function in this way by observing the resistance to capitalism in various social and cultural contexts.

Part III: Resistance to Capitalism

8

Resistance to Capitalism in Nicaragua

In order to be successful, capitalism must defeat the resistance of the people to economic exploitation. At the same time, capitalism must get the people's cooperation in its economic plan.[1]

Pastoral caregivers too often collude with capitalist values by blaming people for the consequences of oppression. Furthermore, they underestimate the creativity and resilience of those who have survived economic vulnerability and violence. In part 3 we look at the resistance to capitalism as a way of understanding both creative resilience and the consequences of oppressive violence. As we understand the historical and social contexts within which people live, we gain respect for their gifts and concern for their oppression. In this light, pastoral care theory and practice can be revised so that the church is more likely to care in ways that empower those who experience family violence and economic vulnerability.

The people of Nicaragua provide a helpful example of how groups in the South have resisted capitalism and have met with the overwhelming power of the North. We will look at three aspects of resistance to capitalism and the responses of the United States to keep Nicaragua in a colonial or neocolonial relationship for the sake of capitalistic gain. Nicaraguans have resisted U.S. economic domination through political and military means, the formation of alternative institutions, and the creation of alternative economic visions. In their struggle, they help us to see the resilient hope that comes from surviving, and they disclose the horrific consequences of violent systems of oppression.

Political and Military Resistance

My first trip to Nicaragua in 1991 was accidental. I was invited to go with a group of American Baptists[2] who had long-term relationships with the Baptist Convention of Nicaragua. For seventy-five years children in U.S. Baptist congregations have heard stories from missionaries and have given their pennies to help the children of that country. Not being Baptist, I did not know much about Nicaragua and its history. However, I was touched deeply when I heard firsthand about the 1979 revolution and the hopes the people had had for new life. I was moved by the stories of suffering caused by the U.S.-sponsored Contra War. My six subsequent trips from 1992 to 2000 were not accidental—I wanted to understand the revolutionary spirit of the people and their struggle for integrity in the midst of U.S. economic domination.

Spanish and U.S. Conquest: I quickly learned that Nicaragua's resistance against oppression had a history. The Spanish invaders came in 1524 and warred against the indigenous people. They named the land *Nicaragua* after the Indian leader Nicarao.[3] The Indian resistance fighters led by Diriangen were defeated by Pedrarias Davila, the first colonial governor.[4] The Spanish conquest was a disaster for the native population of Nicaragua's Pacific region. Within three decades an estimated Indian population of one million plummeted to a few tens of thousands as approximately half of the indigenous people died of contagion with Old World diseases, and 200,000 were sold into slavery in other New World Spanish colonies.[5] After 300 years of direct colonial rule "Central America gained its independence from Spain on September 15, 1821"; the Republic of Nicaragua was formed in 1838.[6]

President James Monroe first articulated the United States' dominance over the Southern Hemisphere on December 2, 1823, in the Monroe Doctrine that attempted to limit European colonization in the West. This doctrine asserted that

> (1) The United States would not interfere in the internal affairs of or in the wars between European powers; (2) the United States recognized and would not interfere with existing colonies and dependencies in the Western Hemisphere; (3) the Western Hemisphere was closed to future colonization; and (4) any attempt by a European power to oppress or control any nation in the Western Hemisphere would be viewed as a hostile act against the United States.[7]

This doctrine meant that the U.S. understood Latin America as a part of its sphere of influence, even though it would be decades before the U.S. could enforce its will against European military force.

In 1847, Cornelius Vanderbilt became the first U.S. investor in Nicaragua, opening the Vanderbilt Accessory Transit Company of boats and overland vehicles that carried passengers from the Caribbean to the Pacific Ocean. Vanderbilt owned "the vessels, hotels, restaurants and land transportation along the entire transit route."[8] During a time of political instability and with the permission of Vanderbilt, William Walker and a group of mercenaries from the United States invaded Nicaragua in 1855 and governed for two years. Even installing himself as president, Walker "declared English the country's official language, and attempted to reinstate slavery in a country that had outlawed it in 1822." Walker was eventually driven out by combined Central American forces and was executed in Honduras in 1860, ending this period of U.S. intervention.[9]

During the second half of the nineteenth century, coffee grown in the highlands by elite nationals and bananas grown on rich lowlands were owned and managed by the United Fruit Company and the Standard Fruit and Steamship Company, both of which dominated the economy of Nicaragua. Thus began the long process of economic control of Nicaragua by the U.S.

The Monroe Doctrine was reaffirmed in 1895 when the U.S. took control of Puerto Rico and Cuba and extended its actual dominance over the Caribbean. President Teddy Roosevelt made his national reputation with the Rough Riders in Cuba and greatly expanded the Monroe Doctrine with the Roosevelt Corollary in 1904.

> Several times during Roosevelt's first years in office, European powers threatened to intervene in Latin America, ostensibly to collect debts owed them by weak governments there. To meet such threats, he framed a policy statement in 1904 that became known as the Roosevelt Corollary to the Monroe Doctrine. It stated that the United States would not only bar outside intervention in Latin American affairs but would also police the area and guarantee that countries there met their international obligations. In 1905, without congressional approval, Roosevelt forced the Dominican Republic to install an American "economic advisor," who was in reality the country's financial director. Quoting an African proverb, Roosevelt claimed that the right way to conduct foreign policy was to "speak softly and carry a big stick." Roosevelt resorted to big-stick diplomacy most conspicuously in 1903, when he helped Panama to secede from Colombia and gave the United States a Canal Zone.[10]

U.S. invasions of Cuba, Puerto Rico, and Colombia sent a strong message to Nicaragua and other Central American nations that they must accept U.S. dominance.

The next direct U.S. military intervention in Nicaragua came in 1909, when the Marines landed to defeat Jose Santos Zelaya, who was trying to continue his presidency of sixteen years. Zelaya was popular with the people of Nicaragua because of his progressive programs and because he canceled the contracts with U.S. companies to take lumber and minerals from Nicaragua. Several influential U.S. citizens pressured the government to do something, and the U.S. Marines were sent to establish a more cooperative government.

U.S. banks took control of Nicaraguan finances, railroads, and communications.[11] Benjamin Zeledon and a small group of military resisters fought against the U.S. Marines, and Zeledon was killed in 1912. At the end he wrote words that are precious to many Nicaraguans: "Each drop of my blood spilled in defense of the nation and its freedom will give life to a hundred Nicaraguans who, like me, will take up arms against the betrayal of our beautiful but unfortunate Nicaragua."[12]

"The Bryan-Chomorro Treaty, signed in 1914 and ratified in 1916, gave the United States exclusive canal privileges in Nicaragua (to prevent competition to the Panama Canal then being built) and the right to establish naval bases."[13] The Liberal party, unhappy with the treaty, continued to resist U.S. control and Marine occupation for the next decade. "In 1927 The Liberal leaders [Sacasa and Moncada] surrendered and signed a U.S. supervised peace treaty. Only General Sandino refused to comply. He assembled an army of peasants and launched a guerrilla war against the U.S. occupational forces."[14]

Augusto Cesar Sandino was born out of wedlock to a single woman; his father was a wealthy landlord. He worked on a banana plantation on the Atlantic Coast. As a guerilla fighter over seven years, Sandino provoked the U.S. into military action that drew international criticism. After the battle of Ocotal in Nueva Segovia, in which U.S. planes bombed civilian targets, President Herbert Hoover decided to withdraw the Marines in 1933. "Sandino and his ragtag guerrillas had accomplished something unthinkable. They had not only won control of a vast territory in northern Nicaragua, but had managed to drive American soldiers from their homeland."[15]

However, before they left, the Marines had trained and equipped the Guardia Nacional with Anastaszio Somoza Garcia as its head. Somoza continued fighting on behalf of the U.S. and the elite Nicaraguans who stood to benefit from betraying the Nicaraguan people. When the Marines left, Sandino was invited for peace talks with President Juan Bautista Sacasa.[16] He returned to Managua on February 2, 1933.[17] "In 1934 Sandino signed for peace with the new president, Sacasa, and returned to the northern mountains to continue organizing peasant cooperatives begun during the war. On February 21, 1934, Sandino was assassinated on the orders of Tacho Somoza."[18]

In 1936 Somoza forced President Sacasa out of office and appointed himself president. This began the tyrannical rule of the Somoza family, which lasted 44 years, from 1936–1979. When his elected term as president was over in 1944, Somoza overthrew President Arguello and made himself dictator. In 1956, a young journalist and poet, Rigoberto Lopez, assassinated Somoza Garcia. The U.S. made sure that the Somoza family continued its control by helping Luis Somoza Debayle (a U.S.-trained engineer) become president until 1963, and then his brother Anastasio "Tachito" Somoza (a West Point graduate) until 1979. The Somoza regime was a most reliable ally for the United States; under Somoza, Nicaragua became a staging ground for U.S.-sponsored invasions of other Latin American countries, including the 1954 CIA coup in Guatemala and the 1961 Bay of Pigs invasion of Cuba.[19] The Somoza family also amassed enormous wealth from their political and military power.

At the peak of their power in the mid-1970s, the Somozas were said to be worth about one billion dollars. They owned more than ten thousand square miles of farm and grazing land in Nicaragua, as well as extensive properties in Guatemala, Honduras, and Costa Rica, and real estate in the U.S. Directly or through intermediaries, they also controlled railroad and steamship lines, factories, fishing fleets, gold mines, lumber companies, and certainly not least, Nicaragua's largest brewery.[20]

Because of its support and complicity with U.S. economic and political dominance, the Somoza family was able to continue and expand the role of the oppressive elite that ruled Nicaragua. In exchange for personal wealth, such an elite was willing to betray the hopes for freedom of fellow citizens. In exchange for favorable trade and economic dominance, the U.S. was willing to support a dictator who kept the people in poverty and brutally suppressed all who tried to exercise their human and civil rights.

Sandinista Revolution and the U.S. Contra War: However, Nicaragua has always been a rebellious country, jealous of its freedom, and unwilling to accept Northern dominance forever. In 1958–1960 a number of armed movements developed, with differing political origins and no single direction. Some were led by the veterans of Sandino's army, some by members of the middle class, such as newspaper editor Pedro Joaquin Chamorro, who staged an armed invasion, which failed to take power. In 1961 the Sandinista National Liberation Front (FSLN) was founded by Carlos Fonseca, Tomas Borge, and Silvio Mayorga, and combined several of the existing armed movements.[21]

By the 1970s the opposition was a well-organized military force against the Somoza government, which increased its widespread repression, torture, and murder through the U.S.-supported and trained Guardia Nacional. The U.S. government continued its 40–year support of the Somoza dictatorship until months before the government fell on July 19, 1979. "In 1976 Carlos Fonseca, founder of the FSLN, was killed in combat with the Guardia Nacional, and Tomas Borge, co-founder, was jailed and put in solitary confinement."[22] Fifty thousand people were killed during the revolution. Most were casualties inflicted by the dictator in defense of his illegitimate government, including his bombing of the barrios in major cities. On June 21, 1979, ABC-TV correspondent Bill Stewart was shot dead by a National Guardsman in Managua."[23] This had a strong effect on U.S. public opinion. As the opposition to Somoza grew stronger, with the U.S. and the Vatican no longer able to support him, he fled the country on July 17 and flew to Homestead Air Force base in Florida.[24] The Sandinistas, led by Daniel Ortega, drove triumphantly into Managua on July 19, 1979, the date that many celebrate today as an important holiday to symbolize resistance to U.S. control.

The revolution brought the Sandinista Party into power, and they set about trying to correct the centuries of misrule and exploitation that had characterized the Nicaraguan situation. Sixty thousand teachers, most of them teenagers, moved into the rural areas and poor barrios on a literacy campaign, practically eliminating illiteracy in a few months. The Sandinistas expropriated the assets of the Somoza family, including "more than one hundred corporations and nearly two million acres of farmland."[25] They also "ordered the nationalization of all banks, credit agencies, and insurance companies, then all export businesses, and then the mining and forestry industries."[26]They intended to make dramatic changes in the way the Nicaraguan economy functioned.

However, almost immediately after the revolution, President Ronald Reagan, with the support of the Nicaraguan elite who had moved to Miami and leaders of the Guardia Nacional who had moved to Honduras, authorized the organizing of a counter-revolutionary force known as the Contras. By 1982, the Contras, trained and financed by the U.S. government, had blown up two bridges in northern Nicaragua.[27] This was the beginning of a costly war that killed 36,000 people, displaced 500,000 people, absorbed 60 percent of the government budget, cost the economy many billions through a blockage and embargo, and destroyed much of the infrastructure of Nicaragua. "Direct material damage from the war inflicted between $1.5 billion and $4 billion in losses...UNO (National Opposition Union) economist Francisco Mayorga has estimated that the U.S. embargo caused an additional $3 billion in losses—this in an economy whose GNP never exceeded $3 billion, even in good times."[28]

The Contra War exacted a terrible cost on the Nicaraguan people. Some estimates of the costs of the Contra War, direct and indirect, are as high as $17 billion. In addition to the military casualties, there were many civilian tragedies because of the way the war was fought. A slogan of Latin American military forces trained in the U.S. is "In order to destroy the fish, it is necessary to drain the lake." This means that the civilian support system that the Sandinista Army used for support had to be attacked directly. Thus, terrorizing, killing, and raping the civilian population, especially community leaders, characterized the war. Thousands of families were disrupted when young men had to leave their studies and jobs to join the mandatory military service, or leave the country to avoid the draft. In addition, there was a rationing system that limited basic products, and there was a continuous fear of being invaded by U.S. military forces. The suffering continues into the new millennium–through the traumatized and disabled veterans, the broken families, the destroyed environment, and children who continue to be killed and maimed by land mines laid by the Contra forces.

After such personal and economic cost, the people of Nicaragua were tired, impoverished, scared, and ready for an end to the war that had lasted almost 15 years. The U.S. supported (politically and financially) the political party opposed to the Sandinistas. UNO (National Opposition Union) was led by Violeta Chomorro, editor of an opposition newspaper and widow of the Director of "La Doce." On February 25, 1990, the people elected the UNO party. "These elections prove the efficacy of Washington's war and belligerence: they demonstrate the effectiveness of low-intensity aggression, of war by proxy, and of international electoral meddling carried out by a rich, powerful country against a poor, vulnerable one."[29]

Arnoldo Aleman Lacayo was the elected president from 1996–2002. Many commentators saw his administration as a return to the policies of Somoza, including the reappropriation of land to the elite, increasing poverty for the people, and decreasing quality of life. U.S. economic control in Nicaragua was solidified through private business and banking with the support of the International Monetary Fund (IMF) and the World Bank. With a pro-U.S. government in power, attention shifted to the following policies to ensure Nicaragua's dependent status as a poor nation within the domination of the U.S. economic system:

- Privatization of government corporations in order to create immediate income and increase efficiency;

- Reduction of government expenditures in education, health care, and social welfare so that debt repayments can be made;

- Legislated free trade that increases foreign investments and makes exports more attractive to foreign-owned businesses within the country.[30]

This brief summary of Nicaragua's history shows the people's continuous resistance to economic exploitation, including a willingness to engage in armed revolt to get rid of invaders and dictators supported by the U.S. It also shows the U.S.'s willingness to support, finance, and organize military forces to maintain its economic and political hegemony over Nicaragua. Some call such policies neocolonialism, which seems accurate. The first point to be learned about market capitalism is that it sometimes engages in military violence to enforce its ideology and practices on those who do not benefit–those persons who live in extreme poverty.

Resistance through Alternative Institutions

In addition to revolt and revolution, the Nicaraguan people have engaged in alternative economic projects, programs that defy the control of capitalism on the one hand, and seek to provide cooperative ways of providing for the needs of the people on the other. In this section, I identify three such projects that are fueled by an alternative vision and contrast them with the projects of market capitalism that are being sponsored by the U.S.

Rancho Ebenezer at Niquinohomo

Rancho Ebenezer is a project to help communities that have an inadequate agricultural or other economic base. Their motto, "Happy are those who live in solidarity, for they will receive solidarity from God," is a poetic interpretation of Matthew 5:7. This solidarity is the opposite of the paternalism that has destroyed the dignity of so many farmers. Francisco Juarez, the director, believes that the peasants in the rural areas will receive little or no benefit from global capitalism in the near future. The economic plan of privatization, reduced government services, and free trade does not include any programs for poor families who live below the subsistence level. And given the economic situation of the last twenty years, which is characterized by inflation and decreasing income, education, health care, and other indices of human quality of life, rural peasants are not likely to see any change soon. So Francisco's plan aims to help these peasants think differently about their future.

If they are not going to be part of the global economy, how will the peasants live? Given their small plots of land of poor quality, modern farming is out of the question. Francisco's dream is a network of small farms that depend on simple crops grown organically and small animals—rabbits, chickens, goats, and pigs. These animals require less land than cattle, and they can live on low-cost feeds that can be grown in smaller spaces. To support small animals, people need training in animal care, growing feed, building adequate cages and/or buildings, managing finances, ecological awareness, and community development. The peasants receive free starter animals if they cooperate with certain expectations: that they attend workshops for one year, that they develop their plots with buildings and crops, and that they promise to provide starter animals for new projects.

At first people are usually skeptical because they are not used to raising small animals this way, especially rabbits and goats. Chickens and pigs are usually allowed to roam free in the villages, without concern for their nutritional needs, and cows are often a sign of wealth in rural areas. People are also skeptical of the financial training and community development. They have lived below subsistence for so long that they doubt any new system will improve their situation. However, some have been courageous enough to try, and their success has encouraged others. The important goal for this project is the production of goods necessary for quality of life, not the income. The success of participating communities is not measured by market indicators, but by indicators of infant nutrition, restoration of the soil, clean water, and care of the environment in general. Rancho Ebenezer now supports 22 rural communities where there is no other help for marginalized peasants.

This project is not radical in its scope, since it affects only a few communities in the country of Nicaragua. However, it is radical in some of its assumptions, namely, that the global economy has no plans for providing for the needs of the poor in Nicaragua, and thus, the poor are forced to develop alternative institutions for their survival. Niquinohomo projects are designed to exist *outside* the global economy, thus providing a radical critique of global capitalism and its mythology of wealth. For now, capitalism can afford to ignore Niquinohomo and such projects because they are insignificant in a $28 trillion global economy.[31] But if large numbers of the world's poor refused to cooperate in the global economy as workers, consumers, and citizens, the legitimacy of capitalism would begin to crumble. Thus, Niquinohomo is a sign of hope for some critics of capitalism.

In contrast to this project in Niquinohomo, global capitalism promotes agribusiness for Nicaragua. The best arable land has been consolidated into large farms (usually owned by politicians and elite families) to grow cash crops for export. Nicaragua exports large amounts of coffee, rice, corn, beans, sugar, and beef and imports rice, flour, oil, and milk.[32] In 1998, Nicaragua exported the equivalent of 39.1 percent and imported the equivalent of 71.5 percent of its GDP of $2 billion.[33] The model of neocolonialism is the same in 2000 as it was during the time before 1979 under Somoza, when agribusiness worked well for capitalism because the Somoza family and other elite Nicaraguans owned most of the arable land, grew crops designed for export, paid the workers less than subsistence wages, and pocketed the profits as their share of doing what the U.S. wanted. Furthermore, the government had a vicious National Guard to repress labor and civil rebellion.

Under the present government, Nicaragua is again moving toward an agribusiness economy. In 1998, I stayed with the Lorenzo family in Chaguitillo. In a town where 50 percent of the adults were unemployed, Jiron Lorenzo and Versis Cruz, husband and wife, felt lucky to be employed by the local coffee processing plant. They had year-round work, he in maintenance and she in cleaning offices. His salary was $83 per month ($4.15 per working day); her salary was $66 per month ($3.30 per working day). This is two or three times the income of the average Nicaraguan. However, their monthly budget required $200 for food, $20 for electricity, $13 for water, and $20 for tuition at the local school for two children, or total expenses of $253. With a combined income of $149, they were left with a deficit of $104 per month. They purchased their home during the years of the Sandinista government, when their agricultural cooperative (now gone) had several good years, so they have fewer expenses for housing than many families. I asked how the six people in their family survived with a deficit budget. They said they manage in two ways: (a) they borrow money and barter services from friends and family when they are short; (b) they hope their daughter, who is in the U.S., will send money. Remittances, or money from relatives who live outside the country, is a source of income for many families. Life on $3 or less per day for peasants who work full-time in agribusiness is the plan of capitalism in Nicaragua. But food for the Lorenzo-Cruz family of six (parents, two children, one son-in-law, and one grandchild) costs $6 per day. Even with two people working full-time, they barely have enough for food. This is what it means to work at a job that pays below subsistence.

In December 1999, The Economic Commission for Latin America and the Caribbean (CEPAL) studied remittances to Nicaragua and found that 20 percent of the Nicaraguan population lives outside Nicaragua. According to other Nicaraguan studies, there are 500,000 illegal Nicaraguan emigrants in Costa Rica[34] and 235,000 Nicaraguans (legal and undocumented) in the United States; 1.8 million people from the six countries of Central America live in the U.S.[35] At least U.S.$200 million come from Costa Rica, and U.S.$400–600 million come from the U.S.A.[36] This amount equals 60 percent of Nicaraguan exports and is more important than international aid. Remittances from outside the country come directly to the population rather than to the government, and thus have more effect on the families' standard of living.

How can so many people live with less than $2 per day? In the rural areas, nature (the ecosystem) subsidizes poverty/misery. In the woods (outside the markets) people find energy resources (firewood), wood for construction, medicine, honey, game for meat, and so on. As the productivity limits of the land are reached and the woods are exhausted, human misery increases. The soil is easily susceptible to erosion and floods, and so the environmental vulnerability to natural disasters increases. The social and economic vulnerability of the population closes the cycle of hopelessness, and the country becomes nonsustainable.[37]

How does capitalism manipulate the Lorenzo family to cooperate with its plan for Nicaragua? In a competitive system where survival is at stake, the Lorenzos are doing better than average Nicaraguans. They have a place to live, food on the table, electricity for television, and education for their children. As long as they don't face any health problems, and as long as their daughter in the U.S. sends them enough money to keep their debt from getting too large, they will survive. More than 50 percent of the adults in Chaguitillo are unemployed. They have no regular source of income and barely survive in what is called "the informal economy," where people trade, barter, and work day labor so they can get food to eat. The Lorenzos are respected members of the community because they are doing slightly better than others. The capitalist ideology of competition can make them feel they have accomplished something, and the danger of such thinking is that they could lose their feelings of solidarity with others in the community. The survival of families such as the Lorenzos shows how some people resist capitalism on a daily basis by sharing their resources with neighbors and extended family.

AEDAF, Asociacion Evangelica de Asesoramiento Familiar (The Evangelical Association for Family Counseling)

AEDAF in Managua is a feminist project for helping poor women, children, and families in Nicaragua. Five Protestant women with training in family counseling and theology have formed this organization to empower women and their families. Believing that women are the poorest of the poor, that gender causes increased vulnerability in the midst of poverty, that the empowerment of women will uplift the whole community, and that the church has an important role to play in all of this, these five courageous professionals have struggled to maintain their services with minimal funding from mainly European NGOs (non-governmental organizations)[38] and U.S. churches. Their willingness to sacrifice more lucrative careers and make their training and personal support available for the poor is a sign of resistance to the commercialization of health care. Women organize to care for one another, children, and men in ways that defy the market forces and show the resilience of the people in the midst of extreme suffering.

AEDAF has been able to maintain an office for nine years where people can come for family counseling; to carry out workshops with poor women on a variety of topics, including self-esteem, marriage, leadership, domestic violence, sexual abuse, and other topics important to women; and to organize conferences to influence other professionals in the community, such as clergy, mental health workers, nurses, health promoters, and so on. As we saw in chapter 2, the AEDAF staff has seen hundreds of women in counseling sessions and workshops over nine years. The stories of Margarita, Soledad, and Juana are examples of what can happen when women get information, support, and empowerment from professionals.

In 1998 I attended an AEDAF workshop on domestic violence. This was the fifth retreat for these thirty women, and they had learned how to do critical thinking about biblical texts, patriarchy, and everyday family life. Most of them had experienced or witnessed domestic violence in their families of origin or families of choice. As one who has attended dozens of such workshops, I was impressed by the level of critical thinking in this group. Their economic vulnerability had given them a perspective from which to deconstruct the myths of oppression under which they lived. They were supportive of one another and appreciative of the AEDAF staff, which provided educational resources and occasions to learn from one another. A taboo topic such as domestic violence received the attention it deserved because of the impact on the lives of women and children, and the women were empowered.

While I attended this workshop, I became aware that there are very few mental health resources for the victims of trauma in Nicaragua. During the Revolution there were clinics that provided a full range of free health care. For example: in the community of Achuapa, where another workshop was held, the Sandinista government established a health clinic with free medical services. For a decade, the people in the surrounding rural areas brought their sick children to the clinic for treatment, mostly for malaria, parasites, and diarrhea caused by unsafe water.

Since the end of the revolution in 1990, the government-run health clinics have been closed or services limited to only those who can pay for treatment and medicines. In 1990, when the UNO, the party supported by the U.S., came into office, one of the first things it did was to begin charging for medical treatment—doctor's visits, medicines, and preventive procedures. This was in accordance with the IMF and the World Bank policies to reduce the cost of government so that more of the taxes can pay off the national debt (Nicaragua's debt is three times the GNP), a policy that reduces or eliminates services to the people. Now, because of global capitalism, there is no accessible medical treatment for the children of Achuapa. People living on less than $2 per day are not counted as those who deserve medical treatment.

One weekend when I was in Achuapa, a teenager in the community committed suicide by consuming rat poison. Living away from her family in order to attend school increased her vulnerability as a young woman, and there were no mental health services. No one recognized the signs of depression, and there were no counselors to visit the school, talk to the other teenagers, help the family work through its shock and grief, and train the community in the principles of mental health. All these aspects of their grief were aggravated by the extreme poverty that dominated their lives every day.

Achuapa needs a project like AEDAF to work long-term on mental health issues for families. While AEDAF raises money in Europe to help women living in the midst of poverty and domestic violence, global capitalism destroys the fragile health system in Nicaragua in order for the country to pay interest on the debt to U.S. banks. AEDAF represents a sign of resilient hope for those it touches and an important form of resistance to market capitalism.

CEPAD, Consejo de Iglesias Evangelicas Pro-Alianza Denominacional (The Council of Evangelical Churches)

CEPAD of Nicaragua was formed in 1972 to respond to the tremendous needs of the population after the earthquake that destroyed downtown Managua, leaving 10,000–15,000 people dead, thousands injured, and thousands of buildings destroyed. This event brought the Protestant churches together in new ways, and the organization has lasted through a revolution, a Civil War, volcanic eruptions, and Hurricane Mitch, which killed more than 2,500 Nicaraguans and displaced more than 100,000 people in October, 1998.[39] Under the leadership of Gustavo Parajon, CEPAD has been involved in many aspects of Nicaraguan life and is one of the most trusted organizations in the midst of the deep suspicions caused by the wars. Their many projects are forms of resistance to war and economic exploitation of the Nicaraguan people.

A credit union for small urban economic projects is among CEPAD's many projects. On one of my first trips, I ate lunch in a restaurant that started with such a loan. Carmelita had used the money to buy a small building across from a government office and began supplying inexpensive lunches and dinners for the workers there. Her business had grown, and she now had two restaurants, which were very small by U.S. standards, but able to provide support for her extended family, most of whose members worked in the restaurant. Carmelita's husband was a pastor of a small Baptist church that could not afford to pay much, even though he had a seminary degree. So Carmelita's business provided a service for the workers and was the primary economic support for her husband's ministry and for their extended family.

Again, this project is not radical in its scope—people borrow money every day in the North to begin small businesses, and many businesses succeed. However, in Nicaragua, banks do not loan to small businesses, especially to those who are poor and have no property for collateral. The banks are more interested in taking land away from the poor, selling it to foreign businesses, and making money from the international trading. Carmelita's restaurant is the opposite of what capitalism has planned for Nicaragua, that is, to provide cheap and docile labor for multinational corporations who cater to U.S. consumers.

In contrast to the micro-loan program of CEPAD, the Zona Franca (Free Trade Zone) operates just a few miles from Carmelita's restaurant. Taiwanese factories are making shirts and pants for U.S. businesses such as Wal-Mart, Sears, and Kmart, and paying 38 cents per hour to the workers. The employees, mostly young women, are worked for ten hours a day, physically abused if they work too slowly, paid no benefits, protected by no safety or environmental regulations, and fired as soon as they show signs of slowing down because of age, pregnancy, or health.

Thirty thousand workers, mostly women, organized themselves into a workers' union to resist their harsh treatment as workers and to offer an alternative vision of what human life should be like. Their hopes can be seen in the Code of Ethics the union presented to the Nicaraguan government for acceptance and enforcement:

(1) Nondiscrimination by race, religion, age, sexual orientation or physical disability; (2) Protection of pregnant women; (3) No violence—psychological, physical, sexual, verbal; (4) Safe environment to prevent accidents; (5) Social security registered with the government for services; (6) Legal salary for overtime.[40]

These demands were necessitated by terrible pay and working conditions. The women get two ten-minute breaks per day with twenty-five minutes for lunch. They have inadequate training and safety precautions to use the dangerous machines. They often work from 7 a.m. to 5 p.m. and often stay later, without extra pay, to finish their quota for that day. The women must work in silence; they need a card to go to the bathroom, and are given limited time to do so. They experience frequent verbal, psychological, physical, and sexual abuse. Women are fired if they become pregnant, a frequent occurrence in a culture where the average woman has 3.9 children.[41]

Carmelita has a much better situation and has a different vision of human life—she owns her own business, makes her own decisions, shares her profits with her family, and contributes as a leader in the community. In contrast, the workers in the Zona Franca are exploited, separated from family and children, and work in dangerous and humiliating conditions for about $3 per day, less than subsistence wage. The Zona Franca is held up as an example of market capitalism at work—business and trade that increases the GNP and enables Nicaragua to pay its debt to the World Bank. Carmelita does not show up on any economic charts, because she barters her way through the day and spends her money to support her extended family. She contributes nothing to international trade and global capitalism.

In this section we have profiled a few projects that represent alternative institutions to those recommended by global capitalism. While these projects will not change the whole situation, they do show the resistance of the people to exploitation, and they are built on values that contradict the views of human life espoused by market capitalism. There àre many other projects, such as those concerned with transportation, teachers, veterans, and health care unions that have directly challenged the neoliberal policies, sometimes by closing down the city of Managua. Without the overwhelming military, economic, and political dominance of the U.S., Nicaragua has the will and creativity to solve many of its own problems.

Resistance through Alternative Economic Visions

Since 1855 Nicaragua has tried various alternative plans to become a viable political economy with reciprocal interdependency rather than total dependency on the United States. Jose Santos Zelaya's plan for a strong national culture with a new canal as its economic base was defeated by the invasion of the U.S. Marines in 1909. Another hope in this century was the Sandinista Revolution in 1979 that became an elected government in 1984. During its brief experiment, before being threatened and then devastated by the U.S. Contra War, the Sandinistas had the following plans.[42]

A Sandinista Vision

Because of the pressing problems of hunger, poverty, health care, education, and underdevelopment in almost every area of life, the Sandinistas moved quickly to change things. Getting the people back on the land where they could grow food for subsistence needs was one of the first priorities. Rejecting the long history of exploitation, they moved to empower the people by providing them with the resources for quality living.

The huge, well-equipped, efficient farms belonging to the Somoza family became state farms; other lands were distributed to peasants in a variety of forms: cooperatives, collectives, and small to medium family farms. Government banks pumped credit into the countryside to encourage production and modernization and provided incentives for various forms of cooperative farming. By tinkering with the pricing structure, the government sought to stimulate production, especially in beans, rice, and corn. And indeed, in the early years of the revolution agricultural production climbed, especially in the staple foods needed to feed a hungry country. On the consumption side of the equation, state subsidies held out the prospect that for the first time in recent history, the poorest two-fifths of the population might be able to consume the minimum daily calories recommended by the UN for a healthy diet. The establishment of free medical care and the inoculation campaigns rectified decades of neglect under the old regime. In the years immediately following the revolution, such programs greatly reduced infant mortality rates and virtually eliminated early death from preventable infectious diseases. In its foreign trade, economic planners actively sought what they called a "comparative advantage"–higher prices on the international markets for coffee, cotton, beef, and bananas– to generate profits that might be reinvested in industrial development projects making the best use of Nicaragua's resources.[43]

While the Contra War sabotaged most of these programs, and some programs were flawed and needed adjustment in vision and implementation through trial and error, this summary describes an alternative vision of economics. Since the end of the revolution in 1990, the Nicaraguan people have been involved in dozens of alternative projects designed to empower the people economically.

A Liberation Theology Vision

Proclamando buenas nuevas a los pobres, "preaching good news to the poor," Luke 4:18, is the motto of CEPAD, the Council of Evangelical Churches of Nicaragua. This text, sometimes called the Manifesto of Jesus, is appropriate because Nicaragua is one of the birthplaces of Liberation Theology. Ernesto Cardenal built a chapel and gathered together a group of campesinos on the island of Solentiname starting in the 1960s, which were some of the worst years of the Somoza tyranny, a time when there was little hope of change. It would be twelve years before the resistance was able to overthrow the forty-year dictatorship supported by the U.S. government.

In long dialogues with parishioners, Cardenal equated the Somoza dictatorship with Herod's tyranny, and compared Sandinista guerrillas to Christ and his apostles. Secretly he became a Sandinista himself and allowed a squad of guerrillas to train at his island sanctuary. The guerrillas launched a bold attack on San Carlos in October 1977, and in retaliation President Somoza ordered the Solentiname chapel destroyed.[44]

Ernesto Cardenal became a favorite of European political theologians, such as Jürgen Moltmann, because of his courage and vision. Johann Baptist Metz knew Cardenal and gave him great praise for inspiring hope, not only in Nicaragua, but also in Europe. "He has eyes for the victims—for the weeping mothers and the wasted children in his exploited people, as well as for the anonymous structures of violence in which a dependence of the third world on the first, a dependence disguised as 'development,' continues to operate."[45] In one of the Bible study sessions Father Cardenal led in Solentiname, he facilitated the group in a discussion of the feeding of the five thousand in Luke 9:10–17. Following are some of the campesinos' interpretations of Luke 9:17, the passage in which Jesus' feeding of thousands results in all the people eating and being filled, after which they filled twelve baskets with the bits that were left.

> *Oscar:* When there is a true community there is equality among everybody. Everybody ate the same; everybody was filled. That ought to happen in our country. In our country there are a lot of us who are hungry. Nobody would have to be hungry if everything in the country belongs to everybody. But here things are the way the devil wants them to be. The devil, who is the Evil One, wants us to be split apart, each one separated by

selfishness. But if we all organize the way God wants, I'm sure nobody would go hungry, because there's enough of everything in the country. There's plenty of food.

Olivia: There'd be not just food left over, like there was there, but medicine, too. But now there are so many of us who are sick, and even dying, because there are no medicines to heal the poor. There are lots of medicines in the country. But they're in the hospitals. For poor people there are no medicines. They won't give them.

Filipe: I think that in our country there's food, there's clothing, there's medicine, there's everything you can want. There's enough. What's wrong is that people have all that stuff not to share but to sell. And the ones that have the things want them to be scarce to earn even more though the people are starving. If you put an end to selfishness there'll be plenty of everything. There'll be education, housing, and produce, a whole lot of eggs, a whole lot of milk and meat, and there'll be lots of teachers, doctors, nurses, facilities so that kids can study for the professions they want. It'll be the multiplication of the loaves and of everything.

Rebecca: He was showing them what love could do in the world, that everybody would have enough. Through his miracle there was enough for everyone, everyone ate, and there was some left over. And that would be the miracle that love would perform in the world. Instead of the situation that we're in, when one person eats and the other doesn't. Selfishness is to blame for the scarcity of everything. Through love there'll be abundance for everybody. He performed that miracle so that we could see what love can do.[46]

This insight offers an alternative vision to capitalism's *homo economicus*. Rather than profit, competition, greed, and consumerism serving as the basis for economic life, why not the deeper values of cooperation, sharing, and community? I believe that all these values are present in human nature. The question is: What kind of virtues and community life do we want to encourage? Just as capitalism says that greed is natural and should be used as the basis for the economic system, so the church often says that love and community are natural in the sense that they are part of the image that God created in every person. How we define natural human needs and desires is a contested area within theology and economics. For example, we observe sacrifices that parents make for their children, or the material help that extended families give to their kin in difficult times, or the charity that flows between people who share common religious beliefs in different countries. How does market capitalism attempt to encourage or manipulate people into buying expensive housing, clothes, electronic equipment, and cars when they know that neighbors near and far are hungry, homeless, lacking medical care, and unemployed? The resistance struggle against market values of greed and competition is a sign of an alternative human vision that I have learned from my accompaniment with the Nicaraguan people.

Summary

Nicaragua is a case study in how people resist capitalism and what this resistance reveals about capitalism as a system of normative values. We saw, first, that the people resisted capitalism in ways that led to military invasion from the United States. The people were looking for ways to become economically viable by protecting their natural environment, planning a canal, and overthrowing the Somoza dictatorship. Second, the people resisted capitalism by developing alternative institutions such as farming with small animals, developing credit unions, and providing pastoral counseling for women and families. These institutions provide ways of living that resist agribusiness, closed health clinics, and the Zona Franca. Third, the people resisted capitalism by developing alternative economic visions. The Sandinista Revolution was an alternative vision of how an economic system can meet the needs of people rather than exploit their labor and ignore their humanity. Liberation Theology is an alternative economic vision based on study of the scriptures and a praxis-based ecclesiology. In the next chapter, we turn to the African American community, where resistance to capitalism has occurred within the United States.

9

African American Resistance to Capitalism in the United States

In the previous chapter we discussed the situation in Nicaragua and contrasted the resistance of the people with the strategies of capitalism to overcome this resistance. We turn now to African Americans in the United States and ask similar questions. By studying the economic oppression of the African American community, we hope to learn more about the nature of the human spirit in its resistance to capitalism, and thus understand people in all social classes who live in various uneasy compromises with it. For more than four hundred years African American women and men have resisted U.S. economic domination through politics and revolt and the creation of alternative economic visions and institutions.

Revolt against Slavery and Racism

Revolt against Slavery

From the beginning of the colonial period, African Americans revolted against slavery. African Americans were first brought to the colonies against their will. The European trade in slaves from Africa to the new world started in 1440, and explorers brought slaves to the Caribbean as early as 1492. "In 1619, John Rolfe, the Norfolk-born first recorder of Virginia, already a grower of tobacco...noted, 'About the last day of August came a Dutch man of war that sold us twenty negroes.'" This comment is usually held to be the first reference to the import of black slaves into what became the United States.[1]

"Herbert Aptheker has listed 250 slave revolts and conspiracies within the area of the continental United States."[2] In addition, there are stories in many of the African American diaries from the eighteenth and nineteenth centuries about personal revolts against white oppressors.

> In 1712, for example, slaves in New York City revolted and killed at least nine whites. And a Virginia plot of 1730 prompted the lieutenant governor to order white men to take their pistols to church with them. A few years later in South Carolina, a group of slaves killed several whites, fired several buildings and set out for Florida, which was held then by Spain.[3]

The successful Haitian revolution in 1804, led by Toussaint L'Ouverture and Jean Jacques Dessalines,[4] inspired many other revolts in the nineteenth century. Denmark Vesey revolted in Charleston, South Carolina, in 1822, and Nat Turner became the most famous of all in Southampton County, Virginia, in 1831.

> On the appointed day, Nat's disciples gathered on the banks of Cabin Pond...About 10 p.m. the conspirators left their retreat and moved to the home of Joseph Travis. They were seven men, armed with one hatchet and a broadax. Twenty-four hours later, there would be seventy men, and at least fifty-seven whites would be dead.[5]

Toni Morrison, in her novel *Beloved,* made famous the story of a mother who killed her own child rather than allow her to be captured by vigilantes and returned to a life of slavery. The novel deals with the long-term consequences of such a violent act for the mother, her family, and the wider community. Angela Davis recovers a historical example of women who revolted against slavery by killing their offspring.

> One may better understand a Margaret Garner, fugitive slave, who, when trapped near Cincinnati, killed her own daughter and tried to kill herself. She rejoiced that the girl was dead—"now she would never know what a woman suffers as a slave,"— and pleaded to be tried for murder. "I will go singing to the gallows rather than be returned to slavery."[6]

Black intellectual leaders, including David Walker, Frederick Douglass, Martin Delany, and H. Ford Douglas, vigorously debated whether revolt was an effective strategy for survival in the racist United States.[7] Sometimes they argued that the U.S. Constitution's values of equality and freedom could provide the protection the community needed. Other times, as in David Walker's *Appeal* of 1829, leaders called for solidarity with liberation movements in Africa through revolt, called for God's judgment upon "the white American nation," and pleaded for the essential unity of all persons of African descent, whether slave or free.[8]

According to Vincent Harding, black resistance leaders often struggled between revolt against white institutions and accommodation that would lead to human rights. This conflict can be seen in the difference between the 1853 National Black Convention in Rochester, New York, where Frederick Douglass addressed resolutions to the white community, and the 1854 Black Convention in Cleveland, where Martin Delany drafted a call to revolutionary action by all African Americans, slave and free. Thus, the debate between Martin Luther King and Malcolm X over whether to engage in violent revolt or nonviolent resistance has a long history of debate within the African American community.[9]

As soon as President Lincoln allowed black units to be formed, 200,000 black men volunteered to fight against the Confederacy, distinguishing themselves in many ways. For the first time African Americans were given legal permission to revolt against the system of slavery and to fight for their freedom.

Revolt against Poverty

The impulse to revolt against racial oppression reemerged in the civil rights movement of 1955–1968. Focusing first on rights such as voting, access to public accommodations, and integration of schools, the protest movement gradually shifted to economic issues when it moved into Chicago in 1966–1968. The Poor People's Campaign of summer, 1968, infused with the anger caused by the assassination of Martin Luther King on April 4, 1968, was an attempt to influence the federal government to make poverty a priority for public policy.

But even in the 1960s, the urge to violent revolt was present and led to a series of urban riots in many U.S. cities. The worst damage occurred in the poorest communities, where whites from outside the local communities owned nearly all the housing and businesses. Absentee landowners and small businesspersons suffered financial loss, and the cost of restoring order to the community was high for the cities. "The number of Black uprisings increased from nine in 1965, 38 in 1966, 128 in 1967, and 131 in the first six months of 1968..." The Black masses were prepared to "take to the streets and thereby declare their hatred for the bondage imposed on them."[10] The Black Panthers were among the most articulate interpreters of the feelings of the black poor. Violent revolt among the poor continues to be a danger in many cities. Riots in the 1990s in Miami and Los Angeles show the continuing resistance of the poor to capitalism.

Black Prisoners

In order to understand the current prison system as it relates to African Americans, we need to understand something of the longer history. Because African Americans constantly revolted against white racism, special systems of punishment for them have been designed and funded by federal and state governments. Manning Marable discusses the history of the criminal punishment system as it has targeted African Americans.

During the time of early slavery, there was little need for a formal justice system for slaves, because every slaveholder was his own judge, jury, and executioner. Those who designed the system knew that the primary threat to slavery was the slave's own wish for freedom. Slavery itself was imprisonment against which African Americans had no formal recourse. As slavery developed into a more public, legal institution in the nineteenth century, the slaveholders created "Negro Courts" for public relations. "In Mississippi, for instance, Blacks charged with noncapital felonies were tried before two justices and five slaveholders. Louisiana Blacks in noncapital felonies were judged by four slaveholders and only one justice."[11] The primary goal of such a system was support of slavery through "speedy verdicts and certain punishments."[12] The desire to protect the capital investments in slaves created a kind of perverse leniency in some cases; in other cases, court-ordered beatings were severe, and death was not uncommon.

After emancipation, the purpose of the criminal punishment system changed. "The Black man/woman was now just another 'competitor' in the labor market. Laws were altered to compensate for the changing status of Black agricultural workers and artisans, to ensure their continued inferior caste status, and to destroy any rebellion with swift punishment. In the autumn months of 1865 a series of Black Codes was ratified to guarantee Black labor subservience."[13] The existence of these laws in themselves showed that African Americans had to be compelled to cooperate with the latest capitalistic plan.

"During this period, the vast majority of Southern Blacks were legally imprisoned for three general offences—any violation of segregation codes monitoring public behavior or activity; any violation of laws governing capitalist agricultural production; and any infraction (misdemeanors and noncapital felonies) against whites."[14] African Americans who violated one of the many rules about where one could be and what one could do, or who had a conflict with a white person, were in danger from the system.

For our purposes, the laws restricting African American participation in agriculture give additional clues about the system of oppression. Sharecropping was a potential gain over slavery, because African Americans had the theoretical possibility of earning enough to eventually buy their own land and become independent. Some whites moved from sharecropping to owning farms, but very few blacks were allowed to succeed. After dividing the crop with the owner and paying off debts, many farmers found themselves with less than they had before, and the system of indebtedness kept them in poverty and virtual slavery. In addition, the peonage system was a set of laws that made it illegal for a sharecropper to leave the land without paying off all the debts. Those who tried to leave could be arrested, put into the convict lease system, and returned to the planters as agricultural workers. The convict lease system itself became a profitable form of slave labor for a number of planters, and because it was profitable for both the planters and the states, the number of convicts increased dramatically.[15] "The segregationist South was steeped in violence. C. Vann Woodward documents that Alabama whites actually spent more money for rifles and pistols than they did for the state's entire supply of farming implements and tools."[16]

Lynching developed as a way to create terror in the African American population so there would be less revolt against the unjust system of white supremacy. While the public myth that lynching was about violent crime, especially the crime of rape against white women, gained notoriety, the real purpose was to discourage "any overt political activity which challenged Jim Crow segregation and the basic system of caste/class rule upon which the entire economy and social order was based."[17] The need for such laws proved that large numbers of blacks were rebellious. Lynching made the legal punishment system more efficient, since revolt against it was undermined by terrorist activity.

> Of the 2,060 Blacks lynched in the U.S. between 1882 and 1903, only 707 were actually charged with "attempted, alleged, or actual rape." 783 were lynched for allegedly murdering whites; 208 were charged with "minor offenses;" 104 were termed "arsonists;" 101 had stolen white property...As an indicator of racial disparity in the use of this violent "deterrent" from 1904–1924, 11 whites and 269 Blacks in Georgia were lynched.[18]

A similar disparity is found after World War II, when legalized courts, long prison sentences, and capital punishment mostly replaced the system of kangaroo justice and lynching. "Although Black males comprised about five percent of the U.S. population in the 1930s, almost 50 percent of all prisoners who were executed during the decade were Afro-American [males]."[19]

The disparity continues. Still today, laws and police occupation punish rebellion and create terror by treating crimes against white persons more severely than crimes against African Americans. From 1976 to July 26, 2000, 654 persons have been executed in the United States: 56 percent white, 35 percent black, 7 percent Hispanic, and 2 percent Native American and Asian. Most of these crimes involved intraracial victims, but in capital cases where there were interracial victims, 11 or 6.6 percent were black and 156 or 93 percent were white. "Almost all capital cases (83 percent) involve white victims, even though nationally only 50 percent of murder victims are white."[20] Thus, the race of the victim continues to make a difference in the severity of the punishment.

National and state governments have increasingly used the death penalty to control the African American community.

> In July, 2000, there were 3,670 death row inmates with California (568), Texas (460) and Florida (391) having almost 40% of the death row population. The death row population has increased from 420 in 1976 to 3,670 in 2000. 46% of these inmates were white; 43% were black, 9% were Hispanic, and 2% were Native American or Asian.[21]

The total prison and jail population in the United States increased from 744,208 in 1985 to 1,802,496 in 1998, an increase of 242 percent. Of that number 41.3 percent were white, 41.2 percent were black, 15.5 percent were Hispanic (black and white), and 2.0 percent were other; 89.2 percent of inmates were male and 10.8 percent were female.[22] This means that a majority of inmates (58.7 percent) are persons of color and 41.3 percent are white in a country that is 74 percent white and non-Hispanic.[23] "Relative to the number of U.S. residents, the rate of incarceration in 1998 was 668 inmates per 100,000 U.S. residents–up from 313 per 100,000 in 1985. At midyear 1998, 1 in every 150 U.S. residents was incarcerated."[24] Even though the crime rate itself fell during the 1990s, and even though crimes are relatively well distributed through the population, black and Hispanic persons are overrepresented in prisons, showing that the prison system is used to control the behaviors of people of color, especially when they revolt against economic and political oppression.

Prisons as punitive institutions designed to oppress people of color can be seen in other ways.

> Blacks comprise over 25 percent of all Americans arrested in a given year. Although Whites are charged with about 72% of all criminal offenses, the criminal justice system tends to "punish" them for certain less serious crimes more so than Blacks and other national minorities...White middle-class Americans are arrested generally for relatively minor property crimes, whereas Blacks are arrested for violent crimes that carry substantial penitentiary sentences.[25]

What we see here is an unfair system that has a long history stemming from slavery and early twentieth century racism.

In this section, we have looked at African American resistance to capitalism and the willingness of the capitalist elite to use violence in defense of its dominance. These stories need to be told so that we can clearly see that capitalism is not a voluntary system supported by the people, but a system that is imposed by violence. White supremacy and capitalism are historically and inherently linked, and this corruption will continue until the white population takes responsibility for its injustice.

Alternative Economics, Institutions, and Visions

Slavery was an economic system designed to obtain the greatest profit from the cheapest labor. Largely because of 250 years of slave labor, the United States became a world economic power. After briefly looking at the debates about the relationship between slavery and capitalism, we will examine the struggles within the black community about the best economic course during the late nineteenth and twentieth centuries.

Was slavery a successful capitalistic venture that created huge profits for U.S. agriculture and industry, or was it an ideological system that depressed the U.S. economy, but persisted because of the elite commitment to feudal values? Eugene Genovese suggested that the planters were tied to a European feudal idea of aristocracy of accumulating wealth and status for themselves. The slave system did not create wealth that provided for the majority of white and black workers, and it put the South at an economic disadvantage with the North, where market capitalism flourished.

James Oakes opposes this view by arguing that the slaveholders were a capitalistic class who knew very well how to manipulate the market system for their economic and political advantage. "They actively embraced the capitalistic economy, arguing that sheer material interest, properly understood, would prove both economically profitable and socially stabilizing."[26] Peter Parish summarizes the consensus of most historians. "There is now broad acceptance that many slave owners made reasonable–and sometimes handsome–profits in the pre–Civil War decades."[27]

For the rest of this section, we will assume that slavery was a capitalist system that produced enormous wealth in the South and the North, and that there is nothing inherent in capitalist theory that prevents slavery of human beings as workers. If capitalism is based on the profit in the interchange between land, labor, and capital, what better system could be devised than one in which labor costs are reduced to the level of bare survival? That most of the transnational corporations are moving production to the poorest countries in the world for cheap labor at subsistence wages is a contemporary expression of the same capitalist logic.

Washington, DuBois, and the Black Women's Club Movement

After the Civil War, the African American community was faced with how to manage its own economic survival within a system that continued to be controlled by white supremacist ideology. This is a complex debate that cannot be easily summarized. In order to simplify it for our purposes, we will look at two time periods: first, the debates during the late nineteenth and early twentieth centuries between Booker T. Washington and W. E. B. DuBois, with additional reference to the women's club movement; the debates during the middle of the twentieth century between Martin Luther King, Jr., and Malcolm X, and the development of womanist thought. In each discussion we will be asking about the particular person or institution's recommendations for the vision and institutions of the African American community within the United States.

The white community chose Booker T. Washington as the most important African American leader during the early decades of the twentieth century. Robert Franklin calls Washington "an adaptive person" because he did not challenge the existence of apartheid laws in the South.[28] Whatever his motives for this approach, he believed that in order to become part of the American society, African Americans needed to organize a firm economic base rather than fight for political rights. In some ways, this was a logical response during the time when African Americans were denied political voice. If capitalism had exploited them by enslaving their labor and preventing them from owning land and the means of production, then freedom from slavery required opportunities to obtain land and the development of wealth necessary to gain a strong economic base for future citizenship. In Washington's opinion, this was best accomplished through education and agricultural production.

Some leaders criticized Washington because, while he was correct about the importance of an economic base for the African American community, he was too optimistic about the benevolence of capitalism and naïve about the future of agricultural production. "His sanguine view of capitalism, his pre–Industrial Revolution educational program, and his pro-rural vision compromised the utility of his answer to the question of black liberation."[29] Washington correctly understood that creating an economic base for the African American community was crucial for its survival as a population in the United States. In this sense he was a forerunner of certain forms of black nationalism such as the Nation of Islam. However, Washington was too optimistic that capitalism would respect an economically strong African American community, and he was mistaken that an economic base could be constructed on an agricultural foundation.

Other black leaders emphasized the importance of economic development in the African American community. After he emigrated from the Caribbean,

> Marcus Garvey was convinced that Washington's strategy could be combined with race nationalism and political militancy to create a self-sustaining Pan-Africanist economic order. DuBois wrote in *Crisis* [1916]: "The main lines of the Garvey plan are perfectly feasible. What he is trying to say and do is this: American Negroes can, by accumulating and ministering their

own capital, organize industry, join the black centers of the south Atlantic by commercial enterprise and in this way ultimately redeem Africa...for black men. This is true. It is *feasible.*"[30]

While DuBois agreed with Washington on the importance of the economic development of the African American community, he sharply criticized Washington for his views on the political dimension of ending black oppression. He believed that as long as African Americans were denied civil rights and a political base to defend themselves against violence and inequities in the political system, they would be prevented from carrying out their economic programs.

Our review of white supremacist violence during the twentieth century gives credence to DuBois's view. For example, the economically successful Greenwood community in Tulsa was destroyed in three days of white rioting, and the community never recovered its former economic strength. The Greenwood district encompassed

> forty-one grocers and meat markets, thirty restaurants, fifteen physicians, five hotels, two theatres, and two newspapers. The black community also included many wealthy blacks who had invested in and profited from oil leases. Some five hundred blacks who owned small parcels with oil resisted all offers and threats made by whites to sell these lands. 'Every increase in the price of oil made the strife more bitter.' In early 1921 prominent blacks had been warned to leave Oklahoma or face the consequences.[31]

When the people discovered that a young man was being lynched, the black community revolted and demanded, with weapons, that the courts be fair. In response to the black revolt, whites attacked, looted, murdered, burned, and destroyed the community.

> When the destruction was over, eighteen thousand homes and enterprises were left in cinder, over four thousand blacks were left homeless, and three hundred people died (both black and white). As Butler understatedly reports "what happened in Tulsa was more than a riot. It was also the destruction of the efforts of entrepreneurs and the end of the Greenwood business district."[32]

White violence against black economic achievements, both official and vigilante, occurred all over the South and North. DuBois saw more clearly than Washington that the terrorism of lynching, riots, and the apartheid legal system in the South, where most African Americans lived, required a political response. Political and economic power always work together.

> With the use of their political power, their power as consumers, and their brainpower...Negroes can develop in the U.S. an

economic nation within a nation, able to work through inner
cooperation, to found its own institutions, to educate its genius,
and at the same time, without mob violence or extremes of race
hatred, to keep in helpful touch and cooperation with the mass
of the nation.[33]

Toward the end of a long and brilliant career, DuBois became
increasingly discouraged because of U.S. white supremacy and looked to
the socialist countries of USSR and China for alternative visions. At age
93, shortly before his death in 1963, he moved to Accra, Ghana, West
Africa and became a citizen of that newly liberated nation.

The Washington vision of African American economic growth
within the capitalist system has been partly successful. "By 1978 the Black
(U.S.) consumer market was the ninth largest in the world."[34] This relative
wealth is a result of African Americans who have jobs within capitalism.
However, when Manning Marable analyzes the ownership of land and
production, the picture is more troubling.

> Black capitalism...must be subdivided into three distinct
> constituencies–the "proletarian periphery"; the intermediate
> Black petty entrepreneurs; and the Black corporate core. Over
> four-fifths of all Black-owned U.S. firms, 82.7 percent of the total
> number, belong to the proletarian periphery.[35]

By "proletarian periphery," Marable means businesses that are small
($3,000–$15,000 per year), owned by one person, have no employees,
and are fragile and likely to go bankrupt within three years.
"Economically and politically, these Blacks are essentially workers who
are attempting to become small businesspersons, struggling against
massive odds to leave the ranks of the proletariat."[36] The other two
groups make up a very small part of the U.S. economy, and the wealth is
concentrated in the hands of a few people. Altogether, black business,
even in 2000, did not provide a reliable economic base for a "nation
within a nation" for the black community.

While Washington and DuBois were debating the best way to uplift
the economic wealth of the black nation, black women were organizing
themselves into the women's club movement. Evelyn Brooks
Higginbotham gives us a picture of this world as she describes the
Woman's Convention (WC) of the National Baptist Convention, founded
in 1900. "In 1903 corresponding secretary Nannie Burroughs [leader
from 1900 to 1961] reported that the WC represented nearly a million
black Baptist women. By 1907 she reported one and a half million."[37]

> The Woman's Convention enabled these large numbers of
> women throughout the nation to establish links with one
> another, plan programs of mutual interest, and define their own
> priorities. The convention established its own educational

institution, the National Training School for Women and Girls, and it also established a Settlement House in Washington, D.C., under the direction of a trained social worker. The black Baptist women also supported secular institutions and organizations that worked for racial and gender advancement, such as the National Association for the Advancement of Colored People (NAACP), the National Association of Colored Women (NACW), and the National League for the Protection of Colored Women.[38]

The National League for the Protection of Colored Women was a secular organization designed specifically to help women during their migration from South to North. The Philadelphia League "assisted more than 450 black women and girls" during the summer of 1905 by providing housing, education, employment information, and supportive community. "Arriving at Ericson Pier in Philadelphia, the migrants were often destitute and vulnerable to 'wharf sharks'–Layten's term for exploitative labor agents and other unscrupulous people."[39]

"In 1900, the AME minister and future bishop Reverend Reverdy Ransom launched the Institutional Church and Settlement House in Chicago, which included a day care center, kindergarten, mothers' and children's clubs, sewing classes, an employment bureau, and a penny savings bank."[40] The importance of the efforts of the black church can be seen when we understand the historical context of the late nineteenth century, the time of especially vicious white violence against African American communities.[41]

> By 1890 it had become clear that the black community would have to devise its own strategies of social and political advancement. In that year Mississippi adopted a disfranchise-ment plan that served as a model to the rest of the south. Disfranchisement formed part of the larger process of "depolitization": literacy tests, poll taxes, and other state election laws, along with social and psychological sanctions such as economic reprisal, violence, and threats of violence, effected the mass removal of blacks from the nation's political life. Political institutions and representative government became simply inaccessible and unaccountable to American citizens who happened to be black...During the 'nadir,' the black communities turned increasingly inward.[42]

In summary, during the early decades of the twentieth century, the African American community had its own vision of its economic life. Alternately accommodating to the capitalist system of white supremacy through programs such as the Tuskegee Institute and programs of the black churches, and resisting through the creation of Black Nationalist plans by leaders such as Marcus Garvey and W. E. B. DuBois, the African

American community sought to follow its own plans. These ideas were continued in the work of Malcolm X and Martin Luther King in the 1950s and 1960s, and continue to inspire intellectual leaders of the early twenty-first century. They have been both affirmed and challenged by the development of womanist thought.

The Great Migration and New Economic Opportunities

From the Civil War to the early twentieth century, most African Americans lived in the agricultural South.

> As late as 1940, 77 percent of all Blacks resided in the former slave states, while only 27 percent of all white Americans lived there. The majority of Black male workers ploughed and planted the fields, harvesting the annual yields of cotton or corn, usually for the benefit of an absent white landlord. In 1910, 57 percent of all Black men and 52 percent of all Black women workers were farmers. Eight percent of the men and 42 percent of the women were employed as domestics or personal servants. Only one sixth of the Black population worked in manufacturing or industries.[43]

In parts of the South, a black economic system was in its beginning stages, with banks supporting small farms and other small businesses. However, the terror that was unleashed was often directed against this rudimentary black economic development, as Ida B. Wells showed in her analysis of the political and economic context of lynching.[44]

Since the Southern political system would not allow African Americans to improve their economic situation, several million African Americans migrated to the North, pushed by harsh working conditions, poverty, and brutal violence, and pulled by the rising opportunities of the industrial North.

> The number of Black people who left the South rose from 454,000 from 1910–20, 749,000 from 1920–30, to 1,599,000 from 1940–50…This was the first generation of Black workers who earned a living primarily from manufacturing, industrial, and commercial labor. In 1940, 28 percent were service workers. Farm employment had dropped to 32 percent. Twenty years later, blue-collar employment increased to 38 percent, and the number of operatives more than doubled. 32 percent were service workers and only 8 percent of all Blacks employed worked in farms.[45]

Those who found jobs in the growing industries of the North became involved in labor unions, and participation in unions continues to be an important value in African American communities today. Most African Americans supported the labor movement and frequently engaged in coalitions with the Democratic political party. While the relationships between Blacks and the unions suffered some tension during the civil rights movement because of the white backlash, most African Americans understood that joining unions often led to higher wages, better working conditions, and a chance for advancement. The statistics show that union organization contributed to economic strength in African American communities.

> The ratio of nonwhite males' to white males' median incomes for all occupations in 1970 was 83 percent in unions and 62 percent outside unions. For blue-collar male workers, the ratio is 90 percent in unions, 72 percent outside unions. For white collar employees, the ratio is 85 percent in labor unions, 70 percent outside unions...There is also a substantial body of research indicating the egalitarian or progressive effects of trade unionism on the dispersion of wages and fringe benefits. The option for personal wage differentials based on favoritism or white racism within specific job categories is greater in nonunion firms than in the unionized sectors of the economy.[46]

In summary, the African American community during the late nineteenth and early twentieth centuries engaged in developing alternative economic visions to market capitalism. Washington, Garvey, DuBois, and the women and men of the black churches have struggled to define a form of economic strength that would sustain the black community. The Great Migration from the rural South to the industrial North was an effort to improve the economic strength of the black community. However, in spite of these efforts, poverty continues to be a prominent feature of the lives of many black families.

King, Malcolm X, and Womanism

The civil rights movement beginning in the 1950s was another attempt to develop an alternative economic vision for the African American community. Martin Luther King, Jr., came from the Atlanta middle-class black religious community and obtained the best education available. When he accepted the pastorate of the Dexter Avenue Baptist Church in Montgomery, Alabama, in 1954, he found himself in the midst of poor people who were prepared to ignite a civil rights movement. Having studied the nonviolent social change movement of Mohandas Gandhi, King was ready to challenge the apartheid system of the South on the basis of the U.S. Constitution. Some commentators see King in the tradition of Frederick Douglass and Booker T. Washington, leaders who sought accommodation to the U.S. political and economic system. For example, in many of his speeches, King appealed to white leaders to live up to the values of the Bill of Rights in the same way that Douglass made his appeal in the nineteenth century. However, when we examine King's economic vision, we see that he also called for revolutionary change in the U.S. economic system. Although the development of his vision was cut short by his assassination on April 4, 1968, he had already moved significantly toward a revolutionary vision by criticizing the Vietnam War and planning for the Poor People's Campaign, both efforts designed to form coalitions between black and white poor people. "In his keynote address to the national Conference for a New Politics on 31 August, 1967, he advanced his analysis of the relationship between racism and economics."[47]

> We have deluded ourselves into believing the myth that capitalism grew and prospered out of the Protestant work ethic of hard work and sacrifices. The fact is that capitalism was built on the exploitation and suffering of black slaves and continues to thrive on the exploitation of the poor, both black and white, both here and abroad...The way to end poverty is to end the exploitation of the poor. Insure them a fair share of the government's services and the nation's resources. We must recognize that the problems of neither racial nor economic justice can be solved without a radical redistribution of political and economic power.[48]

In such statements, King clearly understood the importance of economics in the survival of the African American community.[49] "King concluded finally that the defeat of racial segregation in itself was insufficient for creating a just and decent society for all Americans...Without hesitation, he broke from many of his own advisors and supporters, and like Malcolm, raised many public policy issues which could not be easily resolved within the existing system."[50] In 1967 King fully endorsed the following economic plan called the "Freedom Budget for All Americans." He wrote the introduction to the booklet in which the following objectives were published:

1. To provide *full employment* for all who are willing and able to work, including those who need education or training to make them willing and able.

2. To assure *decent and adequate wages* to all who work.

3. To assure a *decent standing* to those who cannot or should not work.

4. To *wipe out slum ghettos* and provide decent homes for all Americans.

5. To provide *decent medical care and adequate educational opportunities* to all Americans at a cost they can afford.

6. To *purify our air and water* and develop transportation and natural resources on a scale suitable to our growing needs.

7.   To unite sustained *full employment* with sustained *full production and high economic growth.*[51]

This "socialist" vision comports well with what we have read in John Cobb and Herman Daly on how capitalism could function as a market system within a larger moral and political vision. It also comports well with the Sandinista vision for Nicaragua.

Malcolm X was more obviously the 1960s heir of the tradition of Black Nationalism of the nineteenth and early twentieth century. "Nationalists are generally committed to the following goals: a land or territory, a language and culture, common institutions, sovereign government, a common history, love for fellows, devotion to the nation, common pride, hostility to opponents, and hope for the future."[52] After conversion from a life of crime to the Nation of Islam, Malcolm X advocated Black Power, which included, when necessary, violence in opposition to white supremacy. The white media gave his views on violence more coverage than his positive economic vision.

The Nation of Islam has been one of the more successful African American communities in carrying out its economic program. The commitment, discipline, and unity of its members have enabled the Nation of Islam to accumulate land, institutions, and businesses, thus illustrating the ability of an organized group to succeed under capitalism. The problem facing the Nation of Islam has been its exclusiveness, that is, its belief that only African Americans can be members and that people can only benefit from the organization's wealth by becoming members. During his leadership in the Nation of Islam, Malcolm X advocated some of the following goals:

4. We want our people in America whose parents or grand-parents were descendants from slaves, to be allowed to establish a separate state or territory of their own—either on this continent or elsewhere. We believe that our former slave masters are obligated to provide such land and that the area must be fertile and minerally rich.

7. As long as we are not allowed to establish a state or territory of our own, we demand not only equal justice under the laws of the United States, but equal employment opportunities NOW!

8. We want the government of the United States to exempt our people from ALL taxation as long as we are deprived of equal justice under the laws of the land.[53]

After leaving the Nation of Islam in 1964, Malcolm X "made his hajj to Mecca" in March, 1964, thereafter using his new name, El Hajj Malik el Shabazz.[54] In the short time before his assassination on February 21, 1965, Malcolm X, as he continues to be called today, developed a more inclusive economic and political vision. "Malcolm's view of the just society shifted away from being racially separatist, parochial and capitalist to being universalist, Pan-African, quasi-socialist, and public."[55]

> Malcolm displayed a relentless concern for respecting the human dignity, inherent worth, and potential of the poor. He had risen through the ranks of the ghetto-confined underclass and was living evidence of its untapped intellectual and moral wealth...However, Malcolm had clearly lost Muhammad's optimism about capitalism. Peering into a dark future, he sought to envision a socialist America. At least, he thought, such a nation would provide for its poor and actively seek to eradicate the vestiges of racism.[56]

Here we can see the outlines of a similar economic vision that gives preference to the experiences of the poor and builds an economic system that is inclusive of all persons. However, it would be a mistake to see a fully developed economic vision in Malcolm X's words. During most of his public life, he was a minister of the Nation of Islam, which practiced exclusive economics. During his move toward a more international and inclusive perspective, he had too little time to develop an adequate economic perspective. "Although Malcolm spoke approvingly of socialism and disapprovingly of capitalism, his thinking remained primarily antiracist, and class analysis was always secondary."[57]

Meanwhile, the final decades of the twentieth century saw the emergence of the womanist, or black feminist, movement, an activist and intellectual alternative to the racism of white supremacy and the sexism of many black leaders and communities. "The struggle for an Afrocentric feminist consciousness requires embracing both an Afrocentric worldview and a feminist sensibility and using both to forge a self-defined standpoint."[58] While womanism is primarily a movement of African American female intellectuals, its purpose is not just the increase of knowledge, but the concrete liberation of particular people, namely, African American women and men.

> This specialized thought should aim to infuse Black women's experiences and everyday thought with new meaning by rearticulating the interdependence of Black women's experiences and consciousness. Black feminist thought is *of* African American women in that it taps the multiple relationships among Black women needed to produce a self-defined Black women's standpoint. Black feminist thought is *for* Black women in that it empowers Black women for political activism.[59]

Two womanist themes are especially important to our discussion of African American resistance to capitalism. First, African American women are one of the most economically exploited groups in the United

States, and their attempts to overcome this exploitation have often met with insurmountable obstacles. Second, African American women have their own stories to tell about interpersonal violence, especially rape and physical abuse.

During slavery African American women, as a whole, were not treated any better than African American men. Most women were field slaves who worked in the field and did the same work as men. "Around the middle of the nineteenth century, seven out of eight slaves, men and women alike, were field workers. Just as boys were sent to the fields when they came of age, so too were the girls assigned to work the soil, pick the cotton, cut the cane, harvest the tobacco."[60]

Being female during slavery created additional hazards that men did not face, namely sexual assault by white slaveholders and overseers, pregnancy, and responsibility for children under harsh conditions. Some slaveholders made money by selling slaves to other farms, and this created a practice of breeding slaves for economic profit.

> As females, slave women were inherently vulnerable to all forms of sexual coercion. If the most violent punishments of men consisted in floggings and mutilations, women were flogged and mutilated, as well as raped. Rape, in fact, was an uncamouflaged expression of the slaveholder's economic mastery and the overseer's control over Black women as workers.[61]

In order to rationalize such sexual abuse of women, the slave South developed ideologies about African American women that continue to have power in U.S. culture today. Patricia Hill Collins identifies three images that have survived the period of slavery:

> The *mammy* represents the clearest example of the split between sexuality and motherhood present in Eurocentric masculine thought. In contrast, both the *matriarch* and the *welfare mother* are sexual beings. But their sexuality is linked to their fertility, and this link forms one fundamental reason why they are negative images. The matriarch represents the sexually aggressive woman, one who emasculates Black men because she will not permit them to assume roles as Black patriarchs. She refuses to be passive and thus is stigmatized. Similarly, the welfare mother represents a woman of low morals and uncontrolled sexuality, factors identified as the cause of her impoverished state. In both cases Black female control over sexuality and fertility is conceptualized as antithetical to elite white male interests [italics added].[62]

The continuing economic exploitation of black women after the civil rights movement is based on ongoing violation and violence, especially at the workplace. According to womanist scholars, the ideologies of inferiority, sexuality, and color continue to mark women for violence. For example,

> Throughout Afro-American women's economic history in this country, sexual abuse has been perceived as an occupational hazard. In slavery, Black women's bodies were considered to be accessible at all times to the slavemaster as well as to his surrogates. In "freedom," the jobs most frequently open to Black women were as domestic workers. This relegation of Black women to menial jobs did not begin to change until the late 1950s, and there is ample documentation that as maids and washerwomen, Black women have been repeatedly the victims of sexual assault committed by the white men in the families for which they worked. Sexual harassment and sexual extortion are still occupational hazards for working women of *all* racial backgrounds.[63]

Womanist scholars have also disclosed a high incidence of violence against black women and children perpetrated by black men. Black women have been active in the domestic violence movement in every state in the United States. Destructive images create vulnerability in the ongoing black-white tensions, and in the tensions between black women and men. The womanist movement brings such vulnerability to light, and insists that economic empowerment of black women is one of the primary solutions.

Kwanzaa as Resistance

Ritual and education play important roles in such economic empowerment. In a deceptively simple format designed to educate and empower a wide public, including children, about economics, Maulana Karenga and others have developed the theory and ritual of Kwanzaa as part of the Afrocentric movement within African American communities.[64] I reproduce here a version of Kwanzaa by a group of sixth-grade students because of its emphasis on an alternative economic vision. The seven values are celebrated in many homes and churches during seven days at the end of the calendar year to help the community to remember the vision and to support community efforts to continue the struggle for economic justice.

> *Umoja—Unity*: We can work and play together. We must work with the people in our family and in our school and in the community of African American people.
> *Kujichagulia—Self-determination*: It seems hard to say, but I try and try to learn it, and learn that it's about making up my mind to "keep on keeping on" in everything I do.

Ujima—Collective Work and Responsibility: Shared work is teamwork. You help me, and I help you...If you have a problem, you can lean on me...When I have a problem, you are able to help me.

Ujamaa—Cooperative economics: One person alone may not have a lot; but when each person puts in her share of work, wealth, and willpower, everybody has more.

Nia—Purpose: I want a good home and a good school and a good community. I will make a plan every day so I will know what to do to make the good things happen.

Kuumba—Creativity: I create plans for a good home and a good school and a good community...I can create beautiful things, and I will, because inside I am a beautiful person.

Imani—Faith: I believe that sharing together is good. I believe that making up my own mind and sticking to it is good too...I believe that planning and doing the right things is good. All these things help make me beautiful inside. I believe they will help me see the beautiful old people and the little babies that will come in the future.[65]

Summary

I have examined some of the violent and nonviolent revolts against capitalism, briefly considering economic alternatives put forward by African American women and men. In every case, leaders advocate an economic system in which human values of cooperation, inclusiveness, and community assume priority over the capitalistic values of individualism, competition, and supply and demand. Such values have continuity with the scriptures that are common to Jews, Christians, and Muslims. In the next chapter, I look specifically at the resistance to capitalism among women, a story that is often hidden from traditional historians.

10

Women's Resistance to Capitalism in the United States

Introduction

In this chapter I turn my attention to women of various cultures and classes who have struggled for equality in the United States. Women have had trouble understanding themselves as an oppressed class, not because there is a lack of oppression, but because of the lack of a common focus for resistance and activism. Patriarchy is a "totalizing" ideology[1] and so insidious that it has been difficult for women to organize themselves as a group with a firm identity.

Feminism is a movement that helps women understand themselves as an oppressed class and empowers them to work in solidarity with one another for liberation and an alternative future. The feminist slogan "The personal is political" reminds women that patriarchy is enforced in the most intimate systems, namely marriage, family, church, and workplace, and internalized within the psyches and spirits of individual women and men. Women's loyalties to their fathers, mothers, brothers, sisters, husbands, partners, and children, complicated by additional loyalties to culture and social class, may prevent women from organizing as a group. In addition, the sexualization of women contributes to their being considered inferior and makes them vulnerable to sexual and physical violence.

Capitalism demands that women contribute their physical labor to the markets and their biological labor for sexuality and childbearing. In this sense, commodification of women is part of the strategy of capitalism. However, because providing these services for an economic system rather than for the benefit of self, families, and local communities is clearly not in their personal interests, women resist exploitation and seek justice. Therefore, capitalism must depend on systems of control, threat, and violence to make women comply with its requirements.

142

Some of the controls are obvious: systemic poverty for women in poor countries who do not cooperate with global capitalism; poverty and violence for homeless and marginalized women who do not work and maintain respectable families; threats of rape that make women fear being independent; domestic violence against women by husbands and partners; laws that prevent or make it difficult for women who work as waitresses, domestics, and clerical workers to organize labor unions.

Some of the controls are masked in myths about gender and sexuality: romantic stories about true love and living happily ever after within a nuclear family; stories of mothers who sacrifice their careers and health so that their children can make their contributions to society; the sexual fulfillment myths about monogamous sexuality; the media myths that women find pleasure in being sexual objects.

Finally, the control of women within capitalism depends on individual internalization of a system of values and desires that encourages women to value "piety, purity, submission and domesticity,"[2] what Frantz Fanon calls "the colonialization of the mind."[3] Seemingly positive images of women as wives, mothers, housekeepers, and compliant workers, often as volunteers, control the perspectives of many and win their collusion with their own oppression. The ideologies of gender supplemented by the violent consequences of noncompliance effectively control most women. "The promise of goodness functions to trick those who do not benefit from the system into believing that whatever injustices exist can be attributable to the individual's failure to be good rather than to any systemic inequality."[4]

Whenever there is control backed by violence, there is resistance to this oppression among some of the population. In this chapter we focus on women's resistance to capitalism at work and at home. To learn how they have resisted at work I examine the rebellion of women in slavery, the women's movement for political equality, and the organizations of women in unions and immigrant groups. To learn how they have resisted capitalism in the home, especially in terms of sexuality and bearing and raising children, I focus on stories of women who have modified the expectations of women as docile wives, organized shelters and rape crisis centers, and challenged marital rape, sexual harassment, and global prostitution.

Women's Resistance to Exploitation of Labor

Women have resisted exploitation of their labor through violent revolt and through organizational activism. That oppressed groups are kept in place by violence and the threat of violence is obvious in Nicaragua, where the United States and Nicaraguan elites have used military invasion, occupation, murder, and torture to maintain control and keep the Nicaraguan people in an economically dependent and impoverished state. I have documented violent revolt in the African

American community. But such rebellious violence is less obvious for women as a social class: There have been no Marine invasions of independent women's communities to quell their rebellions. There have been no civil wars in which women as a class united and used military means to try to achieve their ends. Yet we know that the oppression of women has been strong, partly because they as well as men have experienced violence based on their race, culture, and class, and partly because all women are oppressed in relation to the economic and political power of men. Women whose ancestors were slaves; women who are Asian, Hispanic, or European immigrants; women who are working class and poor—all have been deprived of rights that are considered fundamental: the right to life, the right to bodily integrity, the right to some control over one's personal life and decisions, the right to food, shelter, and education.

African American Women: Women held in slavery are perhaps the most obvious example of how U.S. women have violently resisted exploitation of their labor and of how violence has been used to control them. There are numerous stories of women in revolt against slavery, some of which we reviewed in the previous chapter. Women were active in the underground railroad that secretly helped slaves escape into Canada over several routes.

> One of the most dramatic escape attempts involved a young woman—possibly a teenager—named Ann Wood, who directed a wagonload of armed boys and girls as they ran for their freedom. After setting out on Christmas Eve, 1855, they engaged in a shoot-out with slave catchers. Two of them were killed, but the rest, according to all indications, made their way to the North.[5]

This story reminds us of Harriet Tubman, the most famous of such leaders, who carried a gun and was prepared to use it. In the deep South, where escape was not always realistic, there were maroon communities deep in the swamps and woodlands, where hundreds of women and men fled for protection and armed themselves in self-defense.[6]

> In 1816 a large and flourishing [Maroon] community was discovered: three hundred escaped slaves—men, women and children—had occupied a fort in Florida. When they refused to surrender themselves, the army launched a battle which lasted for ten days and claimed the lives of more than two hundred fifty of the inhabitants. The women fought back on equal terms with the men. During the course of another confrontation in Mobile, Alabama, in 1827, men and women alike were unrelenting, fighting, according to the local newspapers, "like Spartans."[7]

While some black women were involved in armed resistance, others were engaged in violating the law by seeking education and learning to read. In many states during the nineteenth century, teaching an African American to read and write was a crime punishable by jail time, and much effort was expended, especially in the South, to prevent African Americans from becoming literate. Harriet Jacobs reports that even after she was free and living in the North, she had to write her biography in the attic in the middle of the night lest her northern abolitionist friends find out she was literate and dared to write.[8] The many African American women who sought education and those who worked to make educational opportunities available to others were in fact engaging in acts of resistance. Beginning during Reconstruction, the women's club movement chose education as one of its top priorities. Because of the energy and aspirations of the black community and support from northern liberals, many secondary schools and colleges were formed during the last part of the nineteenth century, some of which remain distinguished colleges today: Howard University, Fisk University, Shaw University, Morehouse and Spelman Colleges, Atlanta Clark University, and many others. Mary McCleod Bethune was one of the leaders of educational efforts for African American women, advising President Franklin Roosevelt on educational policies and founding Bethune College in Florida.

The civil rights movement had a profound impact on the educational aspirations of African American women. The NAACP had advocated desegregation for many years before the *Brown v. Board of Education* decision of the Supreme Court in 1954 started a long process of struggle in the public schools. Another accomplishment of the cvil rights movement was the *Civil Rights Act of 1964*, which provided a legal basis for affirmative action for women of all races. Given the opportunities, African American women surged into new places, filing suit with the federal government when they were blocked, and seeking the educational opportunities to prepare themselves for the future. Since 1960, increasing numbers of African American women have attended college and graduate school; started their own businesses; and entered into professions such as ministry, college teaching, law, medicine, social work, and counseling. By 1990, almost one million African American women had college or graduate degrees from institutions of higher education, and another two million had some college education (U.S. Census, 2000).

Beginning in 1980 there was an effective backlash to these gains. Affirmative action was challenged in many states and at the federal level. When the affirmative action program of the state university system in California was declared illegal, there was a dramatic drop in African American enrollment within two years. The welfare system that provided minimal support for the poorest women was drastically revised in 1996 from welfare to "workfare." This change required even mothers of preschool children to find jobs, thus limiting their ability to attend school.

Poverty and persistent inequality continues for many African American women. While the poverty rate in 1998 was 12.7% for all persons in the U.S., the poverty rate for blacks was 26.1%, and the poverty rate for single black female households was 40.8%.[9]

Nevertheless, African American women have continued to resist under an oppressive capitalistic system by seeking education and working together to "lift as we climb" on behalf of the whole black community.

Women in Trade Unions

Women in the U.S. have been active in labor unions for two hundred years, since the beginning of the Industrial Revolution. Federal and local government policies forced many families to send their younger daughters to the factories to work in poor working conditions. Many of the women who were forced to work in factories were immigrants without adequate legal protection. In nineteenth-century New England they protested the harsh conditions of factory labor, which included long hours, fear of physical punishment and fines if they disobeyed any rules, cold rooms where they had to wear heavy coats in order to keep warm, rotten food, inadequate toilets, and sexual harassment and abuse. Sometimes the women organized and revolted against their conditions.

> The mill women fought back. Beginning in the late 1820s–long before the 1848 Seneca Falls Convention–working women staged "turn-outs" and strikes, militantly protesting the double oppression they suffered as women and as industrial workers. In Dover, New Hampshire, for example, the mill women walked off the job in 1828 to dramatize their opposition to newly instituted restrictions. They "shocked the community by parading with banners and flags, shooting off gunpowder."[10]

Ninety years later, among the Russian Jews in New York, there was discontent over unfair labor practices such as fines and speed-ups for products bound for department stores and mail-order houses. In 1909, Clara Lemlich was one of the leaders of a strike called by the International Lady's Garment Workers' Union (ILGWU). After Lemlich's speech in Yiddish, 20,000–40,000 workers went on strike. Even though they did not accomplish their demands for improved working conditions, the ILGWU was strengthened and the public became more sympathetic to the situation of women workers.[11]

> Elizabeth Ewen observes that the unprecedented uprising had a deeper significance, for it "lifted the work of immigrant women

out of obscurity and into public consciousness." This awareness was accentuated in 1911 when a fire at the Triangle Shirt-Waist Company killed 146 people and injured many more. The employers had ignored the strikers' demands for improved safety arrangements and kept the 800 workers locked inside the factory.[12]

Recently made notorious again through a documentary on the public television network, the Triangle Company fire demonstrated the horrible conditions for working women. The disaster led to drastic changes in labor laws.

Later, during World War II, women proved that they could do a "man's" job. Rosie the Riveter became a central part of U.S. government propaganda that encouraged everyone to do their part. What is less well known is the later pressure on women to give their jobs to the veterans returning from Europe and the Pacific.[13]

Because of the ongoing theoretical and activist work of feminists, the next opportunity for change came with the passage of the 1964 *Civil Rights Act,* which outlawed sex and race discrimination. For the first time, through Title VII of this act, women had a legal claim on equal treatment. The situation of the women of the United Packinghouse Workers of America (UPWA), where women had been discriminated against for years through union-negotiated lower wages, blocked promotions, and jobs that were classified by gender so that they could not apply, is an example of this:

> "I'll tell you the biggest trouble about the women was after the Civil Rights Law was signed," Virgil Bankson remarked in a 1978 interview. "That's when we had trouble with women." Bankson was a retired officer of the United Packinghouse Workers of American (UPWA)...Women's response to the law's passage was significant. By August, 1967, 2,500 sex discrimination complaints had been filed by women workers against unions and employers.[14]

However, the battle for gender equality in the unions was not an easy one. For years, women had endeavored to protect their job security. Their strategy was to pressure employers to designate certain jobs for women only so they could not be taken over by men. They also negotiated special benefits for health and pregnancy so they would not lose their jobs while they were having children. When Title VII outlawed sex discrimination, union women were afraid they would be forced to compete with men and thus lose their jobs. Following this reasoning, Women's Activities Committee members at District 3 of the UPWA urged that separate seniority lists be continued. In an attempt to stave off further losses through automation, they recommended that positions be "frozen...That companies shall not combine female and male jobs...That no portion of a female job be combined with a male job." This last proposal had to do with the fact that automation displaced men as well, leading many of them to work at "women's jobs."[15]

Also undermining the struggle for union women was the lack of sensitivity of professional women who pushed gender equality at all levels without building solid coalitions across classes. Without knowledge of the many decades of union struggles of working-class women, professional women were exerting strong influence on the U.S. government. Because of class differences and lack of communication, many union women opposed the Equal Rights Amendment and helped to defeat it at the state level. However, after years of debate about these issues, union women began to see that gender equality would eventually work in their favor, and they began to work more closely with feminist organizations.

> They came to reject protective measures, along with unequal wages, sex-segregated jobs, and seniority lists. "If we are going against discrimination we go together because this is not a man's union, this is our union," one woman unionist stated in 1956. "This is not a man's world, this is our world. We must unite ourselves together. Divided we fall, united we stand." By the mid-1960s women in the UPWA would look beyond their male coworkers and find their own legal tools to achieve this goal.[16]

In this short review, we see the importance of union women, who have been organizing themselves for equality and protection from capitalism for two hundred years, since the beginning of the factory system. In spite of years of work, unions in the year 2000 represented a smaller percentage of the labor force than ever. Often acting to protect their own income and job security rather than seeing themselves as the vanguard of all working people, they have not successfully organized workers in the service and information industries. Fortunately, the unions are beginning to change their perspectives, and efforts to organize secretaries, waitresses, health care workers, and data entry operators are resuming. We can hope that unions will restore their radical critique of capitalism to counter the transfer of jobs to poor countries where union organizing is usually illegal and controlled by massive military force. Union women will continue to play an important role in defining alternative economic institutions for women.

Immigrant Women

The majority of immigrants during the first half of the twentieth century were women. During the nineteenth century, at least 40 percent of all immigrants were women, and since 1930, a majority have been women.[17]

Prior to 1960, immigrants came primarily from Europe and, in 1960, 90% of all female immigrants had come from [Europe]. Over the subsequent decades, their numbers declined 36 percent–from 4.2 million in 1960 to 2.7 million in 1997...Immigration from other regions of the world began in earnest only in the 1960s and has accelerated...By 1997 four out of every five immigrants had come from non-European countries–primarily Latin America and Asia. Overall the number of immigrant women from Latin America has increased from 450,000 in 1960 to 6.2 million in 1997 and today half of women immigrants are of Latin American origin. Similarly, the number of immigrant women from Asia has increased from 200,000 in 1960 to more than 3 million in 1997.[18]

Many women are motivated to immigrate to the U.S. because of violence such as wars and physical and sexual abuse, and economic issues such as poverty, lack of education and health care, and lack of opportunities for their children. Political conflict and war have severe economic consequences for poor women, who often become refugees. Immigrant women face hardships, such as separation from family, an unfamiliar language, and cultural differences. Those who come to the U.S. often face severe forms of economic exploitation, for large groups of low-skilled, politically vulnerable women who will work for low wages suit the values of capitalism. The population of immigrant workers is available at below-market wages when the economy does well, and they can be discarded during times of recession without consequences, since they lack political power. Despite all this, if they are at all able, immigrants nonetheless send money back to families in their home countries. Nicaraguans in the U.S. send their families $500 million per year in remittances, showing the strong ties that bind family members together.

Immigrant women are also vulnerable to poverty. The wages that look so valuable from the home country do not provide as much economic support as expected. In spite of higher wages, expenses are even higher, and indebtedness leads to a new kind of poverty. In the U.S., immigrant women are disproportionately poor and concentrated in low-paying industries: textile and garment, electronic manufacturing, and domestic service industries. We know that working women as a group, particularly immigrant women, are economically vulnerable in the U.S. Their jobs are not secure; the pay is low; and the benefits are inadequate.

Latino poverty in the nineties increased more than in earlier decades...In 1991, 28.7 percent of all Latinos lived in poverty, compared to 9.4 percent of non-Latinos. From another perspective, Latinos represented nearly 10 percent of the nation's population in 1991; however, they represented almost 19 percent of all persons living in poverty.[19]

In addition to the powerlessness that comes from having a low-paid job, we find that immigrant women are both prone to sexual harassment and coercion from employers, and vulnerable to domestic violence. If a woman is battered by her husband, she may be reluctant to call the police or get a restraining order. If the authorities find problems with immigration status in the family, they can deport the woman, her husband, and her children. Batterers actually use this threat as a part of the emotional abuse in some relationships. Although battering is illegal in the U.S., many immigrant women lack the language skills and safety net of extended families that might provide them with access to help.

The stories of how immigrant women have resisted capitalism give important insights into the relationship of women and capitalism. First, immigration itself is a form of resistance, since individuals are leaving one site of exploitation, hoping to improve their situation. The survival of the extended family is often a motive for immigration.

Second, Hispanic women in particular have been leaders and workers in some labor unions. Dolores Huerta was a leader, along with Cesar Chavez, of the United Farm Workers, organized in 1962, which gained national prominence for its militant action on behalf of farm laborers and for a national boycott of grapes that pressured many large farmers into signing contracts with the union. The willingness of Hispanic workers to join the farm workers' union was a sign of their unhappiness with the wages and work situations. Their efforts resulted in some legal protection and some improvement in the quality of work. However, the exploitation of farm workers is far from over in the U.S.

A third form of resistance to capitalism is the refusal of some Hispanics to assimilate. Many resist by self-consciously holding on to their language and culture. They hold on to the dreams of returning to their homeland, but in changed circumstances where they will have enough resources for their families. Many refuse to adopt English as their primary language, maintain extended families as economic and supportive units, and insist on their national and cultural identity. Vigorous debates about bilingual education, especially in California, show the perceived threat that Hispanics potentially create to the homogenization of capitalism. Some researchers have estimated that Hispanics will make up 15 percent of the U.S. population in the early decades of the twenty-first century, making it the largest ethnic/language group in the U.S.

In summary, we have looked at several groups of women in the U.S. to see how they are engaged in resistance to exploitation of their labor: African American women, women in labor unions, and immigrant women. In each case we have seen how these groups have resisted the exploitation of capitalism and organized themselves into organizations to promote a different kind of life. At the same time, women in all these groups have experienced the violence and exploitation of the capitalistic system. As a group, they suffer inequality in wages, work conditions, and possibilities for advancement. They have never earned more than 75 percent of the average male wage. African American women and Hispanic women suffer high rates of poverty, job insecurity, and sexist forms of exploitation such as harassment and sexual coercion. Capitalism demands compliant workers, which triggers resistance among oppressed groups, in this case women. In this tug-of-war for survival, it is hard for the efforts of working people to win against the overwhelming power of capitalistic systems.

Women's Resistance to Exploitation of Sexuality

Capitalism did not invent patriarchy, the rule of men over women. Patriarchy has been firmly established in nearly all pre-capitalist societies in the world, and sanctioned by official religious doctrines in Christianity, Judaism, Islam, Buddhism, Confucianism, and other world religions. The idea that men are superior in creation and born to be rulers, and that women are inferior and born to be servants of men has a long history.[20] For example, the Christian churches have taught that men have more access to rational and moral reasoning, which makes them more like God, and that the sexual and childbearing functions of women make them more a part of nature. Thus, men have been ordained to be leaders in church, society, and the family, while God has placed women second in this hierarchy, in submission to the authority of men.[21]

However, capitalism has adapted so well to patriarchy that the two systems are now interlocked to such an extent that Maria Mies has chosen to use the term "patriarchal capitalism."

> It is my thesis that capitalism cannot function without patriarchy, that the goal of this system, namely the never-ending process of capital accumulation, cannot be achieved unless patriarchal man-woman relations are maintained or newly created... Patriarchy thus constitutes the mostly invisible underground of the visible capitalist system.[22]

In other words, capitalism has discovered that one of the ways to maintain and control cheap labor is to fuel the alienation between men and women in order to exploit the labor of both women and men. When the first industrial textile factories were built in New England, the laborers were young women sent to the city because they were excess workers from the immigrant farming communities.[23] Likewise, workers today in the free trade zones in Latin America and Asia are largely young women who, working at low wages, assemble consumer products for sale in the U.S. and Europe.

How has patriarchal capitalism managed to "maintain or newly create" gender hierarchies to make women vulnerable to exploitation at work and in the family? This is accomplished through the double bind of the idealization of women as pure, pious, domestic, and submissive and the sexualization of women as loose, amoral, wild, and rebellious. This double bind, enforced by religion, public morality, and the media, gives individual men the power to enforce dominance over women at home and at work. Combined with other systems of oppression—such as white supremacy, heterosexism, ethnocentrism, and other forms of discrimination—many women are trapped in abusive relationships with men and exploitative relationships with employers.

Patriarchal capitalism, therefore, is a system that promotes and benefits from the sexualization, violent abuse, and economic exploitation of women. In order to survive, women have to accommodate to the system that controls their labor and sexuality. They are forced to marry *and* work in low-paying jobs. In modern society, most women are employed in horizontally stratified jobs at the bottom of the economic pyramid: "as secretaries, domestics, nurses, typists, telephone operators, child-care workers, waitresses."[24] The denial of employment and educational opportunities for women through many complex subterfuges results in most being stuck with the jobs they have and not having adequate support for themselves and their children.

Thus, the church, patriarchy, and capitalism have joined forces to devalue women. As a result, men believe they are entitled to women's services and bodies and assume they have been given authority to strike or sexually use women. This tangle of sexual politics has created the male-dominant family that continues throughout her life: A woman is required to subordinate herself to her father as a child, to her husband in marriage, and to her son in old age.[25] And as we are learning, marriages and families are actually the most dangerous places for women. One-third to one-half of women experience domestic violence in families and intimate relationships. More women are raped within the family than outside it.[26] In families and marriages, many men terrorize and enforce female subordination through physical and sexual violence.[27] Patriarchal capitalism is a system in which sexualization, violence, and economic exploitation are interlocked in a way that enables male abusers to exploit women in the family, at work, and everywhere.

Resistance to Domestic Violence

Given these patriarchal ideologies of womanhood, it is not hard to understand why women have violently revolted against their experiences in families. There must have been nineteenth-century women who murdered their husbands because of domestic violence—such self-defense was inevitable among human beings in a culture where men had a legal right to beat women into submission. The story of women's violent revolts against patriarchy and the sanctioned male violence against them has not been fully told.

We have evidence that contemporary U.S. women are responding to domestic violence with violence of their own. In one of the early interventions, Marie Fortune and other feminists in Seattle helped organize a campaign to get a governor's pardon for a woman named Delia, a Hispanic Roman Catholic mother who had killed her husband and was given a life sentence in prison. Women in Seattle, Washington, were able get a public hearing for Delia's story, which included battering, marital rape, physical and sexual abuse of her children, and continued threats to kill her and the children. Over twenty years of abuse Delia went to every resource in the area—extended family, priests and the church, shelters and mental health agencies, police and the courts. When she did not get any effective help, she arranged for someone to kill her husband and prepared herself to go to prison. Cases such as Delia's have mobilized many women and some men to become active in preventing sexual and domestic violence.[28]

> In a study that analyzed all criminally negligent homicides from 1976 to 1987 using The Supplementary Homicide Report (SHR data), Browne and Williams (1993) found that the deaths of approximately 38,649 individuals age 16 and over during this period were the result of one partner killing another (this includes married, common-law, divorced, and dating partners). Of these deaths, 61% of the victims were women killed by male partners and 39% were men killed by female partners. For white couples, the difference was more marked: 70% of the victims were women...Fifty-two percent of all women murdered in the United States between 1980 and 1985 were victims of partner homicide.[29]

These horrifying figures show that men kill their female partners 30–50 percent more often than women kill their male partners, and this accounts for 52 percent of all female homicides. However, these figures also show that women are fighting back against male violence in fairly large numbers: more than 15,000 women killed their partners between 1976 and 1987. The famous story of Lorraine Bobbitt, who used a knife to cut off her husband's penis, is an example of violent revolt today. Such examples and statistics give hints that many women are violently revolting against exploitation because of their gender and sexuality.

Yet this revolt began long before the twentieth century. The Women's Christian Temperance Union (WCTU) was a nineteenth-century progressive political movement aimed at empowering women in relation to male violence. The WCTU argued that women had the right of self-defense, including separation and divorce, against alcoholic husbands. It developed a platform of reform laws that included making alcohol illegal, which contributed to the passing of the eighteenth amendment to the Constitution in 1920. Like other progressive movements, the WCTU eventually lost touch with its more radical roots and began to teach, naively, that removal of alcohol from society would be the cure for male violence and other social problems. Current statistics show that more than 50 percent of male violence against women does not involve alcohol, and even when alcohol is used, it often serves as an excuse rather than a reason.

Women's revolt against sexual and domestic violence became a strong grassroots movement in the last third of the twentieth century. In the 1970s feminist pioneers such as Marie Fortune formed agencies specifically dedicated to ending violence against women. Since 1972, the Center for the Prevention of Sexual and Domestic Violence has engaged in activism and education on the religious issues of violence against women. They organized to obtain a pardon for Delia, advocated for new laws in the state to protect women, and supported shelters in the local community. They actively engaged in national efforts to make family violence more visible, including serving on the advisory board in the Justice Department under Secretary Janet Reno. In addition, they developed videotapes and curricula for churches to use in educating their members about family violence, and they organized training for pastors and other religious leaders.[30]

The case studies in part 1 illustrate some of the ways that women resist exploitation at work and at home. Although her mother took all her money, Soledad began working as a maid when she was eight. As an adult of forty, she was still working as a maid. The combination of exploitative work and abandonment by her husband left her in a desperate situation. The rage that resulted from her trauma often affected her ability to parent her five children and interfered with her work. Her rage can be seen as a kind of revolt against the system that kept her in a vulnerable situation, and her commitment to therapy as a way of developing alternative resources for herself. She consented to the research for this book and allowed herself to be interviewed so that others could learn from her experiences.

Linda Crockett experienced sadistic abuse from her mother and sexual abuse from older boys and men in the community. She survived adolescence by taking drugs and staying away from home. When she got married at 17, she had the internal strength to stop taking drugs and begin to care for her two boys. However, after years of difficult emotional living, she decided to face her experiences of abuse because she was inspired by the El Salvadoran struggle. She sought out a pastoral counselor and soon afterward began speaking out in public about the sexual and physical abuse of children and the terror many children still live in, which she likened to a war zone. She spoke to college classes and church groups and organized a training conference on accompaniment of survivors of abuse. She wrote her story for publication in this volume, and wrote a longer version that was published this year.[31] She is an example of how women move from abuse to activism on behalf of all women.

Women began organizing formal shelters for women affected by domestic violence in 1972 and began talking in consciousness-raising groups about their own experiences.[32] Women from different social classes and ethnic groups discovered they shared the experience of having been victims of male violence. They moved from interpersonal conversations to active resistance, first by taking women into their homes when they were threatened with violence, then organizing agencies with secret residences where victims could stay in safety. At first this required secrecy to make it work, but eventually, the activism included lobbying for changes in state laws so that enraged husbands and boyfriends could not pursue adult women into shelters. Twenty-five years later, the U.S. Department of Justice had a Violence Against Women office advocating for the safety of women in every state. Today there are organized programs at every level to protect women and change the culture that makes violence against them socially tolerated. Unfortunately, it will take many more decades to change the public attitudes about domestic violence, and even longer to change the capitalistic structures that devalue women and make them vulnerable to violence.

Resistance to Sexual Violence

Another common form of violence against women is rape, and the fear of it is an ever-present reality for all women.[33] There is constant danger that a woman can be assaulted in the streets, within her acquaintance circle, or within her family. According to Susan Brownmiller, as quoted in Hester Eisenstein:

> In the minds of women, the knowledge of the possibility of rape act[s] as a powerful form of social control. To keep this knowledge alive, it [is] not necessary for all men to rape all women. This work could be carried out by only a few men...[M]en who commit rape have served in effect as front-line masculine shock troops, terrorist guerrillas in the longest sustained war the world has ever known.[34]

bell hooks argues that analysis of racism leads to an additional understanding of how the facts of sexual violence affect the imagination of the American psyche. As far back as slavery, white people established a social hierarchy based on race and sex that ranked white men first, white women second, though sometimes equal to black men, who are ranked third, and black women last. What this means in terms of the sexual politics of rape is that if one white woman is raped by a black man, it is seen as more important, more significant than if thousands of black women are raped by one white man.[35]

Men, by conscious and unconscious design, use their power to maintain their dominance and are socialized to find this exercise of power in relation to the vulnerability of women an erotic experience. What is organized by patriarchy as a system of power and domination becomes internalized as male sexual desire, which is then projected onto women through obsessions and fantasies. "Incidents of sexual harassment suggest that male sexual desire itself may be aroused by female vulnerability...Men feel they can take advantage, so they want to, so they do."[36]

More than a third of female children are molested and more than half of all women experience rape or attempted rape. Only a small percentage of abusers ever face consequences such as censure, exposure, or jail. The majority of rapists and child molesters are never convicted of a crime.[37] In analyzing the secrecy surrounding the majority of rapes in American society, Angela Davis asks this provocative question:

> Where are the anonymous rapists?...Might not this anonymity be a privilege enjoyed by men whose status protects them from prosecution?...It seems, in fact, that men of the capitalist class and their middle-class partners are immune to prosecution because they commit their assaults with the same unchallenged authority that legitimates their daily assaults on the labor and dignity of working people...The class structure of capitalism encourages men who wield power in the economic and political realm to become routine agents of sexual exploitation. Men who reject this socialization are considered a threat to patriarchy.[38]

The feminist and womanist argument, as I understand it, is that patriarchy is enforced through a combination of forces including economic exploitation, violence, and the sexualization of women. It is this system that begins to explain sexual terrorism in rape, incest, and sexual abuse by professionals. Sexual exploitation is not an aberration of an otherwise fair and just system of commerce and interpersonal relationships. Rather, sexual violence is an integral part of a patriarchal, capitalistic system that is based on the subordination of women and children, and which is interlocked with the oppression of people of color, the poor, gays and lesbians, and other groups.

This enforced subordination of women was challenged by women themselves as they talked about their experiences of rape and subsequently began to develop a strategy of resistance to change the situation for women. Part of this strategy was to: (1) quit blaming oneself; (2) begin telling others about what had happened; and (3) begin pressing charges against rapists. As more women followed this strategy, public pressure developed to enforce the laws and hold rapists accountable.

Such public pressure led to the organization in the early 1970s of rape crisis hotlines and counseling services for victims of sexual assault.[39]

As a result of the resistance of women to rape, nearly every county in the U.S. now has organized services for rape victims. Likewise, state government child protective services provide legal protection and services for children who are sexually abused. However, in spite of the explosion of public information and services, the epidemic of rape continues. Until there is a change in the culture's attitudes toward women and change in how patriarchal capitalism values them, the efforts to prevent rape and sexual assault will be frustrated.

The International Sex Industry

Another arena in which to see women resisting economic vulnerability and family violence is in international trafficking in women. We know about trafficking because women are complaining about what is happening to them, and because many have organized local and international organizations to protect women and educate and change the public attitudes toward this form of violence against women. The Coalition Against Trafficking in Women (CATW) works to educate people about the violence and lies that make trafficking in girls and women possible.[40] End Child Prostitution is a feminist agency that focuses on the exploitation of children in prostitution, pornography, and trafficking.[41] The public has become more aware of the sex industry because victims and their advocates have organized to protest against its existence, and they call on all good people to join them in dismantling it.

A huge global industry is engaged in systematically kidnapping and manipulating women and girls for various forms of enslaved work, including prostitution and pornography. "In the last three years, the Department of Justice has prosecuted numerous 'modern-day slavery' and trafficking cases. The Department's Involuntary Servitude Coordinator alone has prosecuted slavery cases involving over 150 victims."[42] In one case, *United States v. Cadena,* 1998, the following description is given:

> Background/Description: From about February, 1996 to about March, 1998, some 25 to 40 Mexican women and girls, some as young as 14 years old, were trafficked from the Veracruz state in Mexico to Florida and the Carolinas in the United States. The victims had been promised jobs in waitressing, housekeeping, landscaping, childcare and elder care. Upon their arrival, the women and girls were told they must work as prostitutes in brothels serving migrant workers or risk harm to themselves and/or their families.
>
> Confinement: Besides enduring threats, women who attempted to escape were subjected to beatings. Guards used force to keep them in the brothels in order that they pay off their smuggling debt that ranged from $2,000 to $3,000. One woman was locked in a closet for 15 days as punishment for trying to escape.

Additional human rights abuses included: forced prostitution, assault, rape, and forced abortions.

Outcome: In March, 1998, 16 men were indicted in Florida for enslaving the Mexican women and girls in brothels. The men were charged with importing aliens for immoral purposes, transporting women and minors for prostitution, involuntary servitude, visa fraud, conspiracy, and violation of civil rights. The defendants' sentences ranged from 1 to 6 years. The judge ordered that the trafficking organization pay $1 million in restitution. Several of the other key ringleaders had previously fled to Mexico. The victims, who are currently living in Florida at either a shelter or on their own, did receive some money from the traffickers' seized assets in the U.S.[43]

Richard estimates that 700,000 to 2,000,000 women and girls per year are trafficked globally, and that 45,000 to 50,000 women and girls come to the United States through criminal syndicates. Three-fourths of this number come from Southeast Asia, but large numbers also come from Latin America, Eastern Europe, and other regions. These women and girls are trafficked to the U.S. "for the sex industry (prostitution, stripping, peep and touch shows, and massage parlors that offer a variety of sexual services), sweatshop labor, domestic servitude, and agricultural work...also maid services at motels and hotels, peddl[ing] trinkets on subways and buses, and beg[ging]."[44] The average age of the women and girls is twenty years old, with many in their early teens.

The vast majority of women and girls are kidnapped, coerced, or deceived by traffickers. Given the extreme poverty in the countries of origin, families are vulnerable to deception and promises made about the money that will come back to them, and a few are desperate enough to take money for their children. It is hard to estimate the total economic profit in this industry. "Overall profits in the trade can be staggering...Thai traffickers, who incarcerated Thai women and men in the sweatshop in El Monte, California, are estimated to have made $8 million over about six years...Chinese criminal syndicates, living in Malaysia, have also made $5,000 to $7,000 for each Malaysian woman delivered to the U.S."[45]

One reason trafficking in women and girls for the sex industry is difficult to analyze and prevent is because it is so embedded in related industries, such as mail-order bride companies, maid schemes, advertisements for domestic servants at hotels and resorts, and illicit foreign adoptions. The violation of civil rights in these various enterprises varies and involves thousands of men, women, and children. The traffickers are often well organized into crime syndicates that also work in drugs, illicit military equipment, stolen merchandise such as cars, and other schemes. Billions of dollars flow between international banks every year because of such businesses. However, mom-and-pop operations (small tightly knit families) also engage in trafficking for profit and are hard to apprehend.

Even when traffickers are arrested, it is difficult to obtain convictions and get sufficient prison sentences to deter others from engaging in such business. In the *United States v. Cadena* case discussed above, the convicted traffickers got only one to six years in prison for such serious offenses as kidnapping, rape, physical abuse, extortion, and violation of immigration laws. Contributing to the difficulties in convicting traffickers is victims' reluctance to testify because of the trauma they have already experienced and their mistrust and fear of police and other authorities.

Rita Nakashima Brock and Susan Brooks Thistlethwaite's examination of the cultural and theological issues of the sex industries argues that the development of global capitalism since World War II is the primary factor in making the sex industry possible.[46] Although sexual exploitation of women has existed for many centuries, it became a global market during World War II when hundreds of thousands of military troops, especially Japanese and U.S. troops, were stationed all over the world. Wherever military troops were stationed, a sex industry was developed to "entertain the troops" and provide "rest and relaxation." Women from many countries were exploited by this system. The Korean "comfort women" are well known because they have asked for reparations from the Japanese government.[47] The Korean and Vietnamese wars increased the market for commodified sexuality, and now the sex industry serves military personnel, traveling businessmen, and tourists.

The sex industry in the U.S., which includes prostitution, sexually oriented entertainment, and pornography in various forms (cable TV, printed materials, videos, and the Internet) is huge, producing billions of dollars. It is an aspect of U.S. culture that has adapted well to global capitalism, and the lack of moral values in the market system is the perfect context for the sex industry.

Linda Crockett comments on the impact of pornography in the sexual exploitation of women:

> I am reading a book called *Pornography: The Production and Consumption of Inequality.* It is estimated that the video pornography industry alone generated $3.1 billion in rentals & sales in 1995, compared to $2.5 in 1994, and $1.2 in 1991. By now, it is probably a great deal more. Many of the videos produced are no longer low-grade in appearance, but high tech, slick with computer graphics and fast paced editing. Violence is part and parcel of this industry with its huge profits and ever growing market. It is not a surprise that global trafficking in

women (and children) is at such high levels. Most of the women and children involved do so out of economic necessity; there are many people eager to profit from their circumstances; and a market willing to pay to see them exploited. Women are sexualized through advertising, movies, and the construction of gender in middle-class life, and the exaggerated sexual desire creates a market ready for their exploitation. As long as sexuality is a commodity that enhances capitalism and men are given permission to exploit women, there will be a market for exploitation. Whether in the family through incest, or in the marketplace through the sex industry, pornography, and prostitution, women will be in jeopardy.[48]

In summary, women in the U.S. have joined women around the world to resist capitalistic exploitation through political revolt, including violence. This can be clearly seen in the stories of women who resisted during slavery and in the organization of women at every level against physical and sexual violence in the family and within the larger sex industry. In this section, we have also seen how violence is used to control women's resistance. Slavery itself was a violent system, which was replaced by legal and illegal violence after the Civil War. Physical and sexual violence at the interpersonal and family level are means of controlling women as a social class. Finally, global trafficking in women and girls is a form of modern slavery of women, fueled by patriarchal capitalism in its drive for profit and control.

Alternative Economic Visions: Maria Mies

Many feminist scholars have written on the subject of an alternative economic vision and deserve to be noted here: Patricia Hill Collins, who suggests that African American women have a unique perspective and values that can guide an economic vision;[49] Rosemary Ruether, who speaks for many feminists in her vision of alternative Christian economics;[50] Martha Nussbaum, who is working toward a feminist vision of universal human rights;[51] and Saskia Sassen, who encourages coalitions of professional and working women in urban centers to protest exploitation of women as workers.[52] From these scholars, we begin to see the outlines of an alternative economic vision based on women's experiences. In this section, I have chosen Maria Mies as a representative of women who are working toward a comprehensive feminist economic vision.

Maria Mies, a feminist scholar from Germany, worked for many years in India and has made economics the focus of her research. She is one of the few feminist scholars willing to risk a macro-theory of economics as an alternative to "patriarchal capitalism," which she defines as "the relationship between women's oppression and exploitation, and the paradigm of never-ending accumulation and 'growth,' between capitalist patriarchy and the exploitation and subordination of colonies."[53] Noting that the global discovery of violence against women provides a foundation for unity between all social classes and nationalities, she calls for solidarity among women. Together they can organize to end violence against women; they can begin to deconstruct the myth of western femininity that is being used as a club against those in poor countries; and they can retrieve the feminist values from traditional women's cultures, "the remnants of matriarchal or matrilineal traditions, pockets of women's power that may derive from their still communal and collective way of loving and working, or their long tradition of resistance to male, class, and colonial oppression."[54]

Mies suggests the following principles for deconstructing the values of patriarchal capitalism and beginning to construct an alternative feminist economics:

1. Rejection and abolition of the principle of *colonizing dualistic divisions* (between men and women, man and nature);

2. The creation of nonexploitative, nonhierarchical, reciprocal relationships;

3. The regaining of *autonomy over our bodies and our lives*;

4. The rejection of the idea of infinite progress;

5. [The development of] *human happiness* or the *production of life itself*...not a never-ending expansion of wealth and commodities.[55]

We can see in this list of principles some of the core values of the feminist movements over the centuries. There is more at stake than equality between women and men, as important as equality is. Rather, there is an alternative set of values about the way humans relate to one another as workers, investors, and stewards of the land. Emphasizing cooperation, nonviolence, and respect for individual creativity and autonomy will lead to a different vision of human economic life.

Mies suggests a feminist concept of labor. Rather than workers who must sell their skills in the market to obtain money to live, she suggests that work must have intrinsic value for the workers themselves. It must not be defined by the creation of products out of natural resources, especially when those products are sold in foreign markets for profit. Rather, work should be defined as "the production of immediate life."[56] "A feminist concept of labor maintains that work retain its sense of purpose, its character of being useful and necessary for the people who do it and those around them. This also means that the products of this labor are useful and necessary, not just some luxuries or superfluous trash."[57] Such labor will be enhanced if it also includes "a direct and sensual interaction with nature, with organic matter and living organisms."[58]

The principles and understanding of work lead Mies to the foundation of her proposal:

> The first basic requirement of an alternative economy is a changeover, both in overdeveloped and underdeveloped societies, from dependency for the basic subsistence needs–food, clothing, shelter–from economics outside their natural boundaries toward greater *autarky*. Only societies which are to a large extent self-sufficient in the production of these basic necessities can maintain themselves free from political blackmail and hunger. In this, self-sufficiency in food is the first requirement.[59]

This will require a movement of labor back to the land, greater cooperation between women and men in productive agricultural work, an end to violence against women, granting of legal autonomy of women over their own bodies, especially in regard to reproduction, and gender equality in all the chores often labeled as "housework."

All these proposals, Mies acknowledges, will be seen by many as romantic, especially by economists who work with macroeconomic trends using mathematical analysis. Though many people these days say that what is lacking most are visions of an alternative society and economy, when someone like Mies actually dares to formulate some of the basic principles for such a vision, the critique is very often that it is utopian, that it cannot be realized here and now, that it is backward-looking, that it romanticizes a "simpler" life, that it is not progressive.[60] Mies however suggests that such critiques show the degree of our alienation from the realities of life compared with most of the world's population, who live much closer to nature and contend with the daily need to survive. So the catch-22 is that patriarchal capitalism does not meet the basic needs of most human beings, yet any return to addressing such needs is considered naïve.

> People in industrialized societies have particular difficulty in accepting the fact that food still comes out of the earth, that land therefore is the foundation of food production and food security...I realize how difficult it is to explain to people–women and men–in the industrialized world that a subsistence perspective would be a better alternative and that this alternative is already being practiced.[61]

Mies has also been criticized because she advocates a strong and radical consumer movement based on women's importance as consumers in the global economy. "[Some critics] qualified this strategy either as ineffective, individualistic and too weak to challenge the system, or as moralistic and anti-women–why should women again be the ones to make sacrifices while men continue to consume?"[62] Mies counters by saying that she advocates a change in the way women understand themselves as consumers and a greater sense of solidarity with women who produce consumer goods at subsistence wages. A strong consumer movement is not the total strategy for economic change, but it strikes at the heart of contemporary market capitalism, which is based on exploiting poor labor and natural resources in poor countries for the benefit of Northern Hemisphere consumers. Without a huge and dependable consumer market, much of capitalism would have to shift its priorities.

She suggests the following principles for such a consumer movement: (a) every woman can participate with only small changes in buying habits; (b) women can resist products that create or reinforce sexist images of women; (c) women can refuse to buy "products that reinforce women as housewives, supermothers, and sex-objects";[63] (d) women can boycott products that are based on exploitation of poor women; (e) in solidarity with nature, women can boycott lipstick and cosmetics that are based on exploitation of certain animal products. Such a consumer movement will require a massive reeducation campaign, as much of the information necessary for making the above decisions is difficult to find.

> A feminist consumer liberation movement has to start with the lifting of this blindness, with a de-mystification of the commodities, a re-discovery of the exploitation of women, nature, colonies, inherent in these commodities, and effort to transform the market relations which link us *de facto* to women, men, animals, plants, the earth, etc., into *true human relations*. This means to re-discover concrete people behind the abstract commodities...to trace the path a certain commodity has traveled until it reaches our tables or our bodies.[64]

A particularly successful example of such a boycott was the one against Nestlé, which was marketing its baby formulas in poor countries as a replacement for breast milk. As a result of a boycott in the U.S. and Europe, Nestlé changed its policies and encouraged health education that favored breast-feeding. The consumer revolt against tobacco could also move into a global phase that would challenge marketing strategies of this dangerous product aimed at poor people.

Mies suggests two additional strategies: First, the international feminist movement to prevent violence against women can be expanded to increase the solidarity between women in rich and poor countries. Second, women in rich countries can organize a movement to gain control over transnational corporations and the production decisions they make. Working through governments, stockholders, and unions, women could aim to influence decisions such as "automation of production, arms production, the production of dangerous chemicals, and of luxury items." Such changes could also mark beginning steps in creating "new local markets between small, ecologically-oriented producers and urban women."[65]

Conclusion

In the last three chapters we have looked at forms of resistance to capitalism in Nicaragua, in African American communities, and among working-class women in the U.S. We have gained clues about the problems of capitalism as a system of domination from the resistance of certain groups of people. By studying the movements of these groups, we can discover models for creating alternative institutions and visions for human economic life.

In the next part of the book, we turn to the scriptures and the Christian tradition to see what resources they provide for an economic vision. Based on discipleship to Jesus Christ, do the Christian churches have contributions to make? This perhaps abrupt shift of focus is part of the larger aim of this project to plumb the Christian tradition for resources that can help churches to understand the global situation of human beings in the twenty-first century and to begin to design caregiving strategies that are appropriate to the day-to-day experience of contemporary people.

Part IV: Theological Reflection

11

Mark's Critique of Oppressive Political Economies

It is a perennial question for faithful Christian life to ask: What must we render to God, and what can we render to the political economy within which we live? This question assumes that God and the political economy are in conflict fairly often. Whether or not we perceive a conflict depends on our assumptions about what it means to be a believer in God and what knowledge we have about the political economy of which we are a part. That they are competing ideological systems between which we frequently must make a choice is an assumption of this book.

Review

In part 1, I discussed case material related to pastoral care and economics. Many women in Nicaragua suffer from poverty and domestic violence on a daily basis, and programs such as AEDAF and CEPAD work to empower them. Through loan funds, workshops, unions, and cooperatives many women resist their oppression and find a better life for themselves and their children. Meanwhile, in the U.S., working-class women such as Linda struggle with their own kinds of oppression and economic vulnerability. Linda told her story about visiting with peasants in El Salvador and beginning to understand the faith that sustained them through war, violence, and extreme poverty. Her transformation in perspective thrust her into her own healing work. While she had the financial resources for therapy and other educational experiences, she struggled with isolation because of ideologies about women, family, and class. Finally, I shared vignettes from my pastoral counseling with working-class men in the U.S. Workers who are abused in factories and service jobs often carry their woundedness into their family relationships through abusive behaviors. I argued that pastoral care and counseling needs to give more attention to the economic realities in the lives of people.

In part 2, I explored the macro level of economics, that is, the discussions and debates that occur in academic, corporate, and government circles about capitalism and how it should be understood and managed. In part 3 I explored resistance to capitalism and alternative visions of how an economic system might be organized. I looked first at Nicaragua, which has been a site of rebellion and revolt against U.S. capitalism for 150 years. Then I looked at the U.S. African American community, who lived as slaves in North America for 300 years and then as victims of apartheid and racism. Finally I looked at several women's communities from different cultures in the U.S. that have resisted capitalism in many ways—African American women, trade union women, and immigrant women—all of whom have been oppressed and exploited by capitalism and have fought back in creative ways.

Now we come to part 4 of our project: *theological reflection.* I come to this out of a conviction that the ministry of Jesus and his followers represents an alternative vision of human life that provides valuable resources for challenging the dominance of capitalism. What role should the church play in supporting and resisting the various economic options that are available in the world? What kind of care should the church offer to people who are caught in the poverty and oppression of capitalistic dominance?

Render unto God

"Render therefore unto Caesar the things which are Caesar's; and unto God the things that are God's." (Matthew 22:21 with parallels in Mark 12:17 and Luke 20:25; KJV)[1]

The verse that gives the title to this book is used by many as a text on the relation of church and state, parallel to Paul in Romans 13:1 "Let every person be subject to the governing authorities; for there is no authority except from God, and those authorities that exist have been instituted by God." However, rather than focusing narrowly on the issue of church and state, I prefer to follow the interpretation of Ched Myers— that this verse is about the whole political economy of the time, including the unjust distribution of wealth between rich and poor.

Mark was most likely writing at the time of the Jewish rebellion of 66–69 C.E., when the tension between collaboration and rebellion was especially acute. His community felt tremendous pressure to align itself with one or another of the power groups, and this verse from Jesus gives one of the key nonalignment texts of the gospel of Mark. However, it was not a simple nonalignment, because Mark's sympathies were with the rebels against the dominant colonial powers even while he rejected their methods of military revolt. So this verse about the coin applies broadly to the issues of our project.

Both Jesus' hearers and Mark's community would have recognized the trick question that the Pharisees and Herodians put to Jesus. "[The question] was a test of loyalty that divided collaborators from subversives against the backdrop of revolt."[2] To which group are you loyal? Any answer he gave would create trouble with one group or another.[3] That this is an economic as well as a political question can be seen from Mark's choice of words.

> The imperative commonly translated "render" (*apodote*) is widely used in the NT to speak of payment of debt or recompense, but occurs only here in Mark, and is best read as "repay." The sense of the dictum is: "Repay the one to whom you are indebted."...In other words, no Jew could have allowed for a valid *analogy* between the debt Israel owed to Yahweh and any other human claim."[4]

The Greek word *apodote* means repay a debt, which reminds us of the indebtedness of such countries as Nicaragua to first-world powers. If one asked an average Nicaraguan where the national debt comes from, he or she would likely say, "It is Somoza's debt, not ours." The common understanding is that the collaborator Somoza stole the money intended for earthquake relief, and his robbery left the country impoverished and indebted. Or the person might say, "We incurred the debt from the U.S. Contra War," which means that it was a debt imposed by the U.S. as the cost of war, embargo, and blockade. While the Nicaraguan government is legally obligated to repay the debt, it was not incurred by the people through choice, and if justice were done, it would not have to be repaid. Just as the typical Nicaraguan would reject the right of U.S. banks to collect payment on the national debt, so the hearers of Jesus would have rejected the right of the colonial government to collect fees to support their costly occupation.

Within the resistance community of the first century there was a fierce debate about the appropriate means of revolt. In Jesus' time, the zealots were organizing guerilla action and military revolt against Herod and Rome. When Mark wrote the gospel, the rebels had briefly liberated Jerusalem and believed they could stave off future attacks and maintain their independence. Myers believes that Mark was calling for a third way of nonalignment, based on nonviolent resistance, which clearly took the side of the oppressed population but challenged the value system of their rebellion, including faith in military action. Because Mark was opposed to open revolt against Rome, his community was in danger; the rebels controlled Jerusalem, and Rome was soon to attack and reconquer Jerusalem. Mark needed an answer that avoided being "hunted down" by either the rebels or the Romans and that educated his followers about an alternative vision of the political economy for the future. "Those who choose to collaborate with the empire will 'render' according to Caesar's inscription; those who choose to collaborate with the kingdom must 'render' according to the inscription on the cross."[5]

How did Jesus formulate his critique of the dominant economic system of his time? How did he envision an alternative system of values and behaviors for his followers? How did he work to educate the disciple community into his alternative vision so they could become leaders of a new way beyond accommodation and rebellion? In order to answer these questions we must deal with certain issues of biblical interpretation or hermeneutics.

The Nature of Biblical Authority

Jesus is the central religious figure in Christian life, and the Bible is the canonical record of his life, death, and resurrection. As a Christian, I organize my faith and life around the image of Jesus Christ passed on to me through the Bible and the church. I know that Jesus lived in a different time and culture than I do, and I cannot fully trust my own first impressions about him from what I read in the Bible. I have to understand him within the church as a community of interpretation through its preachers, teachers, scholars, and worthy examples. Giving authority to the Bible, or hermeneutics (the study of how interpretations become authoritative for a community),[6] depends on having an understanding of the times and culture of the Bible. Likewise, it depends on having an understanding of the times and culture of the one who is interpreting the Bible. Ched Myers says, "White North American Christians, especially those of us from the privileged strata of society, must come to terms with the fact that our reading site for the Gospel of Mark is empire, *locus imperium.*"[7] I, too am a member of the dominant culture with global influence. By empire, Myers means "the metropolitan domination of the weaker economy (and its political and social superstructure) to ensure the extraction of economic rewards."[8]

However, Mark was not from the privileged elite of the Roman Empire. Myers says, "Whereas I read from the center, Mark wrote from the Palestinian periphery. His primary audience was those whose daily lives bore the exploitative weight of colonialism, whereas mine is those who are in a position to enjoy the privileges of the colonizer."[9] For this reason, as I have argued earlier, the people of Nicaragua, such as the peasants in Solentiname, "will have 'eyes to see' many things that those of us at the center do not."[10]

Mary Ann Tolbert makes the same argument from the perspective of literary criticism. While the author of Mark was literate in a time when most of the population was illiterate, the form of literature he wrote was not elitist, but derived from a popular style intended for the masses.

> [Elitist literature] is written for the literate elite of culture; [popular literature] is accessible to middle- and lower-class masses; one is individualized, subtle, ambiguous, and profound, the other is conventionalized, pellucid, stereotypical, and repetitious; one is an example of self-conscious literate culture, the other of popular culture.[11]

Tolbert suggests that Mark's audience was a popular one that may have included many women who were attracted to the new gospel of freedom.[12] Thus, the highly political nature of the writing is no accident. As we enter into our study of the gospel of Mark, we need to make an effort to untangle the many contradictions involved in interpretation. Myers suggests three themes that can help our endeavor: repentance, "a concrete process of turning away from empire"; resistance against economic empires; and nonviolence.[13]

These themes and assumptions lead to the following view of the gospel of Mark for our times: "Mark [is] an ideological narrative, the manifesto of an early Christian community in its war of myths with the dominant social order and its political adversaries."[14]

The Historical-Economic Context of The Gospel of Mark

Jesus' primary audience was the oppressed peasants of Galilee, who lived in desperate poverty, illness, and hunger. Jesus makes them the subjects of history, and forever ends the "culture of silence of oppressed peoples."[15] The assumption that Jesus was from the poor rather than from the elite is a frequent theme in contemporary worship. Our religious holidays focus on his birth as a homeless person in Bethlehem, his baptism by the outcast John, and his death as a criminal. In spite of these popular images, he has been interpreted primarily as a religious figure for which his social location is romantic but not essential to his message. That is, Jesus could have been born anywhere, and the religious message would have been the same—people can be saved through faith in Jesus Christ. "Confess his name, repent of sins, become an active member of the church, and you will be saved." My interpretation rejects this approach as unbiblical; that is, I believe that an accurate understanding of the New Testament depends on a view of Jesus that accepts the material and historical reality of his life.[16] We need to understand the sociohistorical context of his life in order to understand his role as savior, just as we need to understand the economic realities of those who come to the church for care.

Four things are particularly important about the Bible and first-century Palestine in our context:

1. *Jesus' community and Mark's community.* Several conclusions can be drawn from the date and location of Mark's gospel (Galilee between 66 and 70 C.E.):[17] (a) While not identical, the political and economic realities of Jesus' ministry and Mark's life were similar. Rome was the imperial power, and much of the intrigue of life in Palestine was between the warring factions over accommodation, resistance, and revolt. (b) Mark was writing his gospel in order to argue that Jesus' way of resistance and nonviolence was an appropriate response to oppression for his community just as it had been in Jesus' own day. (c) Mark sympathized with the dispossessed poor of his day and argued that Jesus represented the same social class.

2. *Mixed economy.* We must be careful not to read back into Mark our own assumptions about economic reality. In previous chapters we have engaged in a thoroughly modern discussion of capital, labor, and land as abstract ideas that create systems of wealth on a global scale. These ideas were not available in first-century Palestine. Rather, the economic system was pre-capitalist—a plural economy in a time of transition. Myers describes the economic system of the poor in Palestine as reciprocity, redistribution, and tribute systems.

The reciprocity system comes from the long history of the Israelites as tribal kinship systems within which wealth was freely shared according to certain traditions. "Among members of a family, goods and services were freely given (full reciprocity). Among members of a cadet line within a clan, gifts would be given, but an eye would be kept on the balanced return-flow of countergifts (weak reciprocity)."[18] Families or clans were interdependent economically, and each person got what he or she needed within certain assumptions of what each deserved. Recall the Lorenzo family in Nicaragua described in chapter 7, whose money and resources were pooled, and everyone's survival was the goal. Even the daughter living in North America frequently sent gifts to ensure that her family could repay debts they incurred with neighbors.

The redistribution system originally centered in a religious space. A larger circle of tribes collected resources in a central location, usually the temple, for redistribution during times of hardship, such as during drought or when support for specialized communities of artisans and military forces was needed. This system was initially a creative plan for the health and security of larger communities (remember the dreams of Joseph in Egypt), but later it introduced possibilities for corruption and class conflict. That is, the poor often lost out on their share of resources when the redistribution system was organized in an unfair and exclusive way. Redistribution also made possible the rise of large estates where peasants worked for low wages with little influence over the distribution of resources.

Myers argues that both the reciprocity and redistribution systems were operating in Roman Palestine.[19] The poor survived through reciprocity ethics, that is, sharing whatever they had with family and neighbors so that all had a chance. The temple in Jerusalem was a massive redistribution system, and Galilee was one of the major producers of agricultural goods for the temple economy. Because the system did not function fairly, many of the peasants from Galilee were extremely poor and often stigmatized by the educated elites of Jerusalem. Conflict between the suffering poor and the religious leaders who ran the redistribution system was frequent, and Galilee was often the site of potential banditry and rebellion.[20] The idea that the Messiah might come from Galilee would have been a scandal. It was not unexpected that a peasant leader from Galilee would protest the injustice of the redistribution system, but it was surprising for such a leader to gain a wide hearing with his questions, retorts, and wisdom. Thus, the conflict between Jesus and the religious leaders was economic as well as religious. In fact, making a distinction between religious, economic, and political systems would have been nonsense to Jesus and other first-century leaders.

The tribute system: Overlaying the reciprocal and redistribution systems was the Roman colonial system, which was based on paying tribute to Rome and, frequently, supplying slave labor for the Roman projects. A system was organized to collect these tributes. After paying half their income for rent, the Galilean peasants were subject to taxes from Herod and the temple taxes.[21] Thus, the tax burden on the poor, especially on peasants who produced food products, was enormous. Those who managed to hold on to their land were forced to give most of their produce to Rome and to the temple. Many peasants lost their land because they could not survive with such a burden. This led to the rise of large landowners who hired the landless peasants for meager wages, often below subsistence. Galilee was oppressed on many levels. "This makes it all the more remarkable that rural and village Galilee is placed at the narrative and ideological center of Mark's story, in explicit tension with both Jerusalem and the Hellenistic cities."[22]

3. *Political conflict.* During the time of Jesus, about which Mark was writing, Palestine was occupied by the Roman imperial government and ruled by Herod and Pilate, regional rulers installed by the Romans. The best known Jewish groups were the Chief Priests, Pharisees, Essenes, and Zealots. Myers argues that there were many popular resistance activities whose presence can be deduced from ancient texts, but which are not as obvious in the literature from the period. He refers to the social bandits who helped redistribute wealth to the poor, and *sicarii,* or dagger men, who engaged in assassination of Jewish collaborators. In addition, there

were "numerous spontaneous popular uprisings, not unlike the slave rebellions we know of in Rome. Often these were nonviolent, although usually put down with brutal military force."[23] Myers also argues that there was a third type of resistance, what he calls "action or sign prophets...leaders who performed or promised symbolic acts that heralded liberation," and invoked powerful images such as wilderness and exodus to dramatize their complaints and resistance.[24]

Given the diverse forms of violent and nonviolent resistance to Roman rule and Jewish collaboration, Mark portrayed Jesus' resistance as one type among others. "Mark vigorously engages these popular prophets in a war of myths over the proper interpretation of apocalyptic ideology and practice."[25]

The politics during the time of Jesus was parallel to but different from the politics during Mark's time. When Mark wrote, Palestine continued to be a colony of Rome, and the burden of control through tribute and slave labor kept the masses in extreme poverty. However, his was a later time with its own dynamics, including a successful, though short-lived, revolt and the destruction of the temple in Jerusalem, which changed everything. "Several factors conspired to make the revolt inevitable: the poor economic and political performance of, and endemic corruption within, the Roman colonial administration; the equivocation and exploitation of the collaborating Jewish elite; and the diverse currents of resurgent Jewish nationalism and peasant disillusionment."[26]

Although the revolt successfully gained control of the temple in Jerusalem, disagreements among the Jewish factions and the reassertion of Roman military strength led to eventual defeat.

> Distant from the drama of power-broking and ideological struggle in Jerusalem, [the peasants] were left defenseless before the avenging wrath of the Roman counterinsurgency program, betrayed on the one hand by their regional commander Josephus who defected to the Romans, and on the other by brigand leaders such as John who abandoned Galilee to join the struggle in Jerusalem. It is not difficult to understand, therefore, that someone such as Mark, writing from the perspective of the Galilean poor, might well have brooked little hope in the insurrection.[27]

It might have been apparent to a keen observer that a violent revolution was unlikely to succeed, given the strength and determination of the Roman Empire. Thus, the words of Jesus about nonviolence may have appealed to Mark as a political strategy as well as a theological principle.

4. *The purity and debt systems.* In order to understand Mark's gospel, we need to understand the symbolic order that had been evolving for hundreds of years, namely, the purity and debt systems.

The purity system developed during the long history of Judaism as a set of rules that established religious and ethnic identity. "Jews could be identified by special *times* (Sabbath), special *things* (diet) and special *bodily marks* (circumcision)."[28] Impurity resulted when times, things, or persons were out of place. We are familiar with the cry of the lepers, "unclean, unclean," to alert others to stay away.

While a purity system may seem natural and self-evident to the group whose identity depends on it, it is often difficult for outsiders to comprehend. For example, when we read about the purity rules in Leviticus, we lack a context for understanding how the system worked. In its simplest form, purity assumes that things are supposed to be a certain way, and pollution or impurity occurs when something or someone is out of place. As Myers suggests, a bucket of dirt in a flower pot is considered artful, but the same dirt dumped on the living room rug is not.[29]

We can more easily understand a *debt system* because modern capitalism is based on loans, interest, and obligations to pay what is promised. However, the first-century debt system was very different from ours in the twenty-first century since the poor lived within a reciprocity and redistribution system rather than in a contractual system such as ours. "In Palestine, social power was exclusively determined by kinship and class,"[30] which involved moral obligations to one another. However, the redistribution system was a burden for the poor.[31]

Peasants were required to pay tithes to the Jerusalem temple as part of the redistribution system. In addition, they were required to pay fees and bring sacrifices to the temple priests when they broke the purity laws. The peasants were mostly farmers who could not keep themselves pure according to the law because they had to work for a living and touch unclean things, incurring impurity on a daily basis. As a result, they were expected to pay fees to restore purity whenever they went to temple or synagogue. In addition, anyone who was sick was impure and had to pay certain fees. The Markan stories about lepers, the blind and lame, and the woman with a flow of blood illustrate impurity. Restoring purity was expensive. When Jesus healed such people, he was bypassing the purity system and objecting to the debt system that contributed to the poverty of the poor.

> The major obstacles to rigorous conformity to the demands of the [purity] system for ordinary persons were economic. The daily circumstances of their lives and trades, especially for the peasantry, continually exposed them to contagion, and they simply could not afford the outlay of either time or money/goods involved in ritual cleansing processes.[32]

We are interested here in how the purity and debt systems functioned as a part of economic oppression. While purity had an important identity function for the Israelites, and the redistribution system created short-term debt for the purpose of future security, both systems were turned into systems of oppression in first-century Palestine. In Mark's stories, Jesus frequently criticized how these two systems kept the poor in an economically vulnerable position.

One of the tensions in Palestine was how the peasants, who could not keep themselves unpolluted in the midst of poverty, were to handle their uncleanness. The debate between the Sadducees, Pharisees, and Essenes is important to note here. The Sadducees were the power group in control of the temple, and they benefited the most when the poor brought their sacrifices to purify themselves and their families. Thus, they were conservative in maintaining the purity and debt systems as they were. The Pharisees wanted to reform the system by extending the purity laws into the countryside. However, the struggle between the two groups was also about politics and economics. The Sadducees wanted to maintain their power and privilege centered in the temple; the Pharisees wanted to decentralize the purity and debt systems, which would make their group more essential to the religious practice.[33] "The Essenes responded in yet a third fashion. For them the solution to dilemmas of purity lay not in the present system, nor in reform to a lower common denominator, but in a withdrawal from the social mainstream in order to preserve rigorous observance...All three responses, however, have one crucial goal in common: the purity code itself is upheld as central."[34] Mark's gospel opposes all three groups on the basis of the economic and political interests of the peasants from Galilee.

Because Galilee was one of the primary agricultural regions that produced food for Jerusalem, the burden of tithing was on its shoulders. The peasants knew that the priests were already rich landowners themselves, so the tithing system was an additional injustice on top of unfair rents. The tension between Galilee and Jerusalem had its roots in this injustice, and resentments developed on both sides. The Jerusalem elite looked down on the farmers of Galilee, and the peasants resisted oppression in many direct and indirect ways.[35]

While the Sadducees and Pharisees competed for control of the purity and debt system, and even the Zealots eventually hoped to gain control of it for their own benefit, Mark objected to the system itself. His Jesus called for the overthrow of the temple, not its reform.[36] "Rome's strategy of allowing limited internal autonomy was based upon, as in so many neocolonial formations today, the cooperation of the native aristocracy."[37]

Into this system of colonialism, purity, and debt came alternative strategies for dealing with the interests of various groups. As we saw in part 2, every dominant oppressive system stimulates various forms of accommodation, resistance, and rebellion. This was also true in the first century, when Jesus lived. Myers lists four different approaches to the oppression: (a) *Collaboration.* There was an elite class of leaders, mostly in Jerusalem, who believed that only cooperation with Rome would enable the Jews to survive this period of history. They were willing to trade political and economic allegiance in exchange for limited local autonomy to continue the religious practices in the temple. Their biggest problem was that the unruly masses often revolted.[38] (b) *Renewal.* The Pharisees and Essenes were renewal movements that represented competition to the temple priests. They hoped to build alternative political movements away from Jerusalem, but they did not represent an effective alternative to the "symbolic order" of the past.[39] (c) *Revolt.* The Zealots represented the military overthrow of Rome for the sake of restoring temple-centered Judaism. Their movement was critical of Roman rule and Jewish collaboration, but still maintained hope that the temple redistribution system could work fairly.[40] (d) *Nonalignment.* Asserting that Mark's approach is different from these groups, Myers identifies it as a manifesto that was "alienated, confrontative, and nonaligned."[41]

> I believe Mark's gospel to be such a document, articulating a grassroots social discourse that is at once both subversive and constructive...Though sympathetic to the socio-economic and political grievances of the rebels, Mark was compelled to repudiate their call to a defense of Jerusalem. This was because, according to his understanding of the teaching and practice of a Nazarene prophet, executed by Rome some thirty-five years earlier, the means (military) and ends (restorationist) of the liberation struggle were fundamentally counterrevolutionary.[42]

In this section we have examined the social and economic context for Mark's narrative, both in the time of Jesus and a generation later when the gospel was written. Although the situation had changed in many ways, the same system of Roman-Jewish colonial oppression that had kept the Galilean peasants poor in Jesus' time was still in place in Mark's time. The overlapping economies of the redistribution and tribute systems functioned at a disadvantage to the poor. The people survived mainly through their generous reciprocity with one another, while the redistribution system brought great wealth to the temple elites, and the tribute system brought great wealth to Rome. All this functioned within a symbolic world of purity and debt, a system that had in previous centuries maintained Jewish identity, but which had become corrupt because of its treatment of the poor. This is the social and economic context in which we can understand Mark's story of Jesus.

Mark's Story of Jesus

Mark portrayed Jesus as a popular resistance leader from Galilee with three strategies for bringing religious transformation for his people.

1. *Calling and converting the disciples.* Like many other resistance leaders, Jesus surrounded himself with a group of disciples who would help organize the community and develop symbolic actions to bring change. However, part of the drama of Mark was the slowness of the disciples to understand the vision that Jesus taught and their eventual betrayal when faced with the dangers of confronting the powers. "This tragedy is, however, reversed by the promise that because Jesus lives, the discipleship adventure can continue (Mk. 16:6f)."[43] The work that the disciples cannot endure becomes the work of the church.

2. *Empowering the poor.* Jesus had come to bring healing to the poor, to release them from the bonds of the purity and debt system. Through exorcisms, healings, feedings, and teachings, he spoke to their needs, and they followed him in great numbers. The climax of their relationship was the entry into Jerusalem, which quickly soured when Jesus failed to call for a violent insurrection. The crowds called for the crucifixion of Jesus, who disappointed their revolutionary hopes (Mk. 15:13–14).[44]

3. *Confronting the religious leaders.* From the beginning of his ministry, Jesus confronted the religious leaders by challenging the purity rules and engaging in debates about the meaning of the law. The leaders quickly opposed his ministry and began to plot how they would control or destroy him. They seemed to be outmatched in many of the events, including the entry into Jerusalem; however, by infiltrating the disciple group and conspiring with the Romans, they succeeded in condemning him to death. In their supposed victory, they were shown to the readers of Mark to be corrupt leaders.[45]

It should be noted that all three subplots contribute to the climactic crisis of Jesus' arrest and execution, and are gathered together in the passion narrative.

> In the final scenes of the story we see the defecting disciples, the disillusioned crowd, and the hostile authorities, all juxtaposed to Jesus, who alone goes the way of the cross. These three narrative strands also represent the key aspects in Jesus' program: confronting the old order, bringing liberation to the poor, and constructing an alternative order.[46]

Part I: Confronting the Old Order

For this section, I am following the outline from Myers that shows the literary parallelism.[47]

Events	Jewish side	Gentile side
Inaugural exorcism, fame	1:21–28	5:1–20
Popular ministry	1:29–39	6:54–56
Symbolic healings	5:21–43	7:24–37
Wilderness feedings	6:32–44	8:1–10
Noncomprehension of loaves	6:51f.	8:14–21

The first chapter of Mark introduced themes that will be developed throughout the gospel. The baptism of Jesus of Galilee by John in the Jordan signaled a break with the normal expectations of young men who wanted to be respectable. Myers interprets the baptism of Jesus as a real repentance in terms of rejecting the obligations of citizenship in a colonized state.

> [Jesus' baptism] is a genuine act of repentance. As such it ends his participation in the structures and values of society. It concludes his involvement in the moral order into which he was born...The entire redemptive process of Jewish society as it is maintained by the institutions through which power is ordered,...the totality of the Jewish-Roman social construction of reality, has been terminated. All the debts that have been incurred under this elitist ordering of power and its community life have been cancelled. The death experience of repentance has redeemed Jesus from his comprehensive indebtedness and the prescribed ways and means of discharging his obligations. He has become wholly unobliged.[48]

Soon he called disciples to join him in his unobliged state of existence. "He bade others join him in abandoning all socio-economic responsibility."[49] The apocalyptic dualism of a new order in opposition to an old order is reinforced in many of these opening symbols. After this, Jesus engaged in three forms of ministry: "community building, healing and exorcism, and political conflict."[50]

A series of stories beginning in Mark 5:1 helps us understand the symbolic nature of Jesus' ministry. One of them, the story of the healing of the Gerasene demoniac, is important for several reasons, including its parallel to mental illness in situations of colonization.

> The demoniac represents collective anxiety over Roman imperialism. What Fanon called the "colonization of the mind," in which the community's anguish over its subjugation is repressed and then turned in on itself, is perhaps implied by Mark's report that the man inflicts violence on himself (5:5). The formidable grip by which the powers hold the community is vividly portrayed in the opening lines (5:3–5). Mark carefully uses phrases that he has already loaded with political

significance: no one was able to bind *(deo)* the man, for he had broken his shackles many times; "there was no one strong *(oudeis ischuen)* enough to master him" (5:3f.). This exorcism is thus another key episode in Jesus-the-stronger-one's struggle to "bind the strong man." In the synagogue exorcism he was identified with the scribal class, now with Caesar's armies.[51]

This story is parallel to a previous healing story of the man with the unclean spirit in the synagogue in Capernaum. The two stories, one among the Hebrews and one among the Gentiles, show Jesus' healing of mental illness in a charged political situation. The people in both cases are outcasts because of their strange behavior, and thus in violation of cultural and purity codes in both communities. However, rather than rejecting them as impure, according to the law, Jesus took them seriously and engaged with them.[52] In Jesus' view, they are possessed and can be brought back to their right minds with the right action. What is this possession? Today we can understand it as mental illness brought on by the trauma of poverty and oppression. Those who are mentally ill are members of the community who are living out in their bodies the contradictions of poverty and oppression. When these two men with unclean spirits saw Jesus, they understood that his mission was to challenge the traditional power arrangements, and they tried to disclose his identity to others. However, Jesus commanded the demons to leave, whereupon the men became unpossessed and went about the community proclaiming "how much Jesus had done" for them (Mk. 5:20). The crowds were amazed and frightened in both cases. In Gerasene, the people urged Jesus to leave the community because they were afraid and didn't want to be the center of a rebellion that brought down more oppression on their community. These stories reveal some of the central themes of Jesus' mission–to bring healing to the poor and to challenge the possession of the people by violent ideologies.

Next, Jesus made two dangerous sea crossings where the disciples were afraid and Jesus calmed the winds. Myers reminds us that each sea crossing went back and forth between Jewish and Gentile communities, thus signaling Jesus' rejection of ethnic boundaries that separate the poor of different communities from one another. The primary audience in these stories was the disciples, who became afraid of what would happen to them. Jesus rebuked them for their lack of faith: "Why are you afraid? Have you still no faith?" (Mk. 4:40). Jesus engaged in the task of making the disciples understand that his mission was not a struggle for dominance, but a struggle for a new kind of community where dominance was not normal. Yet they did not understand.[53] How could they understand when Jesus suggested a radical alternative to everything they had known previously?

These harrowing sea stories intend to dramatize the difficulties facing the kingdom community as it tries to overcome the institutionalized social divisions between Jew and Gentile. Through this metaphorical action the community struggles to make the "passage" to integration (hence the difficulty is always en route to the gentile shore). The wind and sea as obstacles derive from the ancient Semitic mythic personification of cosmic forces of chaos and destruction. It is no wonder the disciples demonstrate reluctance: all the power of the established "symbolic universe" of segregation oppose this journey. And no doubt the real-life social hostility to such a project of integration threatened to "drown" the community. But Mark insists that Jesus will rescue this project and silence the winds of opposition.[54]

The sea crossings bracket two healing narratives: the raising of Jairus's daughter and the healing of the woman with a flow of blood, what Myers collectively refers to as "the healing of two daughters." Jairus, a member of the synagogue leadership, asked Jesus to come heal his daughter. On the way, Jesus heard the petition of a "poverty-stricken woman," and he responded to her need. But the delay meant that he arrived too late for Jairus's daughter, who had died. The drama of the story revolves around the contrast between the two healings.[55]

> Jairus was from the elite Jewish class, head of his family and a leader in the synagogue. The fact that he came to Jesus showed the ambivalence among the elite about their position. However, these two stories enabled Mark to show how Jesus treated everyone the same. In contrast to Jairus, the woman who sought healing was poor and an outcast from society.[56]

In these stories, Mark revealed the bankruptcy of the purity and debt systems. Under the law, a woman with a flow of blood was unclean and had to be purified before she could participate in the community. However, her continual flow of blood meant that she could never be included. She had already sought out the authorities of her day for help, and they offered to help her, on a fee-for-service basis. As a result of their incompetent help, she was impoverished and worse off than before. In these few words, Mark showed his attitude toward the purity system, which marginalized people by sets of arbitrary rules, then required payment from them that aggravated their poverty. This woman was a prototype of the peasants of the world. She was defined as unclean, and then was indebted to the system that demanded that she become clean. When Jesus called for the forgiveness of debts, he was talking about women such as this, women who exist in every poor country in the world today.[57]

While Jesus was busy helping the woman with the flow of blood, Jairus's daughter died. Myers suggests that this death was a commentary on the synagogue system. Not only was Jairus's daughter dead, but the temple and synagogue system was sick and about to die. The woman with the flow of blood was a commentary on the bankruptcy of the purity and debt system. Everything the elite leaders had done to help had only made her worse, and along with her, thousands of peasants in Galilee.

> The object lesson can only be that if Judaism wishes to "be saved and live" (5:23), it must embrace the "faith" of the kingdom: a new social order with equal status for all. This alone will liberate the lowly outcast and snatch the "noble" from death..."the tax collectors and prostitutes are making their way into the kingdom of God before you" (Mt. 21:31).[58]

Following these two stories of healing of Jewish women comes the healing of two Gentiles: the Syro-Phoenician woman who confronts Jesus with "even the dogs get the crumbs from the table," and a deaf man who is healed with Jesus' saliva.

The story of the Syro-Phoenician (Gentile) woman illustrates the hostility between Jews and Gentiles. When she came to Jesus for healing for a daughter with an unclean spirit, Jesus said that the children of Israel should be fed before the dogs. However, the woman did not let Jesus get by with this dismissal and asked for the crumbs of the gospel. In response, Jesus respected her wishes and healed her daughter. Until recently, interpreters have ignored the implicit racism in Jesus' statement and viewed him as providing a test of her faith – to see how persistent she would be in her desire for healing. More recently, some interpreters have seen this as a developmental change in Jesus' understanding of his ministry as he moved from a parochial to a more universal vision.[59] The consequence of the story is again to challenge divisions by race, gender, and class that keep the poor from forming communities of solidarity and acting against their oppression.

The final healing act in this section is Jesus' giving the deaf man hearing and speech. In addition to its significance as another occasion for healing a Gentile, it serves as an opportunity for Mark to comment on the disciples' understanding. "Jesus can make the gentile deaf hear, but not, it will turn out, his own disciples!"[60] "Do you have ears, and fail to hear?" (Mk. 8:18). These two pairs of healings demonstrate Mark's mastery in using narrative action to illustrate the ideology of inclusion, which is the cornerstone to the new social order being constructed by Jesus. The social dynamics of status and honor, fundamental in the life of antiquity, have been turned upside down to make way for the outcast Jew and the alien Gentile.[61]

Mark 6:30–42 and Mark 8:1–10 contain two stories of miraculous feedings, which Myers calls "the economics of sharing." I am reminded of the way the peasants of Solentiname in Nicaragua interpreted the narratives about the feedings.

Rebecca: He was showing them what love could do in the world, that everybody would have enough. Through his miracle there was enough for everyone, everyone ate, and there was some left over. And that would be the miracle that love would perform in the world. Instead of the situation that we're in, when one person eats and the other doesn't. Selfishness is to blame for the scarcity of everything. Through love there'll be abundance for everybody. He performed that miracle so that we could see what love can do.[62]

The miracle was that the people discovered a different kind of economic reality. Rather than buying the food in town according to the economic system of the time, Jesus distributed it to the people and urged them to share. And there was enough for everyone, a clear example of the redistribution system that the peasants were quite familiar with. Jesus thus created the eucharistic symbol based on the daily life of the peasants: in the new community, the abundance of God will provide for all by creating a community of economic sharing that responds to the needs of everyone rather than the accumulation of wealth for individual enjoyment.[63] Ernesto Cardenal interprets the scripture in the context of the Nicaraguan peasant reality:

In the Greek there is a single word, *koinonia*, for the Eucharistic communion and for the communion of wealth, the commonwealth, and it's because for the first Christians the two things were the same. Saint Paul says that to place wealth in common is the sacrifice that pleases God, and that is like saying that perfect communism is the true Eucharist ...What this all means (and this is what the disciples probably didn't understand) is that we are called upon to form a humanity with the unity of people, a society in the image of the Trinity.[64]

Myers believes that such values of economic sharing were practiced in the early church and were self-consciously a part of Mark's interpretation of Jesus. "The community re-creates the redistributive system: private ownership of land and houses is abandoned in favor of cooperative economics. This model is not intended to engender corporate affluence, but to provide surplus on behalf of the poor."[65]

In this chapter, I have summarized the reality of the world for Jesus and Mark in terms of economic reality and violence. The overlapping systems of reciprocity, redistribution, and tribute systems created landlessness, extreme poverty, and dependence among the Galilean peasants, the formation community for both Jesus and Mark. Mark reports that Jesus came into this world as an advocate for his community in opposition to the elite religious leaders who cooperated with the colonial system and in opposition to the Zealots who wanted to control the temple. Jesus was "alienated, confrontative, and nonaligned,"[66] representing a third way of challenging the corrupt symbolic order. In chapter 12, we will continue our exploration of the gospel of Mark for its insight into the disciple community of economic sharing, nonviolence, and love.

12

Mark's Alternative Economic Vision

Training the Disciples about Love and Power

In the second part of his gospel, Mark changes the focus of the story from the crowds to the training of the disciples. Jesus begins to explain to the disciples what is going to happen and how they must be willing to follow the way of the cross, which Myers interprets as the way of nonviolent, direct action against the symbolic world of the dominant powers. Their inability to understand the difficulty of the journey of genuine social transformation provides much of the drama of Mark 9:30–10:52.

> A discipleship of the cross makes a difficult demand: the application of nonviolence to every sphere of life. As Gandhi puts it, "If one does not practice nonviolence in one's personal relations with others and hopes to use it in bigger affairs, one is vastly mistaken." Genuine revolutionary transformation occurs "from the bottom up."[1]

Nonviolence of the Heart (Mk. 9:30–50)

> "Whoever wants to be first must be last of all and servant of all."
> (Mk. 9:35)

As they were walking along, Jesus overheard the disciples arguing about who would be the greatest in his kingdom. The repetition of the story twice in this section, 9:33–37 and 10:35–45, shows that Mark considers this conversation important. How will the disciples be able to lead the transformation Jesus has envisioned if they are still engaged in competitive power against one another and are eager to be dominant over those outside the group?

> The way of nonviolence means being attentive to the actual dynamics of social power and privilege among family, friends,

183

and neighbors. The follower of Jesus must expect the fate of a subversive, but the ultimate choice of the cross must also be daily reproduced in the concrete life of the messianic community.[2]

The poor, as represented by the disciples, were aware of their oppression, but having internalized the values of the dominant system, they were confused, left in what Marx calls "false consciousness."[3] They were excited by Jesus' power and the possibility that the system could be changed, but they could not imagine any system except the one they knew, and they could not imagine any improvement except that they would be the elite. So they dreamed of how good it would be when Jesus came into his power and glory and they no longer lived under the heel of the oppressor. What they didn't understand was that Jesus was calling them to a new vision, one in which oppressors and oppressed would be integrated into one community and where the economy would supply an abundance for all. The possibility of such a generous God was beyond their imagination. "The disciples desire glory, honor, and status; they think highly of themselves, more highly indeed than they occasionally think of the One who selected them to be with him...Their values remain those of 'this generation'; they are not on the side of God."[4]

The disciples also did not understand what was involved in moving their community toward such a vision of generosity and abundance. Neither the imaginations of the elite nor of the poor would be changed without struggle and suffering. The structures of power that preserved injustice would not change without exacting a price from those who challenged them. Jesus was shifting his attention from analysis of the power structures that needed to be changed to the disciple community and how it must embody equality, nonviolence, and love.

Nonviolence in the Family (Mk. 10:1–16)

"Whoever does not receive the kingdom of God as a little child will never enter it." And he took them up in his arms, laid his hands on them, and blessed them. (Mk. 10:15–16)

Groups who look to scripture for justification for modern family values easily misinterpret Jesus' teachings about the family. What is usually lacking in such discussions is knowledge of the first-century context of religion and ethics. Some argue that Jesus considered divorce to be against God's holy law; others argue that Jesus practiced gender equality within a first-century context. Myers suggests that we cannot deduce from these concise words a full morality about gender, marriage, and parenting. But we do learn that Jesus' principle of nonviolence applies to the family just as much as it applies to direct political action campaigns against the powers and principalities. In first-century divorce laws, women had no possibility of taking initiative to protect their children or even themselves.

> Mark refuses to overlook the *actual* relations of power, no matter how "sacred" the institution. The "least" in this concrete case is the woman, and Mark is making clear to his community that she can be protected only if she is no longer treated as an object, but as an equal subject, in situations of conflict resolution.[5]

Any community that ignores the problem of violence in the family while advocating nonviolence in public life is living a contradiction. Jesus did not exempt the family from his ethical gaze. The divorce laws of the first century were written to benefit men over women, and Jesus' attempts to empower women in the family are consistent with his attempt to empower women within the disciple community.

Likewise, Jesus applied nonviolence to children and their relationships with parents and other adults within the community. "Jesus rescues children from the margins of the new community and places them at its *center* ('in their midst,' 9:36)...[Children] represent an actual class of exploited *persons*...We must weed out the structures and practices of violence at their roots...The validity of nonviolence must pertain to the most basic building block of human social existence: the family...The child is always the primary victim of practices of domination within the family."[6] A new social order *cannot* be constructed unless and until we have dealt with the very foundations of oppression.

> [A] primary site in which nonviolence must take hold is that of the family/household. The principle of equality obtains in marriage, and must be preserved even in tragic situations of family rupture. Children are recognized to be the primary victims, and the "circle of contempt" in the family system is radically challenged by Jesus' demand that the kingdom be "received as a child."[7]

The ethic of family nonviolence advocated by Jesus can be a major resource for helping the church change its understanding and practices of care for families where there are abusive patterns. Power must be exercised for the purposes of care of those who are vulnerable, not to justify the unjust behaviors of those with social authority, whether men over women, adults over children, or caregivers over persons with disabilities.

Economic Justice for Households (Mk. 10:17–31)

> "You lack one thing; go, sell what you own, and give the money to the poor, and you will have treasure in heaven; then come, follow me." (Mk. 10:21)

This is one of the most difficult verses in the Bible for middle-class Christian families in the U.S. and Europe. Here Jesus should not be interpreted less than literally. How can those with more than their share of the earth's riches become part of the revolutionary movement for justice in the name of Jesus? Persons from middle-class and wealthy situations often have good intentions and would like to act in ways that bring more economic justice in the world. Witness the tremendous works of charity throughout the world and the volunteers who go on work projects to help those in need. The rich young ruler seems at first to be a likely candidate for repentance and resistance to economic injustice. "Good Teacher, what must I do to inherit eternal life?" (Mk. 10:17).

> The man obviously represented fertile ground; he recognized Jesus' authority; he wants to learn; and he had already established his religious zeal by his obedience to the law. In an extraordinary phrase, the narrator notes that "Jesus looking upon him loved him." Jesus responds to the quality of the man; surely, he is the "good earth."[8]

Jesus' answer seems to take the young man's question seriously, and he invited him to become a disciple, leaving everything to join with the disciples in their movement for justice. However, while the young man had followed the rules of piety in his interpersonal life, he had not examined his economic life, and he did not anticipate the changes that following Jesus would entail. Thus, he lived a double life, a split between his private morality in his interpersonal world and his public morality of economic decisions. Mary Ann Tolbert suggests that the parable of the sower provides the answer, especially the image of the seed that landed among the thorns. "The rich man typifies fertile ground in which the seed is sown but no fruit can be produced, for growth of the word is choked off by 'the delight in riches.'"[9] Myers shows us that the issue was complicated by the man's probable role in the first-century economy.

> As we have seen in the discussion of the class structure of Mark's Palestine, landowners represented the most politically powerful social stratum. Within this revelation, the story of the man abruptly finishes, as if the point is obvious. As far as Mark is concerned, the man's wealth has been gained by "defrauding" the poor—he was not "blameless" at all—for which he must make restitution. For Mark, the law is kept only through concrete acts of justice, not the facade of piety.[10]

The rich young ruler, like those of us who are bourgeois Christians, did not want to look at the way in which his riches were obtained or the way in which they were spent. To his detriment, he had limited his search for salvation to a very small area. Now Jesus was bringing home the radical challenge of the gospel. The disciples were shocked by this scene and later engaged Jesus in a debate about wealth. Again they revealed their internalization of the dominant values, which saw the wealthy as somehow successful and more righteous than others. They had made the system work for them; shouldn't they be emulated? No, Jesus says, the kin-dom turns everything upside down.

> Solidarity is extended from the family system to the economic system. *The only* way to salvation for the rich is by the redistribution of their wealth; that is, the eradication of class oppression...What is humanly impossible is not for the God for whom all things are possible.[11]

Jesus is describing liberation from the economic rules of the dominant order in favor of another way of seeing life and community. In that new community, satisfactions beyond all imagination will come.

> "Truly I tell you, there is no one who has left house or brothers or sisters or mother or father or children or fields, for my sake and for the sake of the good news, who will not receive a hundredfold now in this age—houses, brothers and sisters, mothers and children, and fields with persecutions—and in the age to come eternal life. But many who are first will be last, and the last will be first." (Mk. 10:29–30)

Nonviolent Leadership (Mk. 10:32–52)

> "The cup that I drink you will drink; and with the baptism with which I am baptized, you will be baptized; but to sit at my right hand or at my left is not mine to grant, but it is for those for whom it has been prepared." (Mk. 10:39–40)

In this section, Jesus returns to the image of the way of the cross. The disciples do not understand. They again ask for places of honor in the coming messianic kingdom. This leads Jesus into another patient lecture on servant leadership, ending with a dramatic connection between such leadership and the image of the sacraments of eucharist and baptism.

According to Myers, the cup is the symbol of Jesus' blood shed at the crucifixion, and the baptism is the baptism into death. Even the image of sitting at the right or left hand of Jesus points to the men who are crucified alongside Jesus on Golgotha. The disciples are called to share in the life and death of Jesus on the way to Jerusalem, the way of the cross. This is one way that nonviolent leadership becomes true leadership for the new community. "Leadership belongs only to those who learn and follow the way of nonviolence—who are 'prepared' not to dominate but to serve and to suffer at Jesus' side."[12]

Tolbert interprets the cup as a symbol with multiple meanings:

> Jesus' prayer in Gethsemane…comes at a moment of great crisis, for the hour is now upon him; the rhetorical play between the cup of testimony at the supper and the cup of suffering before him provides the audience with a profound sense of the sacrifice he is about to make "for many"; and the agony in his own psyche is appropriately and heroically resolved in favor of God's will.[13]

Recent womanist and feminist scholars have raised questions about the language of sacrifice and suffering.[14] Sacrifice may be a useful image, they remind us, for those in power and leadership positions who would face censure if they tried to change the structures of oppression that affect many oppressed people. However, for those who are oppressed, there are also images in the New Testament about justice, dignity, image of God, protest, and rebellion. We must remember that Jesus did not preach sacrifice to the crowds of poor people. Since those who benefit from empire have written much New Testament scholarship, the images of suffering and sacrifice often function to reinforce unjust power structures by asking the oppressed to sacrifice for the sake of order. This seems to be a major departure from what Jesus' life and teaching were about. If we interpret Jesus within the prophetic tradition of the love and justice of God, it is wrong to use these metaphors to reinforce servanthood and obedience to unjust powers and principalities.

However, Myers's point about the rigorous internal critique that must occur on an ongoing basis within the liberated community of Jesus' followers is important. Nothing corrupts the liberation movement more than the abuses of power by its own leadership.

> A community cannot be resisting the powers' exercise of domination while reproducing their patterns in its own midst. The revolution must come from the ground up, beginning with the primary sites of social oppression: the family and economic existence. If practiced at the base, then conversely, Gandhi argued, nonviolence becomes the "weapon of the masses which enables a child, a woman, or a decrepit old man to resist the mightiest government."[15]

The nonaligned disciple community has to live with many tensions and possible contradictions. While seeking economic justice and liberation from violence for the poor with spiritual and political force (soul-force in Gandhi), the community must practice its own forms of justice and liberation in the hearts of the people, the intimacy of family life, and the leadership. Sometimes community leadership must struggle with internal contradictions and suffer spiritual agony for the sake of community integrity. Otherwise, the disciple community becomes just another unjust social system that mirrors the injustice of the larger systems of economic exploitation and violence.

In this section we have interpreted Jesus' struggle with the disciples as a political struggle–to understand that the way of the cross leads to dangerous confrontation with the powers that can cause torture and death; to understand that the way of nonviolence and servant leadership applies to all levels of life in the new community, including family life and relationships with children. Whoever is the least has a special claim on the whole community. Until the disciples understand the new set of values built around justice, equality, and love, their actions will lead only to a recapitulation of the dominant values in new forms. The "deafness" of the disciples becomes a ploy by Mark that allows Jesus to spell out the details of his new spiritual and political program for humanity.

> And although the disciples do not "take up their cross and follow" Jesus in this story, Mark assures the reader that they will have their own turn at costly confession (13:9–13)...The meaning of the cross is surely better exegeted by sisters and brothers around the world today who work for justice and liberation under repressive regimes. Those who have suffered interrogation and torture by security forces seeking the names of their comrades know the intense psychological and spiritual trauma generated by the temptation to "save oneself."[16]

Jesus' suffering is an apt metaphor for the consequences of oppression. The image provides fertile ground as a form of identification with the poor in Latin American liberation theology. For those who live under extreme oppression, Jesus' suffering is not a mystery, but a description of everyday life. His experience makes him one of the poor, a peasant from Galilee who led a revolt and brought hope to many who seek justice and empowerment today.

The Passion Narrative

Almost forty percent of Mark's gospel focuses on the dramatic events in Jerusalem. Given the abbreviated ending of Mark compared to the other gospels, there is a sense of tragedy. Everything that Jesus has predicted comes together in a climactic ending.

> In the final scenes of the story we see the defecting disciples, the disillusioned crowd, and the hostile authorities, all juxtaposed to Jesus, who alone goes the way of the cross. These three narrative strands also represent the key aspects in Jesus' program: confronting the old order, bringing liberation to the poor, and constructing an alternative order.[17]

The Eucharistic Meal

The last supper, in the upper room, can be interpreted as part of the education of the disciples about the challenges facing the disciple community when it tries to change individuals and society. The fact that the eucharist became the central metaphor for the imperialist church is a hermeneutical problem for any theology that focuses on economic justice and nonviolence. How the official church after Constantine was able to reverse the meaning of Jesus' murder to support the domination of the world is a historical puzzle. In the following section, I follow certain feminist interpretations of Jesus' death as a tragedy that needs to be redeemed by the faithful actions of the historical disciple community. According to Tolbert, "the supper and Gethsemane were especially heavily weighted with forebodings of failure."[18]

Clearly showing that Jesus and the disciples were part of an underground resistance movement with secret signals and hideouts, Jesus instructed his disciples on the arrangements for the supper: look for a man with a jar of water, follow him, use certain code words, go to a large room, and make preparations. Subsequently Jesus begins the meal by predicting betrayal from within the core leadership of the disciples. The disciples were shocked: "They began to be distressed and to say to him one after another, 'Surely, not I?'" (Mk. 14:19). Actually they will all betray Jesus before the night is over.

Jesus then took the bread and the cup and gave it to the disciples. In this act, says Myers, Jesus invited them to live in solidarity with his life and death. Still challenging the dominance of the temple, Jesus showed them another way of symbolizing their love and commitment to God. "In place of the temple liturgy Jesus offers his 'body'—that is, his messianic practice in life and death. It is this very 'sanctuary/body' opposition that will shape Mark's narrative of Jesus' execution."[19] The practice of revolutionary nonviolence is the new religious ritual in place of temple piety and sacrifices by the poor. The temple will eventually be destroyed, but the disciple community will continue in a new form with new values. "The covenant is indeed broken, but will be renewed in Jesus' blood; thus the 'sacrificial lamb' becomes the 'stricken shepherd.'"[20]

Tolbert expresses a feminist awareness in her interpretation that the bread clearly refers back to the various feedings of the poor where everyone had enough to eat. "Feeding the crowds in the wilderness implicitly connected Jesus' mission with Moses and the children of Israel, who were fed manna in the wilderness by a protecting deity."[21] At the last supper the bread symbolized Jesus' body; later Paul would call this the body of Christ, that is, the new community that nourishes the people. The broken body is a body that is damaged by violence. Out of that violence must come a new community that does not damage people through violence, but nurtures them. As a traditional Chinese Christian prayer says:

Help each of us, gracious God, to live in such magnanimity and restraint that the Head of the church may never have cause to say to any one of us, "This is my body, broken by you." Amen.[22]

Likewise, the cup has many levels of meaning. It is the cup of the fellowship meal, the cup of the eschatological banquet, the cup of a New Testament, the cup of giving one's life for the cause of justice, and the cup of violence done against one's body.

> The mention of all present drinking from the same cup should remind the audience of the inappropriate request of James and John following the third passion prediction, because Jesus had asked them if they could "drink from the cup that I drink" (10:38). Here they indeed drink from the literal cup Jesus uses. However, Jesus' question to them had not been literal but metaphorical. It is not the cup of wine at supper that Jesus insists that they must drink; it is, instead, the "cup" he asks God in Gethsemane to remove from his future (14:36) that he and all his faithful followers must share. Yet, while Jesus is agonizing over that metaphorical cup, James and John along with Peter are fast asleep. That cup they will not prove able to drink.[23]

The contrast between the faithful church and the community where violence is tolerated is crucial for understanding the symbolism of the bread and wine. Out of the tragedy of the violence directed against Jesus will come a new vision of a community without violence, a church that lives every day in protest against the violent practices of unjust systems of power.

The paradox of the eucharist is that even though Jesus was executed, his body tortured, and his blood shed by the dominant powers, the subversive ideology–that love is stronger than evil, nonviolence is stronger than military might, and justice is stronger than corruption–will survive. The shepherd was stricken, but the movement for justice cannot be contained. The disciple community will become a force within history that will not be subdued. No matter how much the dominant powers try to kill off the aspirations of the poor and their charismatic leadership, God will raise up leaders from among the poor again and again. "The myth of the Human One overthrowing the rulers of the age is a revolutionary one that legitimizes resistance to the dominant order, and promises its demise."[24]

The Betrayal by the Disciples

One by one the disciples deserted Jesus at the moment of trial, driven by misunderstanding and genuine terror at the violence of the system they had been challenging. First, Judas conspired with the chief priests on the best way to arrest Jesus. Whatever his motives, whether money or to hasten the confrontation that would bring the messianic kingdom, Judas' action is a misunderstanding of the issues at stake. "'For the Son of Man goes as it is written of him, but woe to that one by whom the Son of Man is betrayed! It would have been better for that one not to have been born'" (Mk. 14:21).

> Judas illustrates or symbolizes one possible consequence of a hardened heart: the betrayal of friends...Moreover, the immediately preceding story (14:3–9) demonstrates the proper use of money to finance an act of love, ministry, and gentleness and thus provides a stark counterbalance to Judas.[25]

Next the disciples slept while Jesus agonized in prayer at Gethsemane. Myers suggests that Jesus' agony is genuine: "Jesus is facing his 'destiny' not with contemplative detachment, but with genuine human terror...Jesus admits to his disciples that he is shaken to the core...Jesus would call one more time for solidarity from the inner circle."[26] But the disciples were not able to endure.

Finally, Peter denied that he knew Jesus during the trial, as predicted by Jesus in 14:30. This is the last betrayal. Now all the disciples had betrayed him, and he was completely alone. Can any social transformation come from such a group? We have to wait for the end of the story to see the answer.

The Powerlessness of the Crowds

Throughout the gospel of Mark, the poor are shown as always having been with Jesus. He grew up as one of them in Galilee. He became an itinerant preacher and healer who brought their needs and complaints to the public square. He was bonded to them by birth, family, and adult commitment. At no time in the gospel does Jesus criticize the poor for their needs or their lack of understanding. In contrast to the disciples, Jesus saw them as being like sheep without a shepherd. How were the people going to hear the gospel if there were no preacher? He used his ministry to empower the crowds that followed him from Galilee to Jerusalem.

According to Myers, receiving a popular message about liberation does not magically transform the consciousness of the masses who have been dominated for generations. The transformation of the imagination of the poor requires dedicated work over decades, and a corresponding change in the power structures that allows the creativity of the people to develop. Given an accurate analysis of the profound consequences of oppression for the masses of people, it is not surprising that they were not ready to support Jesus as he went to his death. While they agreed with his analysis that the system kept them oppressed, they were not ready to change their internal values and risk themselves for an uncertain future. When forced to choose, they still had more faith in the violent revolt represented by Barabbas than in the nonviolent revolution of Jesus. They chose the values they knew over the values that they could not yet understand.

Tolbert suggests another possible interpretation of this part of the story:

> It is probably closer to the conventional expectations of the authorial audience to view the crowds as a narrative chorus whose main function is to reflect whatever action is dominating the story at the moment (much the same role played by the chorus in Greek tragedy) than to see them as a character group in Mark who supported Jesus earlier but who now with great fickleness turn against him.[27]

In this case, rather than being malevolent, the crowd must be seen as powerless to stop the tragedy that is taking place before their eyes. While either of these interpretations is possible, it is important to remember the epistemological authority of the experience of the poor, who know firsthand the reality of economic oppression and violence.

The Conspiracy of the Authorities

> We [must recall] the historical "triangle of power relationships" among the Roman administrators, native Jewish aristocracy, and shifting popular allegiances. That the clerical ruling class collaborated fully with the Romans is clear historically. Next we must keep in mind that Rome was forever vigilant about the threat of latent native kingship movements in client territories throughout the empire.[28]

Conspiracy by the authorities against Jesus is a theme within the whole gospel, beginning with 2:16. The first threat to his life comes early: "The Pharisees went out and immediately conspired with the Herodians against him, how to destroy him" (3:6). Their conspiracy turned to murder: "The chief priests and the scribes were looking for a way to arrest Jesus by stealth and kill him" (14:1). The problem they had to solve was the popularity of Jesus with the poor: "For they said, 'Not during the festival, or there may be a riot among the people'" (14:2).

The illegitimacy of their charges is one theme of Mark's story. From a certain angle, we can understand the panic of the religious authorities about Jesus, because he was effectively challenging the symbolic world of purity, debt, and law on which their power was based. From another angle, Jesus was an advocate for the desperately poor Galilean peasants who were dangerously rebellious against the established order. So he could be labeled a bandit (14:48), a blasphemer (14:64), and a zealot (15:18), and his accusers could feel justified in their charges.

However, from Mark's perspective, these passages show the corruption of those in authority. John the Baptist was beheaded because of the drunken oath taken by Herod; Jesus was arrested through bribery of one of the disciples; the chief priests had to summon false witnesses to accuse him.

> Now the chief priests and the whole council were looking for testimony against Jesus to put him to death; but they found none. For many gave false testimony against him, and their testimony did not agree. Some stood up and gave false testimony against him. (14:55–57)

Mark seems to be demonstrating that corrupt power rules by deceit and lies. There is no legitimate reason by which those with power have control of the political and religious resources. They control people and systems through the abuse of power. Those who condemn Jesus to death are corrupt. They crucify the righteous one. And while they succeed in executing Jesus, their power cannot withstand scrutiny and will fall.

> Mark writes with irony in a way that] bonds the audience even more closely with Jesus, who shares the implied author's ideology, and repels the audience away from all of Jesus' opponents, who are depicted as vicious, violent, envious, mean-spirited, hard-hearted, and narrow men.[29]

Unfortunately, especially in the twentieth century, these passages have been used to foster a virulent anti-Semitism that has had tragic consequences.[30]

Mark's larger point is important to remember: that those with economic and political power always argue that their power is legitimately gained and that their decisions are for the benefit of all. But Mark gives witness that those with power in a world of oppression rule only by corruption, and their corruption must be exposed by nonviolent, direct action in order to destroy the symbolic world that makes oppression seem natural and right.

Jesus' Execution and Responses

Jesus was tortured and executed by the Roman colonial government after a legal trial. After Pilate released Barabbas, the torture and humiliation continued. "After flogging Jesus, [Pilate] handed him over to be crucified" (15:15). One dictionary defines flogging as "to beat severely with a whip or rod,"[31]—a form of torture also used on slaves who attempted to escape the South. Then comes the psychological torture.

> And [the soldiers] clothed him in a purple cloak; and after twisting some thorns into a crown, they put it on him. And they began saluting him, "Hail, King of the Jews!" They struck his head with a reed, spat upon him, and knelt down in homage to him. After mocking him, they stripped him of the purple cloak

and put his own clothes on him. Then they led him out to crucify him. (15:17–20)

Picturing police interrogations in dictator countries or in the inner cities of the U.S. help us understand this scene. Torture is more than physical pain; it is a set of behaviors designed to humiliate and break down the personality of the victim. The short- and long-term consequences of such behaviors, physical pain and post-traumatic stress disorders, are well documented in the literature about how police states create terror in large populations.[32]

Finally, they crucified Jesus, and he died.

After the crucifixion comes a series of stories that represent the various groups in response to Jesus. Jon Berquist suggests that Mark's purpose in telling these stories is to confront the readers with the key question of the gospel: "Will we follow Jesus' teachings or not, and will we believe that Jesus is the Son of God, the embodiment of what God wishes to have done in the world?"[33]

Then the women come to the tomb to provide for Jesus' burial. Myers says the women were Galileans who had followed Jesus to Jerusalem and that they fill in the gap left by the betrayal and abandonment of the male disciples. "In other words, not *all* deserted Jesus at Gethsemane. The women now become the 'lifeline' of the discipleship narrative...an alternative to the three men of the former inner circle (Peter, James, and John); they are the true disciples."[34] Tolbert adds:

> Jesus' agony in Gethsemane, his courage at the trial, and his despair on the cross create a deep empathy for him in the audience...Moreover, through irony the author has pilloried both the Twelve and Jesus' opponents, encouraging the audience to look elsewhere for those who will prove faithful to Jesus' heroic example in the face of glaring injustice and evil. When the women are introduced, they become the focus of these hopes, for one so badly wants someone to do well by Jesus.[35]

Resurrection

Of the four gospels, the gospel of Mark has the least to say about the resurrection. Later stories tell of miraculous sightings of Jesus, his body walking through doors, and his appearances in places where he was unexpected. Especially if we use the shorter of the two possible endings to Mark, the focus is on the future of the disciple community. After the death of Jesus, the betrayal by the disciples, the abandonment by the crowds, and the seeming victory of the authorities, how can there be any future? The tomb is empty, but where will they find Jesus again? The young man at the tomb says: "He is going ahead of you to Galilee; there you will see him, just as he told you" (16:7). The short ending says that

Jesus then sent them out from Galilee to the east and the west with the gospel of salvation. Even the longer ending gives only sparse details about Jesus' appearances to Mary Magdalene, two disciples along the road, and the eleven sitting at the table. Afterward the disciples "went out and proclaimed the good news everywhere" (16:20).

Literary analysis of the end of Mark shows interesting insights into the whole gospel. Jesus' ministry originated in Galilee among the poor; now the disciples are ordered to return there, to where their base is found. The future of the disciple community will be in solidarity with their own community, the poor. (16:7).

> The full revelation of the Human One has resulted in neither triumphant victory for the community (as the disciples had hoped), nor in the restored Davidic kingdom (as the rebels had hoped), nor tragic failure and defeat (as the reader had feared). It has resulted in nothing more and nothing less than the regeneration of the messianic mission. If we have eyes to "see" the advent of the Human One we will be able to "see" Jesus still going before us. The "invitation" by Jesus, via the young man, to follow him to Galilee, is the third and last call to discipleship.[36]

However, I disagree with Myers that the story does not have a tragic ending. What could be more tragic than the unjust death of the hero at the end of the story without sufficient redeeming actions? Flora Keshgegian argues that the unresolved grief of the Christian community regarding the crucifixion of Jesus is an ongoing theological issue in churches today.[37] I agree with Myers that the focus of the drama now shifts to the response of the disciple community. In most of the narrative, they have not understood Jesus' vision for a new community that is not modeled on the abuse of power, but creates a new community of economic sharing and nonviolence. Now the reader is also confronted with the same question: "Will we 'flee' or will we 'follow'?"[38] The answer depends on our understanding of Jesus' mission and on our courage to live into the vision he has presented. The way of the cross overturns many of our hopes and dreams of the future, for we are just like the disciples. We want to get into the new kin-dom without going through the struggle that it will take to get there. Those of us who are rich must distribute our wealth to the poor and follow Jesus. Those of us who are poor must give up our dreams of winning the lottery and seek the harder way into the future, solidarity with all who seek justice.

For Mark's readers, the question is also about life after the temple in Jerusalem. After the temple is destroyed, what is left? What is left is the disciple community with its memories of Jesus' body on the cross. "In the Eucharistic moment, Jesus offers his body—that is to say, his practice of justice and acceptance of death—as a new symbolic center, in place of the temple cult."[39] The future of Jesus' movement depends on whether the disciple community can translate Jesus' death into a new vision of economic community that includes all people. This means letting go of all illusions of power based on oppression and exploitation, and committing ourselves to living as Jesus did.

Conclusion

In the last two chapters I have summarized selected parts of the gospel of Mark in relation to the theme of our project: economic vulnerability, family violence, and pastoral theology. With the help of Ched Myers, Mary Ann Tolbert, and other commentators, I have searched for themes that could give perspective on economics and care in a world prone to violence. I discovered that the political economy of the first century was characterized by reciprocity, redistribution, and tribute systems that effectively oppressed the poor. Jesus came from Galilee, one of the areas most oppressed by these systems, and he developed a nonaligned critique of the way oppression was organized. Through healing, parables, symbolic actions, and confrontation of religious and political authorities, he unmasked the ideologies of these systems and called all people to engage in solidarity and care for one another. However, his enemies conspired against him; his disciples betrayed him; the crowds abandoned him; and he was left alone to face torture and death under a police state of terror. Mark, the writer, successfully engages us in sympathizing and identifying with Jesus, and leaves us feeling compelled to do something to correct this horrible tragedy. Thus, we are left with the question of whether we can do anything to redeem this tragedy. The answer lies in the ongoing practice of those who decide to follow Jesus, the disciple community.

Having carefully studied the details of Jesus' historical life, we now turn to the question of ecclesiology. What kind of church follows from the path Jesus laid out for us? What should the church be so that the values of economic justice, nonviolence, and caring community are carried on? How can we live so that the tragic ending designed by Jesus' enemies is not the final answer?[40]

13

A Church Empowered by the Holy Spirit

Introduction

In the previous chapter I reviewed an account of the life of Jesus and the disciple community from the perspective of the historical and economic issues of first-century Palestine. The question at the end of Mark's story is whether the disciple community had been sufficiently transformed to carry on Jesus' work, or whether they would be defeated as have been most other well-intentioned reform movements in history.

How the disciple community carried on Jesus' work after his death and resurrection is the question of *ecclesiology*. That is, how can we describe the kinds of communities that emerged from the chaos of the crucifixion, and how did these communities fare in the coming months, years, centuries, and millennia? Ecclesiology is also the normative question of how human beings who follow Jesus Christ should live together and witness to the world. When Christians gather together in community, they are making a witness about the kinds of communities God desires for humans. The importance of ecclesiology for this project has to do with family violence and economic vulnerability. How does the church confront family and community violence? What kind of economic arrangements should the followers of Jesus engage in?

How the disciple community was and is empowered to become the church that witnesses to Jesus Christ is a question of *pneumatology*, or doctrine of the Holy Spirit. When the disciples received the Spirit at Pentecost, they were empowered to become the church. "They perceived the crucified Jesus in the radiance of the divine glory and power, *doxa* and *dynamis*, and in this exceptional perception they were evidently possessed by the Spirit of Life."[1] The church must be able to distinguish the various spirits at work in the world. For example, what is the spirit of global capitalism in our time, and how should the church, empowered by the Holy Spirit, relate to such a world movement? How does the spirit of capitalism aggravate family violence, and what should the church do to increase the safety of people?

In this chapter, I look at the church empowered by the Holy Spirit from the perspective of the themes of family violence and economic vulnerability. What marks, principles, and values from our study of Jesus can guide our reflections about the church and its witness in a world of economic injustice? What kinds of principles ought to be part of an ecclesiology in a world where family violence is epidemic?

Ecclesiology (Doctrine of the Church)

I am part of a long line of theologians who have reflected on the essential definitions of the church. *Ched Myers* identifies several characteristics of the true biblical church: It must embody a new economic practice of inclusive love and abundance for all people, especially the poor and the Gentiles, and it must embody a new politics of loving justice through shared power and nonviolence. (a) Solidarity with the Poor: Jesus came from the poor, and he articulated the perspectives of the poor all his life. Myers suggests that the table of hospitality is one important image of Jesus' ministry, which became evident when he shared the bread and fish (eucharist) with both Jewish and Gentile crowds.[2] (b) Generosity and Abundance in the New Economic Order: Jesus practiced hospitality and generosity.[3] The God of Jesus Christ, who brought the slaves out of Egypt, is a generous God who provides for the poor. (c) Empowering Leadership within the Community: Mark emphasizes images of servant leadership and forgiveness for members of the community who have "fallen to apostasy."[4] (d) Subversive Politics: Resistance to oppression and evil was a characteristic of Jesus' ministry. The disciple community is called to practice love and to engage in subversive actions in solidarity with the poor.[5] (e) Revolutionary Nonviolence: Genuine revolution—one that embodies equality, justice, and nonviolence—cannot be successful when the resisters adopt the same values and methods of the domination system.[6] Myers's five marks of the church can help us to remember the radical ministry of Jesus and organize the religious life of local communities.

Peter Hodgson interprets five traditional images of the church in light of the new realities of global capitalism: (a) The people of God *(laos theou)*. This biblical image preserves the sociopolitical dimensions of the history and the words of Romans 9:25–26, "Those who were not my people I will call 'my people.'"[7] (b) The body of Christ *(soma tou Christou)*. This image picks up the eucharistic language of the gospels and Paul, as well as the analogy to the body in 1 Corinthians 12.[8] The church should be like the Christian Base Communities of Latin America who side with the poor against the poverty and oppression caused by corrupt governments and multinational corporations. (c) The communion of faith, hope, and love *(koinonia)*. The table of the Lord symbolizes communion of the people with God and with one another. The church is a community where the love and justice of Jesus is a religious practice.[9] (d) The creation of the spirit *(pneuma)*. Paul referred to the church as "the communion of the Holy Spirit" (2 Cor. 13:13; Phil 2:1; 3:3). The Spirit can be understood as an image that empowers individuals in their subversive protest against the requirements of official theology, since the Spirit blows where it wills and its truth is hard to control.[10] (e) The [kin-dom[11]] of God *(basileia tou theou)*.[12]

> The basileia evokes a vision of a radical transformation or reversal of values, standards and orders of life: not the power of money but the power of poverty, not the power of lordship but the power to serve, not the first but the last, not blood relationships but social and ethical relationships, not the logic of reward and punishment, domination and sovereignty, but the logic of grace, liberation and love.[13]

Rosemary Ruether describes the history of the church as a tension between "church as spirit-filled community and church as historical institution."[14] The early charismatic churches suspended many of the rules of status and power in society, such as the rule that women were excluded from full membership, that the poor and Gentiles were unclean and unworthy of leadership, or that those who were ill or demon-possessed were lost. Those with significant social power and wealth were not given special status within the church community. This new spirit depended on accepting the charisms of all persons for the benefit of the whole community. However, these original charismatic communities did not last. "Such experiments with spirit-filled community, anticipating a new order beyond history, are unstable within history."[15] Because of persecution, social pressure, and internal conflicts about how best to organize the church, accommodation to Roman, Hellenistic, and Jewish norms of hierarchy quickly developed. Already in the New Testament, one can see the development of patriarchal Christianity that organized power according to hierarchies that corresponded to the social order. Throughout the history of the church, the rhythm of accommodation and resistance to culture can be clearly discerned. For our purposes, we see that the church as a resistance community has a long narrative that can be a resource for a contemporary doctrine of the church. The church must be a community where God's power is available to women and men, rich and poor in their struggles for equality, justice, and nonviolence.

A Constructive Definition of the Church

The church is the body of Christ, a community of bodies and spirits, of humans and nature, in communion with the Holy Spirit, with the following marks: (1) Inclusive Love; (2) Loving Justice; (3) Nonviolent Resistance to Evil; (4) Multiplicity and Unity; (5) Ambiguity and Goodness.[16]

In this section, I develop my own constructive definition of the church, based on the images from this project on economic vulnerability, family violence, and pastoral theology. The church is the Body of Christ...[17]

You are the body of Christ and individually members of it.
(1 Cor 12:27)

In recent years, the body of Christ has become a favorite image of many Christians because it describes the diversity of gifts, cultures, races, genders, and sexualities within the global church. The unity of the one and the many is emphasized in this image of the body. Even though the people of the church are diverse, they still belong to one body. Overcoming the limitations of economic injustice and violence so the church can become one body is an ongoing challenge. As Christians we become the body of Christ when we practice the values Jesus lived and died for, and when we extend the healing love of the living Christ to all people in the world.

A community...

The church is a community that can be described through images of covenant, relational web, and culture.

Covenant is a rich image throughout the scriptures and history. God formed a covenant with Abraham, Sarah, and Hagar, again with Moses, Aaron, Miriam, and the nation of Israel, and redeemed the covenant through the prophets, including Jesus Christ. God has formed covenants with people of many faiths–Judaism, Christianity, and Islam, but also other religious groups. Covenant is not a contract that is chosen by the individual, but participation in a formation community that shapes personal and corporate identity. A child raised in the church will forever have a particular identity that she or he can assent to, rebel against, or reject, but that becomes an important reference point for the rest of his or her life. Converts who join the church commit themselves to particular beliefs and practices in the promise that their identities will be shaped and new habits will be internalized. Covenant implies a formation that is partially chosen through participation and interaction with others, but partly given by the community context so that the deepest self is formed in ways that are outside of awareness. A church that chooses nonviolence and economic justice in its daily practices will become a community with positive identity-shaping influence on its members and on strangers with whom members interact.

We enter into consciousness as human beings in the midst of the *relational web*. We do not create it. That is, we do not create the relational character of existence. We are connected with all life, in varying degrees of direct and mediated forms of relationships. When we build our many societies (families, churches, clubs, nations) we exemplify the given relational character of existence.[18] The web is a metaphor for the whole pattern that determines the context for an individual's life. Without the web, we cease to exist, because the web is the totality of reality itself.

Culture is another way of describing the content of the relational web. Culture includes the patterns of thought, behavior, language, and symbols that hold a people together, that is, "any society seen in terms of its total human expression,"[19] "[Culture] affects and shapes not only language, the mode of thinking and speaking, but sensibilities of thought, psychical orientation, and thus psychical expectations."[20]

Covenant, web, culture, community, and body are all ways of describing corporate reality in human life, a concept that is difficult to grasp within the individualism of market capitalism. The reality of community is hard to organize and maintain in families and communities where persons are under violent assault. The church holds out the promise of a community that transcends the divisions of gender, race, and economic class and is nonviolent and affirming of all its members.

...of bodies and spirits, of humans and nature

"Bodies and spirits" refers to the physicality and energy of individuals in their relationships with others. Daniel Day Williams discusses the relationship of body and spirit in the following way:

> God is spirit. [Humans], created in God's image, [have] spiritual existence, not as something added to [their] bodily substance, but as the expression of that concrete *body-mind unity* which [they are as persons.] The freedom of spirit is the freedom of God as the ultimate form-giving and life-giving reality. The freedom of [human beings] is also the freedom of spirit, but within the conditions of finite existence.[21] (Emphasis added. Text changed to reflect inclusive language)

Bernard Meland defines *spirit* as the goodness of relationships in human life. "Spirit connotes a depth of sensitivity that forms the matrix of relations in which all life is cast...We may say that spirit is a quality of being which arises out of a particular depth of sensitivity in relations. It is, in other words, a goodness in relationships."[22] "God is faithful; by [God] you were called into the fellowship *(koinonia)* of [God's] son, Jesus Christ our Lord" (1 Cor. 1:9).

Christians, the community of those who confess Christ and follow Jesus in their lives, have been called into the *koinonia*, the economy or household of Jesus Christ. Being a Christian means choosing to value the whole relational web that was created by God. Choosing nonviolence toward the relational web is a decision about one's identity, since the web is torn by violence such as war, poverty, family abuse, and ecological disaster. Choosing economic justice within the relational web means practicing values that are inclusive and move toward equality for all humans and nature.

All humans exist within the web of relationships that includes the natural creation. Our bodies are constantly recycling oxygen, carbon dioxide, water, and food in ongoing interaction with the atmosphere, the mineral world, the surface of the earth, and the animal and plant worlds. The theological traditions that overemphasize human life at the expense of the natural world have resulted in violence and in the exploitation of nature. Our search for nonviolence and economic justice must include the community of both humans and nature.[23]

...in communion with the Holy Spirit

If the Holy Spirit has been a forgotten doctrine among theologians in recent decades, it has never been forgotten among the people. Spiritual revivals of every kind have exploded all over the world as people seek religious answers to the alienation and oppression of their lives. From New Age fascination with indigenous American, Asian, and African religions to the enthusiastic and emotional Pentecostal theologies, people seek knowledge of the Holy Spirit. Christians in communion with the Holy Spirit seek to be faithful to the values of nonviolence and economic justice, and support or oppose market capitalism, depending on whether it fulfills its God-given purpose. But when market capitalism becomes an idol that fosters violence and economic exploitation that benefit the few at the cost of great suffering for the masses, then Christians in communion with the Holy Spirit must resist and oppose such a system.

> The Holy Spirit is not simply the subjective side of God's revelation of himself, and faith is not merely the echo of the Word of God in the human heart. The Holy Spirit is much more than that. It is the power that raises the dead, the power of the new creation of all things; and faith is the beginning of the rebirth of human beings to new life. But this means that the Holy Spirit is by no means merely a matter of revelation. It has to do with life and its source. The Holy Spirit is called "holy" because it sanctifies life and renews the face of the earth.[24]

Marks of the Church [25]

Having defined some of the essential aspects of a doctrine of the church, I turn now to normative marks of the church.

Inclusive love and the limits of inclusivity

The church as a community is characterized by inclusive love. The church includes those who have been excluded and values the interior experience of every person. This requires a radical openness to otherness and difference. The incorporation of what appears to be contradictory constantly creates a new corporate identity.[26]

When experience is defined within a narrow range that does not correspond to the rich variety of individuals, awareness is restricted and persons are marginalized. To be able to engage what is perceived as alien and threatening is difficult, requiring a kind of courage that few individuals or groups can muster. Engaging experiences that threaten a group's identity and cohesiveness is a constant challenge facing any community.

Inclusive love is challenging because of the basic human tendency to exclude whatever makes us uncomfortable. In the face of otherness and difference, we discover aspects of ourselves we don't like. Often we choose to live in a small world where pain is more moderate and our values are more easily supported. Communities that are inclusive of otherness are living deeply out of relational nature of human existence itself and the ambiguity that is part and parcel of flesh-and-blood humanity.

In an inclusive community, the poor and victims of violence are encouraged to give voice to their suffering so it can be shared by others. Such openness gives reality to the experience of individual terror and provides protection from further abuse. In a context of shared suffering, attention can be given to deficiencies that need correction. The community becomes a resource for healing of those who have been damaged by the abuse of power.

In an inclusive community, there is no place where the sinful part of persons can hide. Their attempts to avoid their problems through denial are fruitless, and their access to victims is destroyed. In such a context, perpetrators of violence have to face the inner pain hidden in their symptoms and choose whether to use the community resources that could lead to transformation. Inclusive community destroys the veil of secrecy that makes abuse of power possible.

I use the word *inclusive* in two related senses: (a) the church includes those who have been outcast and marginalized by the dominant culture; (b) the church includes the full range of human experience.

In the first meaning of inclusive, those who are victims of violence and economic vulnerability have a special claim on the church because their marginality is a sign of the failure of human communities, including its economic systems. Jesus represented the poor not because they were more virtuous or faithful but because their cries for justice were valid. They deserved a fair share of the resources available to the human family, and they deserved to be protected from the violence of military actions and the residual violence caused by the breakdown of family and community. Jesus organized a movement that included the poorest of the poor, especially those marginalized because they were unclean: lepers, disabled, the sick, women, children, and Gentiles.

There are limits to inclusivity. It is a practical value that applies to those who are excluded from human society for unjust reasons. Those who are already leaders in the dominant groups, and those who receive privileges because of injustice, cannot sue for inclusion. Jesus reserved very different responses for the poor and for the elite. To be included in a community of economic justice and nonviolence, the elite must repent and be accountable for their power.

In the second meaning of inclusive, the church is called to include the whole range of human experiences. This means acknowledging the voices of children, the experiences of those have been silenced by violence, and the reality of those who have stories that challenge the ethos of the community. This means acknowledging the unconscious experiences of all members of the community as they struggle to live in faithfulness to the Holy Spirit.

Including the full experience of everyone in the community does not require suspending value judgments. Rather, inclusiveness merely opens the dialogue about the core values of the community. In the dialogue that follows acknowledgment of diverse experiences, there must be space and time for sorting out contradictions that could destroy persons and even the community itself. When all aspects of human experience are acknowledged, ugly stories can be told, including stories of perpetrating violence and injustice on others. How else can personal redemption and reconciliation come to individuals unless there is safety for open communication?[27] Silencing those with particular experiences takes the church toward moralistic violence, where persons must conform in silence in order to be accepted. A loving community must be strong enough to be inclusive without losing its moral center.

Loving justice as safety and accountability

The church is a community characterized by loving justice and accountability. Justice is the fair distribution of the resources needed for full life. Safety means that the vulnerable are protected from harm. Accountability means that all are responsible to the larger community for their behaviors. Churches must have the courage to protect the vulnerable and to confront abuse of power within the community and in the larger society. In contrast, unjust communities organize power on the basis of privilege and dominance, so that those who have power are permitted to accumulate resources beyond what they need while others are marginalized and denied basic necessities, including personal safety.

Practicing justice in a community is challenging because of the difficulty persons have in facing their own moral ambiguity. All people like to think of themselves as fair and nonabusive in the way they conduct their lives, and they like to think that their communities function with justice toward all members. The disclosure of injustice is frightening because it discloses deeper realities that create shame and guilt. When a disclosure about violence is made in the church, people often engage in denial and dissociation: denial that such an evil could occur in their group, and dissociation of the facts from any serious consequences for themselves. Often the victim is blamed for exaggeration or lying, and the perpetrator is protected to maintain the good name of the community.[28]

The discussion about whether or not abuse of power exists in a community cannot depend on the perception or honesty of the powerful because the powerful tend to justify themselves at the expense of others. Those who are vulnerable must be given authority to testify about their perceptions. There must be policies and procedures for hearing the testimony of potential victims and norms against which to judge whether abuse of power has occurred.

A just community believes the stories of victims of violence and the poor and provides the resources they need for protection and healing. The church needs trained counselors who know how to work with people who have been victimized by economic injustice and/or family violence, linking victims to healing networks and sharing the costs of healing. Most importantly, victims must not be marginalized because their difficulties are uncomfortable for others. Marginalization and isolation of victims repeat the trauma of victimization.

In a just community, there is accountability for perpetrators of violence and injustice. When there is injury to an individual through abuse of power, the traditional responses to sinners provide the basis for justice. First, there must be confession and full disclosure (truth-telling) of acts of violence against others. This breaks the cloak of secrecy that hides the acts in darkness and prevents support to the victim. Second, there must be repentance and acceptance of adequately rigorous reeducation and healing programs that have real potentiality for healing. A sincere desire to face the pain and evil in one's life and turn in a new direction is the root meaning of repentance. Third, there must be restitution to the victims and the community within a context of full protection for those who are vulnerable. A just community has the conceptual and procedural resources for facing events of abuse of power within its members. Fourth, there must be rigorous standards for reconciliation of sinners back into the community.[29]

One of Jesus' biggest challenges was helping his disciples understand and purge themselves of the values of the dominant system. Although they clearly saw the injustice that made their community subject to violence and oppression, they could see only a reversal of fortunes as the solution. Throughout the gospel of Mark, the disciples assume that their movement will give them opportunities for leadership and prosperity that they have never had before. Twice Jesus hears them arguing over who will have high positions in his kingdom. Even when Jesus is crucified, they fail to understand that his vision requires that the disciple community take a fearless inventory of their own values and habits.

A just church makes a prophetic witness to the larger society on behalf of victims of injustice and violence. The church can advocate the same structures of support and accountability used within its community for implementation in the larger communities. Local, regional, national, and global communities must protect the victims of violence and economic vulnerability and hold those who abuse power to high standards of justice. The church must advocate for public policies and laws at all levels in order to promote justice. For example, Christians in North America need relationships of solidarity with Christians in poor countries such as Nicaragua so they can begin to understand the daily realities of oppression there.

Working for the safety of friends across lines of language, culture, and class not only raises feelings of empathy for the everyday dangers of being poor but also leads to analysis of how U.S. political and economic realities have been responsible for poverty and oppression. Christians can organize together to create safety for the poor and to confront the abuses of power. Solidarity can lead U.S. Christians to engage in political action to change policies toward the poor countries. Wherever there is corruption, whether among the elite of Nicaragua or the politicians of the U.S., the church should be involved in prophetic challenge. The lack of accountability for the rich nations of the world is a core problem in the existence of economic oppression and violence in the world.

Nonviolent resistance to evil

> Jesus' nonviolent resistance to evil discloses that resistance to evil through nonviolence is a fundamental attribute of God and humans.[30]

In Jesus Christ we see constant resistance to evil in his miracles, teaching, criticism of religious leaders, and symbolic actions. Ellen Wondra says of resistance to evil: "For Christians, the resistance of both humanity and divinity to domination is decisively manifest and recognized in Jesus the Christ. In Christ, Christians find the dialectic movement from domination through resistance to transformation both vindicated in history and connected directly with the existence of God."[31]

Jesus' life reveals that resistance to evil is a fundamental characteristic of God, and that his spirit lives on through those who resist evil. Thus, resistance is not just a human response to life's difficulties, but a fundamental attribute of divine and human life. "Resistance mends and motivates the human capacity to engage the very conditions of existence; resistance reveals anew the connection of human being to ongoing history and the transcendence toward which humanity strives. Resistance, then, is one of the elements that constitutes human being itself."[32]

While many stories about Jesus disclose resistance as a part of God's creation of humanity, his death and resurrection require special attention. In an event that would be a failure by most human standards, God's commitment to resistance was disclosed.[33] This is how much Jesus loved the victims of oppression—he loved them enough to die in solidarity with them.

Beginning with his baptism, Jesus acted to resist the dominant religious, economic, and political systems of his day. He was baptized by John for repentance and forgiveness of sins (or debts). He became a child of the wilderness, receiving his wisdom not only from the approved teachers but from the Holy Spirit as well. He called for repentance and spiritual independence from the professionals who decided knowledge and value. Jesus engaged in nonviolent, direct action campaigns designed to challenge the symbolic world that legitimized the violence and economic oppression of the poor.[34]

Throughout history, the Christian church has always had a prophetic calling, and many reform movements have engaged in challenging systems of oppression: the Franciscans, the Hutterites, the Anabaptists, the Quakers, the Black Church, Christian Base Communities, women-church, and so on. The church is called today to engage in nonviolent resistance to evil. As we evaluate expressions of the church, we must look for signs of resistance to evil. What are local congregations doing to challenge the way their community allocates resources? What are local congregations doing to challenge national and international policies that determine who is rich and who is poor?

Resistance to evil must be nonviolent, that is, it must be aimed at challenging the symbolic world of inequality and injustice, rather than advocating violence as a solution. The ends of the church, economic justice, must be congruent with its means, nonviolence.

> The nonviolent resistors can summarize their message in the following simple terms: we will take direct action against injustice without waiting for other agencies to act. We will not obey unjust laws or submit to unjust practices. We will do this peacefully, openly, and cheerfully because our aim is to persuade. We adopt the means of nonviolence because our end is a community at peace with itself. We will try to persuade with our words, but, if our words fail, we will try to persuade with our acts. We will always be willing to talk and seek fair compromise, but we are ready to suffer when necessary and even risk our lives to become witnesses to the truth as we see it.[35]

The church needs to study more actively the philosophy of nonviolent resistance put forth by Gandhi, King, and others, and train cadres of young people who are willing to practice militant nonviolence. Such anticipation of the future work of the church signals solidarity with those who suffer from oppression and violence.

Multiplicity and unity

Jesus' relational love and power reveal the mystery of God's Otherness and proclaim that multiplicity and unity are fundamental attributes of divine and human life.[36]

Multiplicity is the existence of an otherness that cannot be reduced to unity and familiarity. God's love is irreducibly Other in human experience, and it cannot be contained in any unity constructed by human systems. By analogy, human love pulls us into relationships with the multiplicity in the world, and genuine love is open to influence from those who are other.

Unity is a complex nexus of contrasts and contradictions that have been harmonized through faith and courage. God's love seeks unity for all creation, but without sacrificing the multiplicity that is inherent to the creative act itself. God yearns for intimacy with all creation within a bond of unity.

The church of Jesus Christ must find a balance of multiplicity and unity that does justice to the full diversity of God's creation. Every community will have a desire for the unity that was present immediately after Pentecost: "All who believed were together and had all things in common" (Acts 2:44). Unity is important for any community that is trying to generate energy to change things. People working together have more influence than when they are fragmented and alienated. However, the beauty of a unified community comes largely from the amount of multiplicity that can be integrated.[37] "Now there were devout Jews from every nation under heaven living in Jerusalem" (Acts 2:5). The unity at Pentecost was beautiful because of the multiplicity contained in that unity. As the church expanded, the diversity included not only Jews from every nation but women who were not counted and Gentiles from other religions. In our time, we are aware of tremendous multiplicity in the world that must be addressed.

Multiplicity must be a mark of the church. For the sake of this project, we mean especially the multiplicity of poor women, men, and children from every nation in the world, with room for the formerly rich who have repented of their sins of complicity. Jesus invited the rich young ruler to join the disciple community if he would sell his possessions, give the money to the poor, and then follow Jesus. He went sadly away, because he had many possessions. He received the invitation but could not forsake his attachments to wealth and the knowledge that his wealth was fraudulently obtained.

Multiplicity is a value that confronts the church with otherness and difference. The many cannot easily become one[38] when there are contradictions and oppositions between people. Constructing unity where there is otherness and difference requires hard work. For example, the poor challenge the identity of the rich in fundamental ways that must be faced and talked through. If the poor and the rich are to be in community together, there has to be a commitment to sharing deeply the fears and hurts of the past, the kind of truth and reconciliation process that can only be managed through the power of the Holy Spirit.

Ambiguity and goodness

> Jesus' relational love and power reveal the mystery of God's Otherness and proclaim that ambiguity and goodness are fundamental attributes of divine and human life.[39]

Ambiguity is the existence of another morality that cannot be co-opted by those in power, that stands against all systems of power that attempt to oppress others. God's love and power are ambiguous for humans because God contains moral contradictions that cannot be comprehended by human constructions of good and evil. By analogy, human love and power are ambiguous because love strives for a goodness that cannot be limited by human understandings of good and evil. Every morality is tested by the amount of ambiguity it can contain without losing its integrity.

Goodness is the existence of truth and beauty that are harmonized within actual community practice. God's love seeks such truth and beauty and finds it in all times and places. However, goodness is never sought at the expense of reality, and thus, the process of seeking goodness includes high toleration for ambiguity.

Betrayal is part of the drama of the biblical story. All the disciples betrayed Jesus. Paul confesses his sin in one of the most quoted verses of the New Testament: "For I do not do the good I want, but the evil I do not want is what I do" (Rom. 7:19). Honesty about moral ambiguity, the presence of good and evil that has not yet been resolved, is one of the marks of the life of the disciple community. Bringing one's ambiguity into the community for accountability is a sign of faithfulness in the church.

Ambiguity in tension with goodness is a mark of the church. This tension can never be fully resolved. Accepting ambiguity without moral struggle is sloth; asserting moral perfection without knowledge of ambiguity is pride. When we evaluate ourselves and our community on the values of nonviolence and economic justice, no one is innocent and pure. Every member of the church has engaged in destructive behaviors that are damaging to other persons. Every member of the church has an ambiguous relationship with economic resources, through possession and/or desire. The church must be able to tolerate much moral ambiguity in order to resist evil and engage in nonviolent confrontation of injustice. How this ambiguity is dealt with confessionally and ritually must be worked out for the health of the community.

In this section, we have discussed a definition of the church that can guide our reflections of practice. In a world of violence and economic injustice, what kind of church do we need? What is the witness of the scriptures? Having developed such a definition, we are now prepared to discuss some of the various experiments in church life that deal with violence and economic injustice.

Summary

In this chapter, I have presented my constructive views of the doctrine of the church. I defined the empowered church as the body of Christ, a community of bodies and souls, human and nature in communion with the Holy Spirit. I identified five marks of the church that can help us understand the church's role in struggling with family violence and economic vulnerability.

In the next two chapters, I look at some examples of faithful church practice that are in line with my study and begin to spell out the implications for Christian care and counseling.

Part V: Transforming Pastoral Care

14

Pastoral Care with Persons Who Are Vulnerable

Introduction

In these concluding chapters, I turn to practical guidelines for ministry practice. My research has shown that many people in the world live in situations of extreme economic vulnerability where their daily physical needs are met at a subsistence level or less. Many, especially women and children, face threats to their safety and health because of family violence. Economic vulnerability increases this danger when women and children lack the resources to protect themselves. We have seen how the twin dangers of economic vulnerability and family violence make human life difficult and undercut the emotional and spiritual development that God intends for human beings. In addition, we know that both economic oppression and family violence are the result of human sin and thus preventable. If the wealth of the world economy were fairly distributed among the world's population, all would have their basic needs cared for. If those who are temporarily stronger would cease violating the physical integrity of those who are vulnerable, families would no longer be crucibles of violence and abuse.

In my analysis I studied economic oppression and family violence in light of individual and communal resistance to evil. I found organized movements that protest and develop alternative communities in response to oppression, evidence that assertion of the God-given right to live in safety and freedom from oppression is the best marker of the injustice in the world. Vulnerable people resist through silence, language, and action.[1] In pastoral care, we should respect people's resistance to evil and work to empower them with the gospel's message to seek the economic justice and nonviolence that are the promise of God's love.

212

Because representatives of dominant and wealthy societies usually write the theology most of us study, the theories of care for persons who are vulnerable have not been adequately developed. Most theories are overly optimistic about the circumstances within which people live and the choices that they can make to improve their environment. However, economic vulnerability limits choices, and family violence attacks personal agency. How can we challenge the church to develop a more realistic mission for all persons who are vulnerable?

This chapter focuses on the ministry of pastoral care. First, I develop a typology for analyzing forms of difference, injustice, and dominance. Second, I develop strategies of diagnosis and care for individuals caught in situations of economic vulnerability. Third, I review the essential principles for care of persons caught in family violence so that the safety of victims and survivors is paramount. Fourth, I raise some questions about the structures of pastoral counseling in the United States.

Understanding Cultural Differences

During my formal academic training in pastoral theology and counseling during the 1960s and 1970s, I assumed that the principles of pastoral theology and counseling were fairly universal, with variations depending on individual experiences. The following principles continue to be important in our field: (a) Empathy is a basis for understanding and change. People change best when they form trusting relationships with their counselors, and this trust comes when the counselor is accepting, empathic, and authentic. (b) Personal history is important for understanding persons in need of care. I learned to take careful histories of childhood, relationship to parents, physical health, jobs, schooling, and other important experiences. (c) The family system is important for understanding the place of the individual in the family drama. I learned to study family genograms in detail to discover patterns of health and dysfunction. (d) Anxiety, depression, and other symptoms need to be clearly diagnosed, because people are motivated by the stresses of everyday life and respond best when the counselor is interested in the improvement of their lives. I learned to use the *Diagnostic and Statistical Manual* [2] so I could understand the range of human pathology. (e) Religion is an important force in persons' lives and provides a rich resource for healing and wholeness. I learned about various operational theologies that people use in everyday life and how personal faith can be revised to help them have a larger perspective on themselves, others, and the world. In a good counseling relationship, people begin to feel better and begin to understand themselves and their situation differently.

While all these principles are important to me, and I teach them in my courses in pastoral theology and counseling, I have slowly learned to question an assumption behind the above list, namely, that such principles are universal and adequate for all situations. John Cobb criticizes assumptions of universality with the phrase "the fallacy of misplaced concreteness…The problem lies in neglecting the extent to which our concepts are abstract, and therefore also neglecting the rest of the reality from which they have been abstracted…'It means an arbitrary halt at a particular set of abstractions.' (Whitehead)."[3] Talcott Parsons believed that principles of family life, such as an expressive dimension for mothers and a utilitarian dimension for fathers, were universal in all cultures. Freud, Erikson, Piaget, and Kohlberg also believed their theories about sexuality, development, self, and conscience were universal. However, we know now that many psychological theories have a male, western European bias that distorts the experiences of a majority of the world's population.

Abstractions are only ethical when they are contextually applied with full knowledge of their limitations. Emmanuel Lartey helps us understand the relation of cultural diversity and experience when he says that every individual is "like all others, like some others, and like no other…We are all born helpless, grow from dependence toward relative self-management, we relate to other beings and to the physical environment and ten out of ten die!"[4] But these "universal experiences" are not necessarily of more importance than the cultural and individual differences between us. We have learned in the pastoral theology and counseling movement in recent decades that differences of culture and power matter immensely, whether these differences come from language, religion, nationality, gender, race, class, sexuality, disability, or other social locations. How, then, can we develop principles and guidelines for pastoral care that take seriously the reality of economic oppression and family violence?

Cross-cultural counseling has experienced a major revival as the U.S. population becomes increasingly diverse. The 2000 U.S. census found that 29 percent of the U.S. population came from non-European heritage: 34.7 million persons (12.5 percent) in the U.S. identified themselves as being of African descent, 35.3 million (12.7 percent) identified themselves as Hispanic,[5] and 11.2 million (4.0 percent) claimed Asian origins.[6] This multicultural reality has led to an explosion of research and theories about cross-cultural counseling,[7] which encourages counselors to get training in cultural competence to help families cope with multicultural situations. However, the literature continues to be deficient in its analysis of economic vulnerability and family violence. In response to these problems, I have developed the following typology that identifies cultural and economic difference, injustice, and domination, three levels of analysis that I hope will improve our understanding of people who seek care.

Understanding differences

That pastoral counselors should make a careful assessment of cultural and economic differences seems too obvious to mention. But many articles and books have been written as if no important cultural differences exist, as if we know the universal principles that can be applied in every culture beneficially. For example, most articles in the *Dictionary of Pastoral Care and Counseling*[8] are written as if cultural differences are incidental. While there are articles on various kinds of "specialized counseling" (African American, American Indian, Hispanic, women, etc.), most articles hardly mention culture or class as variables in assessment. What do we mean by "culture"? Clifford Geertz defines culture as "an historically transmitted pattern of meanings embodied in symbols, a system of inherited conception expressed in symbolic forms by means of which men [*sic*] communicate, perpetuate, and develop their knowledge about and attitudes toward life"[9] Emmanuel Lartey says, "By culture I shall be referring to the way in which social groups develop distinct patterns of life and give 'expressive form' to their social and material life experience."[10] Many pastoral counselors suspect that careful attention to culture is crucial to diagnosis and treatment in pastoral theology and counseling, but when confronted with situations requiring cultural competence, we often fail to use the skills necessary for careseekers. A recent correspondence with Brenda Ruiz demonstrates my own lack of insight[11] when she shared something about the problems of domestic violence in Nicaragua. By e-mail she wrote:

> I just came home from the workshop on Domestic Violence with the popular health Promoters from Providenic. I am exhausted. People were very attentive and had very good questions. But when it came to the section on interventions I felt very discouraged about what they could do. The system indeed does not lend itself much for timely interventions, especially in the rural areas.[12]

I made some suggestions that have worked in my context, especially encouraging the use of shelters organized by women and counting on the police for intervention. She responded:

> My main reason for worrying about the perpetrators is that as long as they are at large there is very little protection for the victims. Our legal system is not developed well enough to actually restrain the perpetrators adequately and the police resources are very scarce as well, plus there is ample room for payoffs and the use of influences. Women here have fewer alternatives to travel (Nicaragua is indeed a very small country) and because of increasing poverty it is harder for relatives and friends to take in another family, especially if there are many children. There is only one shelter in the country (for about 10 women) and it is in Estelí (2 hours away by car). So the issue of safety is not as easily solved here.[13]

As a consultant on issues of pastoral care and domestic violence in the U.S., I made a number of assumptions in my response to Brenda Ruiz: I assumed the existence of a legal system that understands domestic violence as a crime; I assumed the existence of a network of shelters and crisis services for women; I assumed enough material resources so that people can help one another; and I assumed a middle-class women's movement with political power. I have been to Nicaragua many times, and I know something about the life of the people there, but the assumptions from my U.S. experience are so ingrained in my daily life that it is hard for me to fully understand the cultural and economic differences in Nicaragua. I continue to consult with Brenda to learn how to develop a culturally embedded theory and practice of pastoral theology and counseling. I know that the victims of violence universally want to be free from terror, but assessing the influence of cultural, institutional, and material conditions is a major task. For me, it means radically revisioning my own theories and practices so that they are effective in other cultural situations.

Understanding injustice

Not all differences between persons and groups can be attributed to language, knowledge, attitudes, and social and material experience. Sometimes there are differences that must be characterized as inequalities or injustice. This can be seen in the above example. I am limited in my understanding of the Health Promoters from Providenic in Nicaragua not only because I do not live in Nicaragua, but because I live in a situation of wealth and privilege, and they live in a situation of poverty and injustice. I take for granted the wealth and resources of my situation so that I cannot easily imagine myself as a pastoral counselor with Nicaraguan women. Brenda's exhaustion and feelings of frustration are based on spending extensive time talking with women who have experienced domestic violence in the midst of poverty and on her awareness of a lack of institutional resources. The location of my everyday ministry is quite different, limiting my value as consultant and friend.

My colleague Linda Thomas writes about issues of power and injustice in her research on anthropology and theology in a way that shows her awareness of the injustice that can follow from cultural differences:

> Theological research must be sensitive to the various approaches to culture, but particularly sensitive to the culture of those about whom the topic is focused. This includes, for instance, empirical data about economic conditions. What implications do particular economic conditions have on the state of black people of the period studied as linked to the issues of health care,

employment, and ecology? So often scholarship does not give testimony to the issue of the political economy of the topics represented. It is as if human subjects can be separated from the material reality in which they live. An anthropological approach to theology as it relates to culture will always include a probing of the economic conditions of people as well as an analysis of related issues such as violence.[14]

When cultural difference becomes the occasion for economic difference, we have a potential situation of injustice. Those who control the economic decisions for others often favor one cultural group over another. I became aware of the issues of justice and culture when I was doing research for the book *Balm for Gilead.* Toinette Eugene and I had to learn that in every situation involving sexual and domestic violence, issues of power and injustice had to be addressed alongside issues of culture. One vignette was written by a student about her visit to a public housing project for the poor in Chicago. As an eleven-year-old child, Doris, now the mother of the household, had become pregnant by her mother's boyfriend. Years later she was charged with child abuse after stabbing her own thirteen-year-old daughter with a fork. But she was not worried about going to jail for assault. She knew that the child protective agency did not care enough about women in her social class to follow up on their investigation. She expected she would never see the child protective workers again. Neither would she receive any help from them.[15]

In our reflection, we explored the justice issues involved in this case, noting "the effects of poverty, racism, and a social system that is not serious about helping black people. The federal housing project failed to provide a safe place for her or her family. The schools failed by their ineffective education and interventions when she was in need. Her life was circumscribed by her awareness that a poor black single parent from the projects has very few choices or resources for changing her situation. She is resigned to seeing the patterns of abuse and deprivation repeated into the third generation because nothing can really be done."[16]

In this situation, there are interlocking differences of culture and injustice. A pastoral counselor well trained in African and African American cultures could understand some of the issues in this situation— the language, wisdom, attitudes, and social experience. But there is also injustice based in systems of power. Not only was Doris living in a particular African American culture in Chicago, but she has also been formed by a history of institutional racism and sexism. I am concerned that many pastoral counselors do not know how to analyze power and injustice and thus how to have empathy and provide resources for someone like Doris.

Understanding cultural and economic dominance

Beyond understanding differences and injustice, we must understand the concept of dominance, which aims to destroy the cultural identity of persons and groups. We must understand the resistance among oppressed peoples, which on the surface may appear strident or bizarre, but is actually a strength and resource for healing and theological truth. This is a difficult level to understand and define sufficiently, yet we must make the effort so that our practices of pastoral theology and counseling will be effective.[17] The following definition of cultural domination and oppression developed by an interracial collective in the United States can be helpful:

> The matrix of domination is a system of attitudes, behaviors and assumptions that objectifies human persons on the basis of socially constructed categories such as race, gender, class, etc., and that has the power to deny autonomy, access to resources and self-determination to those persons, while maintaining the values of the dominant society as the norm by which all else will be measured.[18]

According to this definition, dominance depends on (a) a system of reductionistic stereotypes that (b) controls material resources and (c) enforces its own cultural values as normative. In the United States we often use terms such as racism, sexism, classism, and so forth, to describe these forms of dominance. In international events of the twentieth century, the practices of cultural dominance must be understood in many different settings: European Americans against American indigenous peoples, Germans against Jews, Japanese against Koreans, Serbs against Moslem Albanians in Yugoslavia, Rwandans against Tutsis (and vice versa), Zulus against Xhosas, Israelis against Palestinians, United States against Cuba. Wherever injustice based on power differences exists, groups too often struggle for dominance, and use their own culture as a norm to judge, damage, and even commit genocide against other cultures.

But how does such dominance and oppression work in the micro-situations of pastoral theology and counseling? How does a pastoral counselor know when dominance is at work, since the voices from repressed cultures have often been silenced through military and other violent means?

For many years in my practice as a pastoral counselor, I did not hear the voices of women as they struggled to free themselves from the dominance of patriarchy. For all of written history, men have controlled the economy, the politics, the education, and the creation and publication of ideas. In recent decades, women have broken free and started expressing ideas based on years of oppression and collected wisdom. How are individual women finding their voices in the midst of such tensions, and what is pastoral theology and counseling doing to end its own cultural dominance?

Likewise, it has taken me many years to realize the dominance involved in the ideologies of whiteness that pathologize and marginalize other cultures by using white culture as the norm by which "others" are measured. As one who benefits from the dominance of whiteness, I have trouble understanding the cultures of others. Doris, in an earlier example, is invisible to the powers and institutions that control and define language and social practices. It is also difficult for her and other oppressed people to resist the definitions imposed by hostile powers. Frantz Fanon calls this "the colonialization of the mind," that is, the pressure on the oppressed to internalize the oppression by accepting the language, ideas, identities, and values of the oppressors. "The defensive attitudes created by this violent bringing together of the colonised man and the colonial system form themselves into a structure which then reveals the colonised personality."[19]

Most U.S. citizens voice their acceptance of cultural dominance by using the word *American* to refer only to the United States, in fact one of many countries in the Americas. If America means U.S., then what term is available for Mexicans, Central Americans, and Latin Americans? Throughout this book, I have tried to consistently use the awkward phrase U.S. to avoid the appearance of cultural dominance. However, this is only one symptom of the reality of the economic and political dominance of the U.S. throughout the Western Hemisphere, and the tendency of U.S. citizens to discount all others who live here.

Cultural dominance aims at the destruction of cultural identity. Ama Ata Aidoo, a black woman who lived in Europe for many years and is one of Africa's leading writers, gives examples of how cultural dominance threatened her identity in her book *Our Sister Killjoy.*[20] In her story-poem, Sissie, a young woman from Ghana, is visiting Germany when she hears the words "das Schwartze Madchen," in English, "the black girl." The phrase takes her by surprise, until she more closely examines the people around her and notices that they are not black. Her words:

> And it hit her.
> That all that crowd of people going and coming in all sorts of
>   directions had the colour of the pickled pig parts that used
>   to come from foreign places to the markets at home.
> Trotters, pig-tails, pig-ears.
> She looked and looked at so many of such skins together.
> And she wanted to vomit.
> Then she was ashamed of her reaction.
> Something pulled inside of her.

> For the rest of her life, she was to regret this moment when she
> was made to notice differences in human colouring.

She regretted her new knowledge, not just because of her awareness
of color but because color had become, for the first time, a sign of
dominant cultural power. She noticed that she had already internalized
the idea that different shades of color determine the value and material
basis of life for many people in the world. She continues:

> Power, Child. Power.
> For this is all anything is about.
> Power to decide
> Who is to live,
> Who is to die,
> Where,
> When,
> How.

Aidoo raises several questions that are important for understanding
cultural dominance in pastoral theology and counseling:

First, this story illustrates that color is written on the body in a way
that demarcates the differences between groups. For Sissie, this awareness brought a physical response of nausea, then a psychological
response of shame. "For the rest of her life" she regretted that such
knowledge was possible and necessary. She hated this new
epistemology—that she knew how to make judgments between people on
the basis of color.

Second, the story shows that color determines power relationships in
an unjust world—"that someone somewhere would always see in any kind
of difference, any excuse to be mean." This is an experience not unlike
the fall within the garden of Eden—the awareness that difference is related
to power, and power is the occasion for sin and evil in the world. Just as
Adam and Eve discovered they were naked in the midst of sin and felt
ashamed, so Sissie felt ashamed when she first noticed color and realized
that the structures of unjust power were constructed on such differences.

Third, the story illustrates how dangerous the abuse of power based
on difference can be: "Power, Child. Power. For this is all anything is
about. Power to decide who is to live, who is to die, Where, When, How."
People die because they are the wrong color, while other people become
rich because they are the politically correct color.

Aidoo also comments on the negative consequences of English
becoming the dominant global language through military and economic
control and now through computers, television, and movies.

> A common heritage. A
> Dubious bargain that left us
> Plundered of

Our gold
Our tongue
Our life—while our
Dead fingers clutch
English—a
Doubtful weapon fashioned
Elsewhere to give might to a
Soul that is already
Fled.[21]

Cultural and economic dominance is dangerous because it makes the full identity and needs of a careseeking person invisible to the pastoral counselor. When a person has lost her language, her images, her religion, her practices, she will have difficulty communicating her identity in a counseling relationship. When suppressed cultures have been damaged or destroyed by ideological and military power, colonialization of the mind becomes a part of the micro-level interaction between careseeker and caregiver. Retrieval of suppressed cultures and radical critique of dominant cultures must be an aspect of the theories and practices of pastoral theology and counseling.

To summarize, I have described three levels of cultural and economic analysis that are needed in pastoral theology and counseling. The first level is understanding differences. To do this, we must make cultures and economics central modes of analysis with the assumption that many of the traits we think of as the common human condition come from our social reality. We must respect multiplicity in our clients, our communities, and our world. The second level is understanding that cultural and economic differences are often unjustly organized according to race, gender, sexuality, and culture. Individuals and groups live in social situations where resources are limited, and pastoral caregivers who identify with the dominant culture tend to underestimate the amount of injustice that has shaped a person's life. The third level is cultural and economic dominance, that is, the ability of some groups to make their values the norm by which all other cultures are allowed to exist. This is the most difficult level to understand and work with because, in many cases, it has defined individuals and groups out of existence, and destroyed them at the deepest level of spirituality. In *Deliver Us from Evil*, I define evil as "the abuse of power that destroys bodies and spirits."[22] Cultural and economic dominance are important in any understanding of evil.

I am suggesting that pastoral leaders must learn how to do micro-analysis of their ministries in light of these distinctions between cultural and economic differences, injustice, and dominance. When a woman from Nicaragua who has been victimized by family violence seeks pastoral care, the pastoral caregiver must understand the complexities of this encounter. She not only brings her culture of language, religion, and daily practices, but she also represents 500 years of economic oppression and resilient survival. Not only is her life the result of generations of economic injustice, but the U.S. culture continues to dominate and destroy the culture of resistance that has been creatively built up over centuries of rebellion and sacrifice. What has been lost by the person seeking care cannot be seen by the pastoral caregiver without extraordinary sensitivity, especially if he or she is socialized into the dominant U.S. culture and benefits from the economic dominance.

Diagnosis and Care for Individuals and Families in Situations of Economic Vulnerability

The standard criticism of care and counseling as developed in the dominant white cultures of the U.S. and Europe is well known. Behavioristic, psychoanalytic, and human fulfillment theories all make similar assumptions. They tend to be individualistic rather than relational, and they assume a benevolent environment where people can make choices about how to express their sense of initiative and autonomy.[23] As we know from our analysis, these are middle-class assumptions that do not fit the living context of working-class and poor people, the majority of persons in every society in the world. These theories assert that persons can increase their autonomy by strengthening their sense of self and manipulating the environment to their advantage. Missing are a fully developed communal definition of persons, an adequate theory of oppressive social conditions, and a theology of liberation and empowerment. Liberation and feminist scholars during the second half of the twentieth century made significant challenges to these anthropological assumptions, and progress has been made in both theory and practice. But dominant theories and practices vastly misjudge the impact of economic vulnerability and family violence on personality development.

First, pastoral caregivers need to have training in how to counsel with people regardless of their cultural and economic situation. While we have been trained to observe nonverbal communication, increased cultural sensitivity requires paying attention to nonverbal communication in new ways, monitoring one's own nonverbal communication for class bias. Learning how to understand the cultural embeddedness of nonverbal communication is a form of cultural competence that requires workshops and regular supervision. Words and phrases are often impossible to understand outside of their history and culture. This becomes especially evident if the pastoral counselor and parishioner have different native languages. Also, the education level of a person affects the ability to communicate. Those who have not had an opportunity for formal education may have limited vocabulary to express themselves, and they may not be able to comprehend the vocabulary of the counselor. Brenda Ruiz has shared several rules that she uses to remind herself of the nature of empathy with Nicaraguan women in counseling:

1. Use simple language, clear explanations, concrete examples.

2. If you assign tasks to be done at home, they should not be too complicated, and make sure the client understands what the task is.

3. Do not be discouraged if the client does not do the tasks the first time around. This is especially true of abused women who are already overburdened by other tasks.

4. Check with the client about whether the suggestions you make are realistic for her situation, e.g., recommending periodic family outings when the family is not eating well.

5. Help the client understand that unemployment or lack of access to education is not necessarily her fault or her family's fault.

6. Try to explore with the client if there are any possibilities for any community assistance, even at very rudimentary levels, e.g., groups of women taking care of other women's children while they work.[24]

Second, pastoral caregivers need to learn how to do an economic diagnosis in order to assess the impact of economic vulnerability on past development, present functioning, and future dreams of a person who seeks care from the church.

Interview form to assess economic vulnerability

Asking about personal economic situations can be very awkward. Consider Linda Crockett's experience of being poor as a child:

When I was a member of Swamp Lutheran, I was ashamed to invite other people in leadership positions to my house. It seemed everyone on the church council and chairing committees had expensive houses (including the pastor). I did/ do not. Probably some of these people were living way over their means, but nothing in their lives within that congregation would have caused them to be even mildly critical of the capitalist imperative to acquire more and more material goods and wealth (which equates with good and morality).[25]

The following information should be collected first about the pastoral caregiver and discussed with a supervisor. This will help the counselor become aware of how it feels to disclose such personal information about one's economic situation. Then the same questions can be discussed with careseekers during the history and assessment phase of pastoral counseling. For many careseekers, discussing money can be quite sensitive. People with limited resources and/or significant debt may experience deep shame in disclosing this information and blame themselves for being inadequate. Shame about money is part of the ideology that disempowers the poor by inducing shame instead of encouraging critique of the system. Therefore, counselors need to be especially sensitive when asking these diagnostic questions.

I.   Demographic Data: age, gender, race, culture, marital status, family, occupation, religion

II. Social and Economic Class
    A. Socioeconomic status (SES), present time
       1. Education
       2. Occupation
       3. Income
    B. Property, investments, net worth (housing, pension, insurance, cash, investments)
    C. Expenses, liabilities, debts (food, housing, transportation, health care, insurance, education, child-care, fines, legal expenses, credit cards)
    D. Family history (education, occupation, income)
       1. 1st generation, grandparents
       2. 2nd generation, parents, aunts and uncles
       3. 3rd generation, self, partner, and siblings
       4. 4th generation, children (present, dreams for)
    E. Control at work and leisure
       1. Employed, unemployed, history of employment
       2. Full-time, part-time, seasonal, temporary
       3. Day labor, wage labor, salary, level of benefits
       4. Worker, team leader, supervisor, middle management, VP, CEO
       5. Professional/manager, intermediate and junior nonmanual, skilled manual, semi-skilled manual and service, unskilled manual
       6. Vacation, sick days, leisure time, control of schedule at work
       7. Health care coverage, housing, means of transportation

III. Religious Affiliation
    A. Spiritual resources
    B. Theological perspective: fundamentalist, conservative, evangelical, Pentecostal, charismatic, liturgical, social action

      C. Church culture: storefront, independent, denominational
      D. Social class of church: poor, working class, middle class, upper class
      E. Level of training of pastoral leadership

IV. Pastoral Care Experiences
      A. How many times have you talked to a pastoral caregiver about personal or spiritual issues?
      B. How would you evaluate the effectiveness of the pastoral care you have received?
      C. How similar or different were you and pastoral caregivers you have talked to in terms of class, gender, race, culture, other variables?
      D. Give examples of how you have felt understood or misunderstood by a pastoral caregiver.

Discussion

In poor locales such as Nicaragua and poor communities in the U.S., there may be little difference between pastoral caregivers and careseekers, as the whole population suffers from economic oppression, and the opportunities for education and training have been limited. Such a list of questions can provide theoretical tools to understand the oppression that affects the whole community. In these communities, there is often a lack of analytical tools for deconstructing the systems of economic and political power that keep certain populations in positions of economic vulnerability. The list of questions could increase awareness about the causes of oppression and thus help pastoral leaders be more effective with the people they serve. Rather than accepting the individualistic assumptions imported into the community by the media and ideologies of domination from universities, professions, and churches, pastoral leaders could identify with the resistance to evil in the population and learn to embrace theologies that empower rather than oppress the people. Liberation theology in Latin America has provided a literature that moves in this direction,[26] and feminist forms of Liberation theology are emerging, that challenge the patriarchal assumptions of the first generation of Liberation scholars.[27]

    The above questions also can help with the micro-analysis necessary for U.S. pastoral leaders, such as ordained pastors and pastoral counselors in the mainline churches, who have had opportunities for education, economic resources, and social status. Looking at one's own economic situation in relation to the local community and in relation to the world's population is often painful for those who have social privilege and status. But the discrepancies discovered are all the more important to list and analyze. Many pastoral leaders in the wealthy countries discover that they too frequently reflect and serve their middle-class interests rather than Jesus Christ. Becoming aware of the economic differences of various classes of people is crucial to providing effective caregiving in the name of Jesus Christ.

Standard sociological analysis of class is usually done with a formula that includes education, occupation, and income. Those with high socioeconomic status are usually high in all three, although sometimes education and/or occupation are weighted more heavily. For example, clergy are often given high SES regardless of their income because they are held in respect by the local community and have above-average education. Some business people with high incomes are not rated high SES because of the products they deal with or the stigma of dealing with "dirty" money. When working in a poor country such as Nicaragua, the call to ministry might be seen partly as a move toward higher SES even if there is not adequate financial support. In a recent survey of students in my classes, I discovered that almost all of them were improving the SES of their family of origin by going into the ministry and pursuing a master's degree. Interestingly, the children of ordained ministers often seek positions in more lucrative occupations, such as law, medicine, and secular counseling.

Compiling a family history of socioeconomic status is important in evaluating economic vulnerability. A progressive graph toward higher SES can be understood as a family's attempt to improve its situation, as when immigrant children achieve some education and improve their occupational opportunities.

For many other families the intergenerational graph is not progressive. Pastoral caregivers should know the family history. If they discover generation after generation of economic vulnerability, they should wonder if this marginality is not a result of severe oppression over a long period of time. Some sociologists have created a category called the "underclass" to describe this severe form of intergenerational economic oppression. However, the term has come into disrepute because it has been used to "blame the victims" for causing their own economic vulnerability. Politicians use the term to identify the deficiencies in poor communities that make them resistant to charity and responsibility. It is important for pastoral caregivers to know that a significant percentage of the U.S. population has been poor for many generations and that the reason for this poverty is systemic. U.S. market capitalism requires a large pool of impoverished persons, and those who are caught in such oppression should not be blamed for the injustice that is done to them. The widespread poverty in the U.S. and around the world is not caused by deficiencies in the population, but by multiple levels of oppression from which people cannot escape.

In countries such as Nicaragua, where there is extreme poverty, there is very little movement toward higher SES for the majority of the population. Income, education, and lucrative occupations have been out of reach for 80 percent of the Nicaraguan population for 500 years, since the Spanish conquest of the continent. The Sandinista Revolution was a momentary glimpse of the hope and aspirations of the population, but its short-lived existence meant that the majority did not experience any change in their economic situation. When the Contra War sapped their hopes through the loss of life and daily terror, the people voted to end the war rather than trust in an economic plan that had never before benefited them.

Pastoral caregivers need to understand the effects of centuries of extreme poverty on the lives of people. Once we begin to perceive the effects of poverty, how can we continue to urge oppressive psychological theories that emphasize agency, autonomy, and a progressive view of the future? Rather, we must focus on understanding the people's creative resistance, which is based on skills developed over centuries of oppression. What could be seen as self-defeating behaviors according to Northern theories of personality must, instead, be seen as forms of resistance that enhance survival and feed the faith of the people in themselves and in God, in spite of their circumstances.

The above questions suggest that the standard model that measures socioeconomic status (SES) is inadequate. Instead we need to ask additional questions about how much control people have over their work and daily lives. When we look at control over one's life, some surprises emerge. For example, even though the peasant farmers of Nicaragua have to work very hard for their survival, some value the autonomy. They can choose whether to farm the land, herd the cows, buy and sell their products. Lest we make too much of these choices, we need to say that the dangers to survival weigh foremost on the lives of many Nicaraguans. I have stayed overnight with several peasant families, and I know that the women often rise from bed at 3 a.m. to get water from the spring a mile away before it runs out for the day. The men are in the fields from sunup to sundown without any machinery to help them with the farming. So it is important not to romanticize the rural lives of the poor. However, we also have to notice the dignity and pride of some poor people who have developed a culture and a set of habits that include some intrinsic satisfaction. Even if the peasant farmers had access to more capital, some might not change the pattern of their daily lives very much, unless, of course, their lives were dominated by agribusiness.

On the other hand, some middle-income North Americans work in jobs that give them very little control over their daily lives. Some industrial workers spend long hours in dangerous situations where they are treated disrespectfully. Even though their wages are high by world standards, their lives are miserable. Many studies about the dehumanizing effects of industrial jobs have proved that capitalism exacts a high price from some workers for their wages.[28] Without unions, workers all over the world are dehumanized, exposed to dangerous working conditions, and paid only subsistence wages. Within capitalist theory, workers are interchangeable, and the elite who manage the world economy exploit an unlimited supply of temporary workers who have no political power.

The section of the questionnaire that focuses on religious affiliation also features class issues. Forms of church life in all social classes vary, from storefronts to cathedrals in the center of town. Sometimes a large church serves as a center of activity for the working class and poor, as I have seen in Cuernavaca, Mexico, and Managua, Nicaragua. But often, even at the same time, the large church is a center of power for the wealthy, and the poor who attend have very little influence over its forms of worship and programs. Grassroots churches, such as storefronts and some Pentecostal efforts, develop their own forms of religion, sometimes incorporating aspects of pre- and non-Christian culture into their rituals and other practices. Such smaller churches are often stigmatized in dominant Christian cultures as superstitious and even pagan. U.S. television presents snake handlers of Kentucky as exotic or strange, without providing the social and economic history of their faith. Their religion is a curiosity not to be taken seriously as a religious practice, just as the poor communities from which they come are not taken seriously. So this questionnaire can be helpful in increasing the caregiver's awareness of the class structure of the Christian faith, making possible a challenge to the hierarchy of religion from respected to disrespected persons.

Finally, the questionnaire asks about a person's previous experiences of pastoral care. Many who come to a pastoral leader for care have taken such initiative before. These questions direct the caregiver's attention to how effective such caregiving was perceived. My suspicion is that many people who experience economic vulnerability have received patronizing care, lack of empathy, and advice that was inappropriate to their socioeconomic situation. Those who are economically vulnerable are often disempowered by pastoral leaders who act toward them according to their class position. They may sense that they are perceived not only as poor but also as stupid, lazy, and unable to make sound decisions. Some students I have supervised forget their training in empathy when talking with a poor person, launching into giving advice, as if the person is a child who lacks wisdom. Such students do not respect the competencies of those who have survived in an economy in which their existence is optional.[29] Asking about previous pastoral care explores the possibility that previous injuries from the church can be named and mended, allowing the new care to be healing. If the goal of pastoral care for the oppressed provides empowerment, class issues that disempower so many people must be addressed.

It is my hope that this modest proposal on how to evaluate the economic vulnerability of persons seeking care from the church will gospel of nonviolence is an important resource for support of caregivers when they make these moral choices.

(c) *Respect the victim's autonomy.* The person coming for help is already an expert in survival and probably has been strategizing for months or years on the best course of action. By coming for help, she or he is seeking resources that will help. The caregiver should not jump to conclusions about the best action to take, but instead be an adviser who is willing to help. If the victim is a child, making a report to legal authorities is the only effective way to protect the child. In most states, professionals in medical, educational, and legal fields who work with children and families are mandated reporters of child abuse, and this policy of reporting is recommended for clergy and other pastoral leaders as well. Local congregations and judicatories should create policies of required reporting of child abuse. Adult victims, on the other hand, need to retain a sense of agency and make their own decisions about the future. Accompaniment by the caregiver during this process of decision making may be critically important. Instructions on developing safety plans for adult victims are available from most shelters for battered women.

(d) *Promote access to community services.* Some churches are located in communities that have organized services to respond to family violence. Pastoral caregivers must be knowledgeable about local services, such as shelters for battered women, rape crisis centers, child protection agencies, legal authorities, and hospitals. Some churches are located in areas without effective services. Brenda Ruiz reports that this is the case in Nicaragua, where nearly all social services are lacking. In these cases, the church itself should take responsibility for developing services for families experiencing abuse.

(e) *Respect confidentiality.* Confidentiality in situations of family violence requires more than not discussing the situation with others; it requires protecting victims and holding abusers accountable. Protecting adult victims requires a covenant that the caregiver will not take any actions to jeopardize the health and safety of the person, such as talking to the abuser. In this sense, confidentiality is important to observe when working with adults. Pastoral caregivers should not engage in marital or family counseling if one suspects violence. Reporting child abuse is an exception to confidentiality because the life and health of a child is at stake. Holding abusers accountable may require reporting child abuse or alerting other adults that they are in danger. Most pastoral caregivers need special training in how to practice confidentiality while working in the best interests of victims of violence.[32]

Accountability for Abusers: Pastoral caregivers must know how to evaluate a danger of family violence and how to hold abusers accountable. Following are several principles to guide our caregiving with abusers:

stimulate a wider discussion about how the theories and practice pastoral care can be revised.

Principles of Care in Situations of Family Violence

Women's resistance communities have raised the issue of sexual a domestic violence within families as a major issue for church and socie All women are vulnerable to violence, especially in families and intima relationships. When women are economically vulnerable, their jeopar increases because they lack the resources to protect themselves and se healing. As a result of feminist efforts in countering family violence, w see that we must challenge the church to change its understanding an practices. Rather than blame women for bringing violence o themselves, we must understand violence as a part of the fabric o patriarchal capitalism. Because women are vulnerable to family violence the church must act to protect women and prevent violence from occurring.

Pastoral caregivers should have four primary goals when working with families where physical, sexual, and emotional violence is taking place:

1. Safety for the victim(s)

2. Accountability for abusers

3. Healing and mourning losses

4. Reconnection with other persons[30]

Safety for Victims/Survivors: Pastoral caregivers must pay special attention to the safety issues when working with victims of family violence:[31]

(a) *Believe and validate the victim's experience of violence.* The caregiver must listen to the victim, believe the story, acknowledge the feelings expressed, and let the person know that she or he is not alone. This often goes against the natural urge to believe the best about people (i.e., the perpetrator) and to minimize the terrible truths being heard. Many victims report that the first response of the caregiver determines whether they have any hope that their lives can change and whether they have the necessary confidence to take action to seek safety from the violence in their lives. Jesus' care of the poor and marginalized in Galilee and Judea is a model of how a pastoral caregiver can validate the experience of victims of family violence.

(b) *Acknowledge the injustice.* Beyond believing the victim, the caregiver must take a moral position that the violence is wrong. No one deserves to be violated in any way, not by a parent, partner, or any other loved one. Clearly stating that the violence is wrong is important at the crisis stage of intervention. The pastor might say, "I am sorry this has happened to you. Violence should never happen to anyone." Jesus'

(a) *The Violence Must Stop!* Pastoral caregivers must keep a clear focus on the safety of those who are vulnerable, and be willing to confront the abuser with the fact that violent behavior is wrong. Clearly saying "This is violence, and it is wrong" is a form of accountability that is needed.

(b) *Do not accept rationalizations or blaming of the victim.* Most abusers will try to distract the caregiver with stories that try to justify their behavior and blame the victim: the child was misbehaving; my partner was having an affair; my job is very stressful. The caregiver should keep the focus on the violent acts and the need for safety for the vulnerable.

(c) *Do not take the abuser's word that the violence has stopped.* Minimizing and lying are common behaviors for abusers. Usually it will be necessary for family members to separate until there is no more danger of abusive behavior, and trained counselors who talk directly to the victims must make an assessment of the danger.

(d) *Hold the abuser accountable.* Caregivers must be clear that ceasing the violence requires more than promises. It requires actions that promote the safety of victims, such as cooperating with the requirements of other agencies, leaving the home, obeying orders of protection, pleading guilty in court, and attending educational programs. Promises to change are part of the cycle of abuse, and caregivers should not be taken in by such promises. To change, the abuser must accept responsibility for the violence and seek help.

(e) *Offer the abuser hope that change is possible.* Abusive behavior does not have to be a lifetime pattern; abusers can learn to understand their responsibility to protect the vulnerable and to seek healing for their own underlying wounds. Check with the local domestic violence program, crisis hotline, or mental health center to learn where treatment programs are in your area.[33]

There is much more for pastoral caregivers to learn about providing adequate care in situations of family violence. Fortunately, many training and religious resources are available. Every level of church life should be engaged in training church leaders to deal with family violence so they can begin to protect the vulnerable and hold abusers accountable.

Revisions in the Economic Structures of Pastoral Care and Counseling

When the twentieth-century pastoral care movement in the U.S. began around 1920, theories in the church for helping people in difficulty were inadequate. Some pastors had intuitions about principles of care, but such wisdom was not developed and integrated into the training and expectations of pastors. Too often pastors told those with medical illnesses that they lacked faith, or told those in economic vulnerability that they had moral failures such as laziness, alcohol abuse, and so forth. Caregiving often had a heavy moralistic tone of sin and repentance. With the help of the new psychologies, pastors began listening in new ways as people brought their concerns to the church. From this creative beginning, clinical pastoral education in medical centers and professional pastoral counseling in mental health clinics became available for clergy and laity in more affluent communities in the U.S. This movement is now worldwide, and Christian communities in many places are demanding pastoral care and counseling for their suffering people.

However, certain middle-class and professional prejudices were also built into the theories and practices. For example, a fee-for-service system was organized to support pastoral counselors, which made such services available to some people, but excluded others. As a result, pastoral counseling in the U.S. has become a niche market that provides services for people who do not have adequate insurance but seek the personal growth that comes from counseling. However, those without economic resources are largely excluded from care. Another example of the profession's middle-class orientation is that it adopted a one-on-one model of depth counseling that could be very beneficial for certain growth goals, but that limited the number of people one pastoral counselor could see. Furthermore, the field developed the expectation that pastoral counseling would be a long-term relationship that lasted for months or years and thus became prohibitively expensive for even dedicated careseekers. As a result of intensified professionalism with its complex training programs, many pastors have not been competent to practice according to this model of long-term individual counseling. Most pastors of local churches struggle to obtain the minimal educational requirements for leadership, let alone specialize in pastoral counseling. Even though the needs of people for healing are high, the theories of pastoral counseling do not allow this service to be available for most Christians in the world.

I suggest that the pastoral care and counseling model must be revised to take into account the needs of persons in situations of family violence and economic vulnerability. I do not have time to develop such a model here; others have done excellent work in this area.[34] In short, pastoral care of the people of God requires a community model of care that meets people in their social, cultural, and economic situation. Rather than individuals' paying for pastoral care and counseling, the expenses of care must be borne by the whole community. Clinical pastoral education, which brings highly trained teachers and caregivers into hospitals and other institutions to do crisis counseling and promote educational initiatives, has such a model of chaplaincy. Rather than focus on one-to-one counseling, pastoral counselors can train laypersons to engage in support and educational groups for those needing intense healing. Rather than focus on long-term counseling, pastoral counselors can organize the community so that everyone has long-term care through healing groups.

Rather than limit certified pastoral counseling to those with advanced degrees, pastoral counselors can develop a model that trains people at many different levels. For example, the Baptist Seminary in Managua has three degree programs: one for those working at a high school level; one for those working at a college level; and one for those working at a master's level. The curriculum is designed to meet the needs of all three groups of students with the goal of improving their skills as much as possible within the limitations of the students. Pastoral counseling can adopt such a model of training and make it available to a much wider group of church leaders.

Given the high percentage of people in our communities who face family violence and economic vulnerability, the resources of pastoral care and counseling should be more widely available. It is not right that only a small percentage of Christians in mostly middle-class communities can afford it. As the church begins to integrate the insights from decades of research and practice, new models of care can be developed.

In this chapter, I have focused on ministries of care in relation to family violence and economic vulnerability. I have suggested that pastoral care and counseling be changed in practical ways that can make a difference in the lives of many people. First, pastoral caregivers must understand the dynamics of cultural and economic difference, injustice, and dominance so they can understand the careseekers who come to them. Second, pastoral caregivers must make economic vulnerability a part of diagnosis and care plans by asking about income, expenses, family history, and control over family economic life. Third, pastoral caregivers must know more about the principles of care in situations of family violence so that they do more to protect victims and hold abusers accountable. Fourth, pastoral caregivers must examine the economics of their own lives and evaluate their practices. Can those who need care the most afford the services, or does the economic structure of pastoral counseling prevent most from receiving the care of the church? In the next chapter, I look more closely at the practice of ministry within the congregation.

15

The Spirituality of Practicing Goodness

Recently my brother Ed, who is a pastor, wrote to me about a basic change in his understanding of the gospel: "I find myself working on themes from a spirituality perspective. The programs of Shalem [Institute][1] have been very helpful in making the shift from what we 'ought to be doing' to what we are led to do by the grace of God."[2] He said his orientation toward God, himself, and the world has shifted from a heavy weight of responsibility to an attitude of gratitude to God for all good things. Through the grace of God, we are invited to share in the bounty of the creation. So we no longer have to turn away from Jesus, guilty and ashamed for our role in injustice. Rather, we can follow him and become part of the generous new world that is coming into being. The invitation to render unto God what is God's is not an obligation, but an invitation into a richer, fuller life from which we will not want to turn.

During one of my trips to Nicaragua, a group of North Americans and Europeans were discussing the difficulty of living a relational life in a world where so much evil exists. One person said he avoids feeling overwhelmed by such moral dilemmas by concentrating on the issues most immediate to himself—his own integrity and his relationships with friends. He tries to wrestle some mutual satisfaction and pleasure from life.

"What about practicing goodness?" another person asked. He went on to say that a basic need of everyone is to practice goodness so that we know our life is not just for ourselves and a few friends, but also for the good of the world. That simple phrase—practicing goodness—can be a form of faithfulness to the ambiguous life that comes when we follow Jesus.[3]

In this final chapter, I describe the steps in transformation, especially for those who are middle-class. While I have represented the views of oppressed groups in this project, I am aware that most of my readers will be middle-class pastors and church members in the U.S. This is because the book is written in English, in academic style, with the middle-class professional orientation of the author. I am committed to being part of a global church that promotes equality according to gender, race, and class. In this chapter, I focus specifically on the changes necessary for middle-class persons who want to belong to God's global church.

I believe that the spirituality of practicing goodness, especially for the transformation of the world toward economic justice and nonviolence, is not an obligation imposed by God, but a call into God's presence. How do we begin to make changes in the way we think, live, and pray so that the love and power of God are more real in our lives? How do we understand the steps in our own transformation that move us toward an inclusive community of loving justice across barriers of gender? I believe that the transformation we seek is a gradual process of opening ourselves to the grace of God, receiving the witness from those for whom God has made "a way out of no way," and accompanying those who have gained wisdom from their journey. Those who know God's love and power the best are seldom given high status by a world in which the values of competitive greed and violent domination rule. Those who know God best are often surprising: the vulnerable stranger who asks for a place to stay; the wise prisoner who has no hope of being released; the survivor of violence who knows the depths of evil and the resilience of the human spirit.

On the one hand, spirituality is an intensely personal journey as we each seek our own genuine relationship with God. Alfred North Whitehead said, "Religion is what we do with our solitariness." There are moments when each of us is alone with ourselves and God, seeking in our deepest selves a place of peace and integrity. In the moments when we discover that sacred space, we know we are accepted just as we are, and we know how to be and what to do in that moment. At other times, we may not have such full assurance, but we count on memory. Even when we feel utterly alone, our faith reminds us of times when God's presence was so near that we felt no fear, no desire, and no blame.

On the other hand, spirituality is a corporate journey, one that takes place in and through community. At times we are surrounded by a great cloud of witnesses: ancestors who discovered faith in their own lives and passed on that knowledge to us. At such times we join with others in the great hymns of the church, glad to be part of a vast network of believers who try to live with courage in the midst of challenges. We know that we are just one generation in a line that extends as far back as recorded history and extends forward beyond our own children and grandchildren to unborn generations everywhere. We are part of the web of human and natural creation in which God is actively seeking new embodiments of love and power.

I draw on my experiences of transformation through my companions in Nicaragua who have guided me patiently for the last ten years, and my experiences with survivors of violence who have drawn me out of my patriarchal world into a new community of hope. I also draw on the experiences of those who have shared their faith pilgrimages with me over the years of my ministry, some because they needed resources for their own healing and spiritual growth, and some because God sent them at particular times to witness to me in my search for healing and faith. What we get from this pilgrimage is far more valuable than anything we contribute, though the accumulated solidarity of those who practice goodness does make a difference over time.

I have developed a nine-stage theory of spiritual growth that describes the process of transformation available to all persons who respond to the needs of others. As we respond with care to others, their spirit changes us, and this opens up new worlds of spiritual growth for both careseeker and caregiver. The resulting spiritual pilgrimage takes us far from where we started, and as we journey we learn more and more about the nature of God's love and justice. The nine stages are:

1. Open Receptivity

2. Listening and Believing

3. Seeking Knowledge

4. Courage to Act

5. Accompaniment

6. Transformation of Self and Congregation

7. Making Long-term Commitments

8. Prophetic Action

9. Transformation of Worship and Community Life

1. *Open Receptivity.* Spiritual transformation often begins with a simple encounter. Someone comes into our lives with a request for care that triggers our curiosity, anger, hurt, or desire. We cannot let such experiences go, because we know that something incredibly important awaits us. There is much more going on than helping another; it is a step toward engagement in our own journey of transformation.

*Broken Vows*⁴ tells the story of a congregation that decided to get involved in starting a shelter for battered women. The dramatic event that started the congregation in this direction was the pastor's being assaulted by his son-in-law and seriously injured by a knife wound to the head. Rallying behind the pastor, his daughter, and the family, the congregation opened itself to the issue of domestic violence. Quickly they discovered many other survivors of family violence in their community and learned that the services to protect survivors were inadequate. Before long the church found itself committed to taking action.

Rev. Linda Wright Simmons and Larry Clark, of Rockledge Presbyterian Church, Orlando, Florida, visited Project Ebenezer in Ninquinhomo, Nicaragua, as part of a work camp. They expected it to be just one more service project in a series designed to help the youth and adults develop some global sensitivity. But something unexpected happened on this trip. Participating in discussions with director Francisco Juarez and the campesinos affected them more deeply than usual. The result was a long-term commitment to provide labor for new educational buildings and equipment for a veterinary clinic to help deal with indigenous illnesses affecting the small animals.

Open receptivity is a spiritual doorway. When we walk through it we have the opportunity to be blessed by deeply bonded relationships with persons who have experienced economic injustice and violence. We no longer care about these issues in an abstract way. When we are engaged with people across barriers of gender, race, and class, we begin to see ourselves and everything else from new perspectives. Receptivity to others is a way of being receptive to the Holy Spirit and allowing our lives to be transformed every day by God's love.

2. *Listening and Believing.* Open receptivity can be only momentary unless we are ready to listen and believe the voices that are speaking to us. Our lives are full of surprises that we ignore and interesting facts that spark our curiosity and pass on without influence. Even dramatic events can be interesting for a short time, and then we put them out of consciousness. Listening often does not feel like a choice, for we are compelled. But in such moments there are always conflicting voices that tell us to remember our other commitments, that tell us we have too little time to take on something else, that rationalize our wish to draw back in fear and timidity.

Listening to the Nicaraguan people was not comfortable, because they told stories about unrelenting suffering, while at the same time voicing a kind of faith I had never seen before. Tina had lost her husband, son, and daughter in a Contra attack in their mountainous village of fifty people. She took me to the memorial where their names were inscribed. She told of the day airplanes dropped bombs in the valley below, and of the day when the Contra soldiers came out of the woods and she herded as many children as possible to safety down the mountain. She told how her dreams were disturbed by images of her dead family urging her to remember them and to persevere in the struggle by telling the truth about what had happened. She traveled all over the U.S. and Europe telling her story and soliciting solidarity for the people, and then she elected to return to the village, which had no electricity or running water, to be with her people. I had to face the fact that her suffering was caused by the U.S. government, who paid for training and equipping the Contras, and who advised troop commanders how to terrorize the civilian population so they would not be able to support their government and its defensive army. Her story confronted me with my own complicity in her suffering and asked me to change allegiance for the sake of human solidarity. I had to choose whether to listen and believe her story or indulge my denial. I chose to believe, not because she had suffered, but because of the deep spirituality that shone through her words, her eyes, her physical presence. I believed her, and her story settled into my deepest self. Because of the hours we spent together, Tina's words continue to guide me today.

The principle of listening and believing is an important step in the process of spiritual transformation. Johann Baptist Metz calls it listening to the suffering and hope of the people and believing their witness, even if it invites us into uncomfortable spaces.[5]

3. *Seeking Knowledge.* The initial moments of spiritual breakthrough come when we find ourselves receptive to the witness of those who have deep faith through suffering. But these moments of receptivity must be followed by disciplined study and information. What Whitehead calls "the romance of education"[6] is not sufficient to sustain us through the full process of discovery. When entering a new world for the first time, we need guides who know the language and have traveled there before. When I go to Nicaragua, I need help from those who are fluent in Spanish because I cannot understand the subtle ways that people use language. I need drivers who know the roads, who know where to get pure water, who know the places to avoid in order to remain safe. Likewise, we must turn to informed advisers whenever we enter into new spiritual territory. Fortunately, as soon as we enter into the new world, we find wise people who can serve as guides.

Rockledge Presbyterian Church felt compelled to do something to help Rancho Ebenezer. Linda Simmons contacted Larry Clark, a trained veterinarian who worked for the U.S. Department of Agriculture. He had knowledge of animal health and would be able to provide expert advice on the tropical diseases threatening small animals. With Linda's knowledge of solidarity work and Larry's knowledge of veterinary medicine, they were able to develop a plan to provide needed resources for Nicaraguan peasants.

Linda Crockett made a commitment to study Spanish so she would be able to communicate better with the women and men of El Salvador. She studied the history of the country, the history of U.S. policies toward Central America, and the health and welfare statistics from the United Nations. As she continued to visit El Salvador, she became more and more knowledgeable about the needs and the global context within which the people lived.

The principle of seeking knowledge is crucial as a step toward responding to the spiritual awakening in individuals and congregations. God has given us the ability to study the world in depth, to pursue our commitments through books, libraries, Internet resources, workshops, and Bible study. With additional knowledge, we are more prepared to respond to the lure of the adventure.

4. *Courage to Act.* Finding courage to act is a critical turning point. God's invitation often comes in the form of stories of oppression. When we allow ourselves to be drawn into these stories, listen, and believe, and we seek information that helps us understand the context, we are confronted with a choice: whether to act in the direction of engagement and commitment, or to withdraw into the comfortable world we know best.

Until this stage, there is always the option to let the new experiences go as just another interesting form of entertainment. Susan Thistlethwaite and George Cairns call this moment the danger of "theological tourism," that is, the endless consuming of different experiences for the sake of personal enrichment that leads nowhere.[7] Now we are faced with taking a serious step of engagement that leads to more serious commitment. One trip to Nicaragua was interesting, but two or three began to change my life, especially when I tried to use my education and skills to make a genuine contribution to the struggle.

At the moment of decision, we need courage. Other voices will make themselves heard to remind the community that drastic change is about to occur. When Linda Crockett moved beyond reading about El Salvador and told her pastor that she was thinking about going to the war zone to impede the war effort against the peasants, he tried to talk her out of it. He said that she had too many other responsibilities to think about such a dangerous mission, that she should consider her husband, her young children, her job, and her church. When she persisted and asked for a service of blessing, the pastor at first refused, "because the congregation is not ready for this step." Several other members wondered whether she was being duped by communists, and why she felt qualified to challenge U.S. foreign policy. Linda had her own fears about what she was doing and struggled with her doubts about her competence to make this decision. However, she knew that she was called to go to El Salvador. Her initial experiences of hearing the stories of faith in the midst of war led her to the point of conviction. She knew she was at a crossroads, but she also knew that she needed to go on. The pull by the Holy Spirit was stronger than the conservative voices of the status quo. She wanted her life to be about something, and she was determined to go on in spite of the external and internal obstacles. Later, when she decided to enter the war zone of her memories of child abuse, her courage would be needed again.

Courage is required because God invites us into new worlds where we are strangers and will be challenged to grow. To act, we have to trust in God more than ourselves. However, many who have made this journey report that they don't feel courageous, and they don't experience fear as much as the excitement of the invitation from God to become a new person. Courage to act is the doorway into new life, and we must walk through it with faith in what God has in store for us.

5. *Accompaniment.* When we have the courage to act, we find ourselves in a new situation. We put ourselves into the world of the other witnesses, a location where our own authority and resources are limited. Accompaniment on the personal level means staying in close contact through the difficulties and victories of daily life and providing mutual support for one another depending on the needs. On the organizational level, it means working together toward common goals, each contributing what is needed to survive oppression. Accompaniment across boundaries of gender, race, and class means being willing to take risks that might not be understood by one's neighbors, such as opposing U.S. policies toward Nicaragua even when there is no political base in the U.S. for such a position.

Accompaniment can take many forms: Linda visited a church in El Salvador during an attack by the paramilitary; some people build houses with Habitat for Humanity; I helped lead a workshop on domestic violence in Nicaragua. When we accompany the oppressed, we often find ourselves with people who are wiser than we are and who can guide us into new spiritual knowledge. I visited Tina Perez three times in Logartilla. Each time I felt I was in the presence of a spiritual guide. She had survived horrendous evil and ongoing poverty, and she had developed deep faith in God and special sensitivities to the Spirit. She could interpret dreams, give advice, and tell parables that touched my soul. I wanted to be with her because I knew I was in the presence of God.

An inspiring person for me is Herman Ruether, a Christian who has worked to support the labor movement all his life. He has been active in attending meetings, staying informed, and supporting progressive programs by the labor movement. He has especially been supportive of labor organizations who attempt to organize immigrants, working-class women in service jobs, and farm laborers. His life is a model of how an intellectual can also be a Christian activist who accompanies working-class people in their struggles for justice.

The principle of accompaniment has been implemented in many other organizations that work on issues of economic justice and family violence. Activists in Latin America have chosen this term in preference to other possible terms for describing relationships between those who seek empowerment and those who choose to advocate for them. The Chicago Religious Leadership Network practices accompaniment in relation to justice groups in Latin America.[8] The leaders listen carefully to Latin American activists, meet with them to analyze issues, and together develop strategies to confront the governments in the U.S. and Latin America. The Latin American activists have the balance of authority because they are risking their lives every day for justice. When they see U.S. policies that hurt the people, they send an urgent message to the CRLN and other groups to take political action, whether lobbying for a specific law, demonstrating at the School of the Americas, or other actions. These North American groups have committed themselves to accompany Latin America through whatever takes place.

Domestic violence shelters in the U.S. have adopted the image of accompaniment to describe the work of advocates who work with survivors. After decades of work, advocates discovered that they frequently made bad policy decisions when they followed their own intuitions about what was right. When they listened to battered women, however, they could better evaluate the effects of certain laws and policies on domestic violence. For example, advocates had to decide whether to press for mandatory arrest laws. At first it seemed like a good idea because it takes the pressure off the victim to testify in court. But in some cases, women reported that they were less likely to call the police because they lost the choice of whether to press their case in court or not. Especially in poor communities, victims did not want their partner to go to jail, but they did want protection when he became violent. Linda Crockett organized a training conference, "Walking with Survivors of Family Violence: A Call to Accompaniment."[9] The principle of accompaniment is that survivors have special authority to influence the behaviors of advocates who accompany them.

Accompaniment has become the chosen image rather than charity, and is sometimes preferred over the term solidarity. Christians have long been known for extending charity. The outpouring of money and supplies to Nicaragua and Honduras after Hurricane Mitch is an example of charity. The people in the flooded areas needed help, and those with money in the U.S. and Europe felt sympathy for them. As long as charity is understood as a legitimate redistribution of resources in an unjust world, it has a place in the Christian life. Charity, however, has several weaknesses: too often it is the sharing of resources with minimal personal engagement, and it also has a history of paternalism, that is, condescending attitudes by the rich toward those in need. The systemic problem of much charity in the two-thirds world is that the North American and European agencies maintain control over the money they give, often in such a way that it undermines the integrity of the receiving group. For example, churches decide whether and who to send as missionaries to Latin America, rather than sending money so that scholars from Latin America can be trained to do their own work. North American churches define the needs, instead of allowing Central American Christians to determine their own agenda. Projects are selected depending on whether they appeal to donors in North America rather than whether they will work in Central America. While charity has its place, it is severely limited as an image of engagement.

Solidarity is much preferred to charity, because it implies a common cause of correcting injustice and working together in mutual relationships. It continues to be the primary term used in many North American and European programs. However, the term has been criticized for being too sanguine about the differences between North and South, rich and poor. Those who are rich can choose to be in solidarity with the poor according to their own definitions, even if it does not seem like solidarity for those who need support. Accompaniment, on the other hand, signals that the one being accompanied has personal authority in the relationship.

6. *Transformation of Self and Congregation.* When Christians listen and believe, seek more knowledge, and have the courage to accompany those who are vulnerable, they open themselves to the possibility of transformation. What may start as a genuine wish to care becomes instead a process of profound spiritual transformation.

After Linda made numerous trips to El Salvador, experienced the terror of bombing and threats of torture, and sang and worshiped with the Christian leaders who had nothing but their faith to keep them alive, she began to hope that her own life could be healed. In El Salvador, for the first time, she shared her experiences of child abuse. Although Salvadorans lacked the resources to help her through all the stages of healing, they provided the crucial ingredient of hope that moved her beyond despair. When she was home, she sought out a pastoral counselor who had been to Nicaragua and worked with him over six years as she focused on layer after layer of woundedness.

My life has been changed by my accompaniment of survivors such as Linda and the Nicaraguan Christians. I am a different person because of the witnesses who have entered my life and let me into their lives. This book is a result of their impact on me and, in some ways, a report of how much I have been transformed by the experiences. I hope that what I have written will have some impact on others and will enable them to seek opportunities to accompany those who have gained wisdom because of the way God has accompanied them through extreme suffering.

Congregations have been transformed by their actions of accompaniment. I have mentioned the Presbyterian Church that started a shelter for battered women, and the Rockledge Presbyterian Church that accompanied the Rancho Ebenezer Project in Nicaragua. While the changes began with a few people who glimpsed a new form of spiritual life, the practice of goodness eventually involved most of the congregation and led to the transformation of many. These congregations think of themselves as activist churches with a crucial witness to make to their local communities, and the people who attend come partly because they want to participate in such a lively witness. These congregations are not practicing goodness out of guilt, but out of grace and freedom that comes from seeing the new community God is creating, a community of economic justice and nonviolence that includes all people.

7. *Making Long-term commitments.* There are two reasons why people are willing to make commitments to projects of economic justice and nonviolence. First, there is much to gain through long-term practice of goodness. Given people's enormous creativity on these issues, the number of guides and companions is amazing. There is a spiritual depth that can never be exhausted. It is like attending a banquet where all your favorite foods have been exquisitely prepared and are freely available. What conference can I attend this week? What trip to Africa or Latin America can I plan for next year? Who is speaking in the local churches about economic justice and nonviolence? Where are the wise souls gathering, and how can I be a part of their community? After one's life has been transformed by the spiritual wisdom of those who know God through activism, there seem to be endless resources available. Many are motivated to make their lives more simple so they have opportunities to engage in continual spiritual growth.

The second reason for making a long-term commitment is that the changes desired, namely economic justice and nonviolence, take time. There is no lack of issues to be addressed, of policies of governments and corporations to be challenged, of attitudes to be confronted. Bringing about a world in which the poor have their rightful share of the world's resources cannot be done in a few weeks or months. Ending racism will be an ongoing battle for many decades into the future. Preventing violence in families will not be accomplished in a few years. We want our lives to have an impact that is lasting for individuals, nations, and the world. This requires the ability to sustain active involvement for a long time.

There is a risk of burnout during this phase, which happens when people become so tied to certain outcomes that they feel defeated and depressed when these outcomes are not met. A risk of activism is focusing on changing others without also attending to one's own spiritual needs. Our larger goal is to be part of God's movement of love, justice, and nonviolence in the world. The danger of burnout because of too much sacrifice is met on the other side by the danger of self-absorption, or becoming consumers of spirituality. We seek not just the transformation of ourselves but also a closer walk with God in the context of a community that is practicing goodness.

8. *Prophetic Action.* Some changes we seek are systemic. As we have argued throughout this book, the plight of the poor is not their fault, even though they are often blamed for being noncompetitive in the new global markets. Victims of violence do not choose to be abused, but they find themselves captive in situations where they have no control over what happens. Women did not construct patriarchy, which disempowers them solely because they are women. African Americans did not invent white

racism. The patterns of injustice and violence are established by the political economy that determines who is rich and poor, privileged and deprived, powerful and marginalized. Therefore, individual actions of accompaniment, while critically important for ongoing work, are not enough. Systemic change will require concerted efforts of large groups of people working together.

Fortunately, when we reach the stage in our spiritual growth where we are ready to engage in prophetic action, we discover that there are many who have gone before. Non-governmental organizations (NGOs), including churches, are a significant resource for Christians who wish to engage in prophetic action that influences public policy and advocates for social change. For most Christians, the place to start is at the denominational level. Every denominational office has staff that works on social policy issues within the U.S. and on a global scale. For example, the Presbyterian Church (USA) has a policy on economic justice entitled "Hope for a Global Future: Toward Just and Sustainable Human Development."[10] This document has ten goals for economic justice, supported by numerous practical suggestions on how these might be accomplished.

    (a) Sufficient production and consumption

    (b) Full respect for human rights

    (c) Just and effective governance

    (d) Universal and adequate education

    (e) Environmental sustainability and food sufficiency

    (f) Ethical universality with cultural and religious diversity

    (g) Dismantling of warfare and building of peace

    (h) Equitable debt relief

    (i) Just and sustainable international trade

    (j) More and better development assistance[11]

One can easily see from this list that these policies are compatible with the positions I have taken in this book, and in agreement with the seminal work by John Cobb and Herman Daly.[12] The Evangelical Lutheran Church in America has done a similar study and reached similar conclusions.[13]

On issues of family violence, the Presbyterians just recently passed a policy on domestic violence, "Turn Mourning into Dancing! A Policy Statement on Healing Domestic Violence."[14] This statement focuses on child abuse, sibling abuse, dating violence, spouse/partner abuse, and elder abuse, and encourages education, training, and activism at all levels of the church. It is the first comprehensive statement on domestic violence by a major denomination and provides a way for people to become involved in changing systems, not just rescuing individuals. The policy statement is supported by an activist group, Presbyterians Against Domestic Violence Network, that takes the lead in education and training at the national level.[15] Other denominations also have programs on domestic violence that deserve support.

The most important ecumenical agency on domestic violence is the Center for the Prevention of Sexual and Domestic Violence, in Seattle, Washington.[16] It is an award-winning education and advocacy center with an active national staff and position papers on national policy issues. Activists who are interested in prophetic action on domestic violence can support their programs and take advantage of their training opportunities. In addition, most local shelters have training programs for volunteers who are interested in supporting their programs.

Space does not allow me to mention the many parachurch and secular organizations working for economic justice and nonviolence. Best known are groups such as Amnesty International,[17] the Interfaith Agency on Corporate Responsibility,[18] and Habitat for Humanity.[19] All these groups are linked to other progressive groups who provide opportunities for education and activism.

Important for me have been the local agencies in Nicaragua, such as AEDAF (The Protestant Association for Family Counseling), CEPAD (The Council of Evangelical Churches), STB (The Baptist Theological Seminary), and Project Ebenezer. Sometimes it is desirable to have direct contact with agencies in a poor country in order to have counselors who accompany you in your search for the most effective prophetic actions. Prophetic action is a stage in responding to the love of God on issues of economic justice and nonviolence because these values will not be realized without systemic change.

9. *Transformation of Worship and Community Life.* Finally, the pilgrimage toward a spirituality of practicing goodness leads to the transformation of worship and local community life. As one becomes aware of the many forms of injustice in the world, including economic injustice and family violence, there are moments of self-critique and moments of celebration. It is inevitable that worship and liturgy will begin to reflect these new awarenesses.

In moments of self-critique, middle-class congregations look at the manner in which they have accommodated themselves to the capitalist ideology by adopting a corporate model of life with expensive staff and buildings. Every congregation needs to wrestle with these contradictions between success under capitalism and the demands of justice, and to come to some resolution of what balance is right for them. There are many moving stories of churches that have delayed a major building project because they felt called to help start a new congregation in a marginalized community or because they chose mission over property. This does not mean that every expenditure on staff, program, and property is wrong, because decisions not to hire staff and improve buildings can undermine the integrity of the congregation and do not necessarily help restore justice and nonviolence. But the struggle for balance between justice and growth must be considered an important part of the Christian struggle.

When Christians engage in openness, listening, believing, seeking knowledge, courageous action, accompaniment, transformation, long-term commitments, and prophetic action, a new sense of community and self emerges. For me, some of the most moving worship experiences have been in Nicaragua in the midst of the people's witness about the power of God, and with groups of survivors from many social classes and racial groups who have come together to praise God. But experiences of God in worship and in other settings can also exist in the local congregation. Witness the creativity of the recent new hymnals of every denomination with their international hymns, and the creative songs and worship resources by Ruth Duck,[20] Tom Troeger,[21] and Brian Wren.[22] Likewise, other liturgists have made important suggestions for our prayers, poems, sermons, litanies, and sacraments in recently revised books of worship. When we have eyes to see, there are new ideas for worship all around.

Such inclusivity and community have also often been engendered by inclusive language on gender, race, and class. While not universally accepted, it has contributed enormous creativity to local worship, as the following rendition of the Lord's Prayer written by a local congregation exemplifies.

> O God
> Who is within us and beyond us,
> Holy are your names
> Your new earth come
> Your will be done
> On earth as it is in promise.
> Give us this day our daily bread
> And forgive us our Sin
> As we forgive those who sin against us.
> Help us to resist temptation
> And deliver us from evil
> For yours is the New Earth
> And the power and the glory forever. Amen.[23]

The empowerment of the people of God has resulted in the recovery of resources for resistance that are part of indigenous cultures, including music, art, dance, musical instruments, rhythms, stories, and icons. The gospel has taken on new forms in each culture by tapping into the sources of that culture in ways that are compatible with the love and justice of God in Jesus Christ, the values of economic justice and nonviolence.

Christian worship usually includes a period of confession and forgiveness in preparation for receiving the Word of God and participating in the eucharist.[24] This is a solemn moment when we prepare ourselves to meet the most Holy God, before whom we are acutely aware of our limitations. Forms of confession and forgiveness that speak to issues of economics and class, gender and inclusiveness, are beginning to emerge. Of course the needs of persons from the rich countries are different from the needs for those who are disempowered by market capitalism. The following confession from the Taizé Community is appropriate for those persons who are powerful:

> Leader: I confess to God, and in the presence of all God's people, that I have sinned in thought, word, and in deed, and I pray God to have mercy on me.
>
> **People: May God have mercy on you, pardon and deliver you from your sins, and give you time to amend your life.**
>
> **People: We confess to God, and in the presence of all God's people, that we have sinned in thought, word, and in deed, and we pray God to have mercy on us.**
>
> Leader: May God have mercy on you, pardon and deliver you from your sins, and give you time to amend your life.[25]

The advantage of this confession for the powerful is that both the leader and the people confess separately, and both pray for God's mercy. And following the confession, the pardon is conditional; that is, it depends on whether true repentance and changed behavior follow. The crucial words are "*May* God...", that is, *if* one engages in true repentance, may God reconnect you with life. The last phrase, "and give you time to amend your life," is the challenge we need to hear.

However, for the working class and poor who already feel guilty for existing, since the world seems to have no place for them, the confession and forgiveness section should be constructed differently. When Jesus felt the woman's touch, the one who had the flow of blood, he did not first begin with confession and forgiveness. Rather, he said, "Daughter, your faith has made you well; go in peace, and be healed of your disease" (Mk. 5:34). Forgiveness should have a literal meaning in the churches of the poor, namely, that the debts and obligations from the unjust system will be forgiven, and the poor will be liberated. The purpose of confession and forgiveness for the poor must be liberation, the proclamation of jubilee when all God's children will be free. An alternative confession and forgiveness for the poor might look something like this.

> Confession: Leader–During this time of confession, you are encouraged to bring your complaints against God, against the

principalities of this world, and against one another into the presence of God. If you believe that God loves you, and if you trust that God's love will see you through, then come with your honest pleas.

Complaints: based on Psalm 10

Why do you stand so far off, O Lord,

And hide yourself in time of trouble?

The wicked arrogantly persecute the poor,

But they are trapped in the schemes they have devised (etc.).[26]

Forgiveness: (based on Rom. 8:34; 2 Cor. 5:17)

Hear the good news!

Who is in a position to condemn?

Only Christ,

And Christ died for us,

Christ rose for us,

Christ reigns in power for us,

Christ prays for us.

Anyone who is in Christ

Is a new creation.

The old life has gone;

A new life has begun.

Know that God [forgives the debts of the poor].

[Accept God's forgiveness] and be at peace. Amen.[27]

Much creative work has been done on liturgical expressions of confession and forgiveness. These are just a few suggestions in line with the themes of this book to stimulate ongoing theological reflection.

Along with baptism and other sacramental understandings of life, the eucharist is a central ritual in nearly every Christian community in the world. It expresses the mystery of God's love for us that binds us together in community. Too often the eucharist has been spiritualized so that it is detached from economic and other realities of our daily lives. We need words for the eucharist that emphasize the love and justice of God, interpreted in the following way by the Nicaraguan peasants in Solentiname:

William: It seems to me that when he gave them that communion of bread and wine, the bread that is food and the wine that is joy, telling them it was his body and it was his blood, and "go on doing this," it was so that we would also repeat his sacrifice for the cause of the poor—that is, giving his life. "'This is my body" was equivalent to saying, "'This is my life," and the same with blood. And he adds: "'my blood shed." That's what he wanted us to repeat, not to repeat the ritual.

Marita: He also said we'd see him in our neighbor, especially in the poor, in the people. He said, "The poor are me." And for that too you need great faith. There are people who believe that Christ is in the host that they eat, and they don't believe in the Christ that's us.[28]

How can we begin to transform the images and meaning of the eucharist so that it becomes empowering for those who are vulnerable? In a recent eucharist celebration, I used the Emmaus story in Luke 24 as the opening invitation.

> I invite you to the table of the Lord. I pray that we will be like the disciples who were walking to Emmaus and heard Jesus expound the truth of God's revelation in history. When he broke bread and gave it to them, their eyes were opened. Their lives were forever changed because they had seen Jesus, and they understood everything from a new perspective. May we be changed as we break the bread at Jesus' table today.[29]

This invitation picks up a stream of New Testament interpretation of the Last Supper when Jesus instituted the eucharist, namely, the importance of abundant food and breaking bread together around the table. The feeding of the crowds suggests the generosity of God's love and the promise of abundant life for all people. What stronger image could we find for a world in which the majority of people live at or below subsistence and where adequate food is a daily struggle that is too often lost? Jesus offered his disciples the fellowship of his table and the generosity of God's presence in the moment, even when he knew that the evening was going to end badly for all of them. Even though he knew that he could lose his life for the sake of the movement he had started, he took time to share a holy moment with the disciples. This moment was central to their flesh-and-blood relationships.

> This community is our body represented in the bread; this community is our lifeblood represented in the wine we share. As often as you meet together around the table in the presence of God, remember this moment that we share together. Not even death by the force of violence can take away this moment of being together that the church will remember forever.

Perhaps the words of institution could read something like this:

> We give you thanks that the Lord Jesus,
> On the night before he died,
> Took bread,
> And after giving thanks to you,
> He broke it, and gave it to his disciples, saying:
> Take, eat,
> This bread is our body, our shared life in community,
> Our covenant to live together in justice and peace.

Do this in remembrance of our life together.
In the same way he took the cup, saying:
This cup is the new covenant,
Representing our life blood shed for one another,
Our covenant to accompany one another till death.
Whenever you drink this wine,
Do this in remembrance of our life together.[30]

The following litany was written by Christian women in Nicaragua to speak of the unspeakable and multiple forms of violence against the bodies of women and children. The destruction of peasant life caused by the United States Contra War against the Nicaraguan people has continued in the post-war period as society, local communities, and family life have deteriorated under the crushing poverty and oppression.

Remembrances

God,
We remember the bleeding woman
    whose blood converted her into an outcast.
We remember all the unnamed women who exhausted
    themselves working the camps until they bled from their
    hands and feet.
We remember our slave grandmothers,
    beaten and violated by their masters.
We remember our mothers, whose blood nourished us in the
    womb.
We remember our sisters, who died without being given the
    opportunity to see a priest or pastor in the church they
    loved.
We remember the healers, our friends,
    our holy mothers who gave us the ancestral secrets.
We remember the bloody wounds of the women
    who work in manufacturing and prostitution.
We remember all our sisters widowed or without children
    because of the violence of the war and the invasions.
We remember all our sisters and daughters
    whose blood was stained by AIDS.
We remember the women, our mothers, our sisters and their
    daughters, mangled and bloodied in their houses due to
    the evil treatment inflicted on them by husbands and
    lovers.
We remember that these bloody women were moved
    profoundly by Jesus.
We also are moved by the blood of the woman.

Jesus accepted this woman, gave her life and risked himself to
become near when she was alone, dirty and marginalized.
God, we trust that you remember all these women. That you
remember all our names and all the histories of our lives.
That our tears have moved you. We trust also that you
know us and that we are not alone. We trust that you are
always present, although we do not always understand
where and how. For this we wish to ask you: Bless us and
be always for us. Amen.[31]

This litany by and for women in Nicaragua remembers Jesus'
compassion for the woman with the flow of blood (Mk. 5:25–34). Outcast
and despondent, she reached out to him for a miracle, and touching him
revealed a faith that healed her of her physical condition as well as her
social stigma. Likewise, this story can empower the thousands of women
whose flow of blood is brought on by violence, rape, poverty,
malnutrition, and disease. The image of the Nicaraguan women is Jesus
among the people, one of the people, raised up by God from the people.
This Jesus understands the injustice and violence imposed on women,
whatever their social class or economic status. Jesus knows and loves
these women as his mothers, sisters, and daughters and supports their
resistance to the evil they experience.

Conclusion

I have presented a stage theory of transformation that is available to
all persons who respond to the needs of others. What begins as a simple
request for care can develop into a journey of transformation for the
caregiver. As we become more and more involved, we are invited into
new spiritual worlds where the barriers of race, gender and class are
overcome. We come to see that the hierarchies that divide people in the
world, namely rich and poor, male and female, black and white, can be
overcome when persons are together in God's community. Joining this
community requires openness, courage, discipline, and long-term
commitment, but it often begins in a simple request for care.

• • •

This book represents a report on my spiritual pilgrimage. When I
began to accompany Christians of Nicaragua, survivors of family
violence, and recovering perpetrators several years ago, I did not know
the journey would take me through all this. I have been led to study
counseling, economics, and the Bible in new ways. While the journey
itself was long, and at times arduous, my own spirit has been nourished
by the personal encounters, the activism, and the disciplined study. I
believe in God in more profound ways than before, and I know that

God's love and power are at work in the world. Even though there is much suffering that is caused by human evil, there is a resilient Holy Spirit at work in the people. I have been blessed to be involved with God's spirit, and I look forward to the new spiritual insights that come as the journey continues.

Bibliography

Abel, Elizabeth, and Emily Abel, eds. *The Signs Reader: Women, Gender and Scholarship.* Chicago: Univ. of Chicago Press, 1983.

Adams, Carol J. *Woman-battering.* Creative Pastoral Care and Counseling Series. Minneapolis: Fortress Press, 1994.

Adams, Carol J., and Marie M. Fortune. *Violence against Women and Children: A Christian Theological Sourcebook.* New York: Continuum, 1995.

Aidoo, Ama Ata. *Our Sister Killjoy.* Essex, England: Longman, 1977.

American Psychiatric Association. *Diagnostic and Statistical Manual of Mental Disorders.* 4th ed., rev. Washington, D.C.: American Psychiatric Association, 2000.

Andersen, Margaret L., and Patricia Hill Collins, comps. *Race, Class, and Gender: An Anthology.* Belmont, Calif.: Wadsworth, 1995.

Anderson, David A. *Kwanzaa.* New York: Gumbs and Thomas, 1992.

Andolsen, Barbara. *Daughters of Jefferson, Daughters of Bootblacks.* Macon, Ga.: Mercer Univ. Press, 1986.

Aptheker, Herbert. *American Negro Slave Revolts.* New York: Columbia Univ. Press, 1943.

Aquino, Maria Pilar. *Our Cry for Life: Feminist Theology from Latin America.* New York: Orbis Press, 1993.

Archer, John. *Male Violence.* London and New York: Routledge, 1994.

Augsburger, David. *Pastoral Counseling across Cultures.* Philadelphia: Westminster, 1986.

Beneria, Lourdes, and Catherine Stimpson, eds. *Women, Households and the Economy.* New Brunswick, N.J.: Rutgers Univ. Press, 1987.

Benitez-Rojo, Antonio. *The Repeating Island: The Caribbean and the Postmodern Perspective.* Durham, N.C.: Duke Univ. Press, 1996.

Bennett, Lerone, Jr. *Before the Mayflower: A History of the Negro in America 1619–1962.* Chicago: Johnson, 1962.

Berquist, Jon. *Incarnation.* St. Louis: Chalice Press, 1999.

Berthold, Fred, and Bernard Eugene Meland. *The Future of Empirical Theology, Essays in Divinity.* Vol. 7. Chicago: Univ. of Chicago Press, 1969.

Billman, Kathleen D., and Daniel L. Migliore. *Rachel's Cry: Prayer of Lament and Rebirth of Hope.* Cleveland: United Church Press, 1999.

Bolt, Allan. "Roots and Patterns of Our Political Culture." *Envio* 20/240 (2001).

Boserup, E. *Woman's Role in Economic Development.* New York: St. Martin's Press, 1970.

Boyd, Monica. "Family and Personal Networks in International Migration: Recent Developments and New Agendas." *International Migration Review* 3 (1989): 638–70.

Brock, Rita Nakashima. *Journeys by Heart: A Christology of Erotic Power.* New York: Crossroad, 1988.

Brock, Rita Nakashima, and Rebecca Ann Parker, *Proverbs of Ashes: Violence, Redemptive Suffering, and the Search for What Saves Us.* Boston: Beacon Press, 2001.

Brock, Rita Nakashima, and Susan Brooks Thistlethwaite. *Casting Stones: Prostitution and Liberation in Asia and the United States.* Minneapolis: Fortress Press, 1996.

Brown, Joanne Carlson, and Carole R. Bohn, eds. *Christianity, Patriarchy and Abuse: A Feminist Critique.* New York: Pilgrim Press, 1989.

Brownmiller, Susan. *Against Our Will: Men, Women, and Rape.* New York: Simon and Schuster, 1975.

Bruno, Robert. *Steelworker Alley: How Class Works in Youngstown.* Ithaca, N.Y.: Cornell Univ. Press, 1999.

Carby, Hazel. *Reconstructing Womanhood: The Emergence of the Afro-American Woman Novelist.* New York: Oxford Univ. Press, 1987.

Cardenal, Ernesto. *The Gospel in Solentiname.* 4 vols. Maryknoll, N. Y.: Orbis, 1976–1982.

Carney, Thomas F. *The Shape of the Past: Models and Antiquity.* Lawrence, Kans.: Coronado Press, 1975.

Cavanaugh, William T. *Torture and Eucharist.* Oxford: Blackwell Publishers, 1998.

Chinula, Donald M. *Building King's Beloved Community: Foundations for Pastoral Care and Counseling with the Oppressed.* Cleveland: United Church Press, 1997.

Chopp, Rebecca S., and Duane F. Parker. *Liberation Theology and Pastoral Theology.* JPCP Monograph , no. 2. Decatur, Ga.: Journal of Pastoral Care Publications, 1990.

Chopp, Rebecca S., and Mark Lewis Taylor, eds. *Reconstructing Christian Theology.* Minneapolis: Fortress Press, 1994.

Chung, Hyun Kyung. *Struggle to Be the Sun Again: Introducing Asian Women's Theology.* New York: Orbis Books, 1990.

Cicchetti, Dante, and Vicki Carlson, eds. *Child Maltreatment: Theory and Research on the Causes and Consequences of Child Abuse and Neglect.* Cambridge: Cambridge Univ. Press, 1989.

Cobb, John B. Jr., *The Earthist Challenge to Economism: A Theological Critique of the World Bank.* Religion and Politics Series. New York: St. Martin's Press, 1999.

____. *Praying for Jennifer: An Exploration of Intercessory Prayer in Story Form.* Nashville: Upper Room, 1985.

____. *Process Theology as Political Theology.* Philadelphia: Westminister Press, 1982.

____. *Sustainability: Economics, Ecology, and Justice.* Maryknoll, N.Y.: Orbis Books, 1992.

____. *Sustaining the Common Good: A Christian Perspective on the Global Economy.* Cleveland: Pilgrim Press, 1994.

____. *Theology and Pastoral Care.* Creative Pastoral Care and Counseling Series. Philadelphia: Fortress Press, 1977.

Cobb, John B. Jr., and Herman E. Daly. *For the Common Good: Redirecting the Economy toward Community, the Environment, and a Sustainable Future.* Boston: Beacon Press, 1989.

Collins, Patricia Hill. *Black Feminist Thought: Knowledge, Consciousness, and the Politics of Empowerment.* New York: Routledge, 1990.

Cone, James H. *Martin and Malcom in America.* Maryknoll, N.Y.: Orbis Books, 1991.

Conroy, John. *Unspeakable Acts, Ordinary People: The Dynamics of Torture.* New York: Knopf, 2000.

Cooper-White, Pamela. *The Cry of Tamar: Violence against Women and the Church's Response.* Minneapolis: Fortress Press, 1995.

Cornwall Collective. *Your Daughters Shall Prophesy.* New York: Pilgrim Press, 1980.

Couture, Pamela D. *Blessed Are the Poor?: Women's Poverty, Family Policy, and Practical Theology.* Nashville: Abingdon Press in cooperation with the Churches' Center for Theology and Public Policy. Washington, D.C., 1991.

____. *Seeing Children, Seeing God: A Practical Theology of Children and Poverty.* Nashville: Abingdon Press, 2000.

Couture, Pam, and Paul Ballard. *Globalisation and Difference:Practical Theology in a World Context.* Fairwater, Cardiff: Cardiff Academic Press, 1999.

Crockett, Linda. *The Deepest Wound: How a Journey to El Salvador Led to Healing from Mother-Daughter Incest.* New York: Writer's Showcase, 2001.

Davis, Angela. *Women, Culture, Politics.* New York: Vintage, 1990.

____. *Women, Race, and Class.* New York: Vintage, 1981.

D'Cunha, Jean. *The Legalization of Prostitution.* Bangalore: Wordmakers, 1991.

Dean, William, and Larry Axel, eds. *The Size of God: The Theology of Bernard Loomer in Context.* Macon, Ga.: Mercer Univ. Press, 1987.

Death Penalty Information Center. *Prison Population.* www.essential.org/dpic/dpic.html, 2000 [cited July 27, 2000]. Similar information available at www.deathpenaltyinfo.org.

Deere, C. D. "Rural Women's Subsistence Production in the Capitalist Periphery." *Review of Radical Political Economy* 8, no. 1 (1976): 9–17.

Delacoste, Frédérique, and Felice Newman. *Fight Back!: Feminist Resistance to Male Violence.* Minneapolis: Cleis Press, 1981.

Deslippe, Dennis A. *Rights Not Roses: Unions and the Rise of Working-Class Feminism, 1945–80.* Urbana: Univ. of Illinois Press, 2000.

Dines, Gail, Robert Jensen, and Ann Russo. *Pornography: The Production and Consumption of Inequality.* New York: Routledge, 1998.

Dobash, R. Emerson, and Russell Dobash. *Violence against Wives: A Case against Patriarchy.* New York: Free Press, 1979.

____. *Women, Violence and Social Change.* London, New York: Routledge, 1992.

Doehring, Carrie. *Taking Care: Monitoring Power Dynamics and Relational Boundaries in Pastoral Care and Counseling.* Nashville: Abingdon Press, 1995.

DuBois, W. E. B. *W. E .B. Dubois Speaks, 1890–1919.* Vol. 2. New York: Pathfinder Press, 1970.

Duck, Ruth C. *Dancing in the Universe: Hymns and Songs.* Chicago: GIA Publications, 1992.
_____. *Everflowing Streams: Songs for Worship.* New York: Pilgrim Press, 1981.
_____, ed. *Bread for the Journey: Resources for Worship.* Cleveland: United Church Press, 1981.
_____, ed. *Flames of the Spirit: Resources for Worship.* Cleveland: The Pilgrim Press, 1985.
Duck, Ruth C., and Maren C. Tirabassi. *Touch Holiness: Resources for Worship.* Cleveland: United Church Press, 1990.
Edelman, Peter. "Reforming Welfare–Take Two." *The Nation* 274, no. 4 (Feb. 4, 2002).
Edleson, Jeffrey L., and Richard M. Tolman. *Intervention for Men Who Batter: An Ecological Approach.* Vol. 3. Interpersonal Violence. Newbury Park, Calif.: Sage Publications, 1992.
Eisenstein, Hester. *Contemporary Feminist Thought.* New York: Hall and Co., 1983.
Ellsberg, Mary, et al. *Confites en el infierno. Prevalencia y características de la violencia conyugal hacia las mujeres en Nicaragua.* 2d ed. Managua: Red de Mujeres contra la Violencia, 1998.
Evangelical Lutheran Church in America (ELCA). "Give Us This Day Our Daily Bread: Sufficient, Sustainable Livelihood for All: A Study on Economic Life." Chicago: Division for Church and Society, ELCA, 1996.
Falla, Ricardo. "How Dollar Remittances Are Changing a Village." *Envio* (2000): 43–49.
Fanon, Frantz. *The Wretched of the Earth.* New York: Grove Press, 1963.
Fernandez-Kelly, M.P. *For We Are Sold, I and My People: Women and Industrialization in Mexico's Frontier.* Albany: SUNY Press, 1983.
Finn, Daniel. *Just Trading: On the Ethics and Economics of International Trade.* Nashville: Abingdon Press, 1996.
Fiorenza, Elisabeth Schüssler. *Discipleship of Equals: A Critical Feminist Ekklesia-Logy of Liberation.* New York: Crossroad, 1993.
Fortune, Marie M. *Clergy Misconduct: Sexual Abuse in the Ministerial Relationship.* Seattle, Wash.: Center for the Prevention of Sexual and Domestic Violence, 1992.
_____. *Is Nothing Sacred?: When Sex Invades the Pastoral Relationship.* San Francisco: Harper & Row, 1989.
_____. *Keeping the Faith: Guidance for Christian Women Facing Abuse.* San Francisco: HarperSanFrancisco, 1987.
_____. *Love Does No Harm: Sexual Ethics for the Rest of Us.* New York: Continuum, 1995.
_____. *Sexual Abuse Prevention: A Study for Teenagers.* New York: United Church Press, 1984.
_____. *Sexual Violence: The Unmentionable Sin.* New York: Pilgrim Press, 1983.
_____. *Violence in the Family: A Workshop Curriculum for Clergy and Other Helpers.* Cleveland: Pilgrim Press, 1991.
Fortune, Marie M., Denise Hormann, National Clearinghouse on Domestic Violence (U.S.), Center for the Prevention of Sexual and Domestic Violence (Seattle, Wash.), and United States Law Enforcement Assistance Administration. *Family Violence: A Workshop Manual for Clergy and Other Service Providers.* Domestic Violence Monograph Series, no. 6. Rockville, Md.: National Clearinghouse on Domestic Violence, 1981.
Fortune, Marie M., and James N. Poling. *Sexual Abuse by Clergy: A Crisis for the Church,* JPCP Monograph, no. 6. Decatur, Ga.: Journal of Pastoral Care Publications, 1994.
Frampton, Larraine. "Night Colors." Rochester, N.Y.: Colgate Rochester Divinity School, 1992.
Franklin, John Hope, and Alfred A. Moss, Jr. *From Slavery to Freedom: A History of African Americans.* New York: Knopf, 1988.
Franklin, Robert Michael. *Liberating Visions.* Minneapolis: Fortress Press, 1990.
Galloway, Kathy, ed. *The Pattern of Our Days: Worship in the Celtic Tradition from the Iona Community.* New York: Paulist Press, 1996.
Gandhi, Mohandas. *Nonviolence in Peace and War.* 2 vols. Ahmedabad: Navajivan, 1948.
Ganley, Carole, and Anne Warshaw. *Improving the Health Care Response to Domestic Violence: A Resource Manual for Health Care Providers.* San Francisco: Family Violence Prevention Fund, 1995.
Gates, Henry Louis. *The Classic Slave Narratives.* New York: Penguin, 1987.
Gaw, Albert. *Cross-Cultural Psychiatry.* Boston: John Wright, 1982.
Geertz, Clifford. *The Interpretation of Cultures: Selected Essays.* New York: Basic Books, 1973.
Gelles, Richard J., and Murray A. Straus. *Intimate Violence.* New York: Simon and Schuster, 1988.
Giroux, Henry A. *Border Crossings: Cultural Workers and the Politics of Education.* New York: Routledge, 1992.

Glaz, Maxine, and Jeanne Stevenson Moessner. *Women in Travail and Transition: A New Pastoral Care*. Minneapolis: Fortress Press, 1991.

Goffman, Erving. *Asylums: Essays on the Social Situation of Mental Patients and Other Inmates*. Chicago: Aldine, 1962.

Goldberg, Jacob. *Pastoral Bereavement Counseling: A Structured Program to Help Mourners*. New York: Human Sciences Press, 1989.

Gondolf, Edward W., and David M. Russell. *Man to Man: A Guide for Men in Abusive Relationships*. New York: Sulzburger and Graham, 1987.

Goudzwaard, Bob. *Capitalism and Progress: A Diagnosis of Western Society*. Kent: Paternoster Press, 1997.

Goulet, Denis. *Mexico: Development Strategies for the Future*. Notre Dame, Ind.: Univ. of Notre Dame Press, 1983.

Graham, Larry Kent. *Care of Persons, Care of Worlds: A Psychosystems Approach to Pastoral Care and Counseling*. Nashville: Abingdon Press, 1992.

Grant, Jacqueline. *White Women's Christ and Black Women's Jesus*. Atlanta: Scholars Press, 1989.

Greider, Kathleen J. *Reckoning with Aggression: Theology, Violence, and Vitality*. Louisville: Westminster John Knox Press, 1997.

Greider, William. *Who Will Tell the People: The Betrayal of American Democracy*. New York: Simon and Schuster, 1992.

Greven, Philip J. *Child-Rearing Concepts, 1628–1861; Historical Sources*. Primary Sources in American History. Itasca, Ill.: F. E. Peacock, 1973.

——. *The Protestant Temperament: Patterns of Child-Rearing, Religious Experience, and the Self in Early America*. New York: Knopf, 1977.

——. *Spare the Child: The Religious Roots of Punishment and the Psychological Impact of Physical Abuse*. New York: Knopf, distributed by Random House, 1991.

Griffin, David Ray, John B. Cobb, and Clark H. Pinnock. *Searching for an Adequate God: A Dialogue between Process and Free Will Theists*. Grand Rapids, Mich.: W. B. Eerdmans, 2000.

Griffin, Susan. "Rape: The All American Crime." *Ramparts* (1971).

Guberman, Connie, and Margie Wolfe. *No Safe Place: Violence against Women and Children*. Women's Press Issues. Toronto, Ont.: Women's Press, 1985.

Halberstam, David. *The Fifties*. New York: Villard Books, 1993.

Hall, Dinah, ed. *Working Together*. Seattle, Wash.: The Newsletter of the Center for the Prevention of Sexual and Domestic Violence.

Hall, S. "The Local and the Global: Globalization and Ethnicity." In *Culture, Globalization and the World-System: Contemporary Conditions for the Representation of Identity*, edited by Anthony King. Binghamton, N.Y.: SUNY, 1991.

Hall, Stuart, and Brad Gieben, eds. *Formations of Modernity*. Cambrigdge, U.K.: Polity Press and Open University, 1992.

Hampton, Robert L. *Violence in the Black Family: Correlates and Consequences*. Lexington, Mass.: Lexington Books, 1987.

Hanmer, Jalma, Jill Radford, and Elizabeth Anne Stanko. *Women, Policing, and Male Violence: International Perspectives*. London and New York: Routledge, 1989.

Harding, Vincent. *There Is a River: The Black Struggle for Freedom in America*. New York: Vintage, 1981.

Heilbroner, Robert. *The Worldly Philosophers: The Lives, Times, and Ideas of the Great Economic Thinkers*. Rev. ed. New York: Simon and Schuster, 1999.

Herman, Judith Lewis. *Trauma and Recovery*. New York: Basic Books, 1992.

Herren, Ricardo. *La Conquista erótica de las Indias*. Mexico, D.F.: Planeta, 1992.

Higginbotham, Evelyn Brooks. *Righteous Discontent*. Cambridge, Mass.: Harvard Univ. Press, 1993.

Hiltner, Seward. *Preface to Pastoral Theology, The Ayer Lectures, 1954*. New York: Abingdon Press, 1958.

Hodgson, Peter C. *Revisioning the Church: Ecclesial Freedom in the New Paradigm*. Philadelphia: Fortress Press, 1988.

Hondagneu-Sotelo, Pierrette. *Gendered Transitions*. Berkeley and Los Angeles: Univ. of California Press, 1994.

hooks, bell. *Ain't I a Woman: Black Women and Feminism*. Boston: South End Press, 1981.

Horsley, Richard, and John Hanson. *Bandits, Prophets and Messiahs: Popular Movements in the Time of Jesus*. Minneapolis: Winston, 1985.

Houts, Donald C. *Clergy Sexual Ethics: A Workshop Guide.* JPCP Monograph, no. 3. Decatur, Ga.: Journal of Pastoral Care Publications, 1991.

Hunter, Rodney J., ed. *Dictionary of Pastoral Care and Counseling.* Nashville: Abingdon Press, 1990.

Imbens, Annie, and Ineke Jonker. *Christianity and Incest.* Minneapolis: Fortress Press, 1992.

The International Bank for Reconstruction and Development/ The World Bank. *The World Development Report 1999–2000.* New York: Oxford Univ. Press, 2000.

Isasi-Diaz, Ada Maria. *En La Lucha.* Minneapolis: Fortress Press, 1993.

Kahn, Joseph. "Redrawing the Map." *The New York Times,* 25 June 2000, 5.

Karenga, Maulana. *Introduction to Black Studies.* Los Angeles: Univ. of Sankore Press, 1993.

____. *Kwanzaa: A Celebration of Family, Community, and Culture.* Los Angeles: Univ. of Sankore Press, 1998.

____. *Kwanzaa: Origin, Concepts, Practice.* Inglewood, Calif.: Kawaida Publications, 1977.

Kekana, Noko Frans. *Economic Justice in South Africa: Towards a Prophetic Theology of Community Solidarity, Economic Equity and Pastoral Care.* Studies and Reports by the Efsa Institute for Theological & Interdisciplinary Research. Bellville, South Africa: Ecumenical Foundation of Southern Africa, 1995.

Kelber, Werner. *Mark's Story of Jesus.* Philadelphia: Fortress Press, 1979.

Keshgegian, Flora A. *Redeeming Memories: A Theology of Healing and Transformation.* Nashville: Abingdon Press, 2000.

King, Anthony. *Urbanism, Colonialism, and the World Economy: Culture and Spatial Foundations of the World Urban System, The International Library of Sociology.* London: Routledge, 1990.

Kinzer, Stephen. *Blood of Brothers: Life and War in Nicaragua.* New York: Anchor Books, 1991.

Koss, Mary P., Lisa A. Goodman, Angela Browne, Louise F. Fitzgerald, Gwendolyn Puryear Keita, and Nancy Felipe Russo. *No Safe Haven: Male Violence against Women at Home, at Work, and in the Community.* Washington, D.C.: American Psychological Association, 1994.

Kroeger, Catherine Clark, and James R. Beck. *Women, Abuse, and the Bible: How Scripture Can Be Used to Hurt or to Heal.* Grand Rapids, Mich.: Baker Books, 1996.

Krueger, David A. *The Business Corporation and Productive Justice.* Nashville: Abingdon Press, 1997.

Lancaster, Roger N. *Life Is Hard: Machismo, Danger, and the Intimacy of Power in Nicaragua.* Berkeley, Calif.: Univ. of California Press, 1992.

Langs, Robert J. *The Bipersonal Field.* New York: Aronson, 1976.

LaPrensa. "Remittances to Nicaragua." *La Prensa,* Monday, 28 August 2000, 13a.

Lapsley, James. *Salvation and Health.* Philadelphia: Westminster, 1972.

Lartey, Emmanuel Yartekwei. *In Living Colour: An Intercultural Approach to Pastoral Care and Counselling.* London; Herndon, Va.: Cassell, 1997.

Lee, Lee C., and Nolan W. S. Zane, eds. *Handbook of Asian American Psychology.* Thousand Oaks, Calif.: Sage, 1998.

Leehan, James. *Pastoral Care for Survivors of Family Abuse.* Louisville: Westminster/John Knox Press, 1989.

Lerner, Gerda. *The Creation of Patriarchy.* Oxford: Oxford Univ. Press, 1986.

Lim, L. Y. C. "Women Workers in Multinational Corporations: The Case of the Electronics Industry in Malaysia and Singapore." In *Transnational Enterprises: Their Impact on Third World Societies and Cultures,* edited by Krishna Kumar. Boulder, Colo.: Westview Press, 1980.

Livingston, David. *Healing Violent Men: A Model for Christian Communities.* Minneapolis: Fortress Press, 2001.

Lobel, Kerry. *Naming the Violence: Speaking out About Lesbian Battering.* Seattle, Wash.: Seal Press, 1986.

Lofland, John, and Lyn Lofland. *Analyzing Social Settings.* New York: Wadsworth, 1995.

Loomer, Bernard. "On Committing Yourself to a Relationship." *Process Studies* 16, no. 4 (1987).

____. "Two Conceptions of Power." *Criterion* 15 (1976): 12–29.

Loomer, Bernard, William D. Dean, and Larry E. Axel. *The Size of God: The Theology of Bernard Loomer in Context.* Macon, Ga.: Mercer Univ. Press, 1987.

Lorde, Audre. *Sister Outsider.* Freedom, Calif.: Crossing Press, 1984.

MacKinnon, Catherine. *Sexual Harassment of Working Women.* New Haven, Conn.: Yale Univ. Press, 1979.

____. *Towards a Feminist Theory of the State.* Cambridge, Mass.: Harvard Univ. Press, 1989.

Mananzan, Mary John, Mercy Amba Oduyoye, Elsa Tamez, J. Shannon Clarkson, Mary C. Grey, Letty M. Russell, eds. *Women Resisting Violence: Spirituality for Life*. Maryknoll, N.Y.: Orbis Books, 1996.

Marable, Manning. *How Capitalism Underdeveloped Black America*. Boston: South End Press, 1983.

Marciel, David R., and Isidro D. Ortiz, eds. *Chicanas/Chicanos at the Crossroads: Social, Economic, and Political Change*. Tuscon: Univ. of Arizona Press, 1996.

Marin, Elliott, and Vera Amanda Solis. "Badly Fed and Malnourished." *Envio* (August 1996): 26–29.

Marsella, Anthony, Matthew J. Friedman, Ellen T. Gerrity, and Raymond M. Scurfield. *Ethnocultural Aspects of Posttraumatic Stress Disorder: Issues, Research, and Clinical Applications*. Washington, D.C.: American Psychological Association, 1996.

Martin, Joan M. *More Than Chains and Toil: A Christian Work Ethic of Enslaved Women*. Louisville: Westminster John Knox Press, 2000.

McClure, John S., and Nancy J. Ramsay. *Telling the Truth: Preaching about Sexual and Domestic Violence*. Cleveland: United Church Press, 1998.

McCullough, Michael E., Kenneth I. Pargament, and Carl E. Thoresen. *Forgiveness: Theory, Research, and Practice*. New York: Guilford Press, 2000.

McGoldrick, Monica, John K. Pearce, and Joseph Giordano, eds. *Ethnicity and Family Therapy*. New York: Guilford Press, 1982, 1996.

McMullen, Richie, J. *Male Rape: Breaking the Silence on the Last Taboo*. London: GMP Publishers, 1990.

Mead, George Herbert. *Mind, Self and Society*, edited by Charles W. Morris. Chicago: Univ. of Chicago Press, 1962, 1934.

_____. *On Social Psychology; Selected Papers*. Rev. ed. Edited and with an intro. by Anselm Strauss. Chicago: Univ. of Chicago Press, 1964.

Means, Jeffrey. *Trauma and Evil: Healing the Wounded Soul*. Minneapolis: Fortress Press, 2000.

Meilselas, Susan. *Nicaragua: June 1978–July 1979*. New York: Pantheon Books, 1981.

Meland, Bernard Eugene. *Faith and Culture*. London: George Allen and Unwin, 1955.

_____. *Fallible Forms and Symbols: Discourses on Method in a Theology of Culture*. Philadelphia: Fortress Press, 1976.

_____. *The Realities of Faith: The Revolution in Cultural Forms*. New York: Oxford Univ. Press, 1962.

Meland, Bernard Eugene, and Perry D. LeFevre. *Essays in Constructive Theology: A Process Perspective*. Chicago: Exploration Press, 1988.

Metz, Johann Baptist. *The Emergent Church: The Future of Christianity in a Postbourgeois World*. New York: Crossroad, 1981.

Mezey, Gillian C., and Michael B. King, eds. *Male Victims of Sexual Assault*. New York: Oxford Univ. Press, 1992.

Mies, Maria. *Patriarchy and Accumulation on a World Scale*. London: Zed Books, 1998.

Mies, Maria, and Veronika Bennholdt-Thomsen. *The Subsistence Perspective*. London: Zed Books, 1999.

Miles, Al. *Domestic Violence: What Every Pastor Needs to Know*. Minneapolis: Fortress Press, 2000.

Milkman, Ruth. *Gender at Work: The Dynamics of Job Segregation by Sex during World War II*. Urbana: Univ. of Illinois Press, 1987

Miller, Jean Baker, and Irene Pierce Stiver. *The Healing Connection: How Women Form Relationships in Therapy and in Life*. Boston: Beacon Press, 1997.

Moltmann, Jürgen. *The Spirit of Life*. Minneapolis: Fortress Press, 1992.

Morokvasic, Mirjana. "Special Issue on Women Immigrants." *International Migration Review* 18, no. 4 (1984).

Morrison, Toni. *Race-Ing Justice, En-Gender-Ing Power*. New York: Pantheon, 1992.

Morton, Nelle. *The Journey Is Home*. Boston: Beacon Press, 1985.

Mosala, Itumeleng J. *Biblical Hermeneutics and Black Theology in South Africa*. Grand Rapids, Mich.: Eerdmans, 1989.

Moynihan, Daniel P. *The Negro Family*. Washington, D.C.: U.S. Department of Labor, 1965.

Murray, Charles, and Charles Herrenstein. *The Bell Curve*. New York: Free Press, 1994.

Myers, Ched. *Binding the Strong Man: A Political Reading of Mark's Story of Jesus*. Maryknoll, N.Y.: Orbis Books, 1988.

_____. *Who Will Roll Away the Stone? Discipleship Queries for First World Christians*. Maryknoll, N.Y.: Orbis Books, 1994.

Neuger, Christie Cozad. *The Arts of Ministry: Feminist-Womanist Approaches.* Louisville: Westminster John Knox Press, 1996.

———. *Counseling Women: A Narrative Pastoral Approach.* Minneapolis: Fortress Press, 2001.

Nussbaum, Martha Craven. *Sex & Social Justice.* New York: Oxford Univ. Press, 1999.

———. *Women and Human Development: The Capabilities Approach.* Cambridge, U.K.: Cambridge Univ. Press, 2000.

Oliver, Melvin L., and Thomas M. Shapiro. *Black Wealth/ White Wealth: A New Perspective on Racial Inequality.* New York: Routledge, 1997.

Patterson, Morton. *Broken by You: Men's Role in Stopping Woman Abuse.* Cleveland: United Church Publishing House, 1995.

Paymar, Michael. *Violent No More: Helping Men End Domestic Violence.* Alameda, Calif.: Hunter House, 1993.

Pedersen, Paul, ed. *Handbook of Cross-Cultural Counseling and Therapy.* Westport, Conn.: Greenwood Press, 1985.

Pedersen, P. B., et al., eds. *Counseling across Cultures.* Honolulu: Univ. of Hawaii Press, 1989.

Pheterson, Gail, ed. *A Vindication of the Rights of Whores.* Seattle: Seal Press, 1989.

Phillips, Kevin, P. *Arrogant Capital: Washington, Wall Street, and the Frustration of American Politics.* Boston: Little, Brown, 1994.

———. *Boiling Point: Republicans, Democrats, and the Decline of Middle-Class Prosperity.* New York: Random House, 1993.

Poling, J. Nathan. *Casting Spells from the Stage.* Ph.D. diss., Emory University, 1998.

Poling, James Newton. *The Abuse of Power: A Theological Problem.* Nashville: Abingdon Press, 1991.

———. *Deliver Us from Evil: Resisting Racial and Gender Oppression.* Minneapolis: Fortress Press, 1996.

———. "Resisting Violence in the Name of Jesus." *Journal of Pastoral Theology* 7 (1997): 15–22.

Poling, James Newton, and Toinette M. Eugene. *Balm for Gilead: Pastoral Care for African American Families Experiencing Abuse.* Nashville: Abingdon Press, 1998.

Poling, James Newton, and Marie Fortune. *Sexual Abuse by Clergy: A Crisis for the Church.* Decatur, Ga.: Journal of Pastoral Care Publications, 1994.

Poling, James Newton, and Donald E. Miller. *Foundations for a Practical Theology of Ministry.* Nashville: Abingdon Press, 1985.

Poling, James Newton, and Lewis S. Mudge. *Formation and Reflection: The Promise of Practical Theology.* Minneapolis: Fortress Press, 1987.

Poling, James Newton, and Christie Cozad Neuger. *The Care of Men.* Nashville: Abingdon Press, 1997.

Poling, Nancy Werking. *Victim to Survivor: Women Recovering from Clergy Sexual Abuse.* Cleveland: United Church Press, 1999.

Presbyterian Church (USA). *Book of Common Worship.* Louisville: Westminster/ John Knox Press, 1993.

———. "Hope for a Global Future: Toward Just and Sustainable Human Development." Louisville: Office of the General Assembly, 1996.

———. "Turn Mourning into Dancing! A Policy Statement on Healing Domestic Violence." Louisville: 213th General Assembly, Presbyterian Church (USA), 2001.

Procter-Smith, Marjorie. *Praying with Our Eyes Open: Engendering Feminist Liturgical Prayer.* Nashville: Abingdon Press, 1995.

Pryce, Mark. *Finding a Voice: Men, Women and the Community of the Church.* London: SCM Press, 1996.

Quinn, Kathleen M., Illinois Coalition Against Domestic Violence, and Illinois Coalition Against Sexual Assault. *Male Violence Against Women.* Springfield, Ill.: Illinois Coalition Against Domestic Violence and the Illinois Coalition Against Sexual Assault, 1984.

Rainwater, Lee, and William Yancey. *The Moynihan Report and the Politics of Controversy.* Cambridge, Mass.: MIT Press, 1967.

Randall, Margaret. *Sandino's Daughters Revisited: Feminism in Nicaragua.* New Brunswick, N.J.: Rutgers Univ. Press, 1994.

———. *Sandino's Daughters: Testimonies of Nicaraguan Women in Struggle.* New Brunswick, N.J.: Rutgers Univ. Press, 1995.

Raphael, Jody. *Battered Women, Welfare, and Poverty.* Boston: Northeastern Press, 2000.

Reid, Kathryn Goering, and Marie M. Fortune. *Preventing Child Sexual Abuse: A Curriculum for Children Ages Nine through Twelve.* New York: United Church Press, 1989.

Rich, Adrienne. "Compulsory Heterosexuality and Lesbian Existence." In *The Signs Reader: Women, Gender and Scholarship,* ed. Elizabeth Abel and Emily Abel.

Richard, Amy O'Neill. *International Trafficking in Women to the United States: A Contemporary Manifestation of Slavery and Organized Crime.* Washington, D.C.: Center for the Study of Intelligence, Central Intelligence Agency, 1999.

Rocha, Jose Luis. "Masaya Trembles: The Lessons of a Disaster." *Envio* (17 August 2000): 23.

Rocha, Jose Luis, and Ian Criostoplos. "NGOs and Natural Disasters: Gaps and Opportunities." *Envio* (November 1999): 48.

Rosaldo, Renato. *Culture and Truth; the Remaking of Social Analysis.* Boston: Beacon Press, 1993.

Rowbotham, Sheila. *A Century of Women: The History of Women in Britain and the United States.* New York: Penguin, 1997.

Ruether, Rosemary Radford. *Gaia and God: An Ecofeminist Theology of Earth Healing.* San Francisco: HarperSanFrancisco, 1994.

____. *Women and Redemption: A Theological History.* Minneapolis: Fortress Press, 1998.

____. *Women-Church: Theology and Practice of Feminist Liturgical Communities.* San Francisco: Harper and Row, 1985.

Ruiz, Brenda. "Counseling with Women in a Context of Intense Oppression," *The Journal of Pastoral Care* 48, no. 2 (1994).

____. *Violencia contra la mujer y la niñez: Una perspectiva de salud (Violence against Women and Children: A Health Perspective).* Managua: UPOLI, 1998.

Russell, Diana. *The Secret Trauma.* New York: Basic Books, 1986.

Safa, H. I. *The Myth of the Male Breadwinner: Women and Industrialization in the Caribbean.* Boulder, Colo.: Westview Press, 1995.

Sassen, Saskia. *Cities in a World Economy.* Thousand Oaks, Calif.: Pine Forge/ Sage Press, 1994.

____. *The Global City: New York, London, Tokyo.* Princeton, N.J.: Princeton Univ. Press, 1991.

____. *Globalization and Its Discontents: Essays on the New Mobility of People and Money.* New York: The New Press, 1998.

____. *Losing Control? Sovereignty in an Age of Globalization.* New York: Columbia Univ. Press, 1996.

____. *The Mobility of Labor and Capital: A Study in International Investment and Labor Flow.* Cambridge, U.K.: Cambridge Univ. Press, 1988.

Scacco, Anthony M. *Male Rape: A Casebook of Sexual Aggression.* New York: AMS, 1982.

Scharper, Philip, and Sally Scharper. *The Gospel of Art by the Peasants of Solentiname.* Maryknoll, N.Y.: Orbis Books, 1984.

Schechter, Susan. *Women and Male Violence: The Visions and Struggles of the Battered Women's Movement.* Boston: South End Press, 1982.

Schneiders, Sandra. *Women and the Word.* New York: Paulist Press, 1986.

Schreiter, Robert J. *Constructing Local Theologies.* Maryknoll, N.Y,: Orbis Books, 1985.

Schüssler Fiorenza, Elisabeth. *Bread Not Stone: The Challenge of Feminist Biblical Interpretation.* Boston: Beacon Press, 1984.

____. *In Memory of Her: A Feminist Theological Reconstruction of Christian Origins.* 10th ann. ed. New York: Crossroad, 1994.

Schüssler Fiorenza, Elisabeth, and Mary Shawn Copeland, eds. *Violence against Women.* Vol. 1, *Concilium.* Maryknoll, N.Y.: Orbis Books, 1994.

Scribnar, C. S. *Post-Traumatic Stress Disorder.* New Orleans: Bruno Press, 1988.

Sen, Amartya. *Hunger and Public Action.* Oxford, U.K.: Clarendon Press, 1989.

Sen, Amartya, and Jean Dreze. *India: Economic Development and Social Opportunity.* Delhi: Oxford Univ. Press, 1995.

Sennett, Richard, and Jonathan Cobb. *The Hidden Injuries of Class.* New York: Norton, 1972.

Sivard, Ruth Leger. *World Military and Social Expenditures.* Washington, D.C.: World Priorities, 1996.

Smith, Adam. *An Inquiry into the Nature and Causes of the Wealth of Nations, Book One.* New York: Random House, 1776.

Smith, Joan, and Immanuel Wallerstein, eds. *Creating and Transforming Households: The Constraints of the World Economy.* Cambridge, U.K.: Cambridge Univ. Press, 1992.

Solórzano, Irela, et al. *Violencia, Llamemos las cosas por su nombre.* Managua: Puntos de Encuentro, 1995.

Soysal, Yasmin Nuhoglu. *Limits of Citizenship.* Chicago: Univ. of Chicago Press, 1994.

Spain, Daphne. *Gendered Spaces.* Chapel Hill: Univ. of North Carolina Press, 1992.

Spelman, Elizabeth. *Inessential Woman: Problems of Exclusion in Feminist Thought.* Boston: Beacon Press, 1988.

Spielberger, Charles D., and Rogelio Diaz-Guerrero eds. *Cross-Cultural Anxiety*. Washington D. C.: Hemisphere; distributed by New York: Halsted Press, 1976, 1990.

Stackhouse, Max L., Dennis P. McCann, and Shirley J. Rosels, with Preston N. Williams. *On Moral Business: Classical and Contemporary Resources for Ethics in Economic Life*. Grand Rapids, Mich.: Eerdmans, 1995.

Stanko, Elizabeth Anne. *Intimate Intrusions: Women's Experiences of Male Violence*. London and Boston: Routledge & Kegan Paul, 1985.

SteinhoffSmith, Roy Herndon. *The Mutuality of Care*. St Louis: Chalice Press, 1999.

Stoewsand, Corinne. "Women Building Cities." Ph.D. dissertation, Columbia University, 1996.

Stoltenberg, John. *Refusing to Be a Man: Essays on Sex and Justice*. New York: Penguin, 1990.

Stone, Howard W. *Brief Pastoral Counseling*. Minneapolis: Fortress Press, 1994.

Stubbs, Julie. *Women, Male Violence, and the Law*. The Institute of Criminology Monograph Series, ; no. 6. Sydney: Institute of Criminology, Sydney Univ. Law School, 1994.

Sue, Derald Wing, and David Sue. *Counseling the Culturally Different: Theory and Practice*. New York: John Wiley and Sons, 1981.

Sugirtharajah, R. S. *Asian Biblical Hermeneutics and Postcolonialism*. Maryknoll, N.Y.: Orbis Books, 1998.

Switzer, David K. *Pastoral Care Emergencies*. Creative Pastoral Care and Counseling Series. Minneapolis: Fortress Press, 2000.

Tabba, William K. *The Political Economy of the Black Ghetto*. New York: W. W. Norton, 1970.

Takaki, Ronald. *Iron Cages: Race and Culture in Nineteenth Century America*. New York: Oxford Univ. Press, 1990.

Thistlethwaite, Susan. *Sex, Race, and God*. New York: Crossroad, 1989.

Thistlethwaite, Susan B., and George F. Cairns, eds. *Beyond Theological Tourism: Mentoring as a Grassroots Approach to Theological Education*. Maryknoll, N.Y.: Orbis Books, 1994.

Thomas, Hugh. *The Slave Trade*. New York: Touchstone, 1997.

Thomas, Linda Elaine. *Under the Canopy: Ritual Process and Spiritual Resilience in South Africa*. Studies in Comparative Religion. Columbia, S.C.: Univ. of South Carolina, 1999.

Thorne-Finch, Ron. *Ending the Silence: The Origins and Treatment of Male Violence against Women*. Toronto and Buffalo: Univ. of Toronto Press, 1992.

Tolbert, Mary Ann. *Sowing the Gospel: Mark's World in Literary-Historical Perspective*. Minneapolis: Fortress Press, 1996.

Townes, Emilie M. *Womanist Justice, Womanist Hope*. Atlanta: Scholars Press, 1993.

Troeger, Thomas. *Borrowed Light: Hymn Texts, Prayers, and Poems*. New York: Oxford Univ. Press, 1994.

Troeger, Thomas, and Carol Doran Troeger. *New Hymns for the Lectionary: To Glorify the Maker's Name*. New York: Oxford Univ. Press, 1986.

____. *New Hymns for the Life of the Church: To Make Our Prayer and Music One*. New York: Oxford Univ. Press, 1992.

____. *Open to Glory: Renewing Worship in the Congregation*. Valley Forge, Pa.: Judson Press, 1983.

Trouillot, Michel-Rolph. *Silencing the Past: Power and the Production of History*. Boston: Beacon, 1995.

Tsing, Anna Lowenhaupt. *In the Realm of the Diamond Queen: Marginality in an Out-of-the-Way Place*. Princeton, N.J.: Princeton Univ. Press, 1993.

United Methodist Church. *The United Methodist Hymnal: Book of United Methodist Worship*. Nashville: United Methodist Pub. House, 1989.

United Nations Development Programme. *Human Development Report 1999*. New York: Oxford Univ. Press, 1999.

____. *Human Development Report 2000*. New York: Oxford Univ. Press, 2000.

U.S. Census Bureau. *U.S. Census Report*. U.S. government, 1998 [cited September 14 2000].

U.S. Department of Justice. *Prison and Jail Inmates at Midyear, 1998*. Department of Justice, U.S. Government, 1998 [cited September 14 2000].

U.S. Library of Congress. *Nicaragua*. Library of Congress, 2000 [cited September 4, 2000].

Van Beek, Aart. *Cross-Cultural Counseling*. Minneapolis: Fortress Press, 1996.

Vargas, Oscar René. "Badly Fed and Malnourished." *Envio* (1996): 27.

____. *Nicaragua: Despues del Mitch...que?* Managua: CEREN, 1999.

____. *Once años después del ajuste. Resultados y perspectivas*. Managua: Imprimatur, 2001.

____. *Pobreza en Nicaragua: Un abismo que se agranda*. Managua: UPOLI, 1998.

Vernez, Georges. *Immigrant Women in the U.S. Workforce: Who Struggles? Who Succeeds?* Lanham, Md.: Lexington Books, 1999.

Voelkel-Haugen, Rebecca, and Marie M. Fortune. *Sexual Abuse Prevention: A Course of Study for Teenagers.* Cleveland: United Church Press, 1996.

Waetjen, Herman "The Construction of the Way into a Reordering of Power: An Inquiry into the Generic Conception of the Gospel According to Mark." San Anselmo, Calif.: San Francisco Theological Seminary, 1982.

Washington, James Melvin, ed. *A Testament of Hope: The Essential Writings of Martin Luther King.* San Francisco: Harper and Row, 1986.

Watkins Ali, Carroll A. *Survival and Liberation: Pastoral Theology in African American Context.* St. Louis: Chalice Press, 1999.

Weems, Renita J. *Battered Love: Marriage, Sex, and Violence in the Hebrew Prophets.* Minneapolis: Fortress Press, 1995.

____. *Just a Sister Away: A Womanist Vision of Women's Relationships in the Bible.* San Diego, Calif.: LuraMedia, 1988.

Weitzman, Susan. *Not to People Like Us: Hidden Abuse in Upscale Marriages.* New York: Basic Books, 2000.

Weldon, Michele. *I Closed My Eyes: Revelations of a Battered Woman.* Minneapolis: Hazelden, 1999.

Whitehead, Alfred North. *The Aims of Education & Other Essays.* New York: Macmillan, 1929.

Wicks, Robert J., Barry K. Estadt, and Charles Van Engen, eds. *Pastoral Counseling in a Global Church: Voices from the Field.* Maryknoll, N.Y.: Orbis Books, 1993.

Williams, Daniel Day. *The Spirit and the Forms of Love.* New York: Harper and Row, 1968.

Williams, Delores S. *Sisters in the Wilderness: The Challenge of Womanist God-Talk.* Maryknoll, N.Y.: Orbis Books, 1993.

Williams, William A. *Empire as a Way of Life.* New York: Oxford Univ. Press, 1980.

Wilmore, Gayraud. *Black Religion and Black Radicalism.* Maryknoll, N.Y.: Orbis, 1993.

Wilson, William Julius. *When Work Disappears: The World of the New Urban Poor.* New York: Vintage, 1996.

Wimberly, Anne Streaty. "Christian Education for Liberation and Vocation: An African American Perspective." 1993.

____. *The Church Family Sings: Songs, Ideas, and Activities for Use in Church School.* Nashville: Abingdon Press, 1996.

____. *Honoring African American Elders: A Ministry in the Soul Community.* The Jossey-Bass Religion-in-Practice Series. San Francisco: Jossey-Bass, 1997.

____. *Soul Stories: African American Christian Education.* Nashville: Abingdon Press, 1994.

Wink, Walter. *Engaging the Powers: Discernment and Resistance in a World of Domination.* Minneapolis: Fortress Press, 1992.

____. *Naming the Powers: The Language of Power in the New Testament.* Minneapolis: Fortress Press, 1984.

____. *Unmasking the Powers: The Invisible Forces That Determine Human Existence.* Philadelphia: Fortress Press, 1986.

Winquist, Charles. *Practical Hermeneutics: A Revised Agenda for Ministry.* Atlanta: Scholars Press, 1980.

Wondra, Ellen. *Humanity Has Been a Holy Thing: Toward a Contemporary Feminist Christology.* New York: Univ. Press of America, 1994.

Wren, Brian. *Faith Looking Forward: The Hymns & Songs of Brian Wren.* Oxford: Oxford Univ. Press, 1983.

____. *Faith Renewed: 33 Hymns Re-Issued and Revised.* Carol Stream, Ill.: Hope Publishing, 1995.

____. *Praising a Mystery: 30 New Hymns.* Carol Stream, Ill.: Hope Publishing, 1986.

Yellin, Jean Fagan, ed. *Harriet A. Jacobs: Incidents in the Life of a Slave Girl Written by Herself.* Cambridge, Mass.: Harvard Univ. Press, 1987.

Yoder, John Howard. *The Politics of Jesus,* 2d Rev. ed. Grand Rapids, Mich.: Eerdmans, 1993.

Notes

Introduction

[1]Author's rendering.

[2]James Poling, *The Abuse of Power: A Theological Problem* (Nashville: Abingdon Press, 1991); *Deliver Us from Evil: Resisting Racial and Gender Oppression* (Minneapolis: Fortress Press, 1996); with Toinette Eugene, *Balm for Gilead: Pastoral Care for African American Families Experiencing Abuse* (Nashville: Abingdon Press, 1998).

Chapter 1: Economics, Violence, and Care

[1]Ched Myers, *Binding the Strong Man: A Political Reading of Mark's Story of Jesus* (Maryknoll, N.Y.: Orbis Books, 1988). See chapters 12 and 13 for further analysis of the gospel of Mark with the help of Myers's commentary.

[2]Original definition by author.

[3]I am thinking here of the global depression of the 1930s. See John Maynard Keynes's analysis of stagnation in chapter 6.

[4]*The American Heritage Dictionary of the English Language,* 3d ed. (Boston: Houghton Mifflin Company, 1992), 583.

[5]I am thinking of John Steinbeck in the United States, Pat Barker in England, and many other authors of fiction.

[6]Adapted from Jose Luis Rocha, "Masaya Trembles: The Lessons of a Disaster," *Envio* (August 17, 2000): 23, quoting Lorenzo Cardenal.

[7]Jose Luis Rocha, and Ian Criostoplos, "NGOs and Natural Disasters: Gaps and Opportunities," *Envio* (November 1999): 48.

[8]The Team Nitlapan-Envio, "Sketches of an Unexpected Tragedy," *Envio* (November 1998): 5.

[9]*Working Together To Prevent Sexual and Domestic Violence,* the newsletter of the Center for the Prevention of Sexual and Domestic Violence, Seattle, Wash., vol. 21, no. 3 (Spring 2001): 1.

[10]Adapted from Carole Warshaw and Anne Ganley, *Improving the Health Care Response to Domestic Violence: A Resource Manual for Health Care Providers* (San Francisco: Family Violence Prevention Fund, 1995), 16.

[11]*The American Heritage Dictionary of the English Language,* 3d ed. (Boston: Houghton Mifflin, 1992), 2131.

[12]Ibid., 1994.

[13]However, for discrete populations, the rates can be higher. Brenda Consuelo Ruiz found rates as high as 50 to 77 percent among small samples of nursing students in Nicaragua. Similar studies of prison populations, persons with mental illnesses, and persons living in war situations also show increased rates of traumatic violence.

[14]Mary P. Koss, Lisa A. Goodman, Angela Browne, Louise F. Fitzgerald, Gwendolyn Puryear Keita, and Nancy Felipe Russo, *No Safe Haven: Male Violence against Women at Home, at Work, and in the Community* (Washington, D.C.: American Psychological Association, 1994).

[15]Rocha, "Masaya Trembles," 16.

[16]For a careful discussion of the race and class issues of family violence, see Robert L. Hampton, *Violence in the Black Family: Correlates and Consequences* (Lexington, Mass.: Lexington Books, 1987). See also Mary P. Koss et al., *No Safe Haven.*

[17]Two recent books have exploded the myth that family violence does not occur in middle-class families, and they also help to explain the silence about such violence. Michele Weldon, *I Closed My Eyes: Revelations of a Battered Woman* (Minneapolis: Hazelden, 1999); Susan Weitzman, *Not to People Like Us: Hidden Abuse in Upscale Marriages* (New York: Basic Books, 2000).

[18]For an excellent summary of family violence and poverty in the United States, see Jody Raphael, *Battered Women, Welfare, and Poverty* (Boston: Northeastern Press, 2000).

[19]Pamela D. Couture, *Seeing Children, Seeing God: A Practical Theology of Children and Poverty* (Nashville: Abingdon Press, 2000), 14–15. See also Pamela D. Couture, *Blessed Are the Poor?: Women's Poverty, Family Policy, and Practical Theology* (Nashville: Abingdon Press in cooperation with the Churches' Center for Theology and Public Policy in Washington D.C., 1991).

[20]Ibid., 28–29.

[21]Ibid., 34.

[22]Ibid., 29–31.

[23]Ibid., 118.

[24]Ibid., 118.

[25]Original definition by author.

[26]*The American Heritage Dictionary of the English Language,* 3d ed. (Boston: Houghton Mifflin Company, 1992), 2117.

[27]Ibid., 1325.

[28]Seward Hiltner, *Preface to Pastoral Theology, The Ayer Lectures, 1954* (New York: Abingdon Press, 1958).

[29]James Lapsley, *Salvation and Health* (Philadelphia: Westminster, 1972).

[30]Emmanuel Yartekwei Lartey, *In Living Colour: An Intercultural Approach to Pastoral Care and Counselling* (London; Herndon, Va.: Cassell, 1997), 9–10, See also Clifford Geertz, *The Interpretation of Culture: Selected Essays* (New York: Basic Books, 1973), 89: Culture is "an historically transmitted pattern of meanings embodied in symbols, a system of inherited conception expressed in symbolic forms by means of which men *(sic)* communicate, perpetuate, and develop their knowledge about and attitudes toward life."

[31]Lartey, *In Living Colour,* 11.

[32]Ibid., 9

[33]Lapsley, *Salvation and Health.*

[34]Carrie Doehring, *Taking Care: Monitoring Power Dynamics and Relational Boundaries in Pastoral Care and Counseling* (Nashville: Abingdon Press, 1995).

[35]Marie M. Fortune, *Love Does No Harm: Sexual Ethics for the Rest of Us* (New York: Continuum, 1995).

Chapter 2: Pastoral Counseling of Domestic Violence Victims in Nicaragua

[1]All names and other personal information have been changed to protect the identities of the clients.

[2]Organización Panamericana de la Salud y Organización Mundial de la Salud, *Situación de Salud en las Américas. Indicadores Básicos* (Managua: Ultradesigns, 1999), 4.

[3]Oscar René Vargas, *Once años después del ajuste. Resultados y perspectivas* (Managua, Imprimatur, 2001), 17.

[4]Oscar René Vargas, *Nicaragua: Después del Mitch...qué?* (Managua: CEREN, 1999), 27.

[5]Oscar René Vargas, *Pobreza en Nicaragua: Un abismo que se agranda* (Managua: UPOLI, 1998), 66.

[6]Vargas, *Once años después del ajuste,* 87.

[7]Ibid., 46 and 47.

[8]Ibid., 132 and 134.

[9]Fondo de Población de las Naciones Unidas, *Estado de la población mundial 1999: Resumen ejecutivo Nicaragua* (Managua, 1999), 26.

[10]Vargas, *Once años después del ajuste,* 38 and 39.

[11]Ibid., 109.

[12]Ibid., 138.

[13]Ibid., 144.

[14]Ibid., 12.

[15]Ibid., 75

[16]Ricardo Herren, *La Conquista erótica de las Indias* (Mexico, D.F.: Planeta, 1992), 22.

[17]Ibid., 38.

[18]Ibid., 27.

[19]Irela Solórzano et al., *Violencia, Llamemos las cosas por su nombre* (Managua: Puntos de Encuentro, 1995), 88.

[20]Mary Ellsberg et al., *Confites en el infierno. Prevalencia y características de la violencia conyugal hacia las mujeres en Nicaragua,* 2d ed. (Managua: Red de Mujeres contra la Violencia, 1998), 63.

Chapter 3: A Story of Healing and Liberation

[1]Linda uses her real name, and her therapist's name is Jim. For clarity, her therapist is not the author of this book. A longer version of Linda Crockett's story is published as Linda Crockett, *The Deepest Wound: How a Journey to El Salvador Led to Healing from Mother-Daughter Incest* (New York: Writer's Showcase, 2001).

[2]Jim is a pastoral counselor in Pennsylvania.

Chapter 4: Pastoral Care and Vulnerability

[1]Marie M. Fortune, "A Five-Year Long Range Plan for Leadership Development," *Working Together to Prevent Sexual Domestic Violence* 21/3 (Spring 2001): 1.

[2]Judith Lewis Herman, *Trauma and Recovery* (New York: Basic Books, 1992).

[3]Pamela D. Couture, *Seeing Children, Seeing God: A Practical Theology of Children and Poverty* (Nashville: Abingdon Press, 2000).

[4]Mary P. Koss, Lisa A. Goodman, Angela Browne, Louise F. Fitzgerald, Gwendolyn Puryear Keita, and Nancy Felipe Russo, *No Safe Haven: Male Violence against Women at Home, at Work, and in the Community* (Washington, D.C.: American Psychological Association, 1994), 24.

[5]Judith Orr, "Hard Work, Hard Lovin', Hard Times, Hardly Worth It: Care of Working-Class Men" in *The Care of Men,* ed. James Newton Poling and Christie Cozad Neuger (Nashville: Abingdon Press, 1997), 70–91.

[6]Ibid., 71.

[7]Ibid., 72.

[8]Ibid., 75.

[9]Ibid.

[10]Ibid.

[11]Ibid.

[12]Stan Gray, "Sharing the Shop Floor" in *Race, Class, and Gender: An Anthology,* comp. Margaret L. Andersen and Patricia Hill Collins (Belmont, Calif.: Wadsworth, 1995), 505.

[13]Ibid., 506.

[14]Pamela D. Couture, *Blessed Are the Poor?: Women's Poverty, Family Policy, and Practical Theology* (Nashville: Abingdon Press in cooperation with the Churches' Center for Theology and Public Policy Washington D.C., 1991).

[15]Ibid., 73.

[16]Ibid., 38

[17]Ibid.

[18]Ibid.

[19]Ibid.

[20]Ibid.

[21]Ibid.

[22]Ibid., 163.

[23]Ibid., 166.

Chapter 5: The Connection between the Unjust Distribution of Wealth and Vulnerability

[1]Bureau of the Public Debt, Parkersburg, W.V., http://www.publicdebt.treas.gov/opd/opd.htm for July, 2001.

[2]Development Programme United Nations, *Human Development Report 2000* (New York: Oxford Univ. Press, 2000), 139–40.

[3]Ibid., 269, 279. "At the PPP rate, one dollar has the same purchasing power over domestic GDP as the US dollar has over US GDP…PPP rates allow a standard comparison of real price levels between countries" (281).

[4]Ibid., 136. Note: By straight GNP, Nicaragua ranked 130th in 1994, Ruth Leger Sivard, *World Military and Social Expenditures* (Washington, D.C.: World Priorities, 1996).

[5]United Nations, *Human Development Report 2000,* 157. The U.S. is ranked number 1 in GNP.

[6]Ibid., 129 for wording of this sentence.

[7]Ibid., 159.

[8]Ibid.

[9]Ibid., 180, PPP$ of 2,142.00 (purchasing power parity = the amount that can be bought in U.S. dollars accounting for regional differences). Ibid., 159. PPP$ is artificially

created to help persons from the rich countries understand the minimal purchasing power in countries where the standard of living is cheaper. For example, $2,142 would be considered extreme poverty within the U.S.

[10]Oscar René Vargas, *Nicaragua: Despues del Mitch...que?* (Managua: CEREN, 1999), 40, 42.

[11]Ibid., 38.

[12]Oscar René Vargas, "Badly Fed and Malnourished," *Envio* (1996): 27.

[13]Vargas, *Nicaragua: Despues del Mitch...que?* 170.

[14]Ibid., 159.

[15]United Nations, *Human Development Report 2000,* 170.

[16]The International Bank for Reconstruction and Development/The World Bank, *The World Development Report 1999-2000* (New York: Oxford Univ. Press, 2000), 237.

[17]United Nations, *Human Development Report 2000,* 220.

[18]Ibid., 220, 225.

[19]Vargas, "Badly Fed and Malnourished," 27.

[20]United Nations, *Human Development Report 2000,* 239.

[21]Ibid., 184, 204; Vargas, *Nicaragua: Despues del Mitch...que?* 20.

[22]Development Programme United Nations, *Human Development Report 1999* (New York: Oxford Univ. Press, 1999), 45.

[23]"Remittances to Nicaragua," *La Prensa,* 28 August 2000.

[24]Vargas, *Nicaragua: Despues del Mitch...que?* 77.

[25]United Nations, *Human Development Report 2000,* 163.

[26]United Nations, *Human Development Report 1999,* 36.

[27]Susan Meilselas, *Nicaragua: June 1978–July 1979* (New York: Pantheon Books, 1981), Appendix.

[28]Ibid.

[29]"World Court Sides with Justice," *Envio* (July, 1986).

[30]Irela Solórzano et al., *Violencia, Llamemos las cosas por su nombre* (Managua: Puntos de Encuentro, 1995), 88. Mary Ellsberg et al., *Confites en el infierno. Prevalencia y características de la violencia conyugal hacia las mujeres en Nicaragua,* 2d ed. (Managua: Red de Mujeres contra la Violencia, 1998), 63.

[31]United Nations, *Human Development Report 2000,* 177.

[32]Ibid., 202.

[33]Ibid., 205.

[34]Ibid., 205.

[35]Ibid., 186, 188.

[36]Ibid., 159.

[37]Ibid., 178, 180.

[38]Ibid., 165.

[39]Ibid., 161.

[40]U.S. Census Bureau, 1998 census estimates, Washington, D.C.

[41]United Nations, *Human Development Report 2000,* 172.

[42]Ibid., 163.

[43]Ibid., 172.

[44]Ibid.

[45]Ibid.

[46]Ibid., 149.

[47]Ibid., 172.

[48]United Nations, *Human Development Report 1999,* 188.

[49]Ibid., 192.

[50]Ibid.

[51]Mary P. Koss, Lisa A. Goodman, Angela Browne, Louise F. Fitzgerald, Gwendolyn Puryear Keita, and Nancy Felipe Russo, *No Safe Haven: Male Violence against Women at Home, at Work, and in the Community* (Washington, D.C.: American Psychological Association, 1994); Diana Russell, *The Secret Trauma* (New York: Basic Books, 1986).

[52]Mary P. Ross, *Journal of Interpersonal Violence* 8, no. 2 (June 1993): 198–222.

[53]Dante Cicchetti and Vicki Carlson, eds., *Child Maltreatment: Theory and Research on the Causes and Consequences of Child Abuse and Neglect* (Cambridge: Cambridge Univ. Press, 1989), 48.

[54]Ibid., 98–99.

[55]Richard J. Gelles and Murray A. Straus, *Intimate Violence* (New York: Simon and Schuster, 1988), 104.

Chapter 6: Theories of Capitalism and the Distribution of Wealth

[1]The International Bank for Reconstruction and Development/The World Bank, *The World Development Report 1999–2000* (New York: Oxford Univ. Press, 2000), 13–14.

[2]Daniel Finn, *Just Trading: On the Ethics and Economics of International Trade* (Nashville: Abingdon Press, 1996), 196.

[3]Ibid., book jacket.

[4]Robert Heilbroner, *The Worldly Philosophers: The Lives, Times, and Ideas of the Great Economic Thinkers,* rev. ed. (New York: Simon and Schuster, 1999).

[5]Ibid., 20–21.

[6]Ibid., 26–27.

[7]Ibid., 28.

[8]Ibid.

[9]Adam Smith, *An Inquiry into the Nature and Causes of the Wealth of Nations, Book One* (New York: Random House, 1776), quoted in Max L. Stackhouse, Dennis P. McCann, and Shirley J. Rosels, with Preston N. Williams, *On Moral Business: Classical and Contemporary Resources for Ethics in Economic Life* (Grand Rapids, Mich.: Eerdmans, 1995), 213.

[10]Heilbroner, *The Worldly Philosophers,* 54–56.

[11]Ibid. 89-90.

[12]See William Greider, *Who Will Tell the People: The Betrayal of American Democracy* (New York: Simon and Schuster, 1992); Kevin Phillips, *Arrogant Capital: Washington, Wall Street, and the Frustration of American Politics* (Boston: Little, Brown, and Company, 1994); and Kevin Phillips, *Boiling Point: Republicans, Democrats, and the Decline of Middle-Class Prosperity* (New York: Random House, 1993).

[13]Heilbroner, *The Worldly Philosophers,* 97.

[14]Ibid., 100.

[15]Ibid., 101.

[16]Ibid., 105f.

[17]Ibid., 163.

[18]Ibid., 173. In the next chapter, John Cobb and Herman Daly question the decisions about what indexes are measured by the GNP and suggest alternatives that also depend on mathematics.

[19]Ibid., 190.

[20]Ibid., 197.

[21]Ibid.

[22]Ibid., 203.

[23]Ibid., 235.

[24]Ibid., 248–49.

[25]Ibid., 250.

[26]Ibid., 251–52.

[27]Ibid., 270–71.

[28]Ibid., 270.

[29]Development Programme United Nations, *Human Development Report 1999* (New York: Oxford Univ. Press, 1999), 25.

[30]Heilbroner, *The Worldly Philosophers,* 286.

Chapter 7: A Christian Critique of Market Capitalism

[1]Original definition by author.

[2]Daniel Finn, *Just Trading: On the Ethics and Economics of International Trade* (Nashville: Abingdon Press, 1996), 63–76.

[3]David A. Krueger, *The Business Corporation and Productive Justice* (Nashville: Abingdon Press, 1997), 29–30.

[4]John B. Cobb, Jr., and Herman E. Daly, *For the Common Good: Redirecting the Economy toward Community, the Environment, and a Sustainable Future* (Boston: Beacon Press, 1989), 159.

⁵Ibid., 165.

⁶Ibid.

⁷Ibid., 161.

⁸Ibid., 139.

⁹Ibid., 453.

¹⁰Development Programme United Nations, *Human Development Report 2000* (New York: Oxford Univ. Press, 2000). OEDC countries have 920 million people out of 4,017 million people in the world (226); OEDC countries have a GNP of $23 trillion out of a world GNP of $28 trillion (205).

¹¹John B. Cobb, Jr., *Sustaining the Common Good: A Christian Perspective on the Global Economy* (Cleveland: Pilgrim Press, 1994), 70–71. See also Presbyterian Church (USA), *Hope for a Global Future: Toward Just and Sustainable Human Development* (Louisville, Ky.: Office of the General Assembly, 1996), 20-30, for a narrative of these international agencies since 1970.

¹²Cobb, *Sustaining the Common Good,* 72.

¹³Ibid., 72–73; Presbyterian Church (USA), *Hope for a Global Future,* 21.

¹⁴Cobb, *Sustaining the Common Good,* 73–74.

¹⁵Ibid., 74; United Nations, *Human Development Report 2000,* 222.

¹⁶Cobb, *Sustaining the Common Good,* 74–75.

¹⁷Cobb and Daly, *For the Common Good,* 231.

¹⁸Cobb, *Sustaining the Common Good,* 78.

¹⁹The International Bank for Reconstruction and Development/The World Bank, *The World Development Report 1999–2000* (New York: Oxford Univ. Press, 2000), 236–37.

²⁰Presbyterian Church (USA), *Hope for a Global Future,* 21.

²¹Cobb and Daly, *For the Common Good,* 290.

²²Cobb, *Sustaining the Common Good,* 76; Presbyterian Church (USA), *Hope for a Global Future,* 21.

²³Cobb, *Sustaining the Common Good,* 78.

²⁴Presbyterian Church (USA), *Hope for a Global Future,* 22.

²⁵Ibid., 45–56. See also Rosemary Radford Ruether, *Gaia and God: An Ecofeminist Theology of Earth Healing* (San Francisco: HarperSanFrancisco, 1994).

²⁶World Bank, *The World Development Report 1999–2000,* 13–14.

²⁷Cobb, *Sustaining the Common Good,* 71. See Denis Goulet, *Mexico: Development Strategies for the Future* (Notre Dame, Ind.: Univ. of Notre Dame Press, 1983), 70–71.

²⁸William K. Tabba, *The Political Economy of the Black Ghetto* (New York: W. W. Norton, 1970), 53.

²⁹United Nations, *Human Development Report 2000,* 281.

³⁰Daniel P. Moynihan, *The Negro Family* (Washington, D.C.: U.S. Dept of Labor, 1965). See rebuttal in Lee Rainwater and William Yancey, *The Moynihan Report and the Politics of Controversy* (Cambridge, Mass.: MIT Press, 1967).

³¹Manning Marable, *How Capitalism Underdeveloped Black America* (Boston: South End Press, 1983), 7.

³²Melvin L. Oliver and Thomas M. Shapiro, *Black Wealth/White Wealth: A New Perspective on Racial Inequality* (New York: Routledge, 1997).

³³Ibid., 28.

³⁴Ibid., 14.

³⁵Ibid.

³⁶John Hope Franklin and Alfred A. Moss, Jr., *From Slavery to Freedom: A History of African Americans* (New York: Knopf, 1988), 238.

³⁷Ibid., 38.

³⁸Ibid., 17, 39.

³⁹Ibid., 41.

⁴⁰William Julius Wilson, *When Work Disappears: The World of the New Urban Poor* (New York: Vintage, 1996), 165.

⁴¹Peter Edelman, "Reforming Welfare–Take Two," *The Nation* 274, no. 4 (Feb. 4, 2002), 16.

⁴²Oliver, *Black Wealth/White Wealth,* 43.

⁴³Ibid., 44.

⁴⁴Ibid., 169.

⁴⁵Marable, *How Capitalism Underdeveloped Black America,* 62.

Chapter 8: Resistance to Capitalism in Nicaragua

[1] Original definition by author.

[2] My trip was sponsored and financed by Colgate Rochester Divinity School and the American Baptist Churches. The organizer was Lowell Fewster, ABC minister. I am grateful for the opportunity these Christians gave me.

[3] Susan Meilselas, *Nicaragua: June 1978–July 1979* (New York: Pantheon Books, 1981).

[4] Stephen Kinzer, *Blood of Brothers: Life and War in Nicaragua* (New York: Anchor Books, 1991), 23.

[5] *Encyclopedia Britannica*, s.v. "Nicaragua, History" (*Encyclopedia Britannica* Web page, 2000 [cited September 4, 2000]). "200,000" is the number of persons enslaved according to the U.S. Library of Congress, s.v. "Nicaragua" (Library of Congress, 2000 [cited September 4, 2000]).

[6] Kinzer, *Blood of Brothers: Life and War in Nicaragua*, 23.

[7] *Encyclopedia Britannica*, s.v. "Monroe Doctrine" (*Encyclopedia Britannica* Web page, 2000 [cited September 4, 2000]).

[8] Library of Congress, "Nicaragua."

[9] Roger N. Lancaster, *Life Is Hard: Machismo, Danger, and the Intimacy of Power in Nicaragua* (Berkeley, Calif.: Univ. of California Press, 1992), 1.

[10] *Encyclopedia Britannica*, s.v. "Theodore Roosevelt, Foreign Policy" (*Encyclopedia Britannica* Web page, 2000 [cited September 4, 2000]).

[11] Meilselas, *Nicaragua: June 1978–July 1979.*

[12] Kinzer, *Blood of Brothers: Life and War in Nicaragua*, 27.

[13] *Encyclopedia Britannica*, "Nicaragua, History."

[14] Meilselas, *Nicaragua: June 1978–July 1979.*

[15] Kinzer, *Blood of Brothers: Life and War in Nicaragua*, 30.

[16] Ibid., 30.

[17] Lancaster, *Life Is Hard: Machismo, Danger, and the Intimacy of Power in Nicaragua*, 2.

[18] Meilselas, *Nicaragua: June 1978–July 1979.*

[19] David Halberstam, *The Fifties* (New York: Villard Books, 1993), 385.

[20] Kinzer, *Blood of Brothers: Life and War in Nicaragua*, 33.

[21] Meilselas, *Nicaragua: June 1978–July 1979.*

[22] Ibid.

[23] Ibid.

[24] Kinzer, *Blood of Brothers: Life and War in Nicaragua*, 70.

[25] Ibid., 76.

[26] Ibid., 76.

[27] Ibid., 97.

[28] Lancaster, *Life Is Hard: Machismo, Danger, and the Intimacy of Power in Nicaragua*, 7.

[29] Ibid., 8.

[30] John B. Cobb, Jr., *Sustaining the Common Good: A Christian Perspective on the Global Economy* (Cleveland: Pilgrim Press, 1994), 76.

[31] Development Programme United Nations, *Human Development Report 2000* (New York: Oxford Univ. Press, 2000), 205.

[32] Elliott Marin and Vera Amanda Solis, "Badly Fed and Malnourished," *Envio* (August 1996).

[33] Development Programme United Nations, *Human Development Report 2000,* 212.

[34] Oscar René Vargas, *Nicaragua: Despues del Mitch...que?* (Managua: CEREN, 1999), 77.

[35] Ricardo Falla, "How Dollar Remittances Are Changing a Village," *Envio* (2000).

[36] "Remittances to Nicaragua," *La Prensa,* Aug. 28, 2000.

[37] Special thanks to Gustavo Ruiz, economist in Managua, for the insights of this paragraph.

[38] Non-governmental organization (NGO) is the official title given to any agency that works in the two-thirds world outside of government. It includes churches, secular relief agencies, and many small groups of people who want to make a difference for poor people.

[39] United Nations, *Human Development Report 2000,* 253.

[40] Translated by James Poling. I received this code of ethics directly from one of the organizers when I visited their union office.

[41] Oscar René Vargas, *Once años después del ajuste. Resultados y perspectivas* (Managua: Imprimatur, 2001), 87.

[42]There is substantial criticism of the Sandinista Revolution, not only from the opposition but also from those who have been committed to the Sandinista Party or the Revolution. For example, see Allan Bolt, "Roots and Patterns of Our Political Culture," *Envio* 20/240 (2001).

[43]Lancaster, *Life Is Hard: Machismo, Danger, and the Intimacy of Power in Nicaragua,* 13.

[44]Kinzer, *Blood of Brothers: Life and War in Nicaragua,* 217.

[45]Johann Baptist Metz, *The Emergent Church: The Future of Christianity in a Postbourgeois World* (New York: Crossroad, 1981).

[46]Ernesto Cardenal, *The Gospel in Solentiname,* vol. 2 (Maryknoll, N.Y.: Orbis Books, 1978), 155–56.

Chapter 9: African American Resistance to Capitalism in the United States

[1]Hugh Thomas, *The Slave Trade* (New York: Touchstone, 1997), 174.

[2]Lerone Bennett, Jr., *Before the Mayflower: A History of the Negro in America: 1619–1962* (Chicago: Johnson, 1962), 101.

[3]Herbert Aptheker, *American Negro Slave Revolts* (New York: Columbia Univ. Press, 1943), quoted in Bennett, *Before the Mayflower,* 103–4.

[4]Michel-Rolph Trouillot, *Silencing the Past: Power and the Production of History* (Boston: Beacon, 1995). Antonio Benitez-Rojo, *The Repeating Island: The Caribbean and the Postmodern Perspective* (Durham, N.C.: Duke Univ. Press, 1996).

[5]Bennett, *Before the Mayflower,* 122.

[6]Herbert Aptheker, "The Negro Woman," *Masses and Mainstream* 11, no. 2 (1944): 11, quoted in Angela Y. Davis, *Women, Race, and Class* (New York: Vintage Books, 1981), 21.

[7]Adapted from James Newton Poling, *Deliver Us from Evil: Resisting Racial and Gender Oppression* (Minneapolis: Fortress Press, 1996), 47–48.

[8]Vincent Harding, *There Is a River: The Black Struggle for Freedom in America* (New York: Vintage, 1981), 86.

[9]Ibid., 179–94.

[10]Manning Marable, *How Capitalism Underdeveloped Black America* (Boston: South End Press, 1983), 208.

[11]Ibid., 108.

[12]Ibid.

[13]Ibid., 109.

[14]Ibid., 110.

[15]Ibid., 111.

[16]Ibid., 114.

[17]Ibid., 115.

[18]Ibid., 117–18.

[19]Ibid., 121.

[20]Death Penalty Information Center, *Prison Population* (www.essential.org/dpic/dpic.html, 2000 [cited July 27, 2000]). Similar information available July 2002 at www.death penaltyinfo.org.

[21]Ibid.

[22]U.S. Government Department of Justice, *Prison and Jail Inmates at Midyear, 1998* (Department of Justice, U.S. Government, 1998 [cited September 14, 2000]).

[23]U.S. Census Bureau, *U.S. Census Report* (U.S. Government, 1998 [cited September 14, 2000]).

[24]Department of Justice, *Prison and Jail Inmates.*

[25]Marable, *How Capitalism Underdeveloped Black America,* 127–28.

[26]James Oakes, quoted in ibid., 316.

[27]Peter Parish, quoted in ibid., 313.

[28]Robert Michael Franklin, *Liberating Visions* (Minneapolis: Fortress Press, 1990), 11.

[29]Ibid., 24.

[30]Marable, *How Capitalism Underdeveloped Black America,* 146–47.

[31]Melvin L. Oliver and Thomas M. Shapiro, *Black Wealth/White Wealth: A New Perspective on Racial Inequality* (New York: Routledge, 1997), 49–50.

[32]Ibid., 50.

[33]W. E. B. DuBois, *W .E. B. Dubois Speaks 1890–1919,* vol. 2 (New York: Pathfinder Press, 1970), 84, quoted in Franklin, *Liberating Visions,* 59.

[34]Marable, *How Capitalism Underdeveloped Black America,* 158.

[35]Ibid., 156.

[36]Ibid.

[37]Evelyn Brooks Higginbotham, *Righteous Discontent* (Cambridge, Mass.: Harvard Univ. Press, 1993), 161.

[38]Ibid., 162–63.

[39]Ibid., 181.

[40]Ibid., 173–74.

[41]Cf. James Newton Poling and Toinette M. Eugene, *Balm for Gilead: Pastoral Care for African American Families Experiencing Abuse* (Nashville: Abingdon Press, 1998).

[42]Higginbotham, *Righteous Discontent*, 4–5.

[43]Marable, *How Capitalism Underdeveloped Black America*, 33.

[44]Emilie M. Townes, *Womanist Justice, Womanist Hope* (Atlanta: Scholars Press, 1993).

[45]Marable, *How Capitalism Underdeveloped Black America*, 34.

[46]Ibid., 41.

[47]Franklin, *Liberating Visions*, 127.

[48]Ibid.

[49]Gayraud Wilmore, *Black Religion and Black Radicalism* (Maryknoll, N.Y.: Orbis Books, 1993).

[50]Marable, *How Capitalism Underdeveloped Black America*, 210.

[51]Franklin, *Liberating Visions*, 129.

[52]Ibid., 80.

[53]Franklin, *Liberating Visions*, 87, quoting from Elijah Muhammad, *The Final Call,* formerly *Muhammad Speaks Newspaper* (Chicago: Muhammad Temple of Islam No. 2), back page of each issue.

[54]Franklin, *Liberating Visions*, 78.

[55]Ibid., 97.

[56]Ibid., 100-101.

[57]James H. Cone, *Martin and Malcolm in America* (Maryknoll, N.Y.: Orbis, 1991), 284.

[58]Patricia Hill Collins, *Black Feminist Thought: Knowledge, Consciousness, and the Politics of Empowerment* (New York: Routledge, 1990), 28.

[59]Ibid. ,32.

[60]Davis, *Women, Race, and Class*, 4.

[61]Ibid., 7.

[62]Collins, *Black Feminist Thought*, 78.

[63]Angela Y. Davis, *Women, Culture, Politics* (New York: Vintage Books, 1990), 47.

[64]Maulana Karenga, *Kwanzaa: Origin, Concepts, Practice* (Inglewood, Calif.: Kawaida Publications, 1977).

[65]David A Anderson, *Kwanzaa* (New York: Gumbs and Thomas, 1992), 56.

Chapter 10: Women's Resistance to Capitalism in the United States

[1]Erving Goffman, *Asylums: Essays on the Social Situation of Mental Patients and Other Inmates* (Chicago: Aldine, 1962).

[2]Hazel Carby, *Reconstructing Womanhood: The Emergence of the Afro-American Woman Novelist* (New York: Oxford Univ. Press, 1987), 23.

[3]Frantz Fanon, *The Wretched of the Earth* (New York: Grove Press, 1963).

[4]J. Nathan Poling, *Casting Spells from the Stage* (Ph.D. diss.,: Emory University, 1998), 165–66.

[5]Angela Y. Davis, *Women, Race, and Class* (New York: Vintage Books, 1981), 21.

[6]Maroon is a term "for plantation slaves who had run away to live free in uncultivated parts. The English word is taken from the French word *marron*, runaway Black slave." *The American Heritage Dictionary of the English Language*, 3d ed. (New York: Houghton Mifflin, 1992), 1102.

[7]Ibid., 22.

[8]Jean Fagan Yellin, ed., *Harriet A. Jacobs: Incidents in the Life of a Slave Girl Written by Herself* (Cambridge, Mass.: Harvard Univ. Press, 1987).

[9]U.S. Census Bureau, *U.S. Census Report* (U.S. government, 1998 [cited September 14 2000]).

[10]Davis, *Women, Race, and Class*, 55.

[11]Sheila Rowbotham, *A Century of Women: The History of Women in Britain and the United States* (New York: Penguin, 1997), 45.

[12]Ibid., 45.

[13]David Halberstam, *The Fifties* (New York: Villard Books, 1993), especially chap. 39.

[14]Dennis A. Deslippe, *Rights Not Roses: Unions and the Rise of Working-Class Feminism, 1945–80* (Urbana: Univ. of Illinois Press, 2000), 67.

[15]Ibid., 86.

[16]Ibid., 87–88.

[17]Ibid., 2.

[18]Georges Vernez, *Immigrant Women in the U.S. Workforce: Who Struggles? Who Succeeds?* (Lanham, Md.: Lexington Books, 1999), 19–29.

[19]Refugio I. Rochin and Adela de la Torre, "Chicanas/os in the Economy: Issues and Challenges since 1970," in *Chicanas/Chicanos at the Crossroads: Social, Economic, and Political Change,* ed. David R. Marciel and Isidro D. Ortiz (Tuscon: Univ. of Arizona Press, 1996), 68–69.

[20]Gerda Lerner, *The Creation of Patriarchy* (Oxford: Oxford Univ. Press, 1986).

[21]Rosemary Radford Ruether, *Women and Redemption: A Theological History* (Minneapolis: Fortress Press, 1998).

[22]Maria Mies, *Patriarchy and Accumulation on a World Scale* (London: Zed Books, 1998), 38. See also Maria Mies and Veronika Bennholdt-Thomsen, *The Subsistence Perspective* (London: Zed Books, 1999).

[23]Davis, *Women, Race, and Class.*

[24]Adrienne Rich, "Compulsory Heterosexuality and Lesbian Existence," in *The Signs Reader: Women, Gender and Scholarship,* ed. Elizabeth and Emily Abel (Chicago: Univ. of Chicago Press, 1983), 149.

[25]There is a common Confucian saying that explicitly teaches young Asian women and men that this hierarchy is natural and important for the smooth operation of society.

[26]Diana Russell, *The Secret Trauma* (New York: Basic Books, 1986), 60.

[27]Hester Eisenstein, *Contemporary Feminist Thought* (New York: Hall and Co., 1983), 31 (summarizing Susan Griffin, "Rape: The All American Crime," *Ramparts* [1971]).

[28]Marie M. Fortune, *Sexual Violence: The Unmentionable Sin* (New York: Pilgrim Press, 1983). For further information, contact the Center for the Prevention of Sexual and Domestic Violence, 2400 N. 45th St., Suite 10, Seattle, WA 98103 (www. cpsdv.org). Delia tells her own story in the award-winning video "Broken Vows," produced by the center.

[29]This is from Mary P. Koss, Lisa A. Goodman, Angela Browne, Louise F. Fitzgerald, Gwendolyn Puryear Keita, and Nancy Felipe Russo, *No Safe Haven: Male Violence against Women at Home, at Work, and in the Community* (Washington, D.C.: American Psychological Association, 1994), 72–73. The article cited is A. Browne and K. R. Williams, "Exploring the Effect of Resource Availability and the Likelihood of Female-Perpetrated Homicides," *Law and Society Review* 23:75–94.

[30]Center for the Prevention of Sexual and Domestic Violence, 2400 N. 45th St., Suite 10, Seattle, WA 98103 (www.cpsdv.org).

[31]Linda Crockett, *The Deepest Wound: How a Journey to El Salvador Led to Healing from Mother-Daughter Incest* (New York: Writer's Showcase, 2001).

[32]See Eisenstein, *Contemporary Feminist Thought,* for an excellent summary of the history of the women's movement and the discovery of sexual and domestic violence.

[33]This section adapted from a booklet by James Newton Poling and Marie Fortune, *Sexual Abuse by Clergy: A Crisis for the Church* (Decatur, Ga.: Journal of Pastoral Care Publications, 1994).

[34]Susan Brownmiller, *Against Our Will: Men, Women, and Rape* (New York: Simon and Schuster, 1975). Quoted in Eisenstein, *Contemporary Feminist Thought,* 30.

[35]bell hooks, *Ain't I a Woman: Black Women and Feminism* (Boston: South End Press, 1981), 52–53.

[36]Catherine MacKinnon, *Sexual Harassment of Working Women* (New Haven, Conn.: Yale Univ. Press, 1979), 149.

[37]Russell, *The Secret Trauma.*

[38]Davis, *Women, Race, and Class,* 199–200.

[39]See Eisenstein, *Contemporary Feminist Thought* for a summary of this history.

[40]CATW, PO Box 9338, N. Amherst, MA 01059 (www.catwinternational.org).

[41]ECP, End Child Prostitution, www.ecpatusa.org. See also A-STOP, Alliance for Speaking Truths on Prostitution, 1901 Portland Ave, Minneapolis, MN 55404 (www.a-stop.org).

[42]Amy O'Neill Richard, *International Trafficking in Women to the United States: A Contemporary Manifestation of Slavery and Organized Crime* (Washington, D.C.: Center for the Study of Intelligence, Central Intelligence Agency, 1999), 47.

[43]Ibid.

[44]Ibid., 3.

[45]Ibid., 19–20.

[46]Rita Nakashima Brock and Susan Brooks Thistlethwaite, *Casting Stones: Prostitution and Liberation in Asia and the United States* (Minneapolis: Fortress Press, 1996).

[47]See Chung Hyun Kyung, "Your Comfort vs. My Death," in *Women Resisting Violence: Spirituality for Life,* ed. Mary John Mananzan, Mercy Amba Oduyoye, Elsa Tamez, J. Shannon Clarkson, Mary C. Grey, Letty M. Russell (Maryknoll, N.Y.: Orbis Books, 1996), 129–40. See also the journal *International Activities Against Military Sexual Slavery by Japan,* especially vol. 5, no. 1, "Kim Hak-Soon Finished Her 'Han-filled' Life."

[48]Linda Crockett, personal communication.

[49]Patricia Hill Collins, *Black Feminist Thought: Knowledge, Consciousness, and the Politics of Empowerment* (New York: Routledge, 1990).

[50]Rosemary Radford Ruether, *Women-Church: Theology and Practice of Feminist Liturgical Communities* (San Francisco: Harper and Row, 1985).

[51]Martha Craven Nussbaum, *Sex & Social Justice* (New York: Oxford Univ. Press, 1999), and *Women and Human Development: The Capabilities Approach* (Cambridge, U.K.: Cambridge Univ. Press, 2000).

[52]Saskia Sassen, *Cities in a World Economy* (Thousand Oaks, Calif.: Pine Forge/Sage Press, 1994), and *Globalization and Its Discontents: Essays on the New Mobility of People and Money* (New York: The New Press, 1998).

[53]Mies, *Patriarchy and Accumulation on a World Scale,* 1.

[54]Ibid., 209.

[55]Ibid., 211–12.

[56]Ibid., 216.

[57]Ibid., 218.

[58]Ibid.

[59]Ibid., 219.

[60]Ibid., xvii.

[61]Ibid., xvii, xviiii.

[62]Ibid., xv.

[63]Ibid., 225.

[64]Ibid., 227.

[65]Ibid., 228.

Chapter 11: Mark's Critique of Oppressive Political Economies

[1]All biblical quotations in this chapter are taken from the *New Revised Standard Version Bible* (NRSV) unless otherwise noted. This text is taken from the *King James Version* (KJV), which was used frequently in churches during my childhood and gives a translation that is familiar to many Christians.

[2]Ched Myers, *Binding the Strong Man: A Political Reading of Mark's Story of Jesus* (Maryknoll, N.Y.: Orbis Books, 1988), 310.

[3]Mary Ann Tolbert, *Sowing the Gospel: Mark's World in Literary-Historical Perspective* (Minneapolis: Fortress Press, 1996), 251.

[4]Ibid., 311–12.

[5]Ibid., 386.

[6]For more detail on my views of biblical hermeneutics, see James Newton Poling, *Deliver Us from Evil: Resisting Racial and Gender Oppression* (Minneapolis: Fortress Press, 1996), 148–57.

[7]Myers, *Binding the Strong Man,* 5.

[8]William A. Williams, *Empire as a Way of Life* (New York: Oxford Univ. Press, 1980), 7f., quoted in Myers, *Binding the Strong Man,* 6.

[9]Myers, *Binding the Strong Man,* 6.

[10]Ibid., 7.

[11]Tolbert, *Sowing the Gospel,* 60.

[12]Ibid., 73.

[13]Myers, *Binding the Strong Man,* 8.

[14]Ibid., 31.

[15]Ibid., 39–40.

[16]See Itumeleng J. Mosala, *Biblical Hermeneutics and Black Theology in South Africa* (Grand Rapids, Mich.: Eerdmans, 1989); and John Howard Yoder, *The Politics of Jesus*, 2d rev. ed. (Grand Rapids, Mich.: Eerdmans, 1993).

[17]Myers, *Binding the Strong Man*, 41.

[18]Thomas F. Carney, *The Shape of the Past: Models and Antiquity* (Lawrence, Kans.: Coronado Press, 1975), 167, quoted in Myers, *Binding the Strong Man*, 48.

[19]Myers, *Binding the Strong Man*, 49.

[20]Ibid., 53.

[21]Ibid., 51–52.

[22]Ibid., 54.

[23]Ibid., 58–60.

[24]Ibid., 62.

[25]Ibid.

[26]Ibid., 65.

[27]Ibid., 69.

[28]Ibid., 75.

[29]Ibid., 71.

[30]Ibid.

[31]Ibid., 52.

[32]Ibid., 75–76.

[33]Ibid., 76.

[34]Ibid., 77.

[35]Richard Horsley and John Hanson, *Bandits, Prophets and Messiahs: Popular Movements in the Time of Jesus* (Minneapolis: Winston, 1985), 61, quoted in Myers, *Binding the Strong Man*, 79.

[36]Myers, *Binding the Strong Man*, 80.

[37]Ibid., 81.

[38]Ibid., 80–81.

[39]Ibid., 70, 82–83.

[40]Ibid., 83–85.

[41]Ibid., 85.

[42]Ibid., 87.

[43]Ibid., 120.

[44]Ibid., 120–21.

[45]Ibid., 121.

[46]Ibid.

[47]Werner Kelber, *Mark's Story of Jesus* (Philadelphia: Fortress Press, 1979), 30f., quoted in Myers, *Binding the Strong Man*, 188.

[48]Herman Waetjen, "The Construction of the Way into a Reordering of Power: An Inquiry into the Generic Conception of the Gospel According to Mark" (San Anselmo, Calif.: San Francisco Theological Seminary, 1982), 6, quoted in Myers, *Binding the Strong Man*, 129.

[49]Myers, *Binding the Strong Man*, 132.

[50]Ibid., 139.

[51]Ibid., 193–94.

[52]Tolbert, *Sowing the Gospel*, 134 n. 16.

[53]Ibid., 101.

[54]Myers, *Binding the Strong Man*, 197.

[55]Ibid., 200; Tolbert, *Sowing the Gospel*, 168–70.

[56]Myers, *Binding the Strong Man*, 201.

[57]Ibid., 201–2. See the litany by Nicaraguan women in chap. 15.

[58]Ibid., 202–3.

[59]Sandra Schneiders, *Women and the Word* (New York: Paulist Press, 1986); Tolbert, *Sowing the Gospel*, 185.

[60]Myers, *Binding the Strong Man*, 205.

[61]Ibid.

[62]Ernesto Cardenal, *The Gospel in Solentiname*, vol. 2 (Maryknoll, N.Y.: Orbis, 1978), 155–56.

[63]Myers, *Binding the Strong Man*, 206.
[64]Cardenal, *The Gospel in Solentiname*, 157.
[65]Myers, *Binding the Strong Man*, 442.
[66]Ibid., 85.

Chapter 12: Mark's Alternative Economic Vision

[1]Ched Myers, *Binding the Strong Man: A Political Reading of Mark's Story of Jesus* (Maryknoll, N.Y.: Orbis Books, 1988), 257.
[2]Ibid., 260.
[3]See Henry A. Giroux, *Border Crossings: Cultural Workers and the Politics of Education* (New York: Routledge, 1992), 183–96, for a discussion of contemporary Marxist arguments about culture and education.
[4]Mary Ann Tolbert, *Sowing the Gospel: Mark's World in Literary-Historical Perspective* (Minneapolis: Fortress Press, 1996), 209.
[5]Myers, *Binding the Strong Man*, 266.
[6]Ibid. 267–68.
[7]Ibid., 286.
[8]Tolbert, *Sowing the Gospel*, 157.
[9]Ibid.
[10]Myers, *Binding the Strong Man*, 274.
[11]Ibid., 275.
[12]Ibid., 278.
[13]Tolbert, *Sowing the Gospel*, 215.
[14]Rita Nakashima Brock and Rebecca Ann Parker, *Proverbs of Ashes: Violence, Redemptive Suffering, and the Search for What Saves Us* (Boston: Beacon Press, 2001); Rita Nakashima Brock, *Journeys by Heart: A Christology of Erotic Power* (New York: Crossroad, 1988); Joanne Carlson Brown and Carole R. Bohn, eds., *Christianity, Patriarchy and Abuse: A Feminist Critique* (New York: Pilgrim Press, 1989); Jacqueline Grant, *White Women's Christ and Black Women's Jesus* (Atlanta: Scholars Press, 1989); James Newton Poling, *The Abuse of Power: A Theological Problem* (Nashville: Abingdon Press, 1991); Delores S. Williams, *Sisters in the Wilderness: The Challenge of Womanist God-Talk* (Maryknoll, N. Y.: Orbis Books, 1993).
[15]Mohandas Gandhi, *Nonviolence in Peace and War*, 2 vols. (Ahmedabad: Navajivan, 1948), 41, quoted in Myers, *Binding the Strong Man*, 287.
[16]Myers, *Binding the Strong Man*, 285–86.
[17]Ibid., 121.
[18]Tolbert, *Sowing the Gospel*, 212.
[19]Myers, *Binding the Strong Man*, 364.
[20]Ibid., 365.
[21]Tolbert, *Sowing the Gospel*, 213.
[22]United Methodist Church, *The United Methodist Hymnal: Book of United Methodist Worship* (Nashville: United Methodist Pub. House, 1989), nos. 640, 642.
[23]Tolbert, *Sowing the Gospel*, 213–14.
[24]Myers, *Binding the Strong Man*, 391.
[25]Tolbert, *Sowing the Gospel*, 211
[26]Myers, *Binding the Strong Man*, 366.
[27]Tolbert, *Sowing the Gospel*, 278–79 n. 13.
[28]Myers, *Binding the Strong Man*, 373.
[29]Tolbert, *Sowing the Gospel*, 278.
[30]Ibid.
[31]*The American Heritage Dictionary of the English Language*, 3d ed. (Boston: Houghton Mifflin, 1992), 697.
[32]See William T. Cavanaugh, *Torture and Eucharist* (Oxford: Blackwell, 1998); and John Conroy, *Unspeakable Acts, Ordinary People: The Dynamics of Torture* (New York: Knopf, 2000).
[33]Jon L. Berquist, *Incarnation*, Understanding Biblical Themes (St. Louis: Chalice Press, 2000), 128.
[34]Myers, *Binding the Strong Man*, 396.
[35]Tolbert, *Sowing the Gospel*, 296.
[36]Myers, *Binding the Strong Man*, 399.
[37]Flora A. Keshgegian, *Redeeming Memories: A Theology of Healing and Transformation* (Nashville: Abingdon Press, 2000). A similar argument is made by Rita Nakashima Brock

and Rebecca Ann Parker in *Proverbs of Ashes: Violence, Redemptive Suffering, and the Search for What Saves Us* (Boston: Beacon Press, 2001).

[38]Myers, *Binding the Strong Man*, 401.

[39]Ibid., 406.

[40]James Newton Poling, *Deliver Us from Evil: Resisting Racial and Gender Oppression* (Minneapolis: Fortress Press, 1996), 104–5.

Chapter 13: A Church Empowered by the Holy Spirit

[1]Jürgen Moltmann, *The Spirit of Life* (Minneapolis: Fortress Press, 1992), 66.

[2]Ched Myers, *Binding the Strong Man: A Political Reading of Mark's Story of Jesus* (Maryknoll, N.Y.: Orbis Books, 1988), 439.

[3]Ibid., 441–42.

[4]Ibid., 435.

[5]Ibid., 435–36.

[6]Ibid., 437–38.

[7]Peter C. Hodgson, *Revisioning the Church: Ecclesial Freedom in the New Paradigm* (Philadelphia: Fortress Press, 1988), 29.

[8]Ibid., 29.

[9]Ibid., 32.

[10]Ibid.

[11]I am substituting the word kin-dom for kingdom based on a proposal from Rosemary Ruether. However, Hodgson uses the word kingdom in his book.

[12]Hodgson, *Revisioning the Church*, 35.

[13]Ibid., 36.

[14]Rosemary Radford Ruether, *Women-Church: Theology and Practice of Feminist Liturgical Communities* (San Francisco: Harper and Row, 1985), 11.

[15]Ibid., 23.

[16]Original definition by author.

[17]Parts of the following section are adapted from James Newton Poling, *Deliver Us from Evil: Resisting Racial and Gender Oppression* (Minneapolis: Fortress Press, 1996), 115–17.

[18]Bernard Loomer, "On Committing Yourself to a Relationship," *Process Studies* 16, no. 4 (1987): 257–58.

[19]Ibid., 8.

[20]Ibid., 5.

[21]Daniel Day Williams, *The Spirit and the Forms of Love* (New York: Harper and Row, 1968), 3.

[22]Bernard Eugene Meland, *The Realities of Faith: The Revolution in Cultural Forms* (New York: Oxford Univ. Press, 1962).

[23]Rosemary Radford Ruether, *Gaia and God: An Ecofeminist Theology of Earth Healing* (San Francisco: HarperSanFrancisco, 1994).

[24]Moltmann, *The Spirit of Life*, 7–8.

[25]Parts of the following section are adapted from Poling, *Deliver Us from Evil*, 156–68.

[26]Charles Winquist, *Practical Hermeneutics: A Revised Agenda for Ministry* (Atlanta: Scholars Press, 1980). Dr. Winquist suggests that the depth of experience becomes available when one attends to the cracks and fissures in language and perception.

[27]See David Livingston, *Healing Violent Men: A Model for Christian Communities* (Minneapolis: Fortress Press, 2001), for an interesting discussion of reconciliation in relation to perpetrators of violence.

[28]Judith Lewis Herman, *Trauma and Recovery* (New York: Basic Books, 1992), 7–8.

[29]David Livingston, *Healing Violent Men*.

[30]Original definition by author.

[31]Ellen Wondra, *Humanity Has Been a Holy Thing: Toward a Contemporary Feminist Christology* (New York: Univ. Press of America, 1994), 330.

[32]Ibid., 329.

[33]Ibid., 333.

[34]Myers, *Binding the Strong Man*, 70.

[35]Martin Luther King, Jr., quoted in *A Testament of Hope: The Essential Writings of Martin Luther King*, ed. James Melvin Washington (San Francisco: Harper and Row, 1986), 149.

[36]Original definition by author.

[37]For Alfred North Whitehead, beauty occurs in the harmony of contrasts and former contradictions.

[38]Alfred North Whitehead coined the phrase "the many becoming one and increased by one" to describe the process of becoming.

[39]Original definition by author.

Chapter 14: Pastoral Care with Persons Who Are Vulnerable

[1]James Newton Poling, *Deliver Us from Evil: Resisting Racial and Gender Oppression* (Minneapolis: Fortress Press, 1996), 103.

[2]American Psychiatric Association, *Diagnostic and Statistical Manual of Mental Disorders,* 4th ed., rev. (Washington, D.C.: American Psychiatric Association, 2000).

[3]John B. Cobb, Jr., and Herman E. Daly, *For the Common Good: Redirecting the Economy toward Community, the Environment, and a Sustainable Future* (Boston: Beacon Press, 1989), 36–37.

[4]Emmanuel Yartekwei Lartey, *In Living Colour: An Intercultural Approach to Pastoral Care and Counselling* (London; Herndon, Va.: Cassell, 1997), 12.

[5]*Chicago Tribune,* 8 March 2001, 1.

[6]U.S. Census Bureau, March 8, 2001, based on 1999 estimated figures with a total population of 276.9 million persons.

[7]Albert Gaw, *Cross-Cultural Psychiatry* (Boston: John Wright, 1982); Paul Pedersen, ed., *Handbook of Cross-Cultural Counseling and Therapy* (Westport, Conn.: Greenwood Press, 1985); Monica McGoldrick, John K. Pearce, and Joseph Giordano, eds. *Ethnicity and Family Therapy* (New York: Guilford Press, 1982, 1996); Charles D. Spielberger and Rogelio Diaz-Guerrero, *Cross-Cultural Anxiety* (Washington, D.C.: Hemisphere; distributed by New York: Halsted Press, 1976, 1990); Derald Wing Sue and David Sue, *Counseling the Culturally Different: Theory and Practice* (New York: John Wiley and Sons, 1981).

[8]Rodney J. Hunter, ed., *Dictionary of Pastoral Care and Counseling* (Nashville: Abingdon Press, 1990).

[9]Clifford Geertz, *The Interpretation of Cultures: Selected Essays* (New York: Basic Books, 1973), 89; see Linda Elaine Thomas, *Under the Canopy: Ritual Process and Spiritual Resilience in South Africa,* Studies in Comparative Religion (Columbia, S.C.: Univ. of South Carolina, 1999).

[10]Lartey, *In Living Colour: An Intercultural Approach to Pastoral Care and Counselling,* 9. See also Stuart Hall and Brad Gieben, eds., *Formations of Modernity* (Cambridge, U.K.: Polity Press and Open University, 1992), 229–37; David Augsburger, *Pastoral Counseling across Cultures* (Philadelphia: Westminster, 1986); Robert J. Wicks, Barry K. Estadt, Charles Van Engen, eds., *Pastoral Counseling in a Global Church: Voices from the Field* (Maryknoll, N.Y.: Orbis Books, 1993); Pedersen, *Handbook of Cross-Cultural Counseling and Therapy* ; Lee C. Lee and Nolan W. S. Zane, eds., *Handbook of Asian American Psychology* (Thousand Oaks, Calif.: Sage Publications, 1998).

[11]Brenda Ruiz, *Violencia contra la mujer y la ninez: Una perspective de salud (Violence against Women and Children: A Health Perspective)* (Managua: UPOLI, 1998). Also see Brenda Ruiz, "Counseling with Women in a Context of Intense Oppression," *The Journal of Pastoral Care* 48, no. 2 (1994).

[12]Personal communication, June 16, 1999.

[13]Personal communication, June 23, 1999.

[14]Linda Thomas, "Theology and Culture," paper written for faculty discussion, February 22, 1999, Garrett-Evangelical Theological Seminary, Evanston, Ill.

[15]James Newton Poling and Toinette M. Eugene, *Balm for Gilead: Pastoral Care for African American Families Experiencing Abuse* (Nashville: Abingdon Press, 1998), 80.

[16]Ibid. 97–98.

[17]See ibid., xi–xii.

[18]Poling, *Deliver Us from Evil,* 8, adapted from The Cornwall Collective, *Your Daughters Shall Prophesy* (New York: Pilgrim Press, 1980), 39.

[19]Frantz Fanon, *The Wretched of the Earth* (New York: Grove Press, 1963), 204.

[20]The following quotes are from Ama Ata Aidoo, *Our Sister Killjoy* (Essex, England: Longman, 1977), 12–13.

[21]Ibid., 29.

[22]Poling, *Deliver Us from Evil,* 100.

[23]See the following for well-developed arguments on issues of gender, race, and class: Christie Cozad Neuger, *The Arts of Ministry: Feminist-Womanist Approaches* (Louisville: Westminster John Knox Press, 1996); Carroll A. Watkins Ali, *Survival and Liberation: Pastoral Theology in African American Context* (St. Louis: Chalice Press, 1999).

[24]Personal communication, summer, 2001.

[25]Personal communication, summer, 2001.

[26]Ernesto Cardenal, *The Gospel in Solentiname*, vol. 2 (Maryknoll, N.Y.: Orbis, 1978).

[27]Elsa Tamez in *Women Resisting Violence: Spirituality for Life*, ed. Mary John Mananzan, Mercy Amba Oduyoye, Elsa Tamez, J. Shannon Clarkson, Mary C. Grey, Letty M. Russell (Maryknoll, N.Y.: Orbis Books, 1996).

[28]Robert Bruno, *Steelworker Alley: How Class Works in Youngstown* (Ithaca, N.Y.: Cornell Univ. Press, 1999); Richard Sennett and Jonathan Cobb, *The Hidden Injuries of Class* (New York: Norton, 1972).

[29]Audre Lorde, *Sister Outsider* (Freedom, Calif.: Crossing Press, 1984), 42, "We were not meant to survive."

[30]Judith Lewis Herman, *Trauma and Recovery* (New York: Basic Books, 1992).

[31]These principles for working with victims were developed at the Center for Prevention of Sexual and Domestic Violence, Seattle, Wash. See the 2001 General Assembly Policy of the Presbyterian Church (USA), "Turn Mourning into Dancing! A Policy Statement on Healing Domestic Violence" (Louisville: 213th General Assembly, Presbyterian Church [USA], 2001), available from the Presbyterian Church Office, 100 Witherspoon Street, Louisville, KY 40202.

[32]Adapted, Domestic Violence Project, 6308 8th Ave., Kenosha, WI 53143.

[33]Adapted, Mennonite Central Committee, Domestic Violence Task Force, 134 Plaza Dr., Winnipeg, Manitoba, Canada, R3T 5K9.

[34]Effective discussions of these issues can be found in Christie Cozad Neuger, *Counseling Women: A Narrative Pastoral Approach* (Minneapolis: Fortress Press, 2001); Roy Herndon SteinhoffSmith, *The Mutuality of Care* (St Louis: Chalice Press, 1999); and Howard W. Stone, *Brief Pastoral Counseling* (Minneapolis: Fortress Press, 1994).

Chapter 15: The Spirituality of Practicing Goodness

[1]Shalem Institute for Spiritual Formation, Inc., 5430 Grosvenor Lane, Bethesda, Maryland 20814, Telephone: (301) 897-7334, http://www.shalem.org.

[2]Personal communication, August 13, 2001.

[3]These two paragraphs were originally published in James Newton Poling, *Deliver Us from Evil: Resisting Racial and Gender Oppression* (Minneapolis: Fortress Press, 1996), 175.

[4]*Broken Vows*, a videotape on domestic violence from The Center for the Prevention of Sexual and Domestic Violence, 2400 N. 45th Street, Suite 10, Seattle, WA 98103, 206-634-1903.

[5]Johann Baptist Metz, *The Emergent Church: The Future of Christianity in a Postbourgeois World* (New York: Crossroad, 1981).

[6]Alfred North Whitehead, *The Aims of Education & Other Essays* (New York: Macmillan, 1929).

[7]Susan B. Thistlethwaite and George F. Cairns, eds., *Beyond Theological Tourism: Mentoring as a Grassroots Approach to Theological Education* (Maryknoll, N.Y.: Orbis Books, 1994).

[8]Chicago Religious Leadership Network on Latin America, 4750 N. Sheridan Rd., Suite 429, Chicago, IL 60640, 773-293-2964.

[9]October 27–29, 2000, sponsored by the Samaritan Counseling Center, Lancaster, Penn.

[10]Presbyterian Church (USA), "Hope for a Global Future: Toward Just and Sustainable Human Development" (Louisville: Office of the General Assembly, 1996).

[11]Ibid., chap. 7, 95–143.

[12]John B. Cobb, Jr., and Herman E. Daly, *For the Common Good: Redirecting the Economy toward Community, the Environment, and a Sustainable Future* (Boston: Beacon Press, 1989).

[13]Evangelical Lutheran Church in America (ELCA), "Give Us This Day Our Daily Bread: Sufficient, Sustainable Livelihood for All: A Study on Economic Life" (Chicago: Division for Church and Society, ELCA, 1996).

[14]Presbyterian Church (USA), "Turn Mourning into Dancing! A Policy Statement on Healing Domestic Violence" (Louisville: 213th General Assembly, Presbyterian Church [USA], 2001), available from the Presbyterian Church Office, 100 Witherspoon Street, Louisville, KY 40202.

[15]Presbyterians Against Domestic Violence Network, Presbyterian Health and Welfare Association, 100 Witherspoon St., Louisville, Ky. 40202, www.pcusa.org.

[16]Center for the Prevention of Sexual and Domestic Violence, 2400 N. 45th Street, Suite 10, Seattle WA 98103 206-634-1903, www.cpsdv.org.

[17]Amnesty International USA, 322 Eighth Avenue, New York, NY 10001, 212-807-8400, http://www.amnesty-usa.org.

[18]Interfaith Center on Corporate Responsibility, 475 Riverside Dr., Rm. 550, New York, NY, 10115, 212-870-2295, http://www.iccr.org.

[19]Habitat for Humanity International, 121 Habitat St., Americus, GA 31709, http://www.habitat.org.

[20]Ruth C Duck, and Maren C. Tirabassi, *Touch Holiness: Resources for Worship* (Cleveland: United Church Press, 1990); Ruth C. Duck, *Dancing in the Universe: Hymns and Songs* (Chicago: GIA Publications, 1992); Ruth C. Duck, *Everflowing Streams: Songs for Worship* (New York: Pilgrim Press, 1981); Ruth C. Duck, ed., *Bread for the Journey: Resources for Worship* (Cleveland: United Church Press, 1981); Ruth C. Duck, ed., *Flames of the Spirit: Resources for Worship* (Cleveland: The Pilgrim Press, 1985).

[21]Thomas Troeger, *Borrowed Light: Hymn Texts, Prayers, and Poems* (New York: Oxford Univ. Press, 1994); Thomas and Carol Doran Troeger, *New Hymns for the Lectionary: To Glorify the Maker's Name* (New York: Oxford Univ. Press, 1986); Thomas and Carol Doran Troeger, *New Hymns for the Life of the Church: To Make Our Prayer and Music One* (New York: Oxford Univ. Press, 1992); Thomas and Carol Doran Troeger, *Open to Glory: Renewing Worship in the Congregation* (Valley Forge, Pa.: Judson Press, 1983).

[22]Brian Wren, *Faith Looking Forward: The Hymns & Songs of Brian Wren* (Oxford: Oxford Univ. Press, 1983); Brian Wren, *Faith Renewed: 33 Hymns Re-Issued and Revised* (Carol Stream, Ill.: Hope Publishing, 1995); Brian Wren, *Praising a Mystery: 30 New Hymns* (Carol Stream, Ill.: Hope Publishing, 1986).

[23]Printed by permission of the Wheadon United Methodist Church, Evanston, Ill., pastor Rev. Andres Ulman. This prayer has been developed over a period of years and used regularly in worship. It is an example of liturgical reform that comes from a practicing community rather than a scholar's mind.

[24]Carol J. Adams and Marie M. Fortune, *Violence against Women and Children: A Christian Theological Sourcebook* (New York: Continuum, 1995).

[25]Adapted from "An Act of Prayer" in *The Pattern of Our Days: Worship in the Celtic Tradition from the Iona Community,* ed. Kathy Galloway (New York: Paulist Press, 1996).

[26]Adapted from Presbyterian Church (USA), *Book of Common Worship* (Louisville: Westminster/ John Knox Press, 1993), 619.

[27]Ibid., 57.

[28]Philip Scharper, and Sally Scharper, *The Gospel of Art by the Peasants of Solentiname* (Maryknoll, N.Y.: Orbis Books, 1984), 52.

[29]Original by author.

[30]Original adaptation by author from the Presbyterian Church (USA), *Book of Common Worship,* 127.

[31]Adapted from a sermon in "Network in Liturgy," Council of Latin American Churches. Received from Brenda Consuelo Ruiz, pastoral counselor with AEDAF (Asociacion Evangelica de Asesoramiento Familiar–The Protestant Association for Family Therapy) in Managua. Translated from Spanish by James N. Poling, "Resisting Violence in the Name of Jesus," *Journal of Pastoral Theology* 7 (1997).

Index